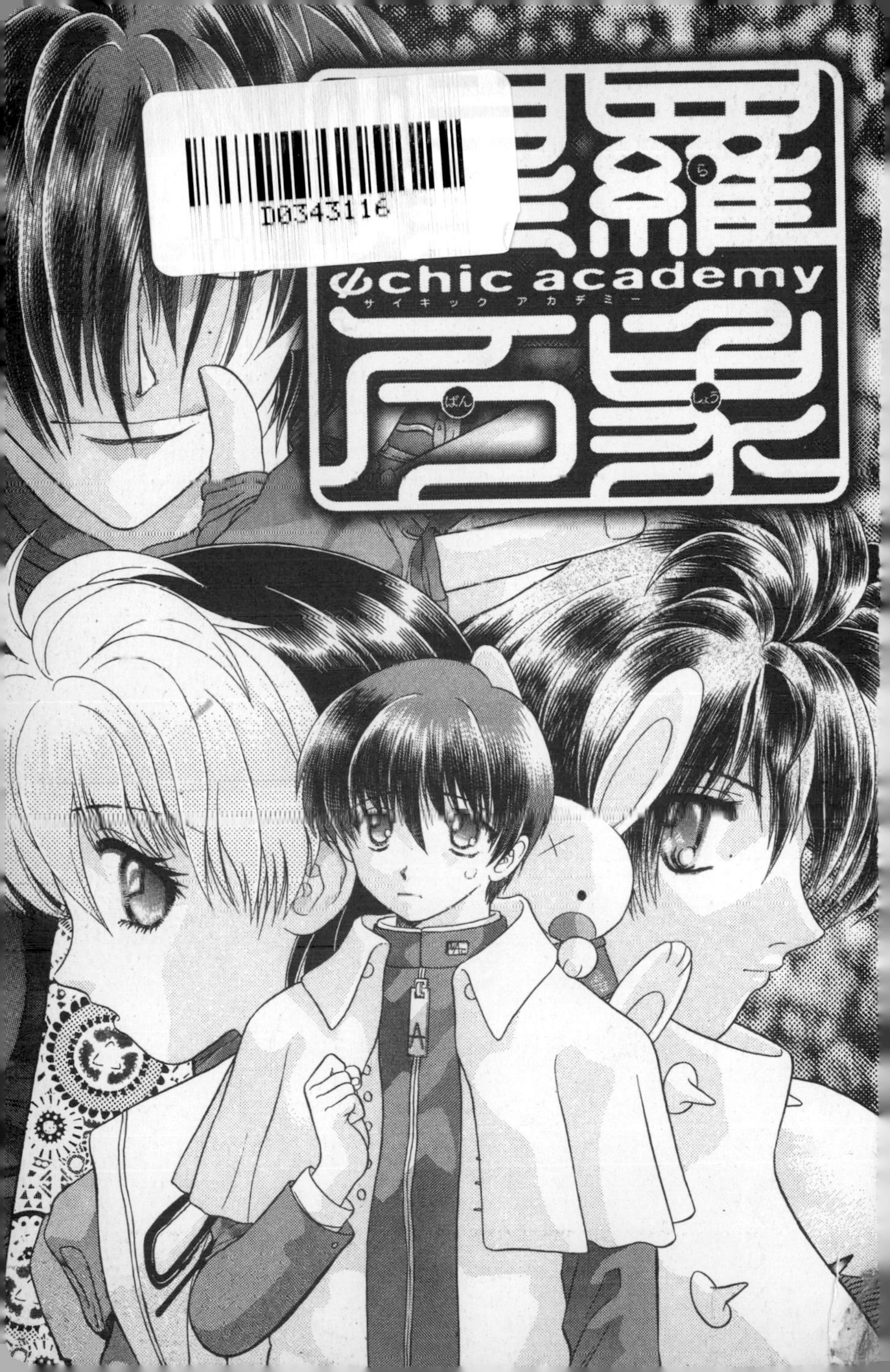
羅
ψchic academy
サイキック アカデミー
万象

PSYCHIC ACADEMY

VOLUME 2

BY
KATSU AKI

Los Angeles • Tokyo • London

Translator - Jan Scott Frazier
English Adaptation - Nathan Johnson
Associate Editor - Arthur Milliken
Retouch and Lettering - Jose Macasocol, Jr.
Cover Layout - Anna Kernbaum

Editor - Luis Reyes
Digital Imaging Manager - Chris Buford
Pre-Press Manager - Antonio DePietro
Production Managers - Jennifer Miller and Mutsumi Miyazaki
Art Director - Matt Alford
Managing Editor - Jill Freshney
VP of Production - Ron Klamert
President & C.O.O. - John Parker
Publisher & C.E.O. - Stuart Levy

Email: info@TOKYOPOP.com
Come visit us online at www.TOKYOPOP.com

A  Manga

TOKYOPOP Inc.
5900 Wilshire Blvd. Suite 2000
Los Angeles, CA 90036

Psychic Academy Vol. 2

ISBN: 1-59182-622-5

First TOKYOPOP printing: May 2004

10 9 8 7 6 5 4 3 2 1

Printed in the USA

PSYCHIC ACADEMY

Story Thus Far...

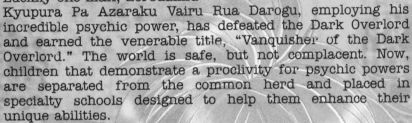

In the near future, the discovery of psychic abilities has run congruously with the threat of evil forces. Luckily one man, Zerodaimu Kyupura Pa Azaraku Vairu Rua Darogu, employing his incredible psychic power, has defeated the Dark Overlord and earned the venerable title, "Vanquisher of the Dark Overlord." The world is safe, but not complacent. Now, children that demonstrate a proclivity for psychic powers are separated from the common herd and placed in specialty schools designed to help them enhance their unique abilities.

Ai Shimoi was perfectly happy NOT being gifted so. However, pressured by his parents and with a filial reputation thrust upon him by his brother—the aforementioned Vanquisher of the Dark Overlord—Ai enrolls in the Psychic Academy. He has already made some new friends, and has become reacquainted with an old one, but his life there is a difficult one. Ai is dealing with new powers, a new school, and perhaps worst of all, the onset of adolescence. And to make matters worse, every goon with a psychic axe to grind wants to take a stab at the hotshot new kid. Luckily he has the support of his old friend Sahra, his roommate Telda, the stern but caring Mew and a strange bunny, Master Boo, who vows to train the young buck in the psychic arts.

Exams are just beginning, but Ai has to deal with a host of distractions...not the least being a bevy of beautiful women wreaking havoc on his addled adolescence.

CONTENTS

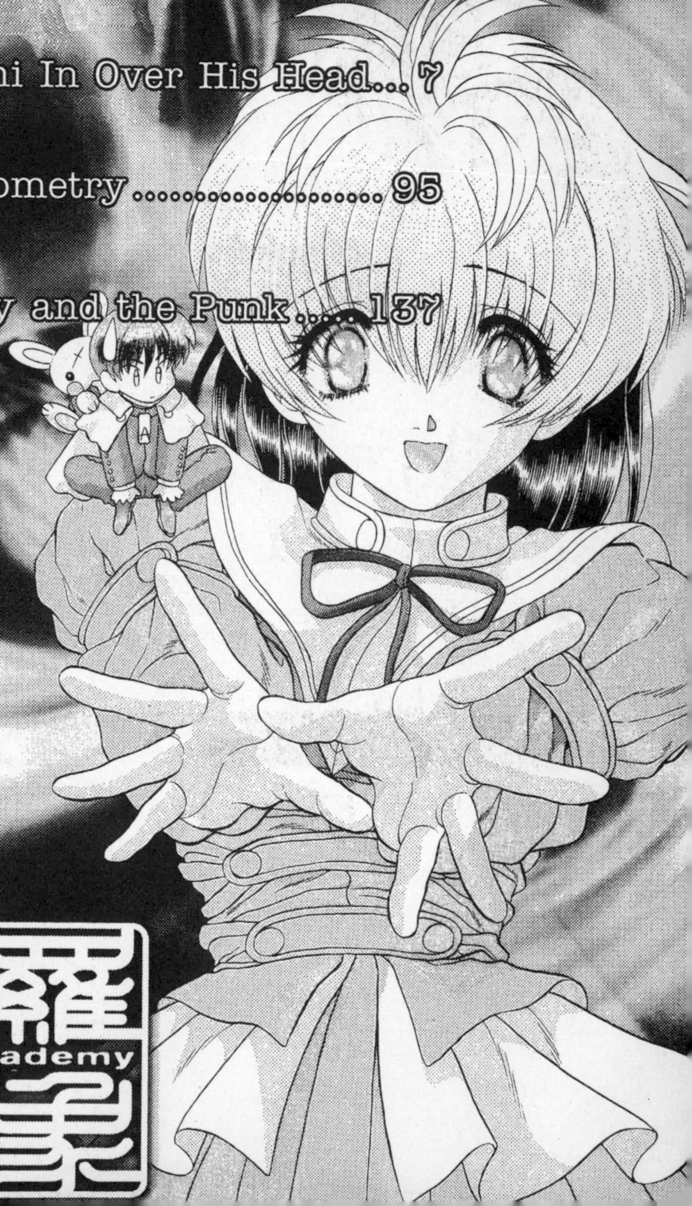

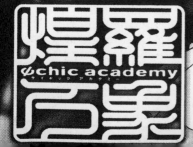

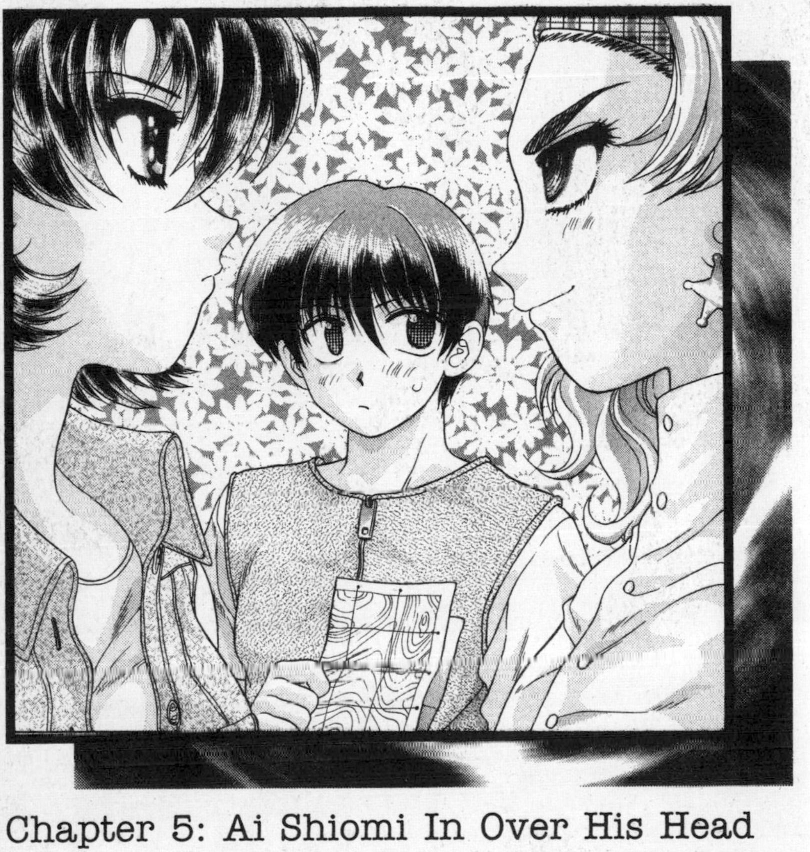

Chapter 5: Ai Shiomi In Over His Head

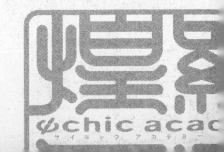

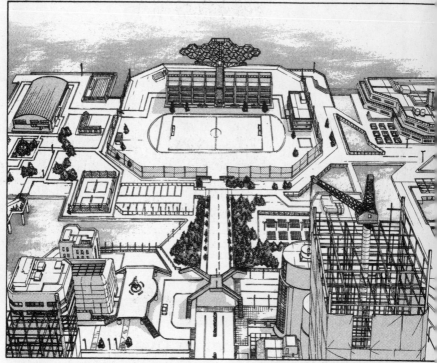

カリ

カリ

8

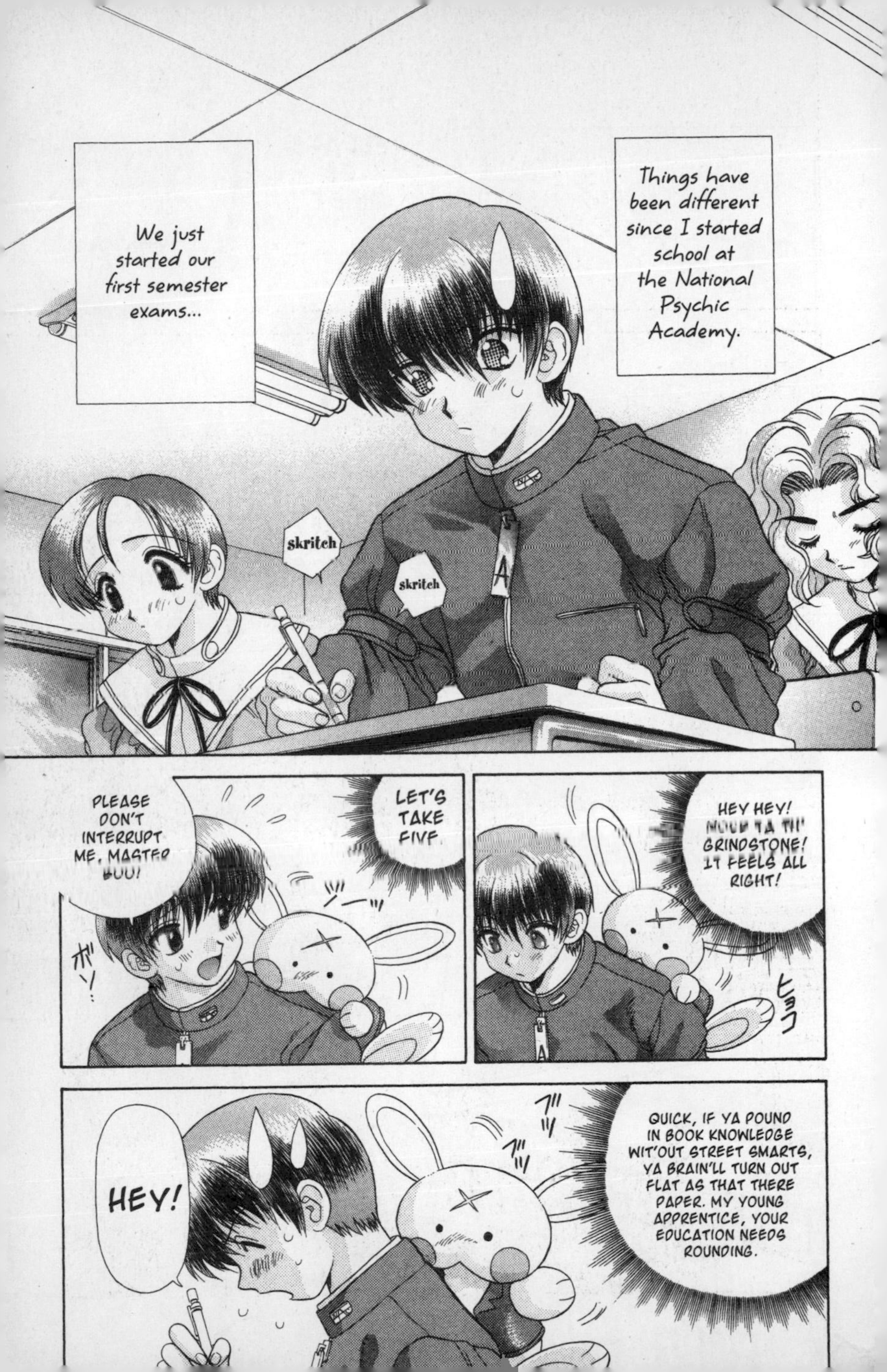
Things have been different since I started school at the National Psychic Academy.
We just started our first semester exams...
skritch
skritch
HEY HEY!
GRINDSTONE! IT FEELS ALL RIGHT!
LET'S TAKE FIVE.
PLEASE DON'T INTERRUPT ME, MASTER BUU!
QUICK, IF YA POUND IN BOOK KNOWLEDGE WIT'OUT STREET SMARTS, YA BRAIN'LL TURN OUT FLAT AS THAT THERE PAPER. MY YOUNG APPRENTICE, YOUR EDUCATION NEEDS ROUNDING.
HEY!

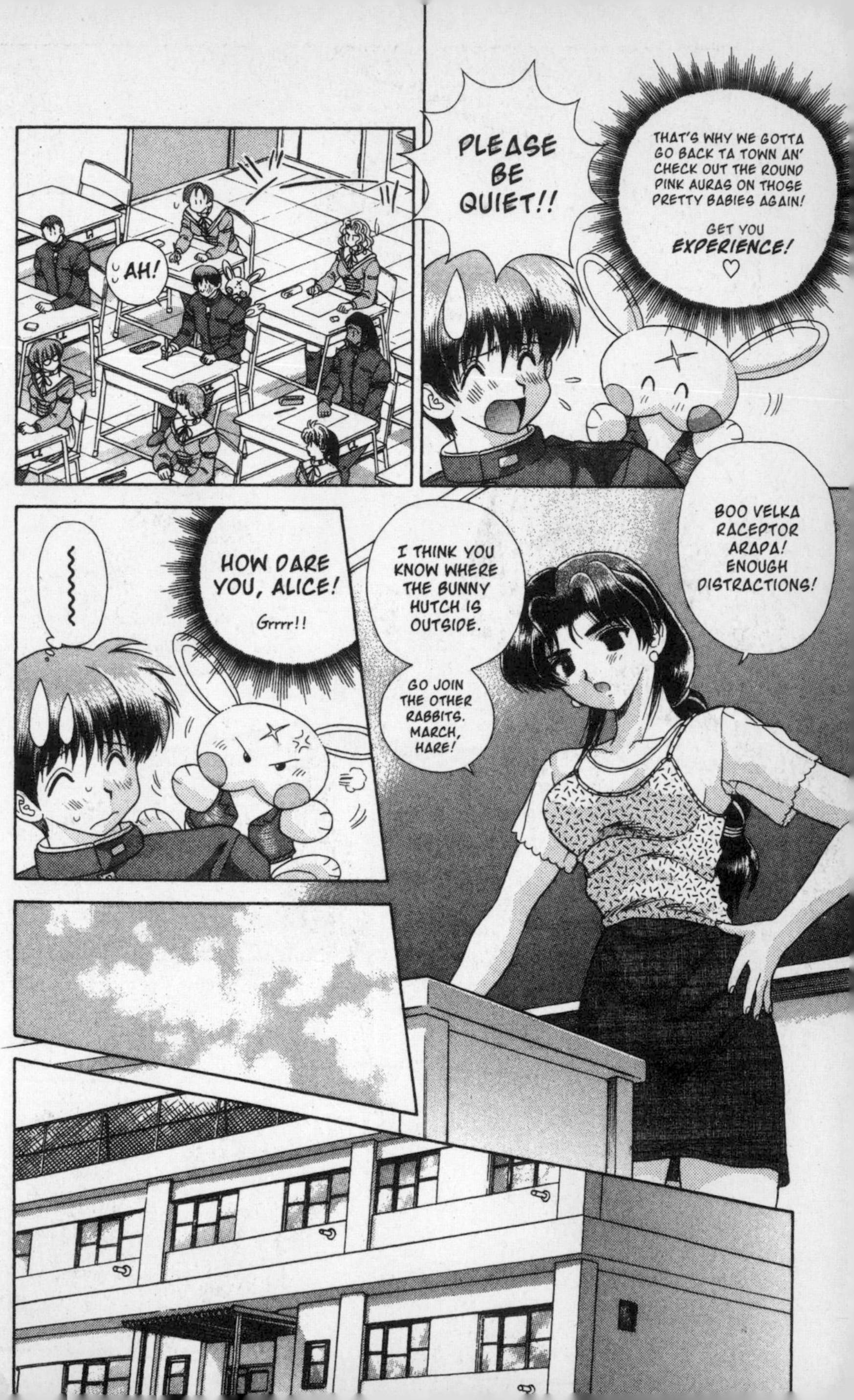
THAT'S WHY WE GOTTA GO BACK TA TOWN AN' CHECK OUT THE ROUND PINK AURAS ON THOSE PRETTY BABIES AGAIN!
GET YOU EXPERIENCE! ♡
PLEASE BE QUIET!!
AH!
BOO VELKA RACEPTOR ARAPA! ENOUGH DISTRACTIONS!
I THINK YOU KNOW WHERE THE BUNNY HUTCH IS OUTSIDE.
GO JOIN THE OTHER RABBITS. MARCH, HARE!
HOW DARE YOU, ALICE!
Grrrr!!

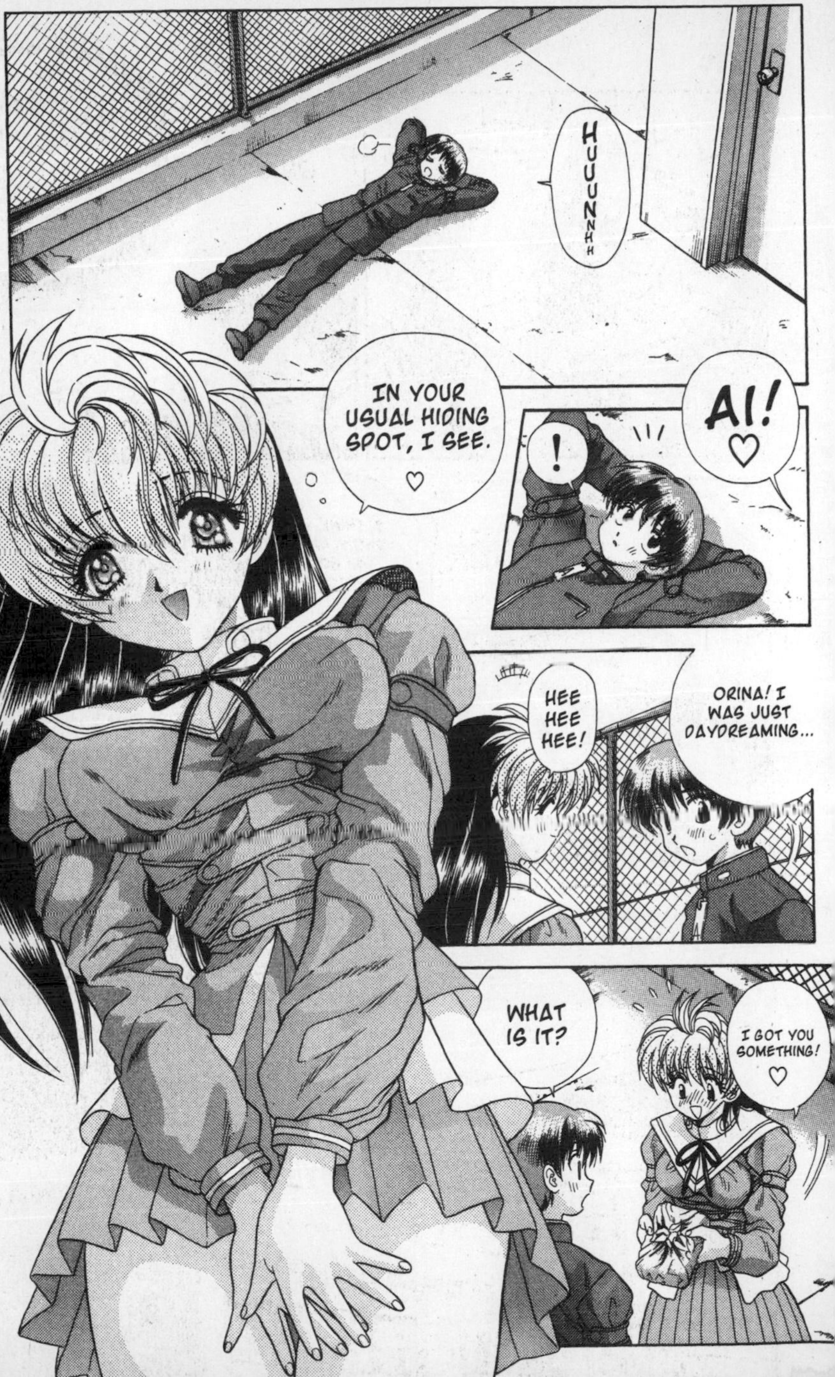
HUUUNNHH
IN YOUR USUAL HIDING SPOT, I SEE. ♡
AI! ♡
!
ORINA! I WAS JUST DAYDREAMING...
HEE HEE HEE!
I GOT YOU SOMETHING! ♡
WHAT IS IT?

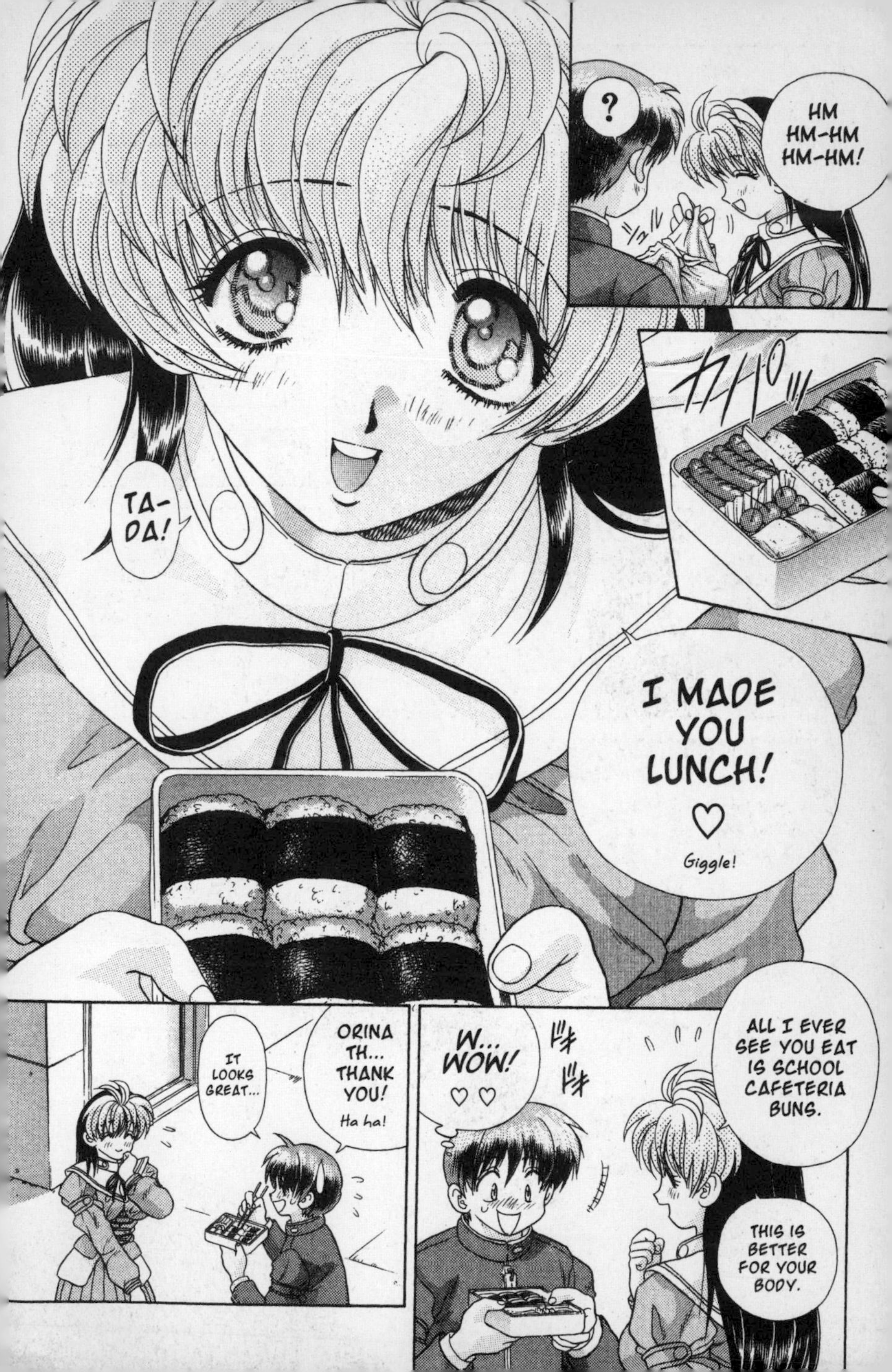

HM HM-HM HM-HM!
?
TA-DA!
I MADE YOU LUNCH! ♡
Giggle!
ALL I EVER SEE YOU EAT IS SCHOOL CAFETERIA BUNS.
W... WOW! ♡♡
ドキ ドキ
THIS IS BETTER FOR YOUR BODY.
ORINA TH... THANK YOU!
Ha ha!
IT LOOKS GREAT...

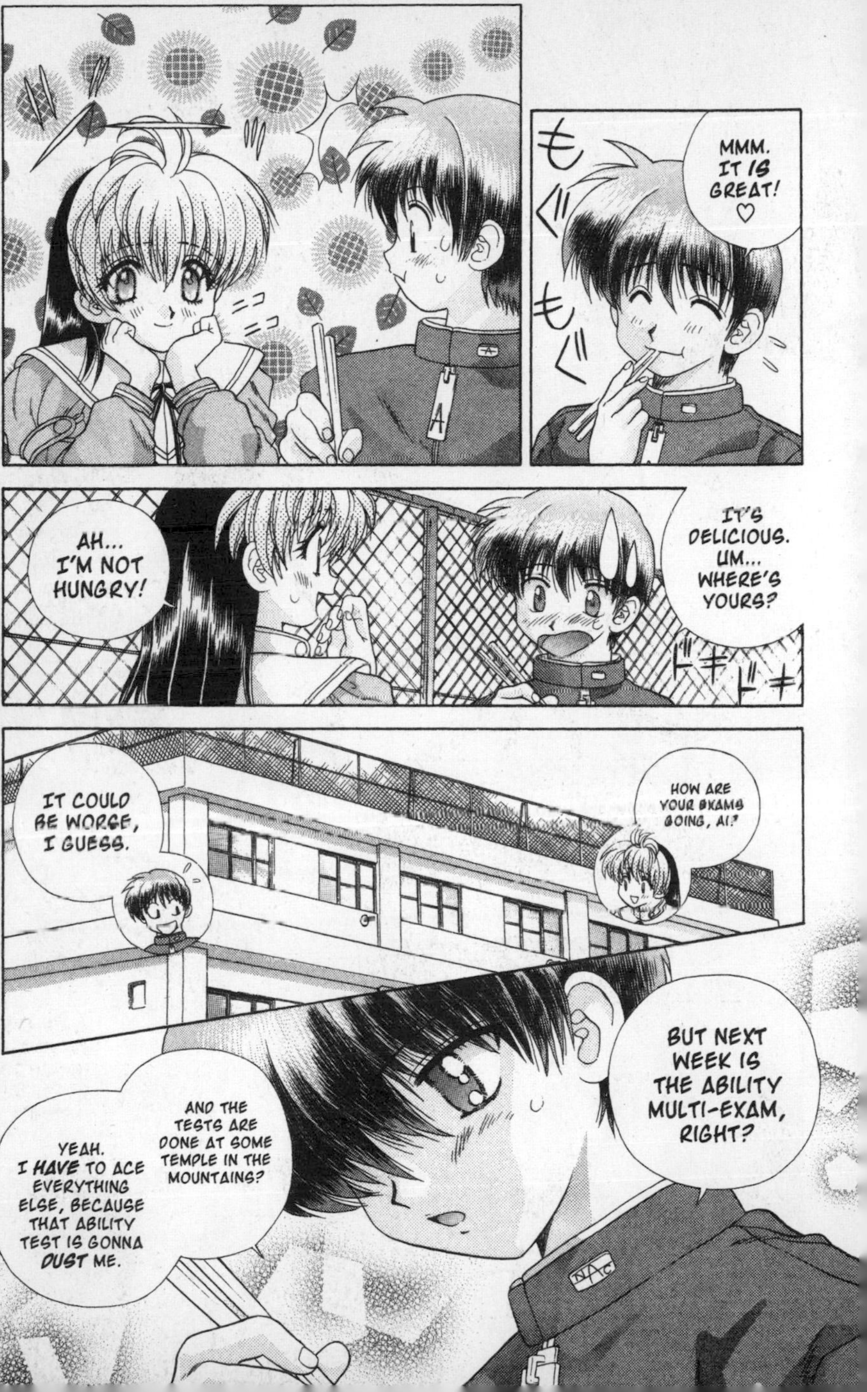
MMM. IT IS GREAT! ♡
もぐもぐ
ニコニコ
IT'S DELICIOUS. UM... WHERE'S YOURS?
ドキドキ
AH... I'M NOT HUNGRY!
HOW ARE YOUR EXAMS GOING, AI?
IT COULD BE WORSE, I GUESS.
BUT NEXT WEEK IS THE ABILITY MULTI-EXAM, RIGHT?
AND THE TESTS ARE DONE AT SOME TEMPLE IN THE MOUNTAINS?
YEAH. I HAVE TO ACE EVERYTHING ELSE, BECAUSE THAT ABILITY TEST IS GONNA DUST ME.

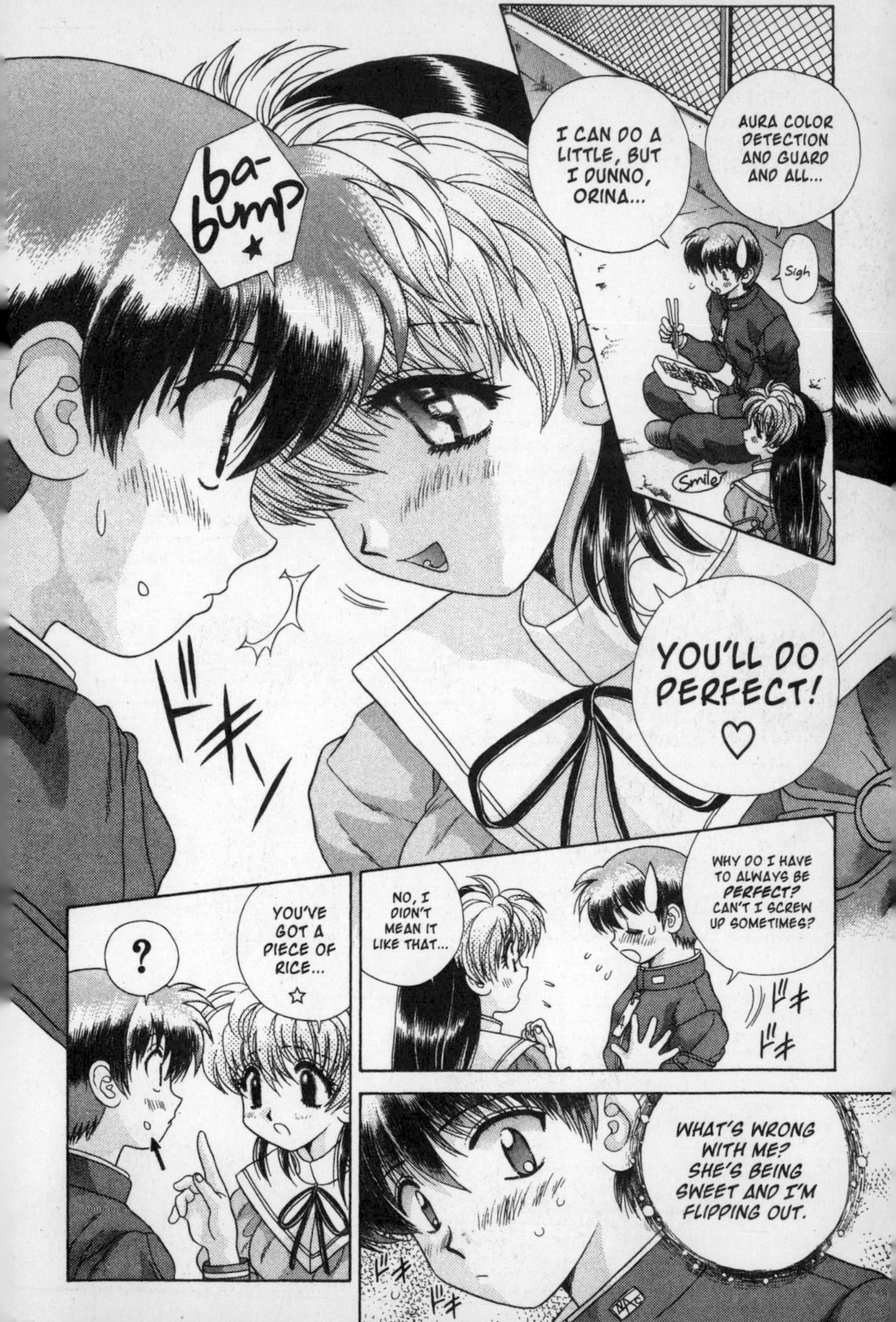
AURA COLOR DETECTION AND GUARD AND ALL...
I CAN DO A LITTLE, BUT I DUNNO, ORINA...
Sigh
Smile
YOU'LL DO PERFECT! ♡
ba-bump ★
ドキッ
WHY DO I HAVE TO ALWAYS BE PERFECT? CAN'T I SCREW UP SOMETIMES?
NO, I DIDN'T MEAN IT LIKE THAT...
ドキ ドキ
WHAT'S WRONG WITH ME? SHE'S BEING SWEET AND I'M FLIPPING OUT.
ドキ ドキ
YOU'VE GOT A PIECE OF RICE... ☆
?

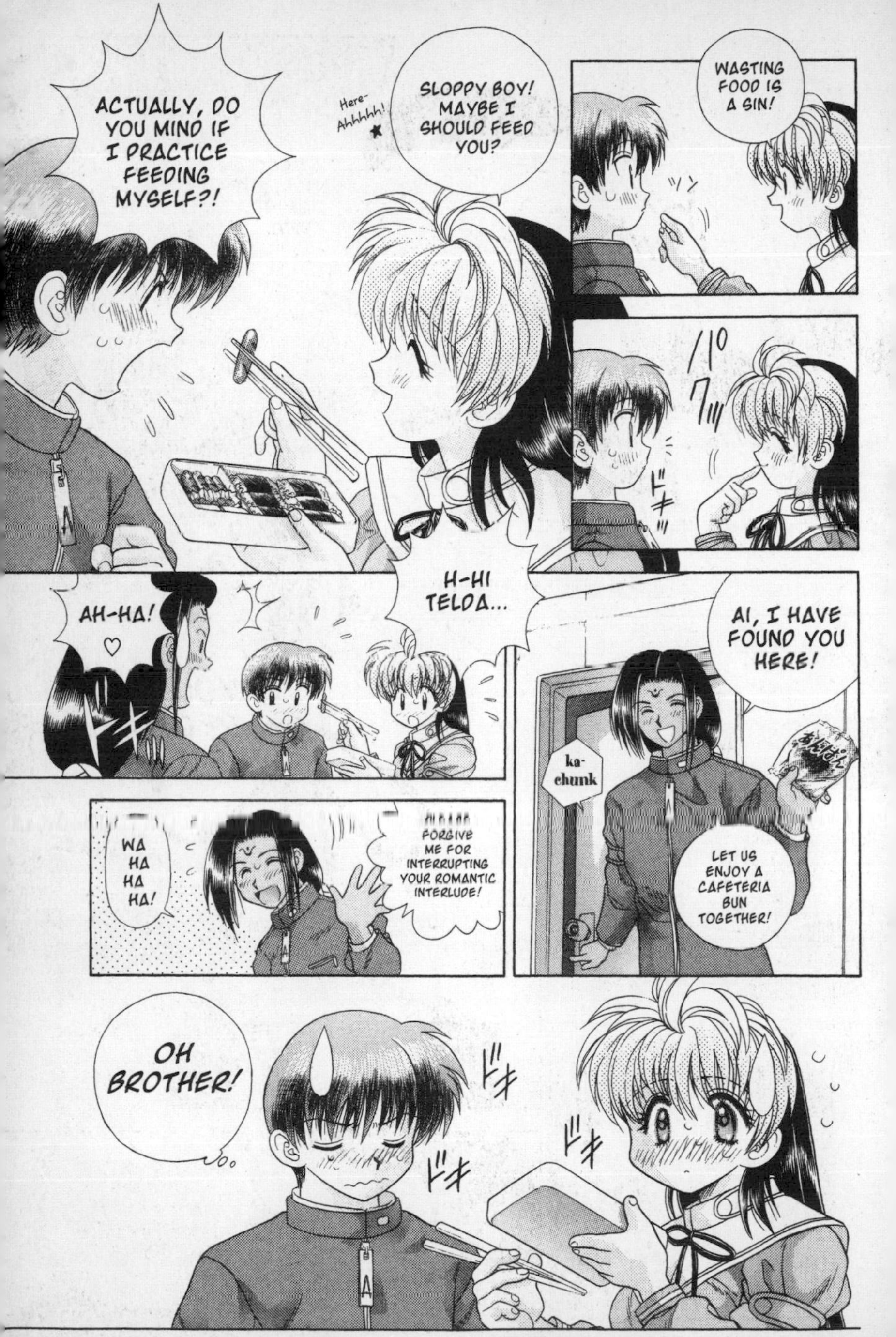

WASTING FOOD IS A SIN!
ツン
パク
ドキ
SLOPPY BOY! MAYBE I SHOULD FEED YOU?
Here- Ahhhhh!
ACTUALLY, DO YOU MIND IF I PRACTICE FEEDING MYSELF?!
AI, I HAVE FOUND YOU HERE!
ka-chunk
LET US ENJOY A CAFETERIA BUN TOGETHER!
H-HI TELDA...
AH-HA!
FORGIVE ME FOR INTERRUPTING YOUR ROMANTIC INTERLUDE!
WA HA HA HA!
OH BROTHER!
ドキ
ドキ
ドキ

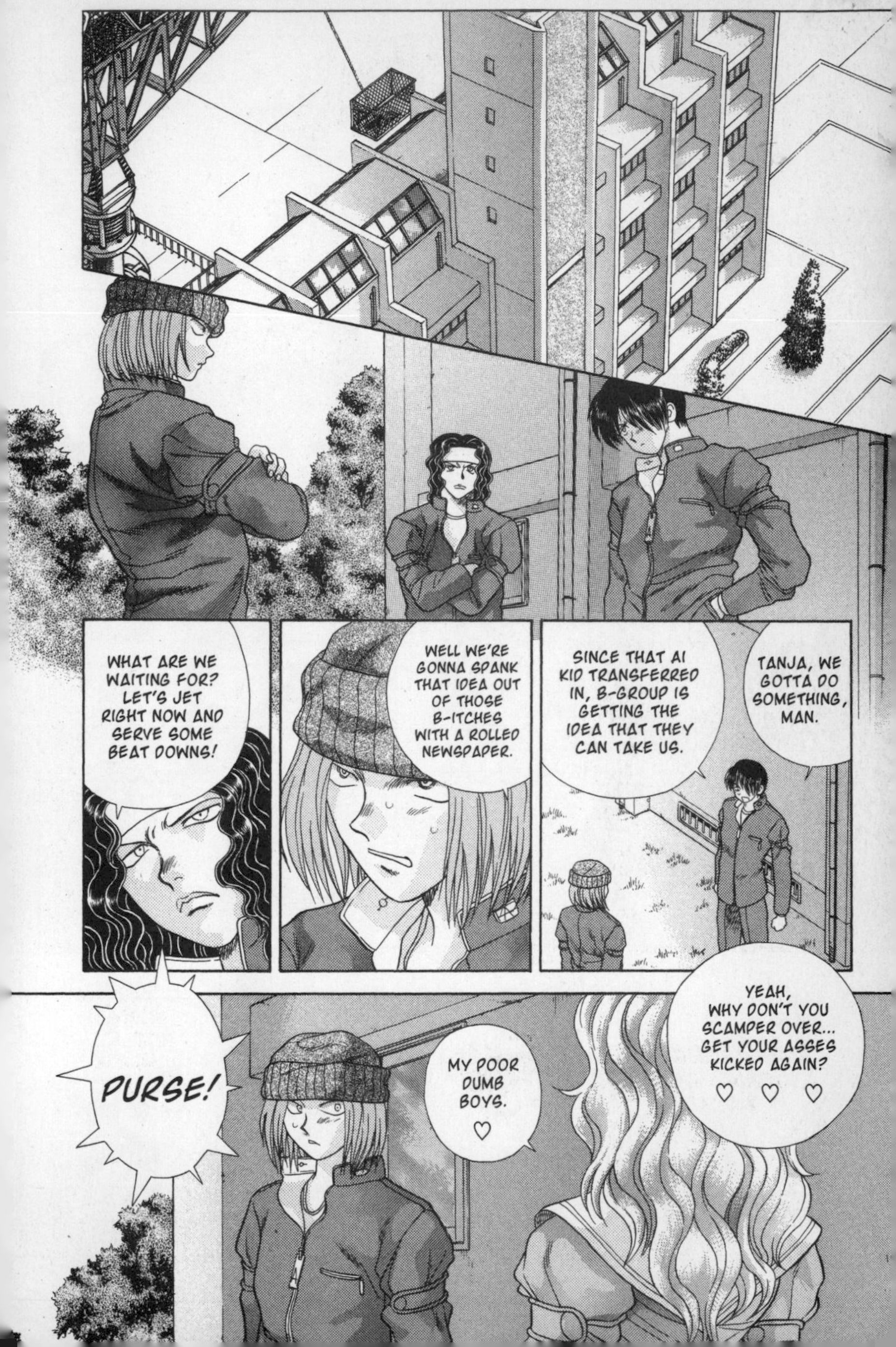
TANJA, WE GOTTA DO SOMETHING, MAN.
SINCE THAT AI KID TRANSFERRED IN, B-GROUP IS GETTING THE IDEA THAT THEY CAN TAKE US.
WELL WE'RE GONNA SPANK THAT IDEA OUT OF THOSE B-ITCHES WITH A ROLLED NEWSPAPER.
WHAT ARE WE WAITING FOR? LET'S JET RIGHT NOW AND SERVE SOME BEAT DOWNS!
YEAH, WHY DON'T YOU SCAMPER OVER... GET YOUR ASSES KICKED AGAIN? ♡ ♡ ♡
MY POOR DUMB BOYS. ♡
PURSE!

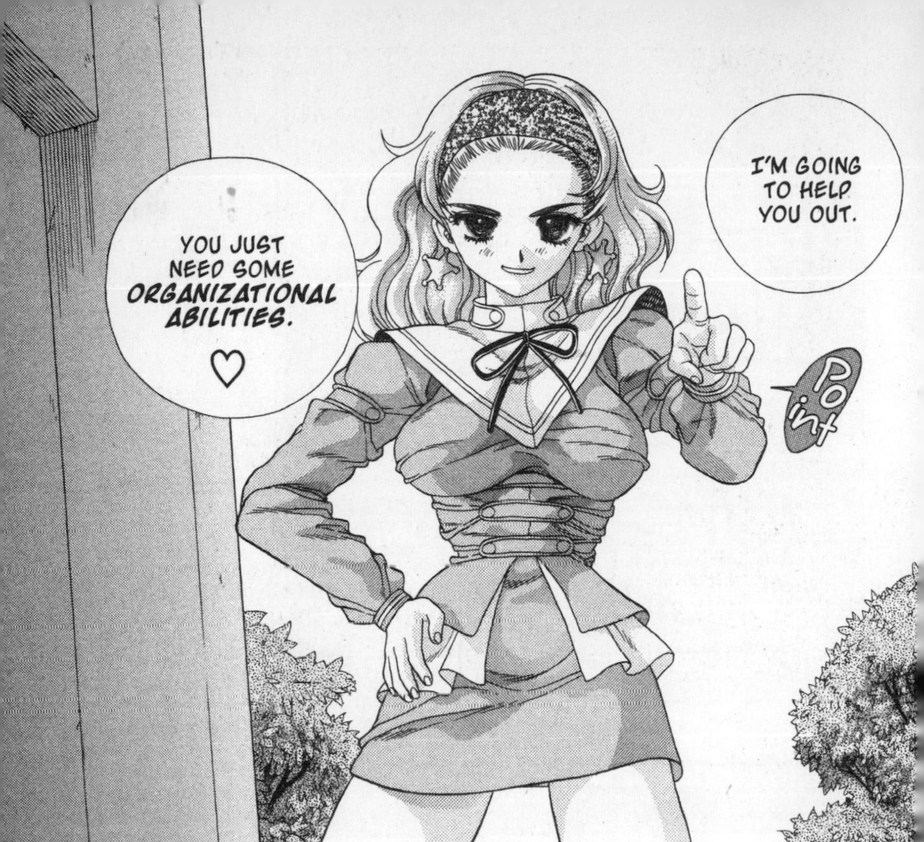
I'M GOING TO HELP YOU OUT.
Point
YOU JUST NEED SOME ORGANIZATIONAL ABILITIES. ♡

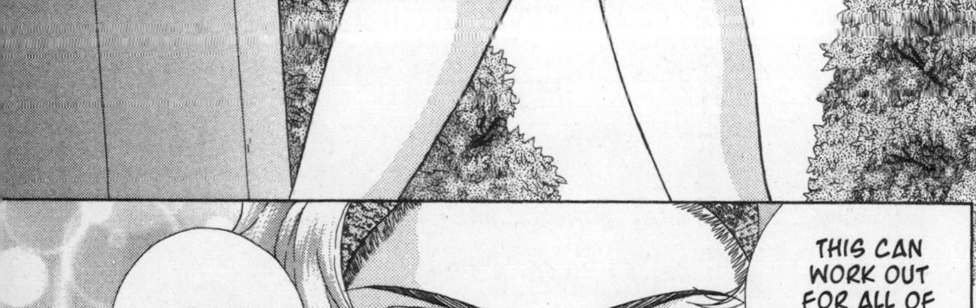
THIS CAN WORK OUT FOR ALL OF US. SEE, THERE'S THIS GIRL IN B...
...I JUST CAN'T STAND ANYMORE.

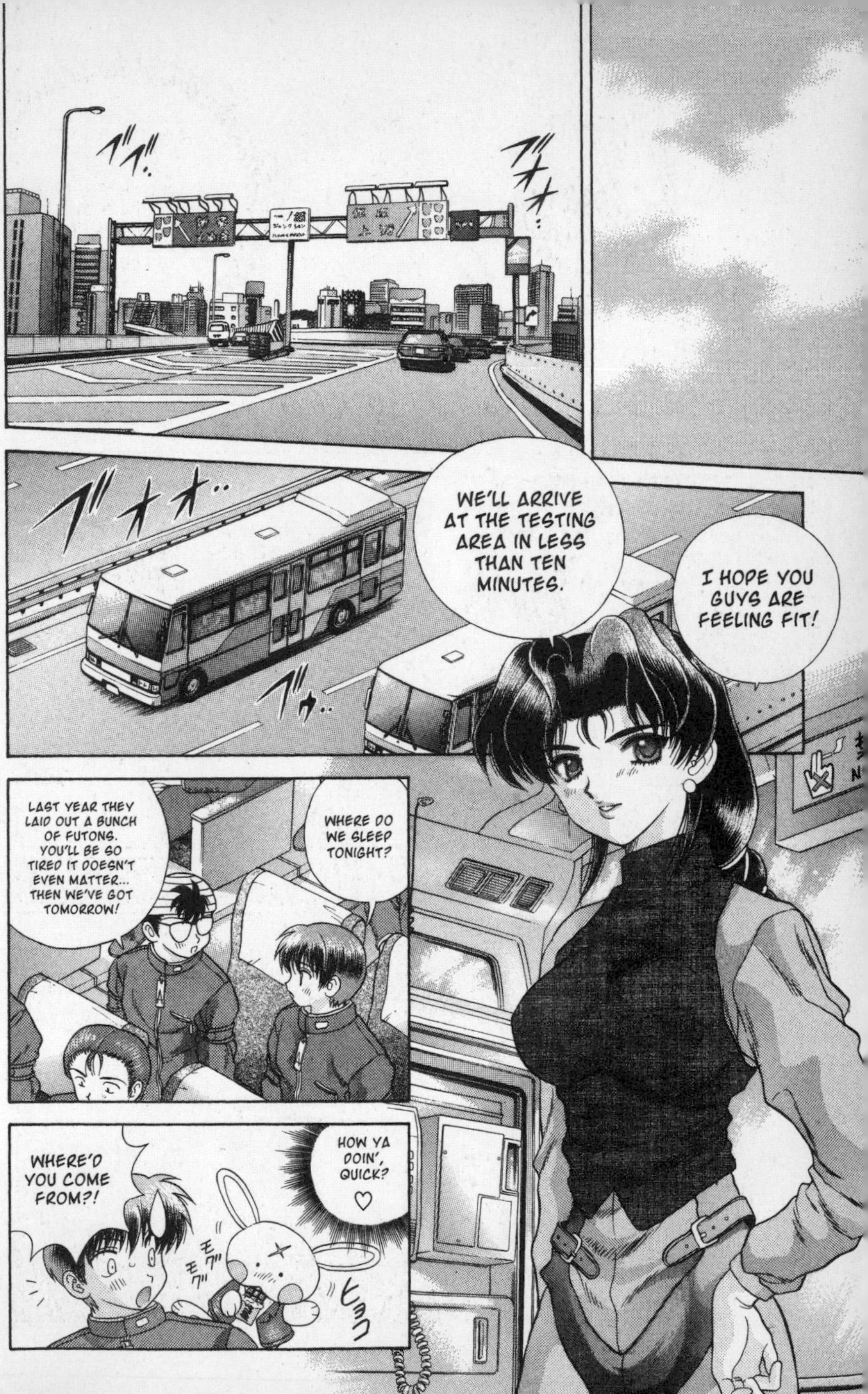
WE'LL ARRIVE AT THE TESTING AREA IN LESS THAN TEN MINUTES.
I HOPE YOU GUYS ARE FEELING FIT!
WHERE DO WE SLEEP TONIGHT?
LAST YEAR THEY LAID OUT A BUNCH OF FUTONS. YOU'LL BE SO TIRED IT DOESN'T EVEN MATTER... THEN WE'VE GOT TOMORROW!
HOW YA DOIN', QUICK? ♡
WHERE'D YOU COME FROM?!

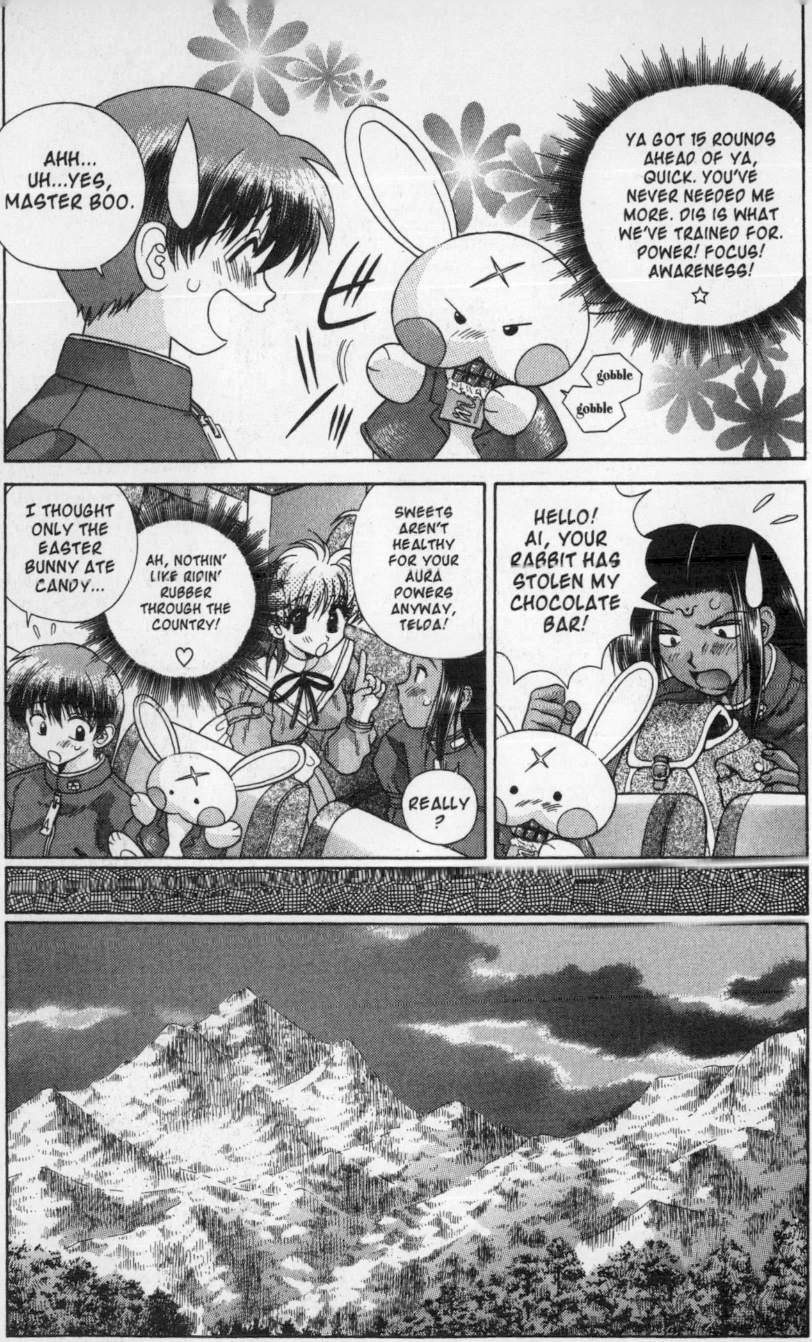
YA GOT 15 ROUNDS AHEAD OF YA, QUICK. YOU'VE NEVER NEEDED ME MORE. DIS IS WHAT WE'VE TRAINED FOR. POWER! FOCUS! AWARENESS! ☆
AHH... UH...YES, MASTER BOO.
gobble
gobble
HELLO! AI, YOUR RABBIT HAS STOLEN MY CHOCOLATE BAR!
SWEETS AREN'T HEALTHY FOR YOUR AURA POWERS ANYWAY, TELDA!
REALLY ?
AH, NOTHIN' LIKE RIDIN' RUBBER THROUGH THE COUNTRY! ♡
I THOUGHT ONLY THE EASTER BUNNY ATE CANDY...

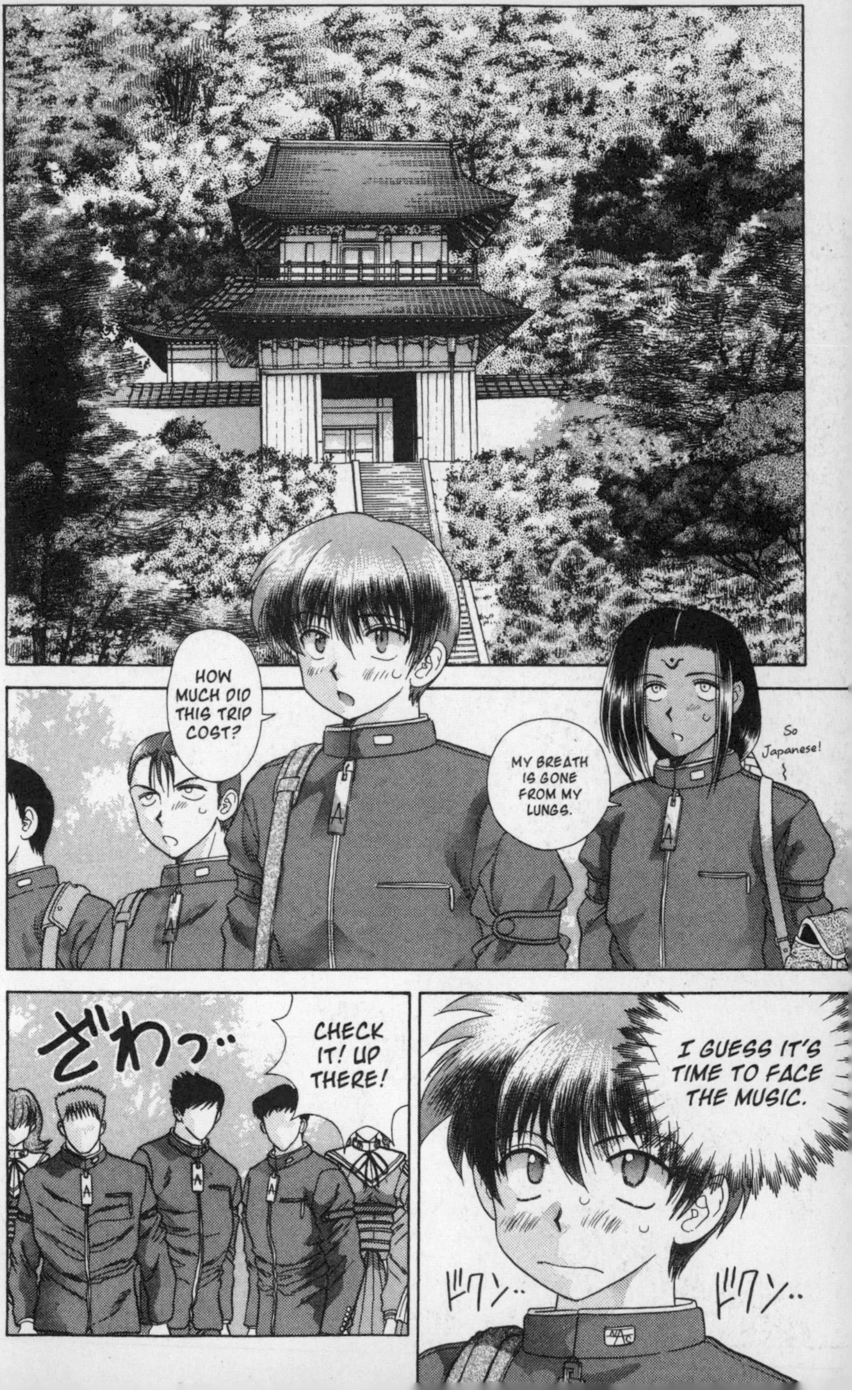
So Japanese!
MY BREATH IS GONE FROM MY LUNGS.
HOW MUCH DID THIS TRIP COST?
I GUESS IT'S TIME TO FACE THE MUSIC.
ドクン‥
ドクン‥
CHECK IT! UP THERE!
ざわっ

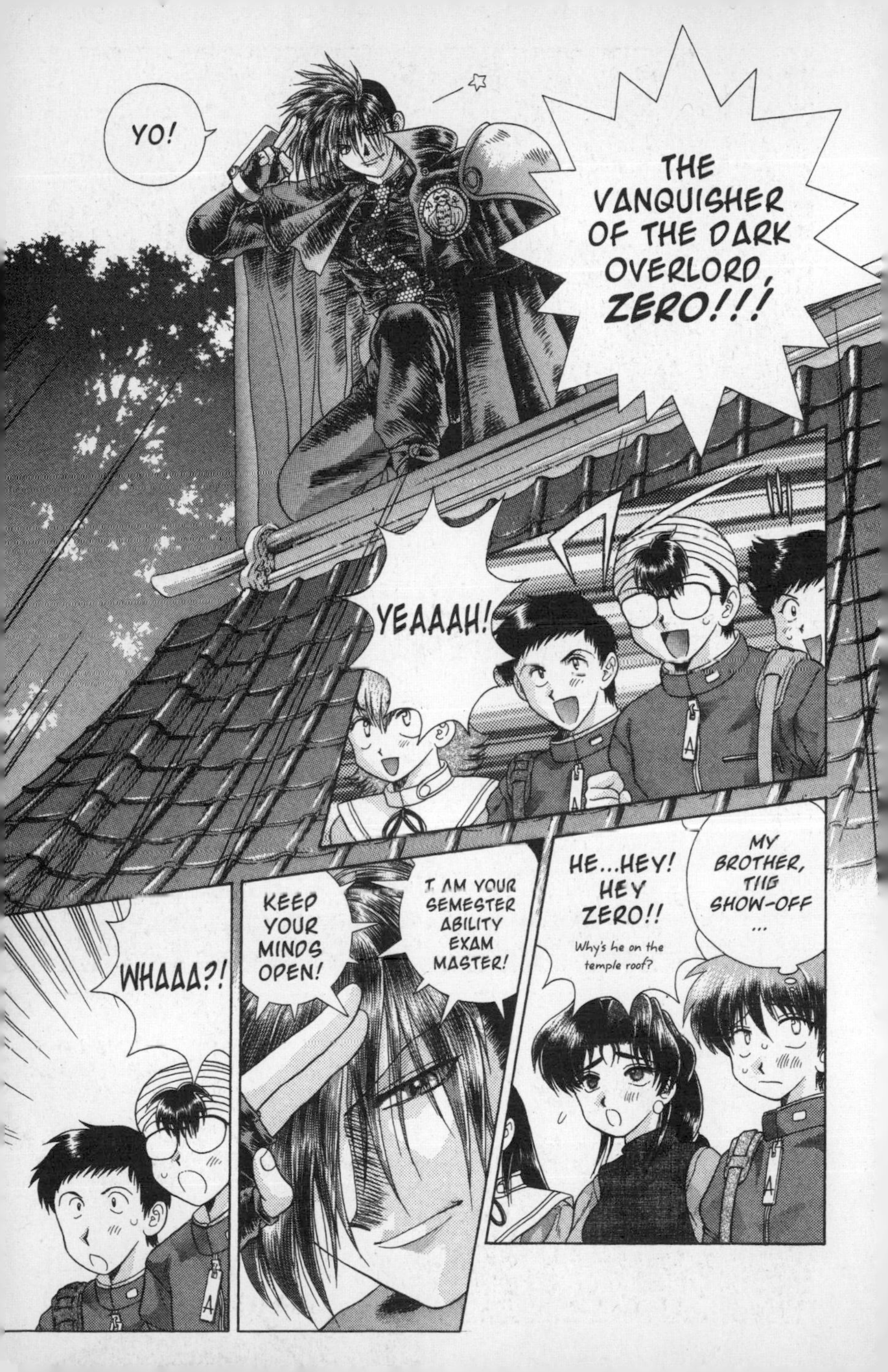
THE VANQUISHER OF THE DARK OVERLORD, ZERO!!!
YO!
YEAAAH!
MY BROTHER, THE SHOW-OFF ...
HE...HEY! HEY ZERO!!
Why's he on the temple roof?
I AM YOUR SEMESTER ABILITY EXAM MASTER!
KEEP YOUR MINDS OPEN!
WHAAA?!

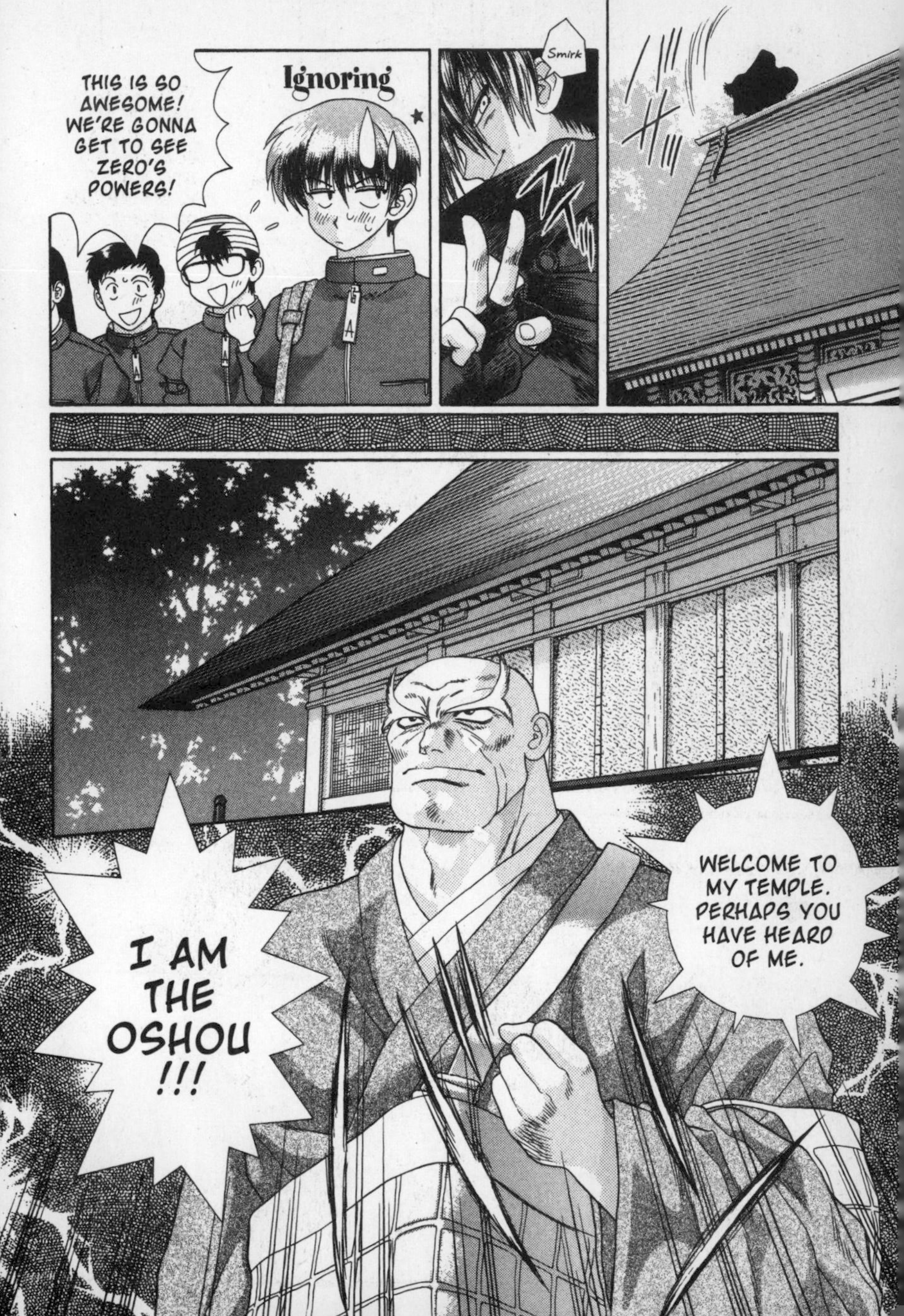
Smirk
Ignoring
THIS IS SO AWESOME! WE'RE GONNA GET TO SEE ZERO'S POWERS!
WELCOME TO MY TEMPLE. PERHAPS YOU HAVE HEARD OF ME.
I AM THE OSHOU !!!

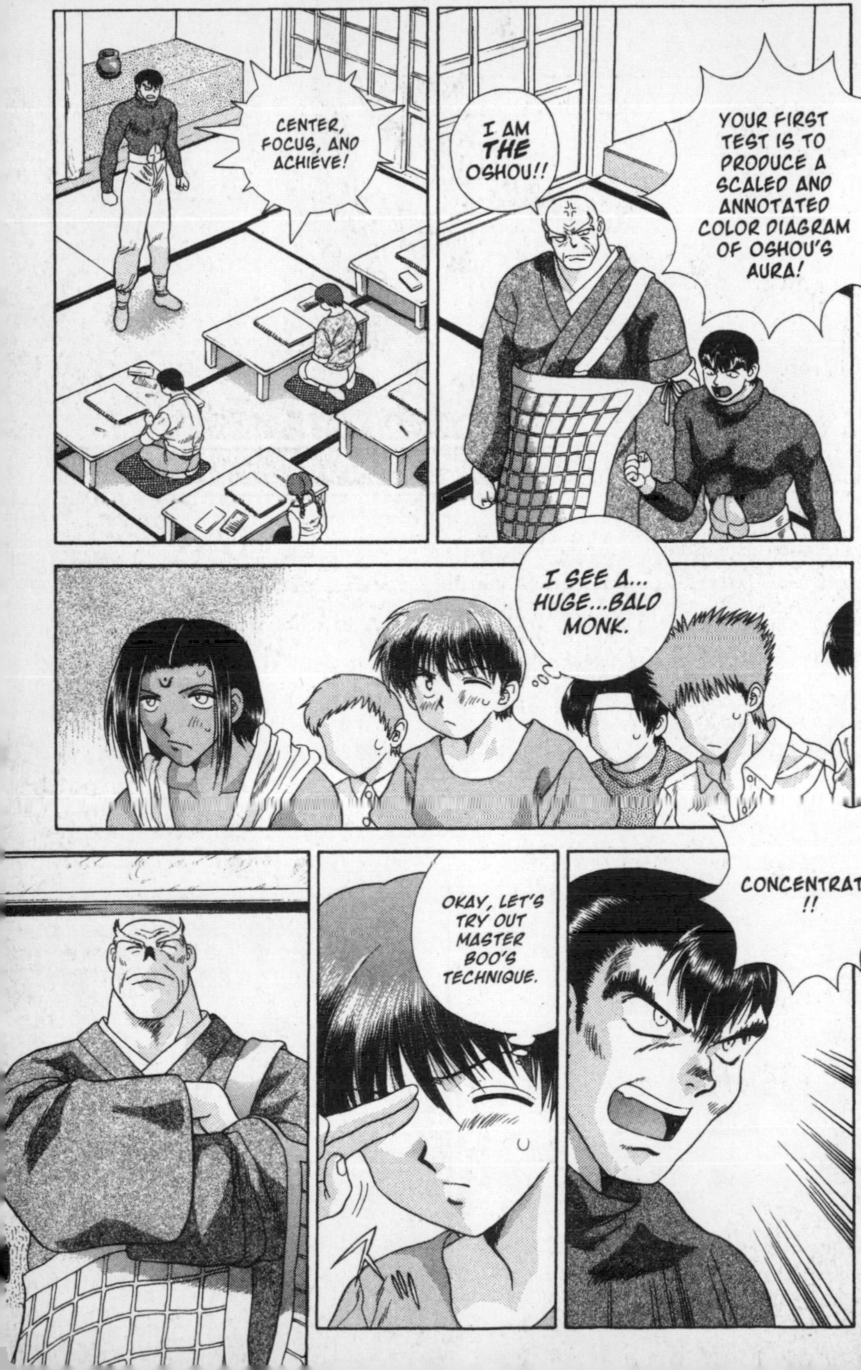
YOUR FIRST TEST IS TO PRODUCE A SCALED AND ANNOTATED COLOR DIAGRAM OF OSHOU'S AURA!
I AM THE OSHOU!!
CENTER, FOCUS, AND ACHIEVE!
I SEE A... HUGE...BALD MONK.
CONCENTRATE!!
OKAY, LET'S TRY OUT MASTER BOO'S TECHNIQUE.

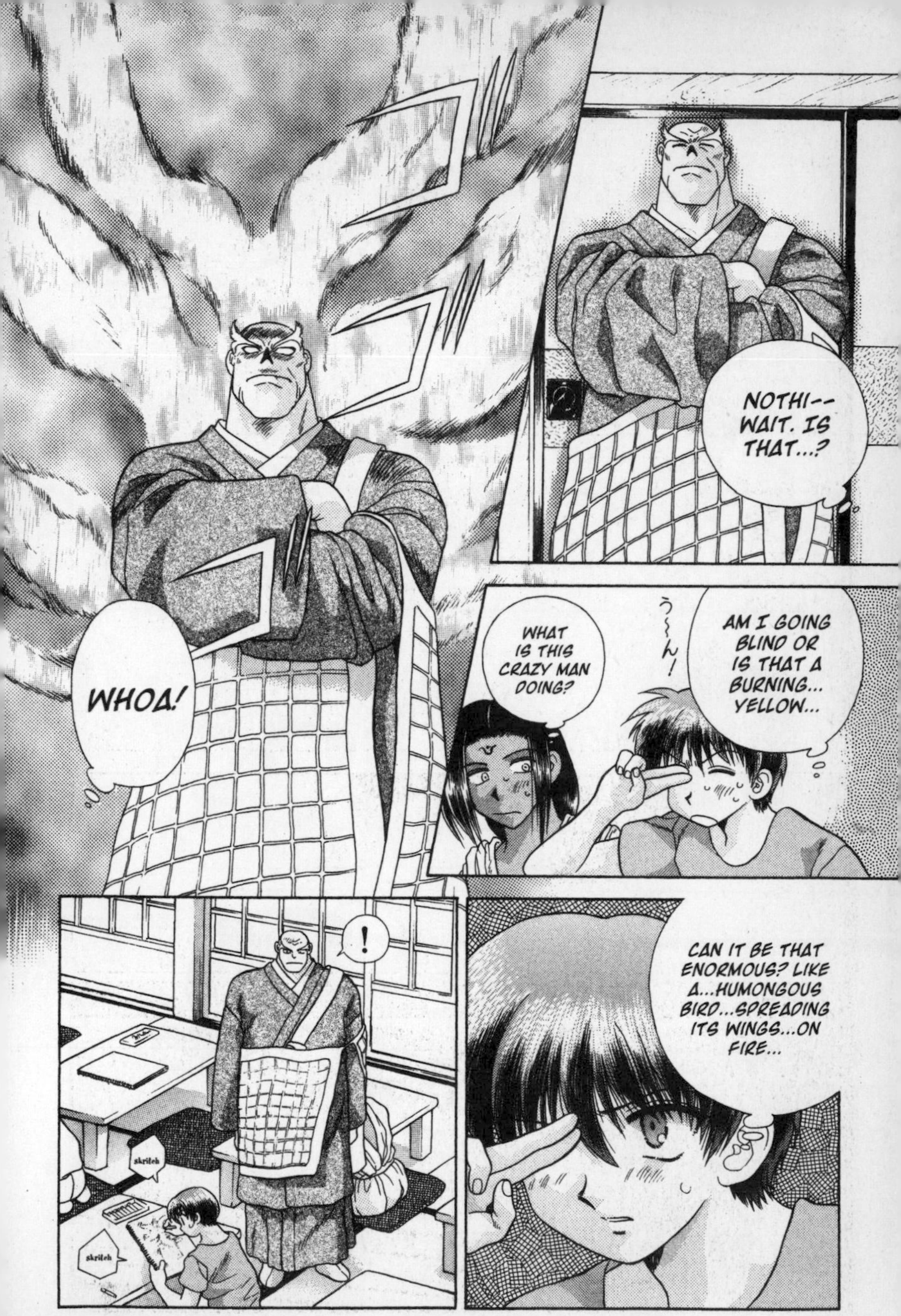
NOTHI--
WAIT. IS
THAT...?
AM I GOING
BLIND OR
IS THAT A
BURNING...
YELLOW...
う～ん!
WHAT
IS THIS
CRAZY MAN
DOING?
WHOA!
CAN IT BE THAT
ENORMOUS? LIKE
A...HUMONGOUS
BIRD...SPREADING
ITS WINGS...ON
FIRE...
!
skritch
skritch

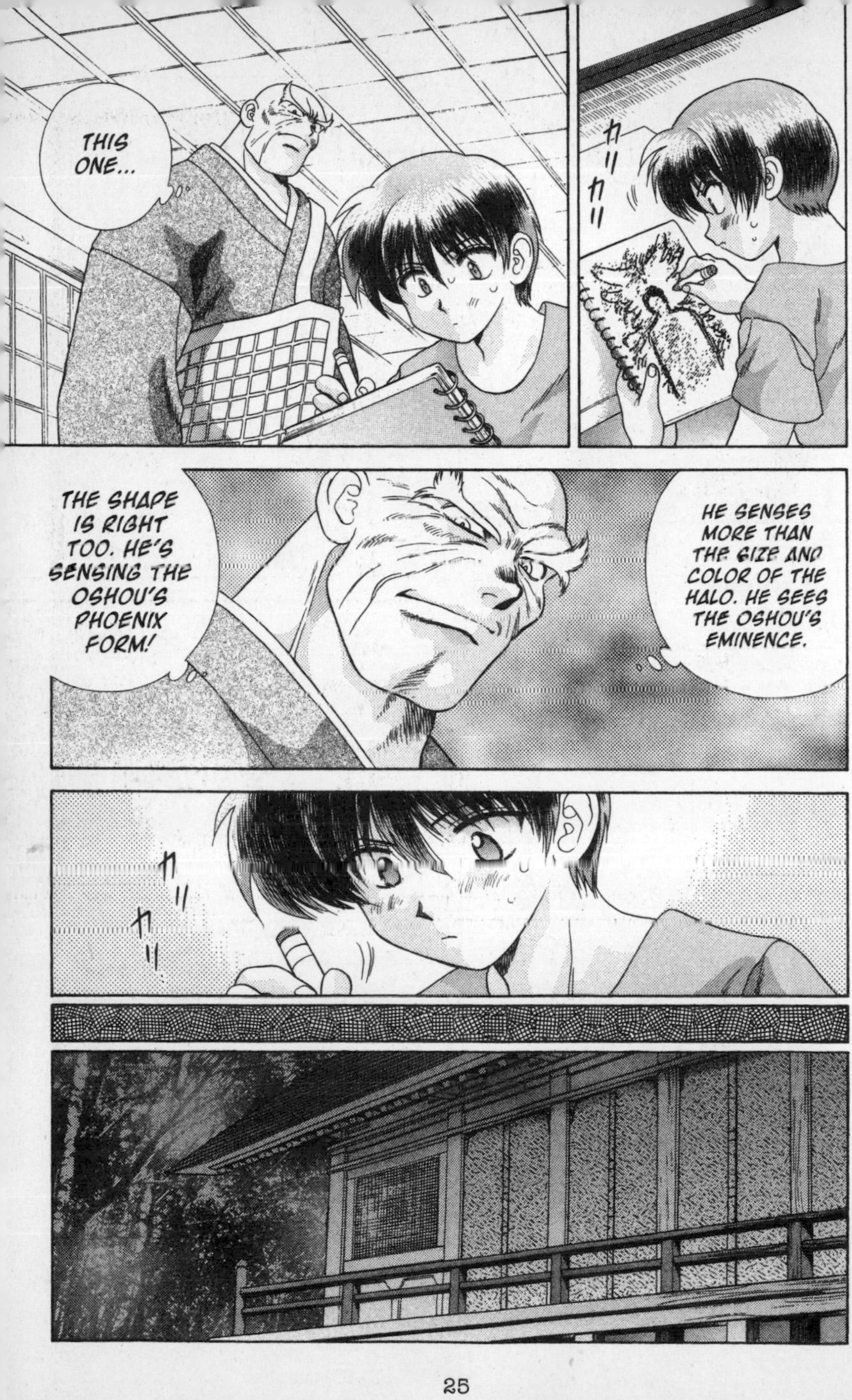
カリ カリ
THIS ONE...
HE SENSES MORE THAN THE SIZE AND COLOR OF THE HALO. HE SEES THE OSHOU'S EMINENCE.
THE SHAPE IS RIGHT TOO. HE'S SENSING THE OSHOU'S PHOENIX FORM!
カリ カリ

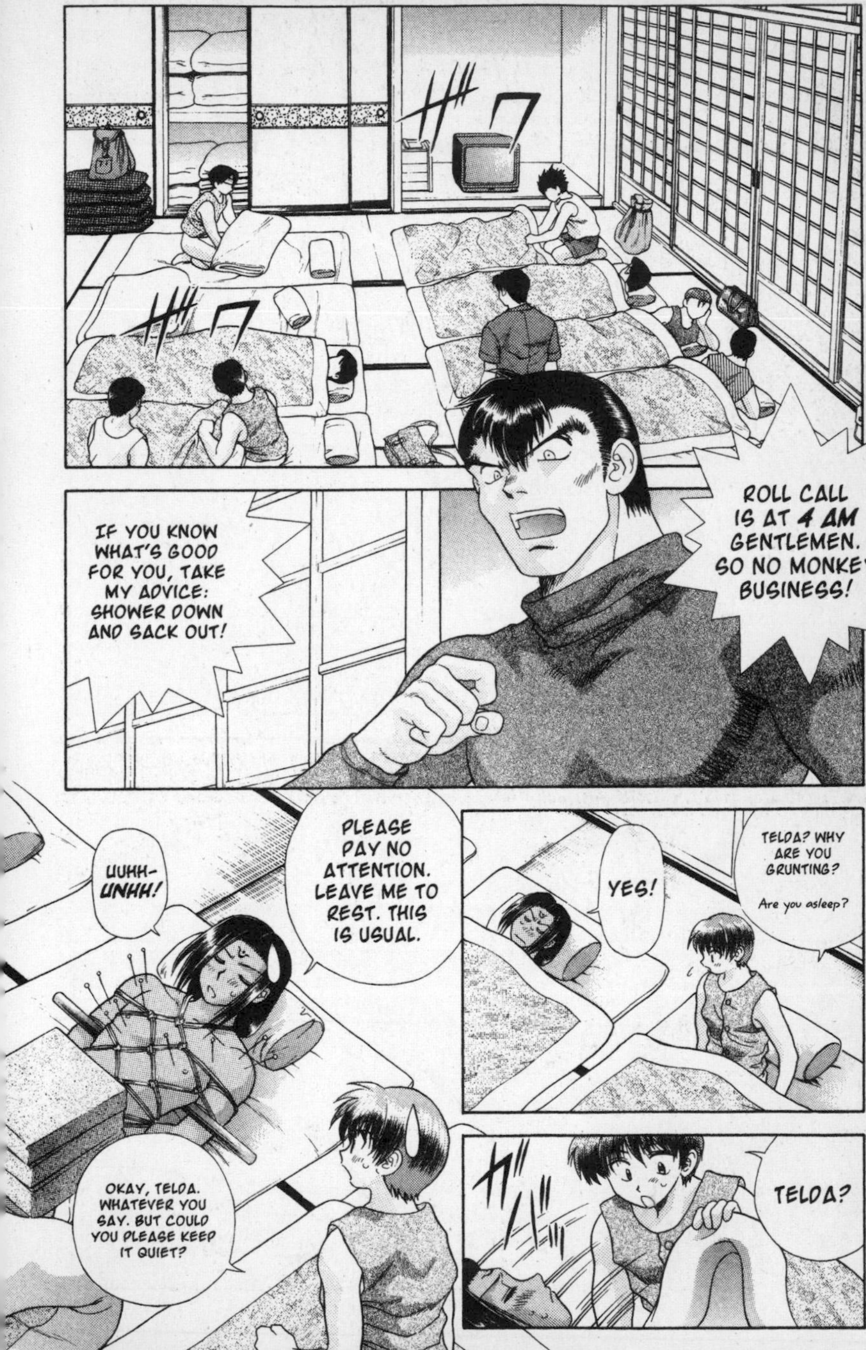
ROLL CALL IS AT 4 AM GENTLEMEN. SO NO MONKEY BUSINESS!
IF YOU KNOW WHAT'S GOOD FOR YOU, TAKE MY ADVICE: SHOWER DOWN AND SACK OUT!
TELDA? WHY ARE YOU GRUNTING?
Are you asleep?
YES!
TELDA?
PLEASE PAY NO ATTENTION. LEAVE ME TO REST. THIS IS USUAL.
UUHH-UNHH!
OKAY, TELDA. WHATEVER YOU SAY. BUT COULD YOU PLEASE KEEP IT QUIET?

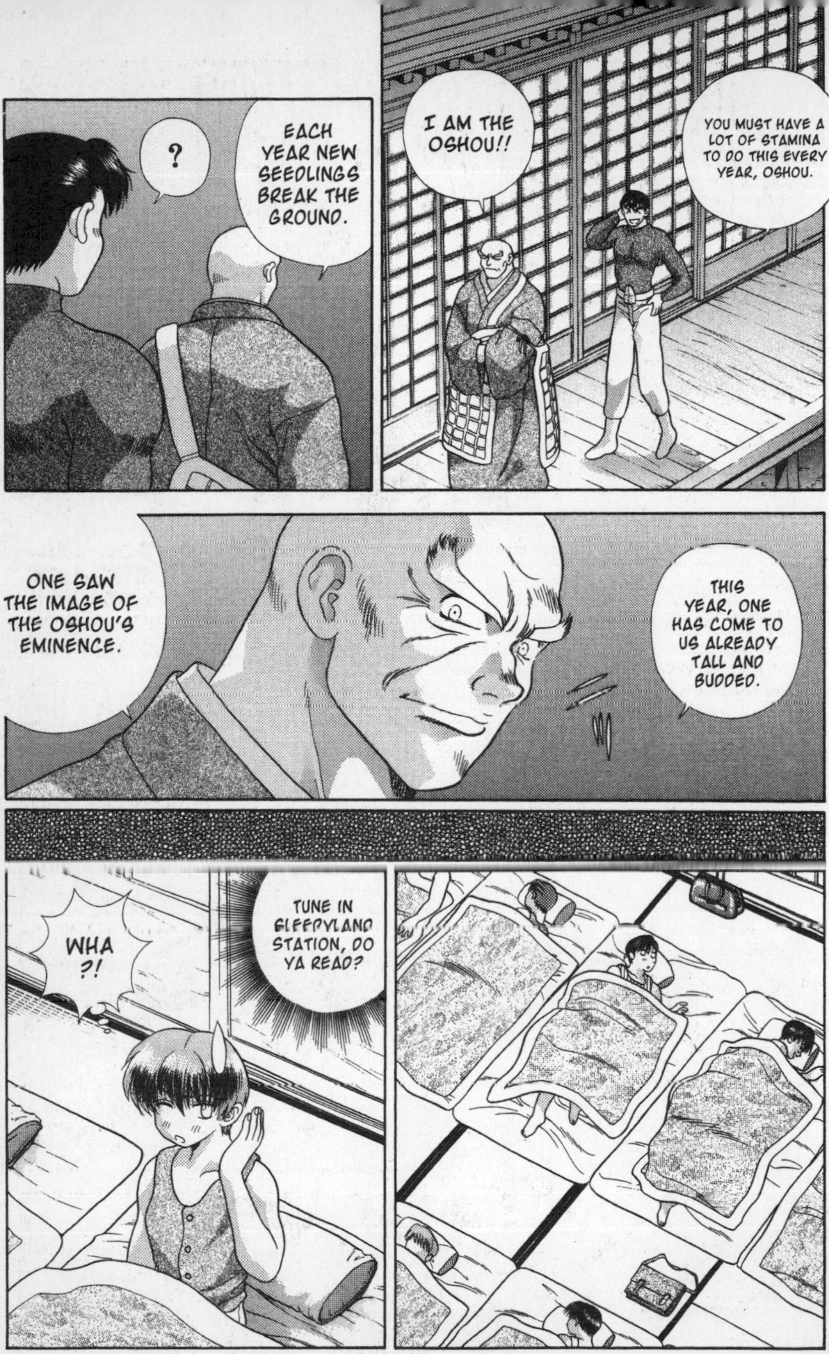
YOU MUST HAVE A LOT OF STAMINA TO DO THIS EVERY YEAR, OSHOU.
I AM THE OSHOU!!
EACH YEAR NEW SEEDLINGS BREAK THE GROUND.
?
THIS YEAR, ONE HAS COME TO US ALREADY TALL AND BUDDED.
ONE SAW THE IMAGE OF THE OSHOU'S EMINENCE.
TUNE IN SLEEPYLAND STATION, DO YA READ?
WHA ?!

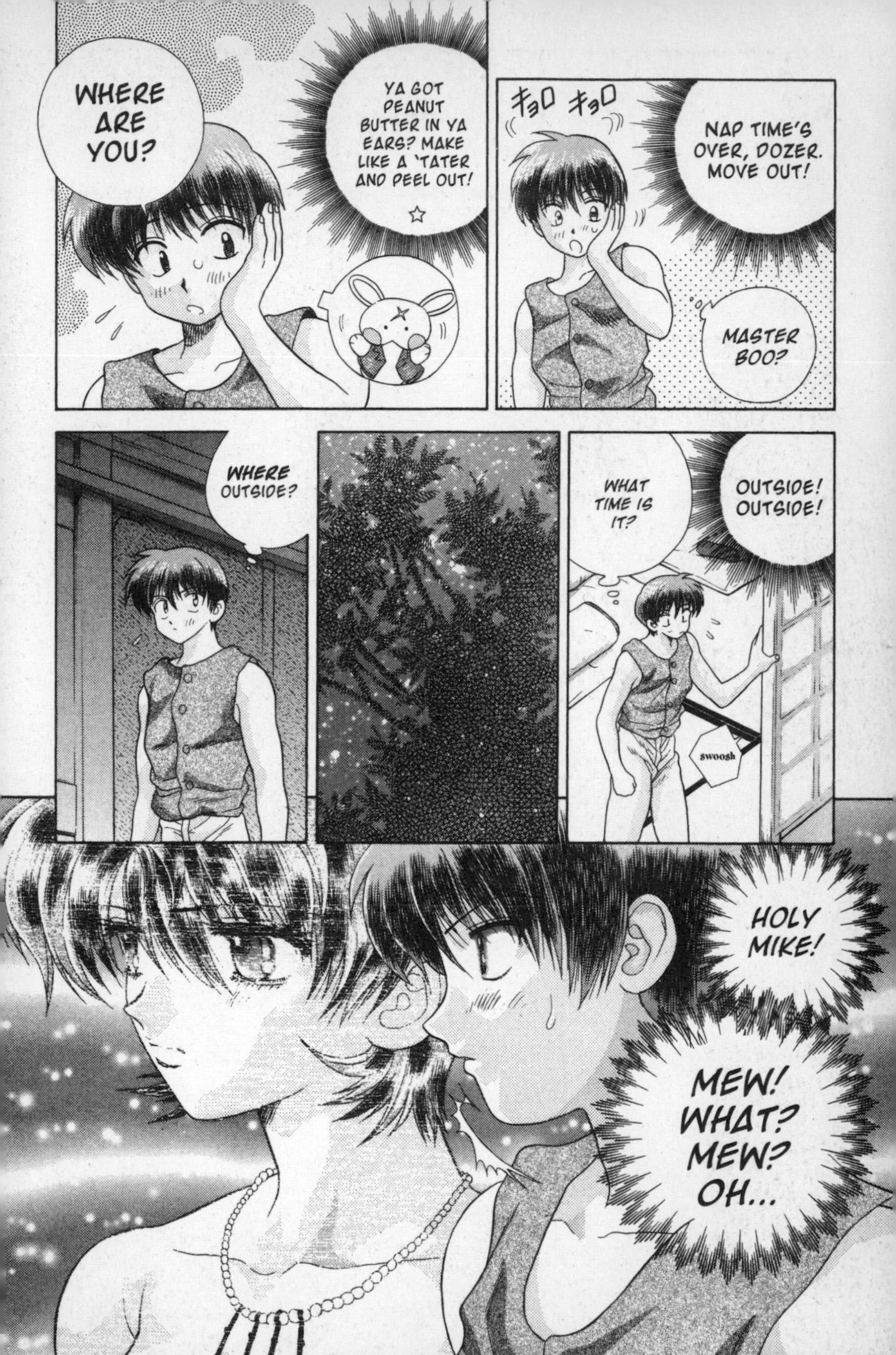
キョロ キョロ
NAP TIME'S OVER, DOZER. MOVE OUT!
MASTER BOO?
YA GOT PEANUT BUTTER IN YA EARS? MAKE LIKE A 'TATER AND PEEL OUT! ☆
WHERE ARE YOU?
OUTSIDE! OUTSIDE!
WHAT TIME IS IT?
swoosh
WHERE OUTSIDE?
HOLY MIKE!
MEW! WHAT? MEW? OH...

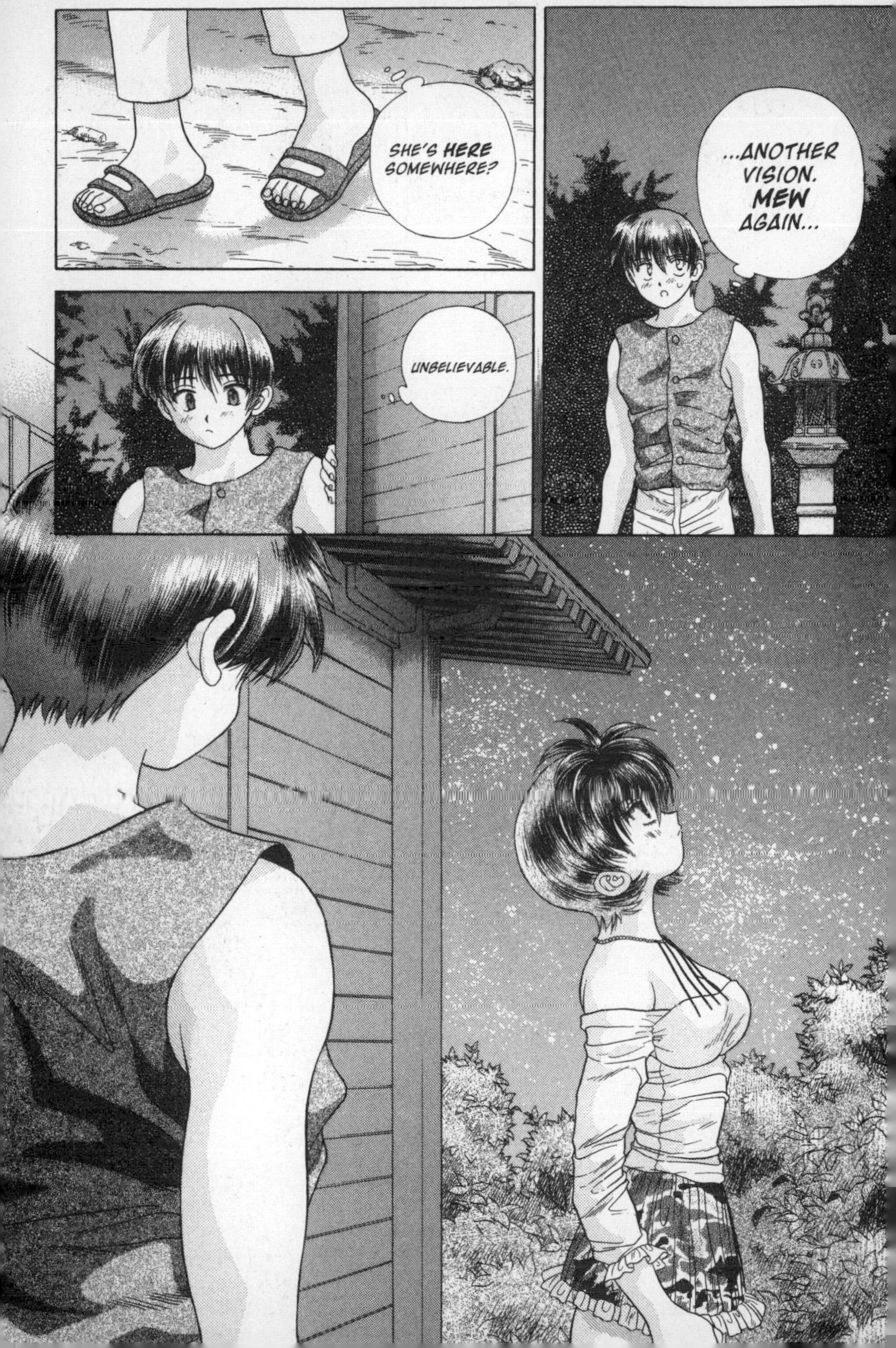
...ANOTHER VISION. MEW AGAIN...
SHE'S HERE SOMEWHERE?
UNBELIEVABLE.

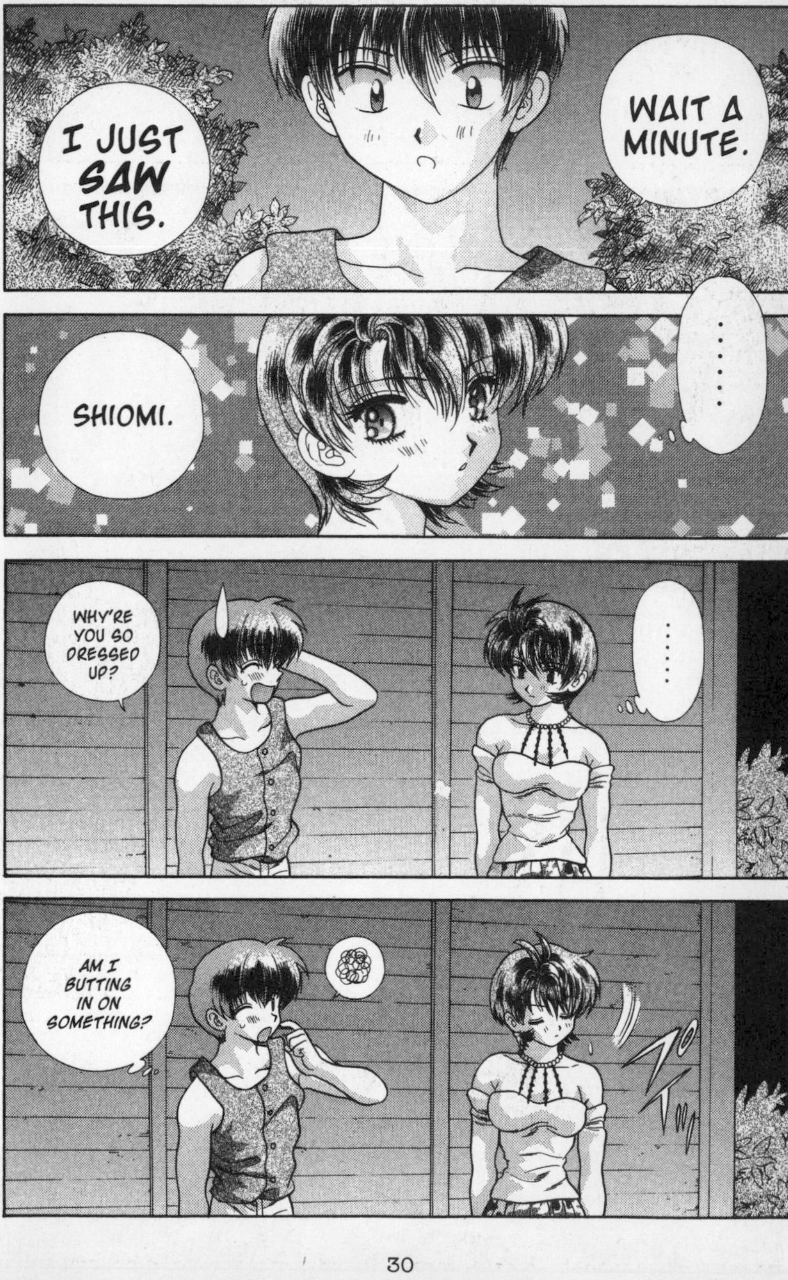
WAIT A MINUTE.
I JUST SAW THIS.
......
SHIOMI.
......
WHY'RE YOU SO DRESSED UP?
AM I BUTTING IN ON SOMETHING?

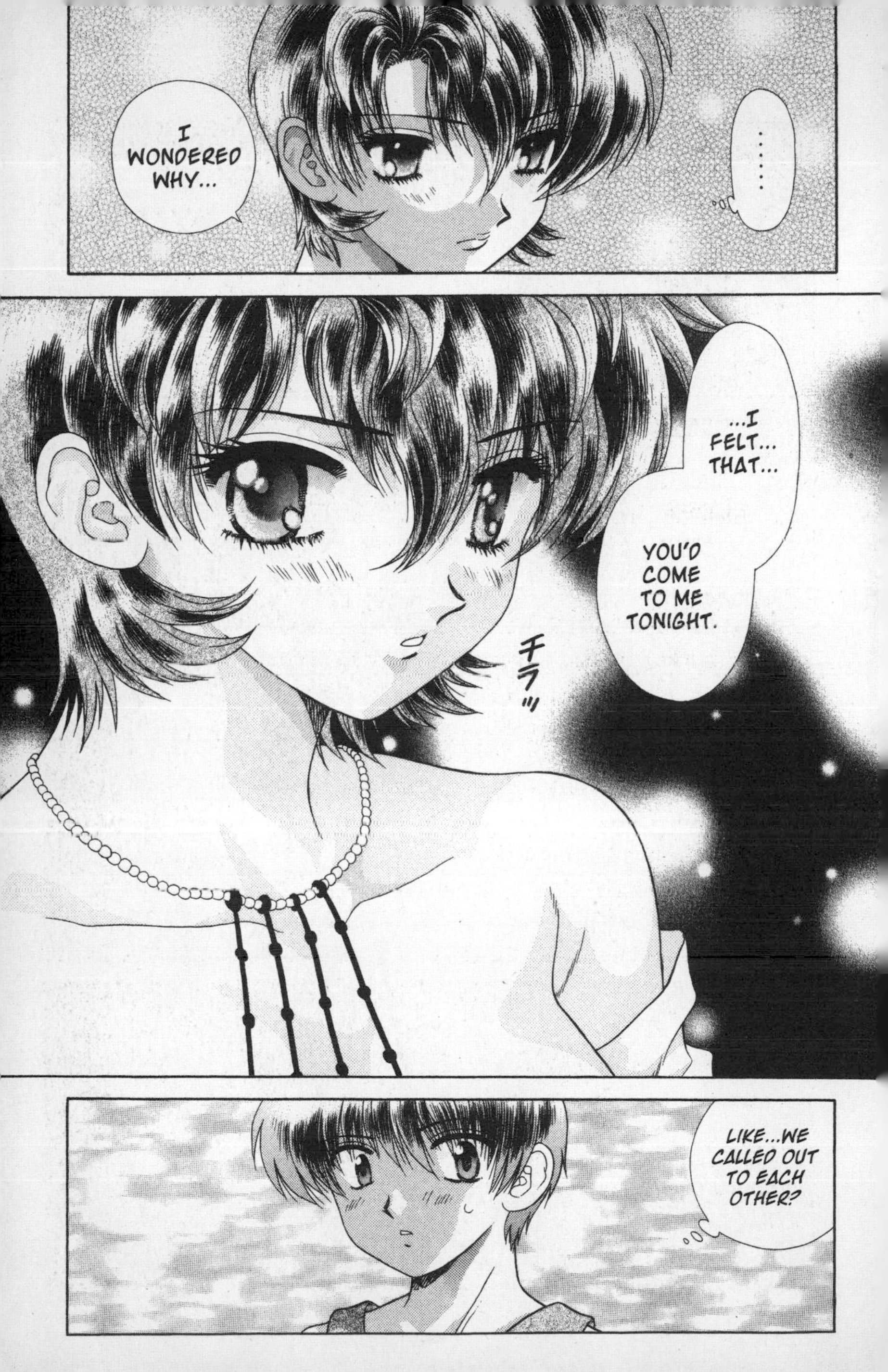
......
I WONDERED WHY...
...I FELT... THAT...
YOU'D COME TO ME TONIGHT.
チラッ
LIKE...WE CALLED OUT TO EACH OTHER?

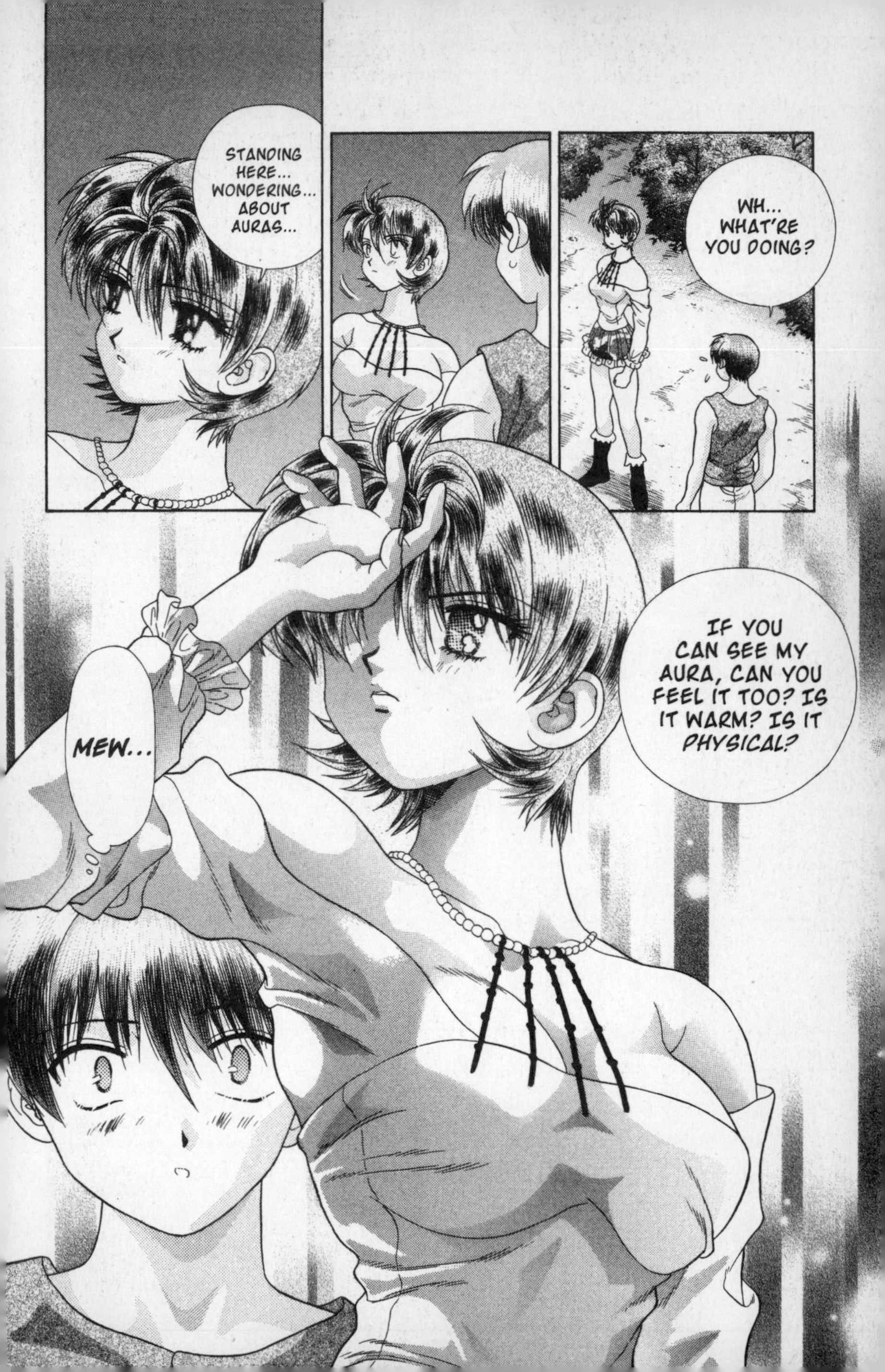
WH... WHAT'RE YOU DOING?
STANDING HERE... WONDERING... ABOUT AURAS...
IF YOU CAN SEE MY AURA, CAN YOU FEEL IT TOO? IS IT WARM? IS IT *PHYSICAL?*
MEW...

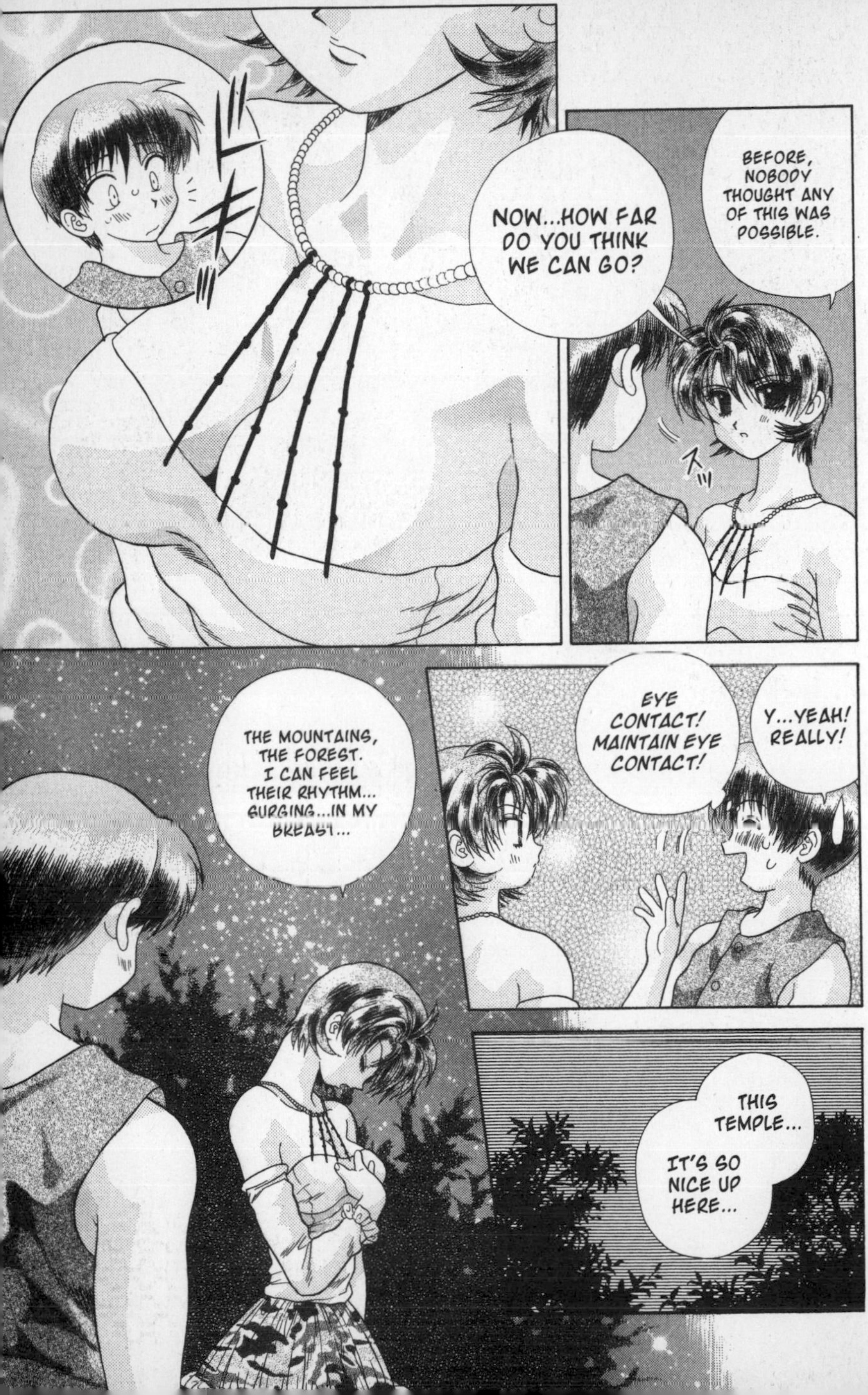
BEFORE, NOBODY THOUGHT ANY OF THIS WAS POSSIBLE.
NOW...HOW FAR DO YOU THINK WE CAN GO?
Y...YEAH! REALLY!
EYE CONTACT! MAINTAIN EYE CONTACT!
THIS TEMPLE...
IT'S SO NICE UP HERE...
THE MOUNTAINS, THE FOREST. I CAN FEEL THEIR RHYTHM... SURGING...IN MY BREAST...

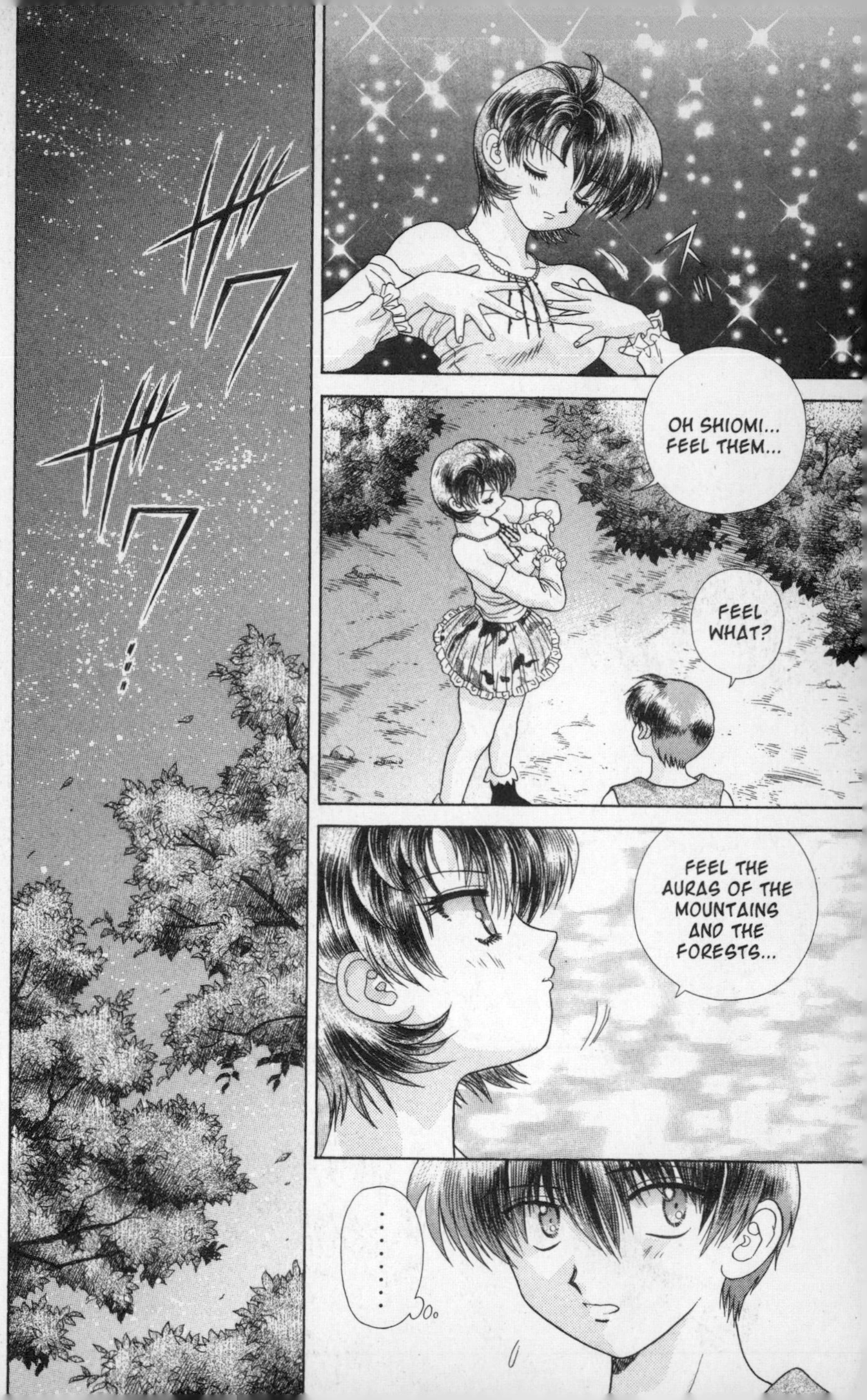
OH SHIOMI... FEEL THEM...
FEEL WHAT?
FEEL THE AURAS OF THE MOUNTAINS AND THE FORESTS...
......
ザワ
ザワ

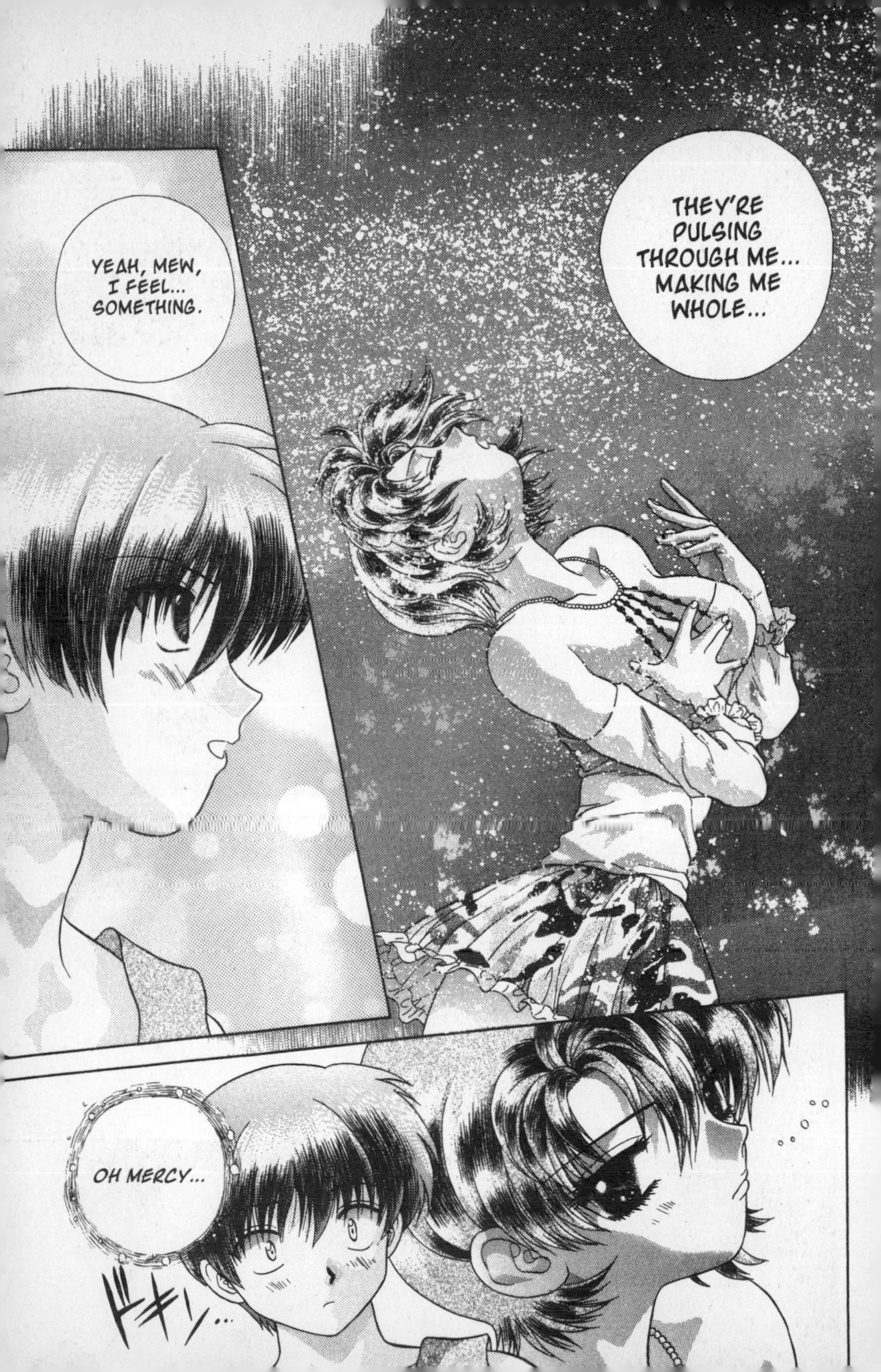
THEY'RE PULSING THROUGH ME... MAKING ME WHOLE...
YEAH, MEW, I FEEL... SOMETHING.
OH MERCY...

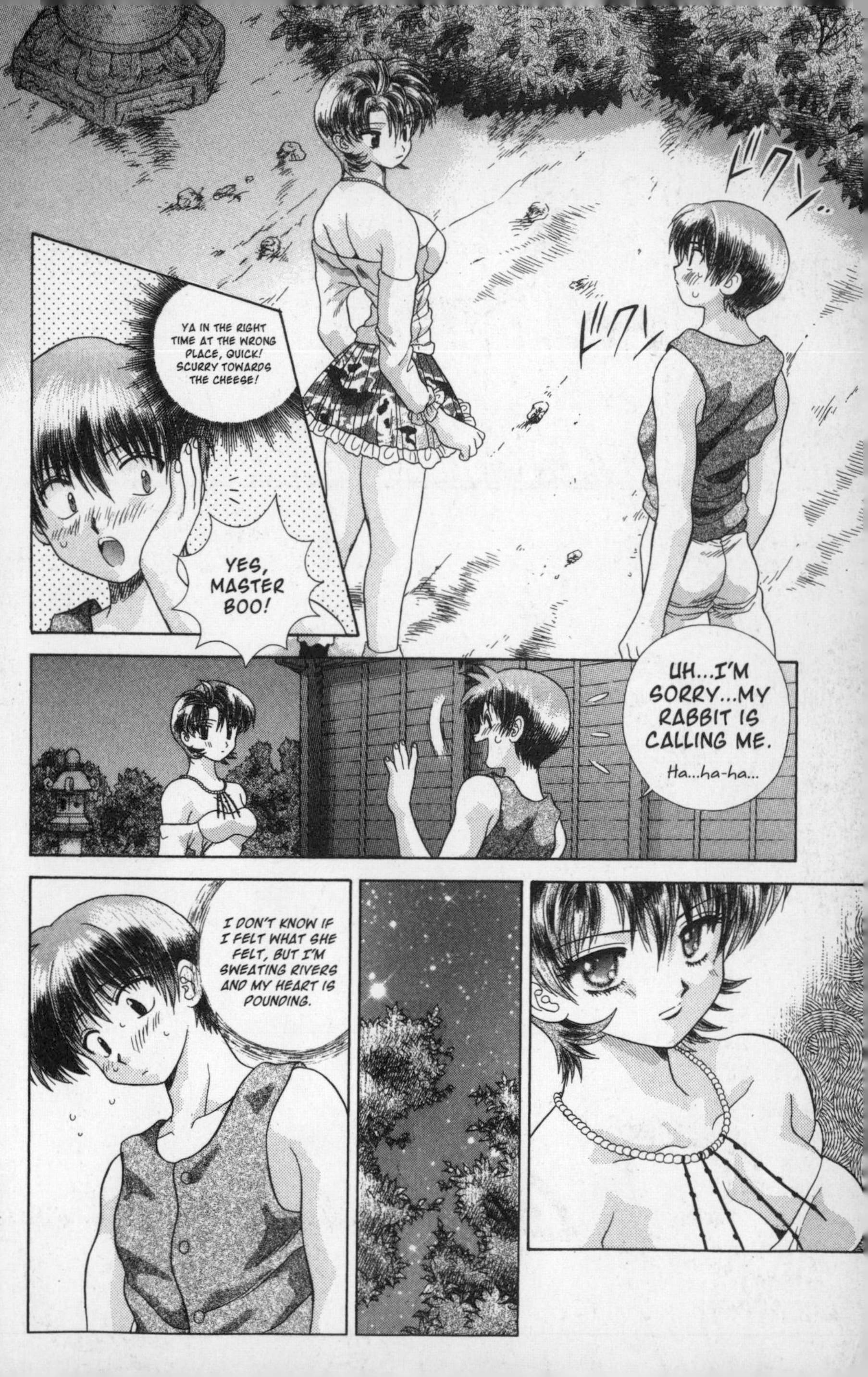
ドクン..
ドクン
YA IN THE RIGHT TIME AT THE WRONG PLACE, QUICK! SCURRY TOWARDS THE CHEESE!
YES, MASTER BOO!
UH...I'M SORRY...MY RABBIT IS CALLING ME.
Ha...ha-ha...
I DON'T KNOW IF I FELT WHAT SHE FELT, BUT I'M SWEATING RIVERS AND MY HEART IS POUNDING.

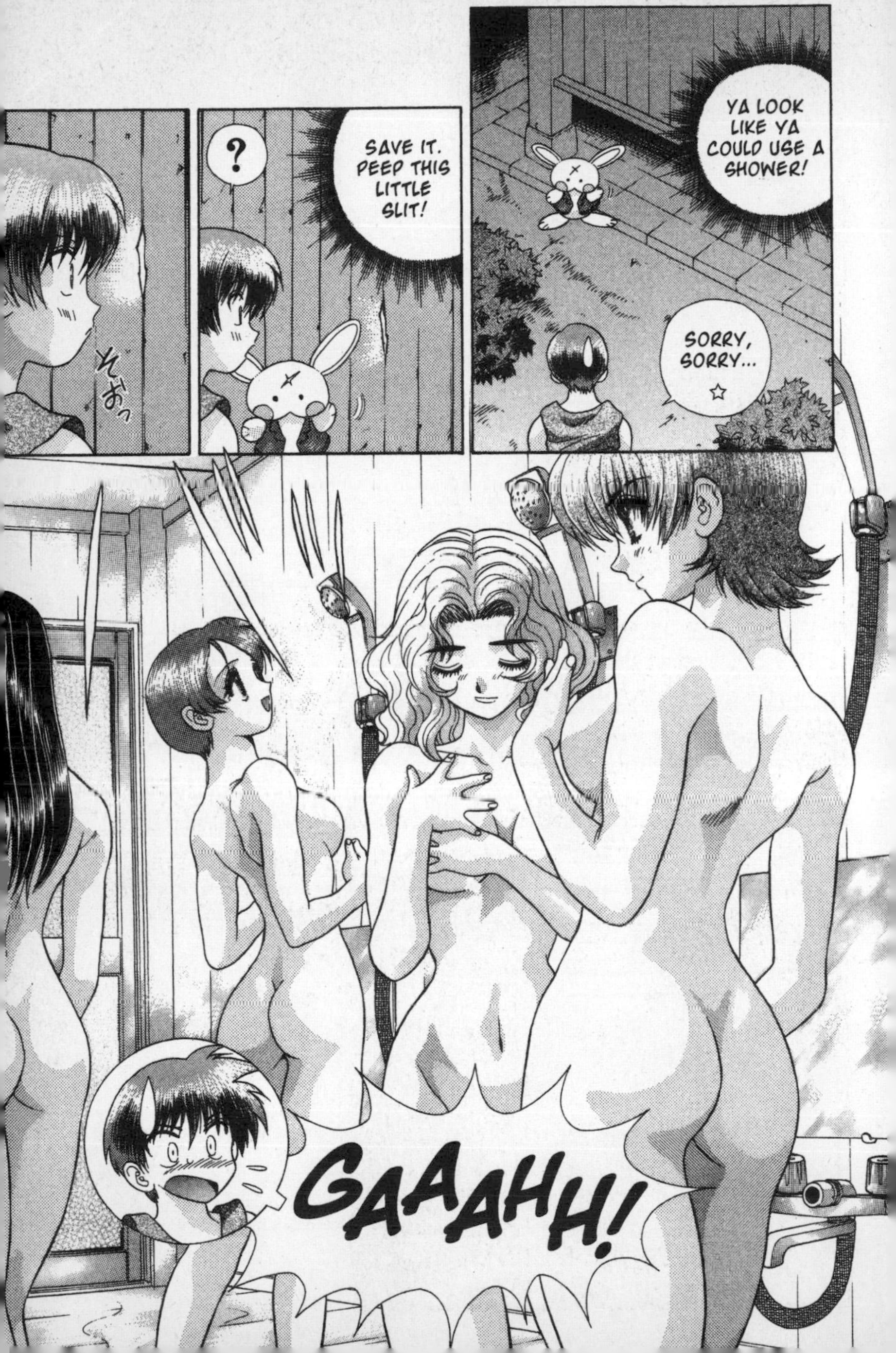
YA LOOK LIKE YA COULD USE A SHOWER!
SORRY, SORRY... ☆
SAVE IT. PEEP THIS LITTLE SLIT!
?
ぞおっ
GAAAHH!

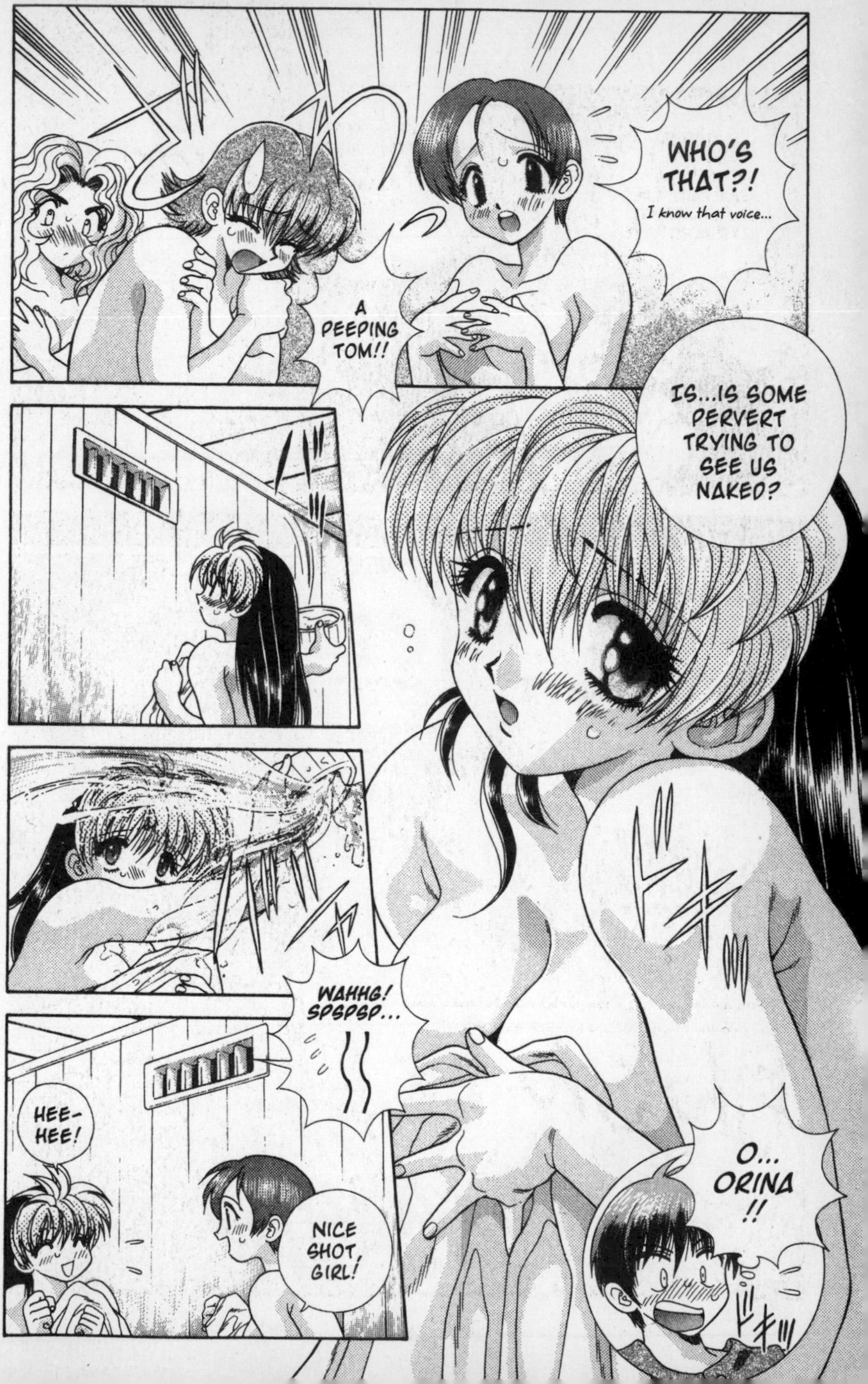
WHO'S THAT?!
I know that voice...
A PEEPING TOM!!
IS...IS SOME PERVERT TRYING TO SEE US NAKED?
O... ORINA !!
WAHHG! SPSPSP...
NICE SHOT, GIRL!
HEE-HEE!

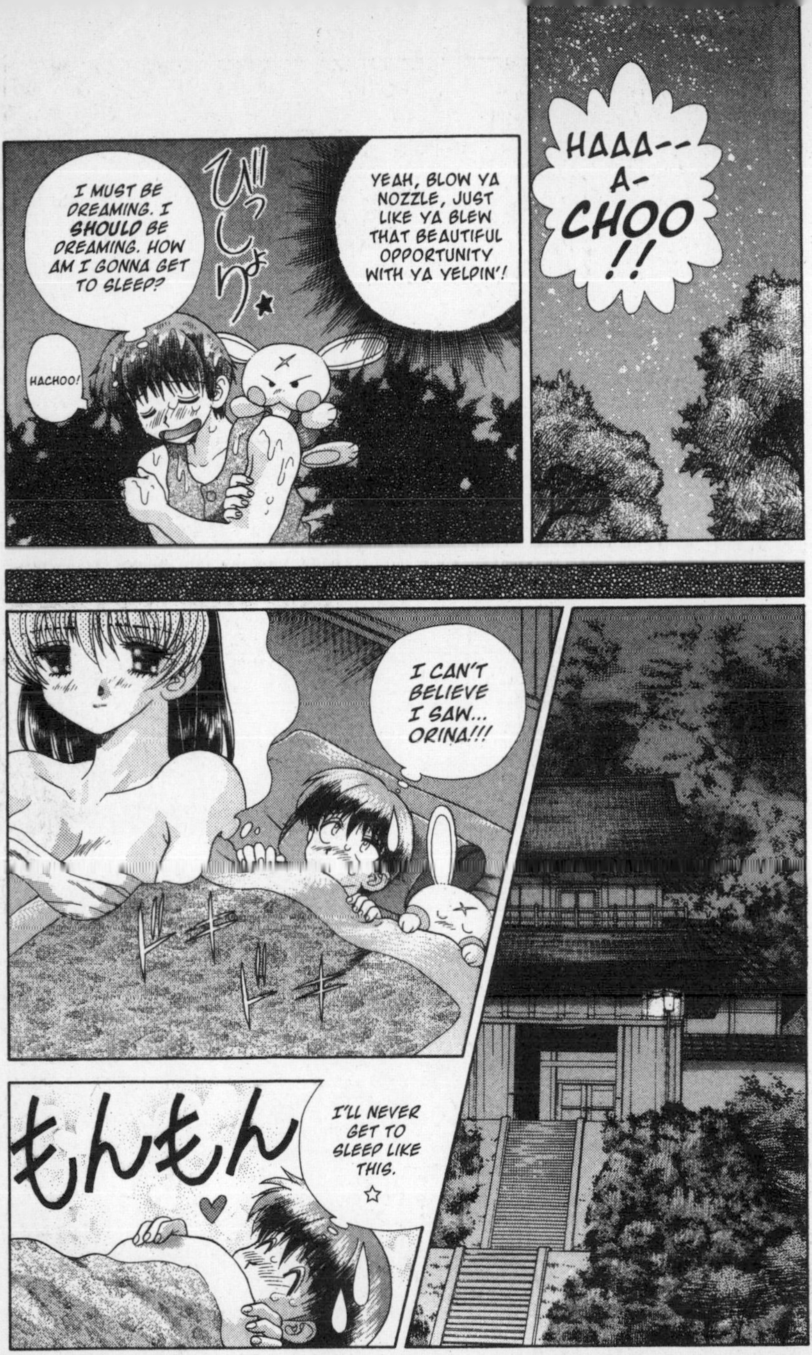
HAAAA--A-CHOO!!
YEAH, BLOW YA NOZZLE, JUST LIKE YA BLEW THAT BEAUTIFUL OPPORTUNITY WITH YA YELPIN'!
びっしょり
I MUST BE DREAMING. I SHOULD BE DREAMING. HOW AM I GONNA GET TO SLEEP?
HACHOO!
I CAN'T BELIEVE I SAW... ORINA!!!
ドキドキ
I'LL NEVER GET TO SLEEP LIKE THIS. ☆
もんもん

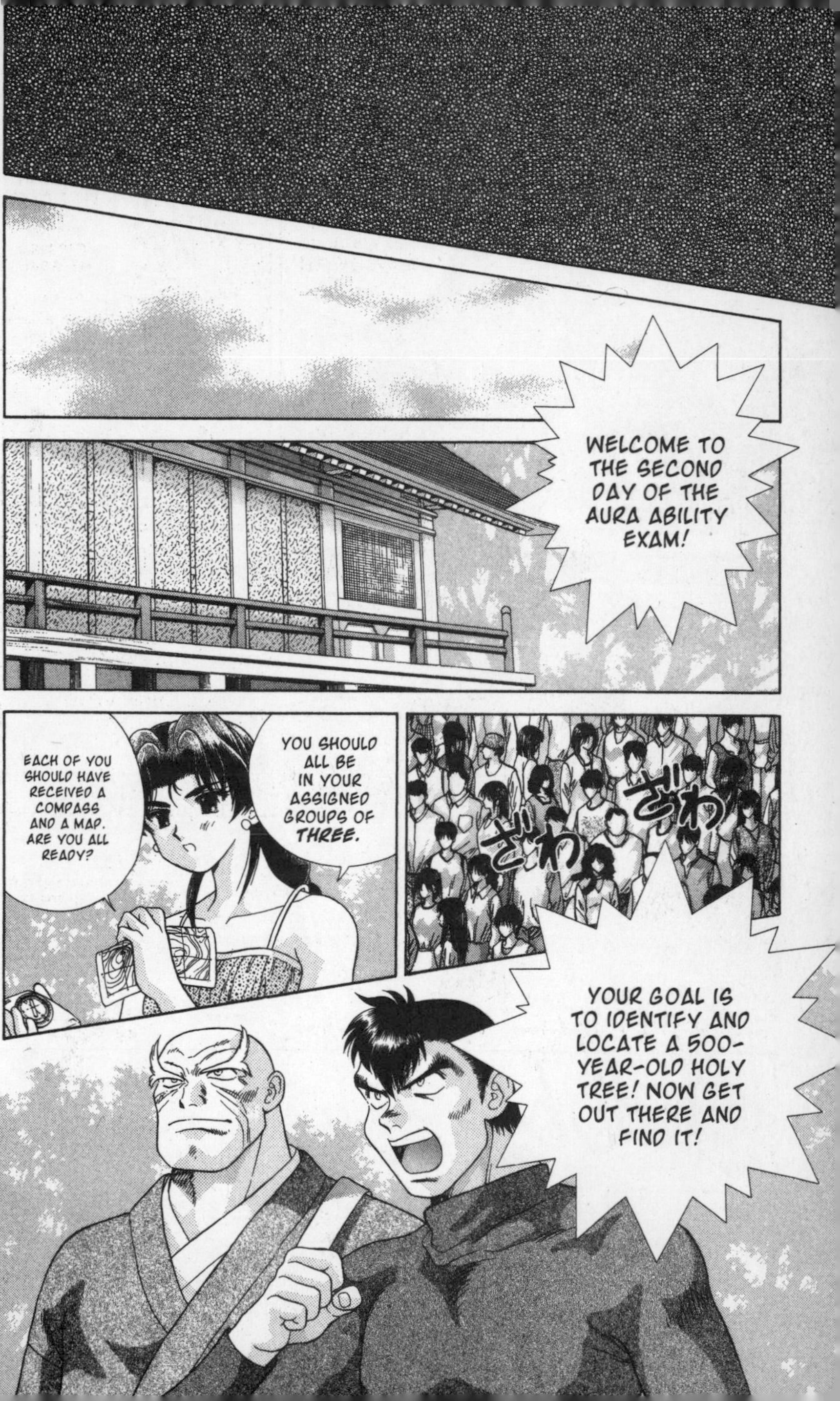
WELCOME TO THE SECOND DAY OF THE AURA ABILITY EXAM!
ざわ ざわ
YOU SHOULD ALL BE IN YOUR ASSIGNED GROUPS OF THREE.
EACH OF YOU SHOULD HAVE RECEIVED A COMPASS AND A MAP. ARE YOU ALL READY?
YOUR GOAL IS TO IDENTIFY AND LOCATE A 500-YEAR-OLD HOLY TREE! NOW GET OUT THERE AND FIND IT!

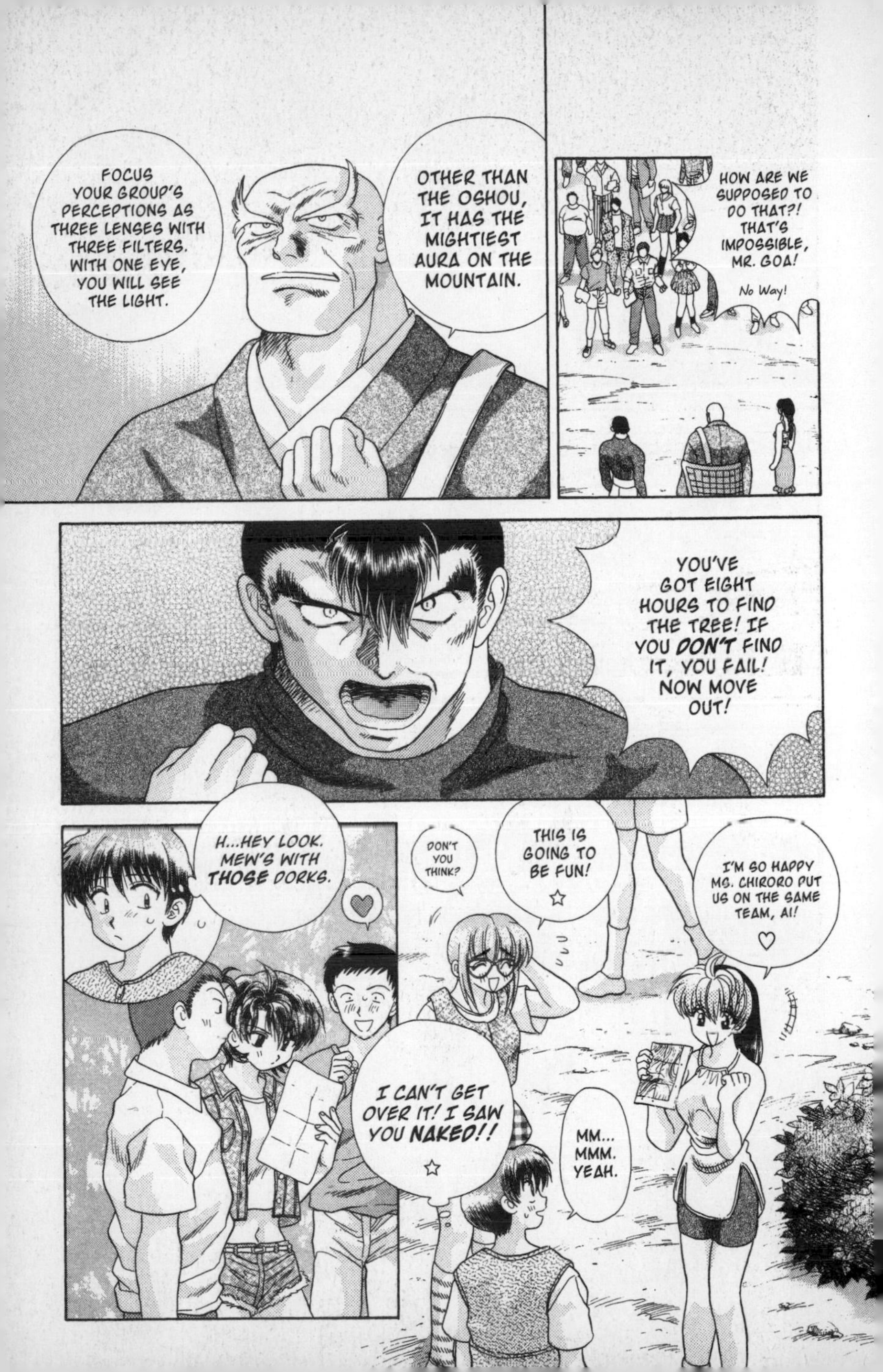
HOW ARE WE SUPPOSED TO DO THAT?! THAT'S IMPOSSIBLE, MR. GOA!
No Way!
OTHER THAN THE OSHOU, IT HAS THE MIGHTIEST AURA ON THE MOUNTAIN.
FOCUS YOUR GROUP'S PERCEPTIONS AS THREE LENSES WITH THREE FILTERS. WITH ONE EYE, YOU WILL SEE THE LIGHT.
YOU'VE GOT EIGHT HOURS TO FIND THE TREE! IF YOU DON'T FIND IT, YOU FAIL! NOW MOVE OUT!
I'M SO HAPPY MS. CHIRORO PUT US ON THE SAME TEAM, AI! ♡
THIS IS GOING TO BE FUN! ☆
DON'T YOU THINK?
MM... MMM. YEAH.
I CAN'T GET OVER IT! I SAW YOU NAKED!! ☆
H...HEY LOOK. MEW'S WITH THOSE DORKS.

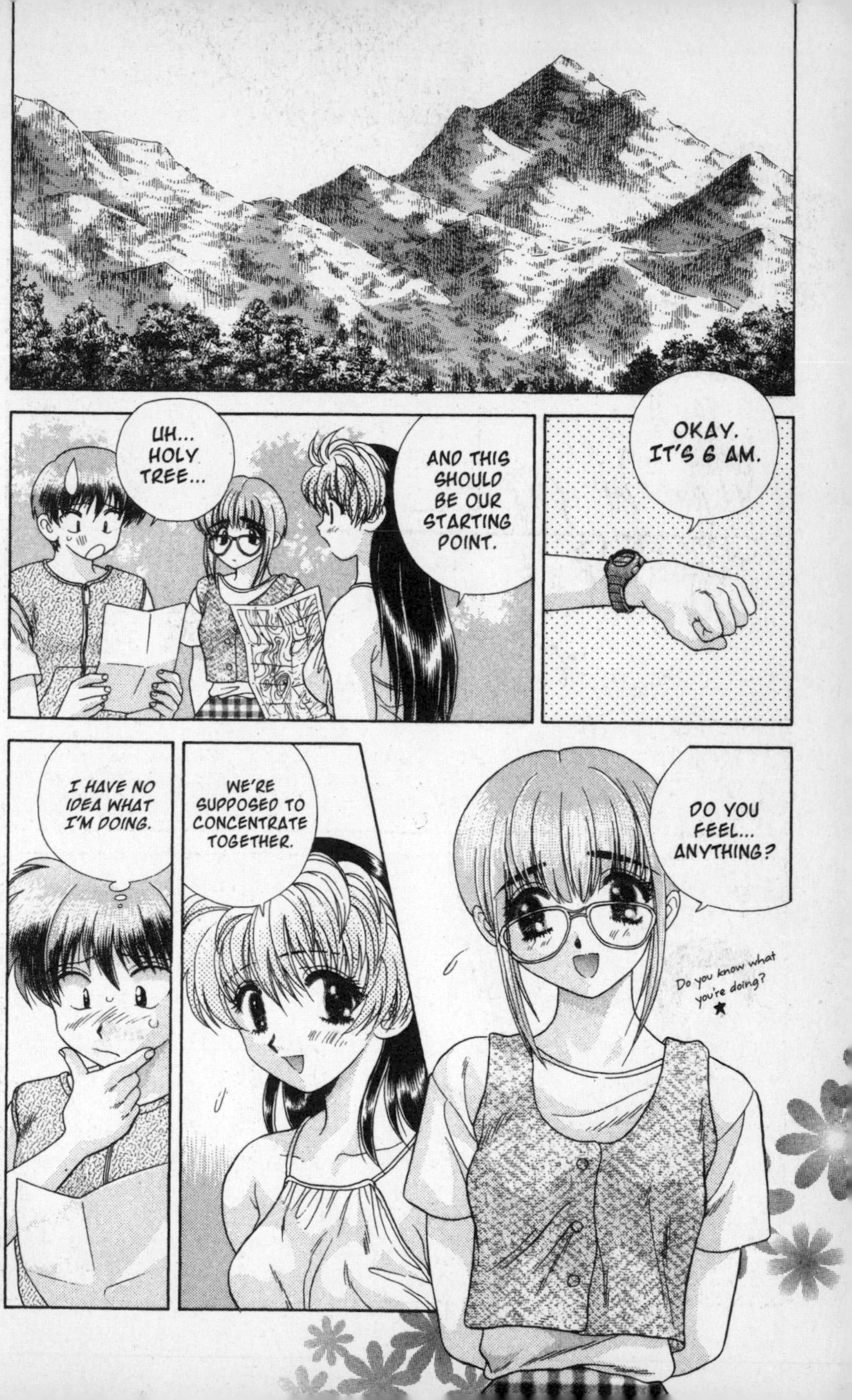
OKAY. IT'S 6 AM.
AND THIS SHOULD BE OUR STARTING POINT.
UH... HOLY TREE...
DO YOU FEEL... ANYTHING?
Do you know what you're doing? ★
WE'RE SUPPOSED TO CONCENTRATE TOGETHER.
I HAVE NO IDEA WHAT I'M DOING.

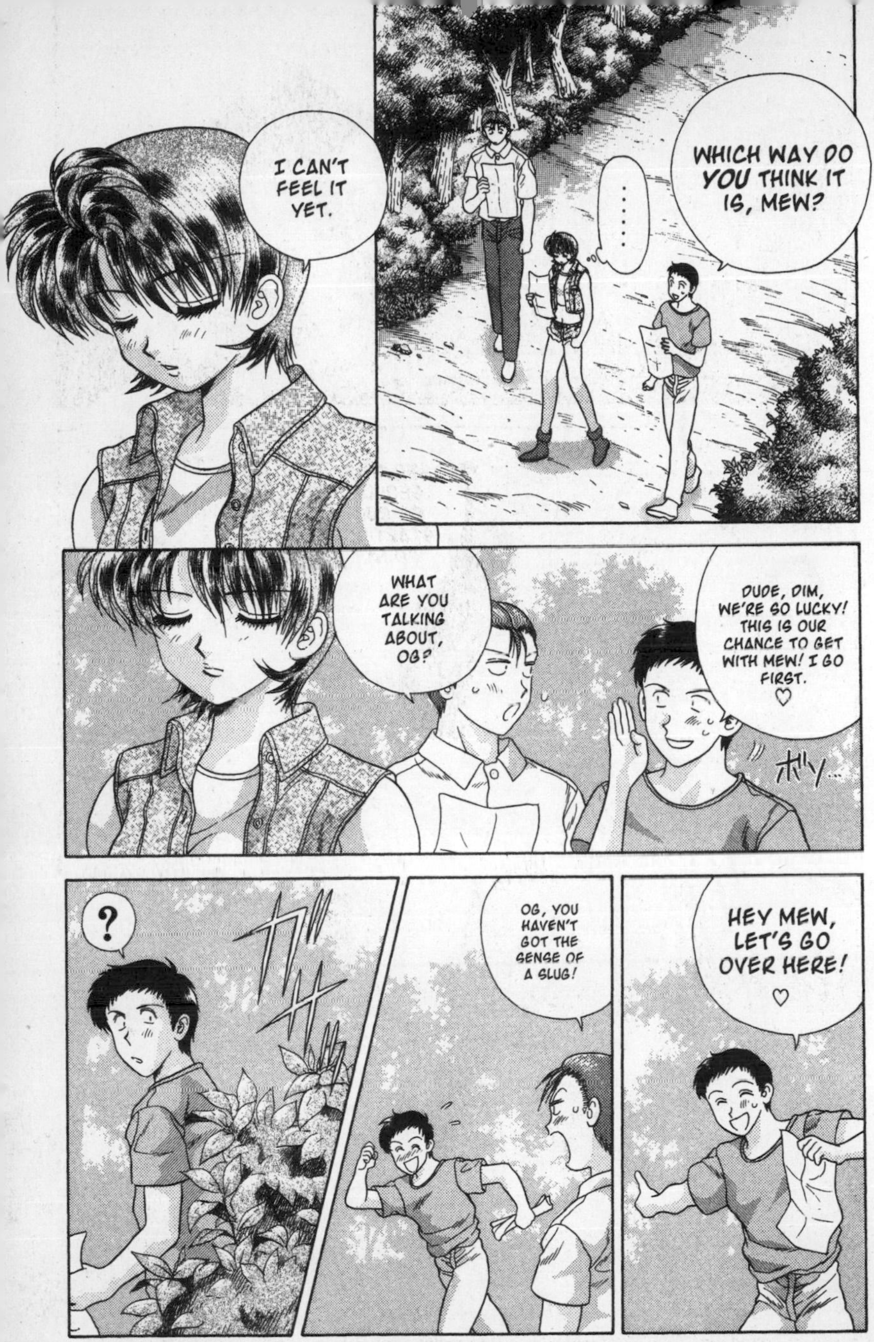
WHICH WAY DO YOU THINK IT IS, MEW?
......
I CAN'T FEEL IT YET.
DUDE, DIM, WE'RE SO LUCKY! THIS IS OUR CHANCE TO GET WITH MEW! I GO FIRST. ♡
ボソ…
WHAT ARE YOU TALKING ABOUT, OG?
HEY MEW, LET'S GO OVER HERE! ♡
OG, YOU HAVEN'T GOT THE SENSE OF A SLUG!
?

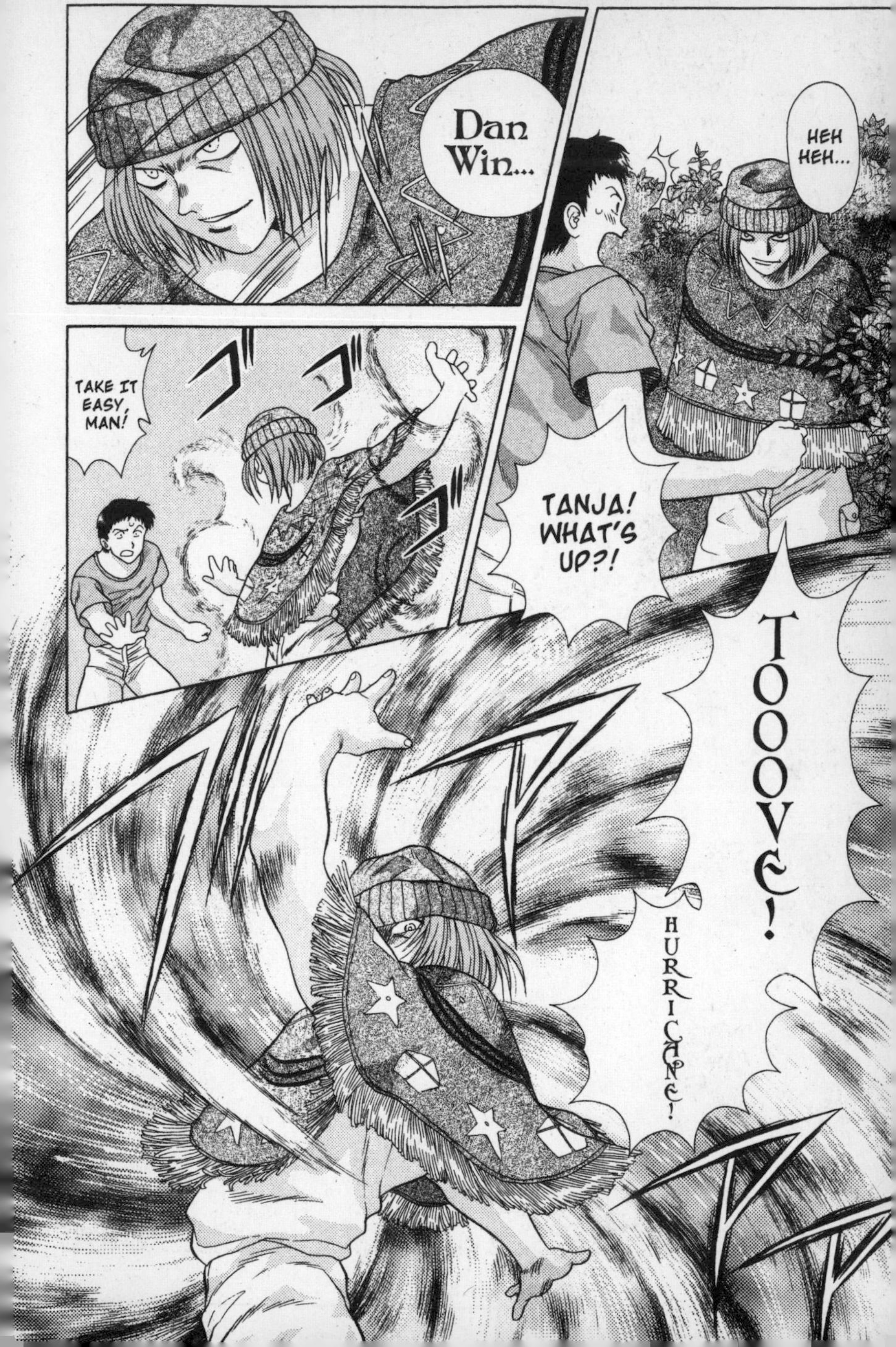
HEH HEH...
TANJA! WHAT'S UP?!
Dan Win...
ゴ ゴ ゴ
TAKE IT EASY, MAN!
TOOOVE!
HURRICANE!

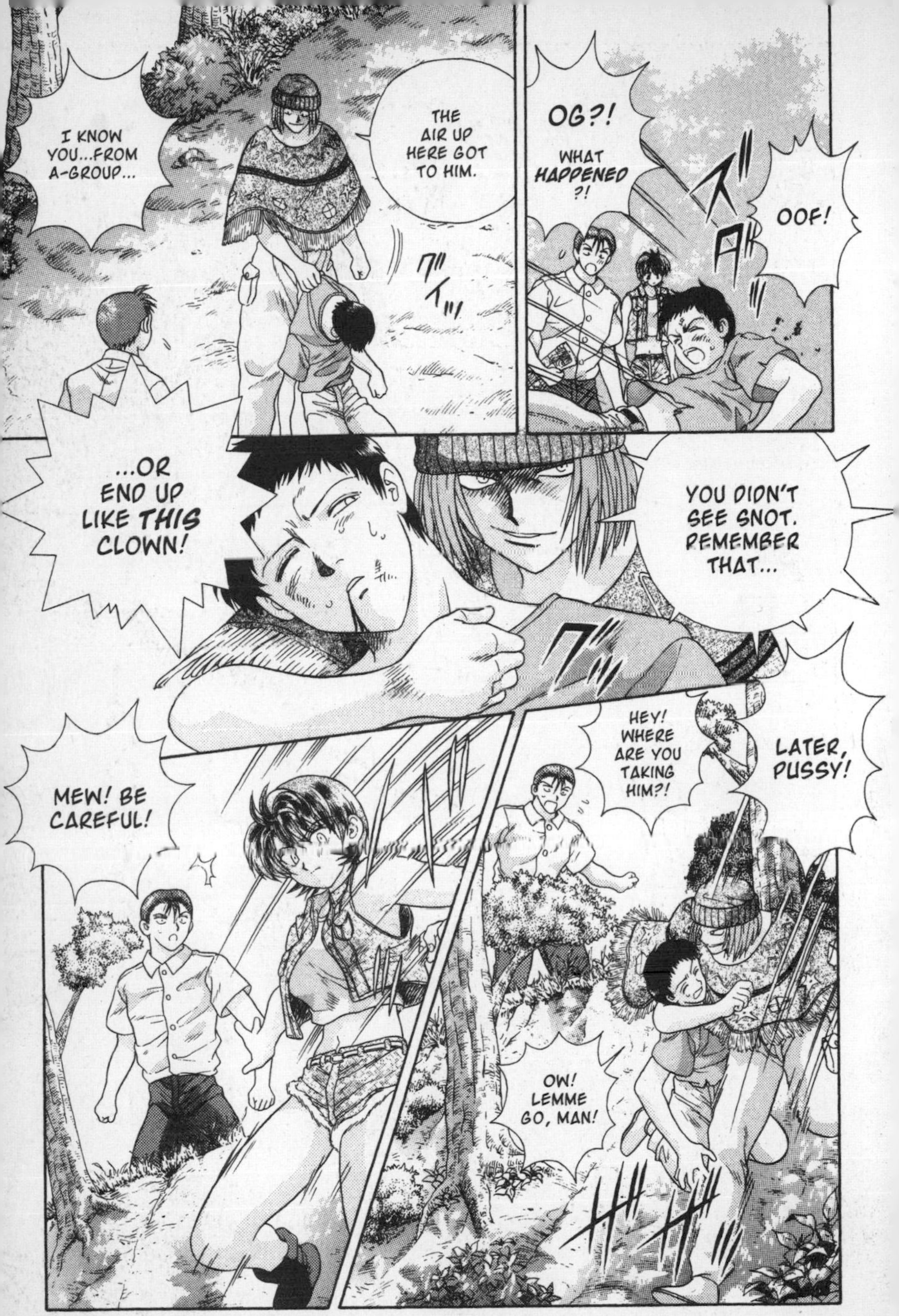
OOF!
OG?!
WHAT HAPPENED?!
THE AIR UP HERE GOT TO HIM.
I KNOW YOU...FROM A-GROUP...
YOU DIDN'T SEE SNOT. REMEMBER THAT...
...OR END UP LIKE THIS CLOWN!
LATER, PUSSY!
HEY! WHERE ARE YOU TAKING HIM?!
OW! LEMME GO, MAN!
MEW! BE CAREFUL!

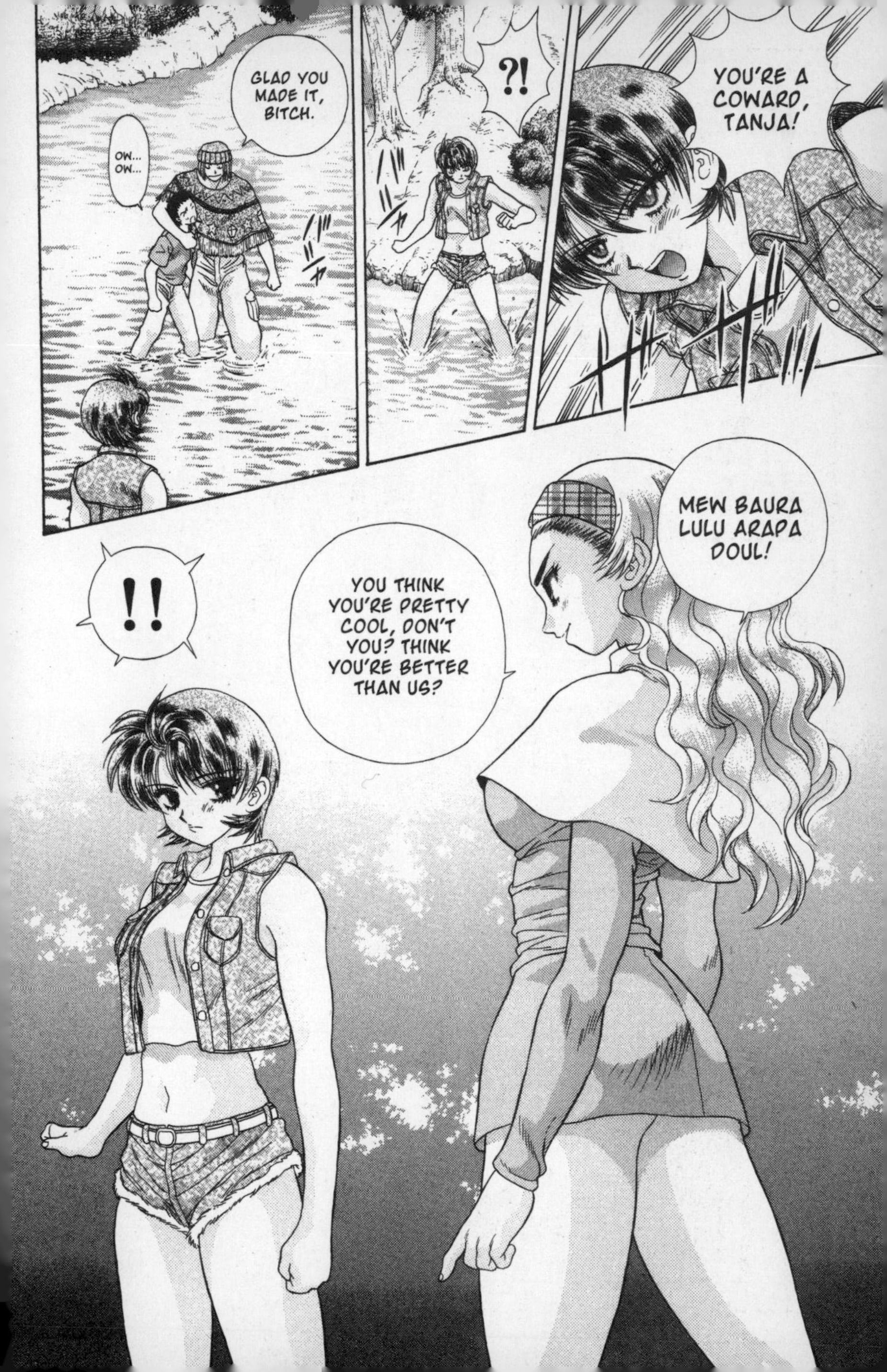
YOU'RE A COWARD, TANJA!
?!
GLAD YOU MADE IT, BITCH.
OW... OW...
MEW BAURA LULU ARAPA DOUL!
YOU THINK YOU'RE PRETTY COOL, DON'T YOU? THINK YOU'RE BETTER THAN US?
!!

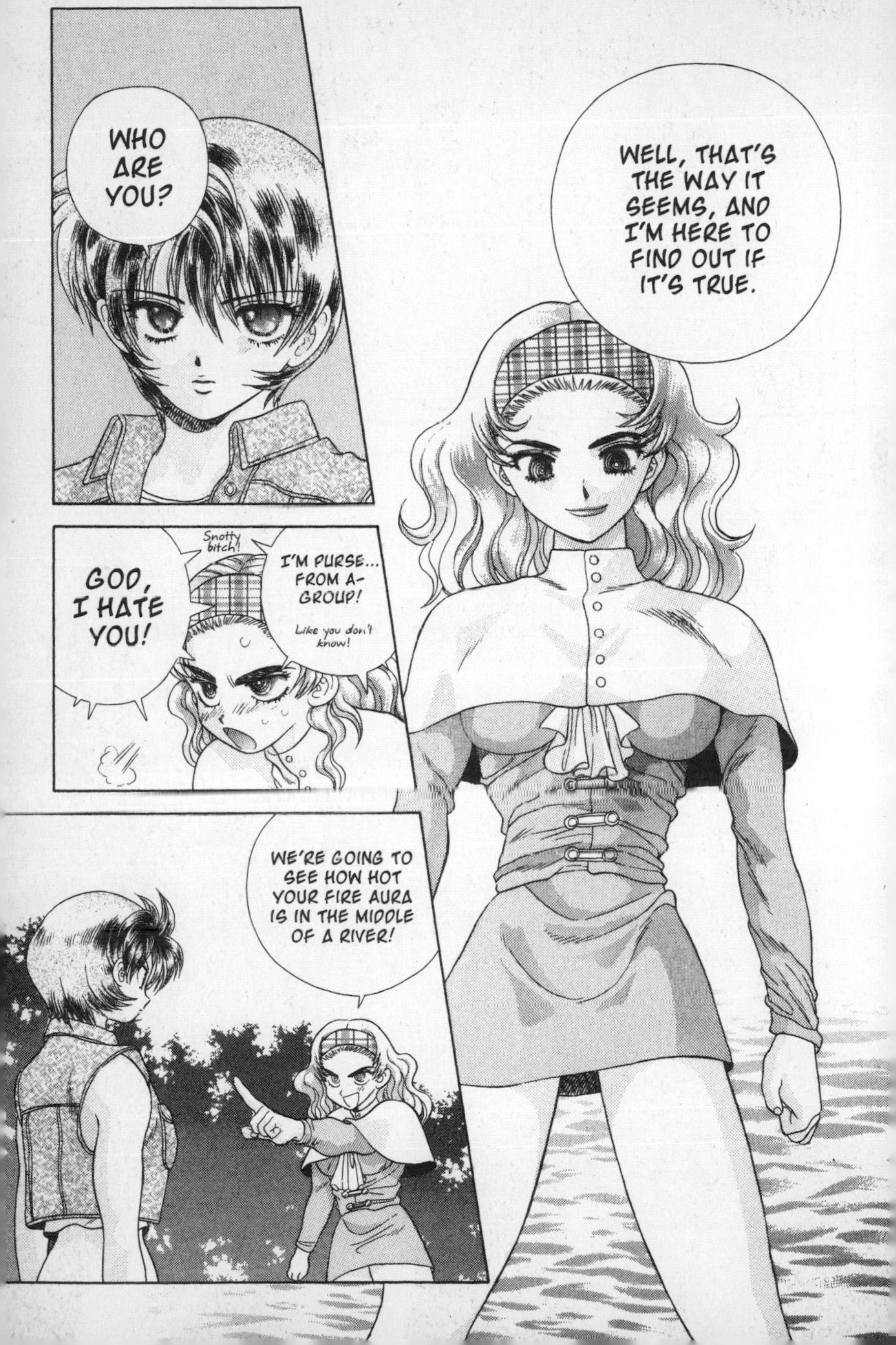
WELL, THAT'S THE WAY IT SEEMS, AND I'M HERE TO FIND OUT IF IT'S TRUE.
WHO ARE YOU?
I'M PURSE... FROM A-GROUP!
Like you don't know!
Snotty bitch!
GOD, I HATE YOU!
WE'RE GOING TO SEE HOW HOT YOUR FIRE AURA IS IN THE MIDDLE OF A RIVER!

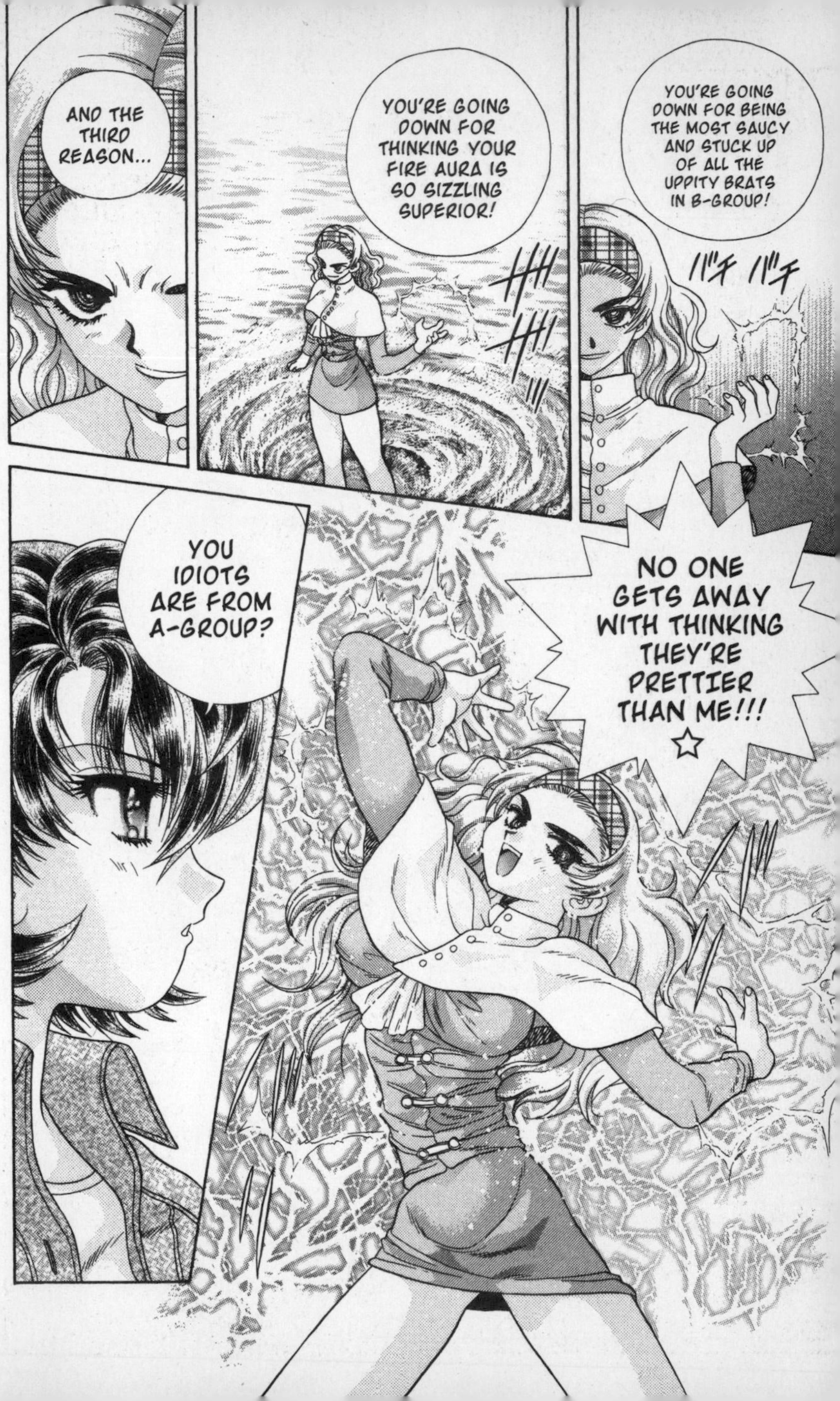
YOU'RE GOING DOWN FOR BEING THE MOST SAUCY AND STUCK UP OF ALL THE UPPITY BRATS IN B-GROUP!
バチ バチ
YOU'RE GOING DOWN FOR THINKING YOUR FIRE AURA IS SO SIZZLING SUPERIOR!
AND THE THIRD REASON...
NO ONE GETS AWAY WITH THINKING THEY'RE PRETTIER THAN ME!!! ☆
YOU IDIOTS ARE FROM A-GROUP?

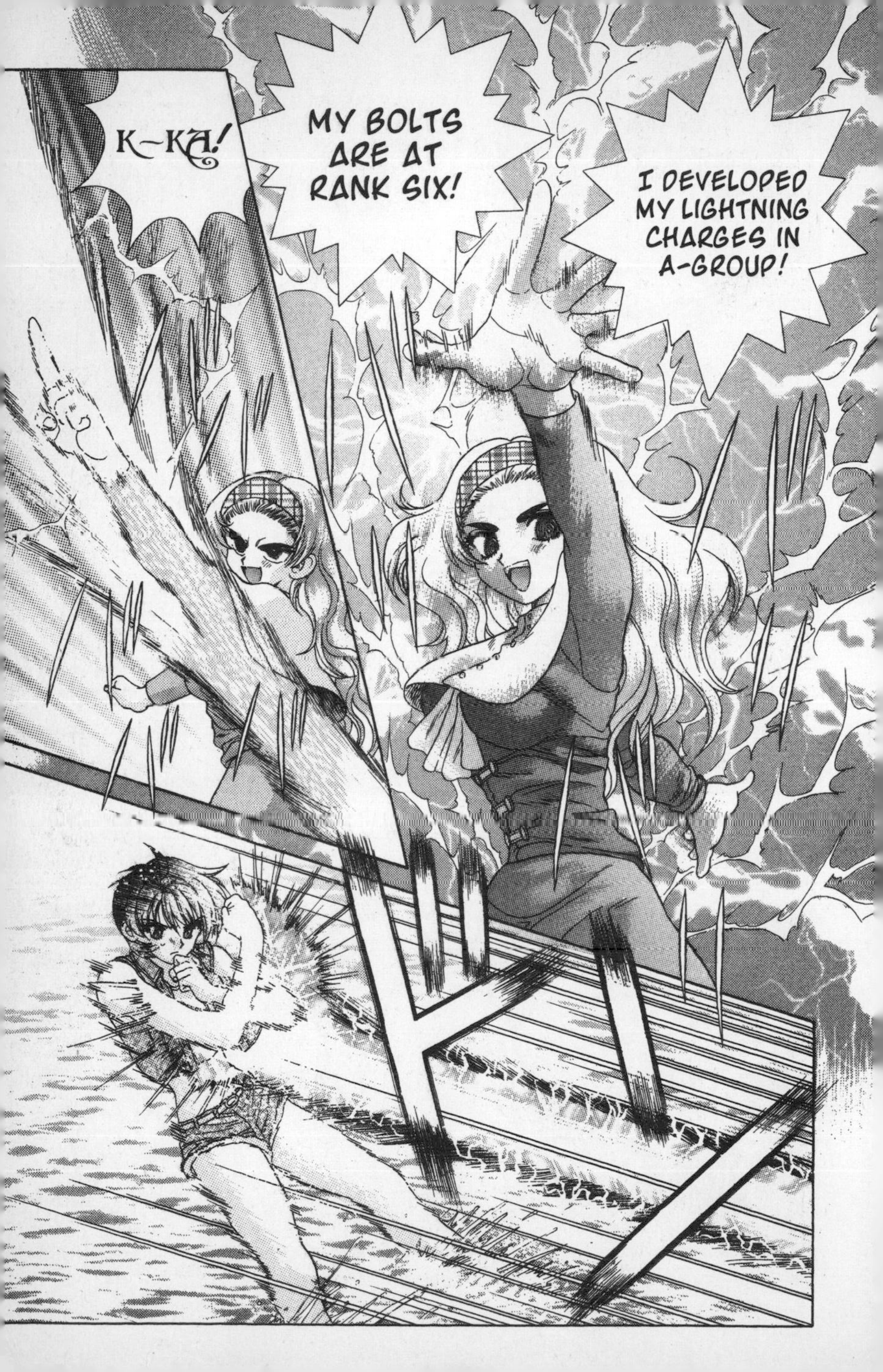
I DEVELOPED MY LIGHTNING CHARGES IN A-GROUP!
MY BOLTS ARE AT RANK SIX!
K-KA!

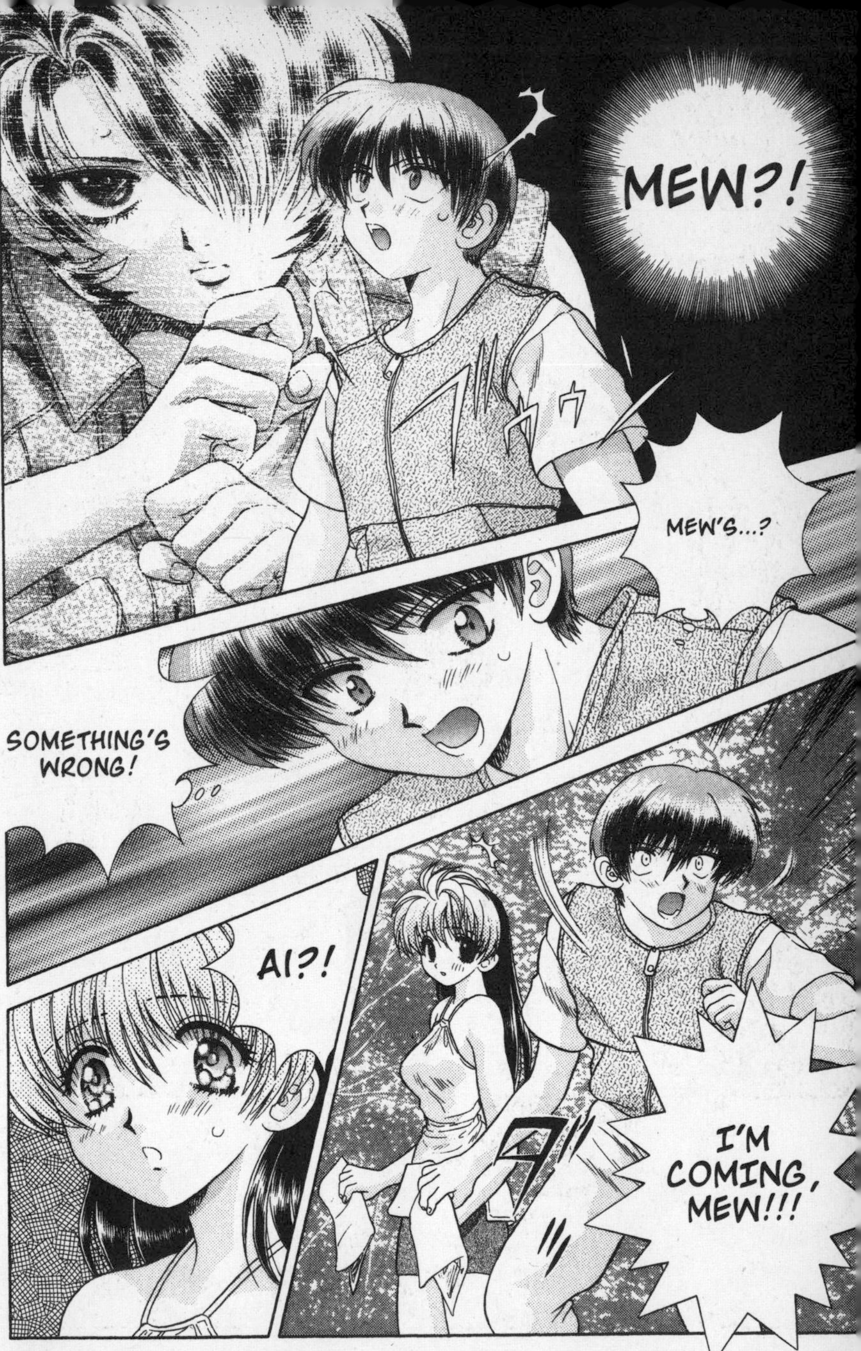
MEW?!
MEW'S...?
SOMETHING'S WRONG!
I'M COMING, MEW!!!
AI?!

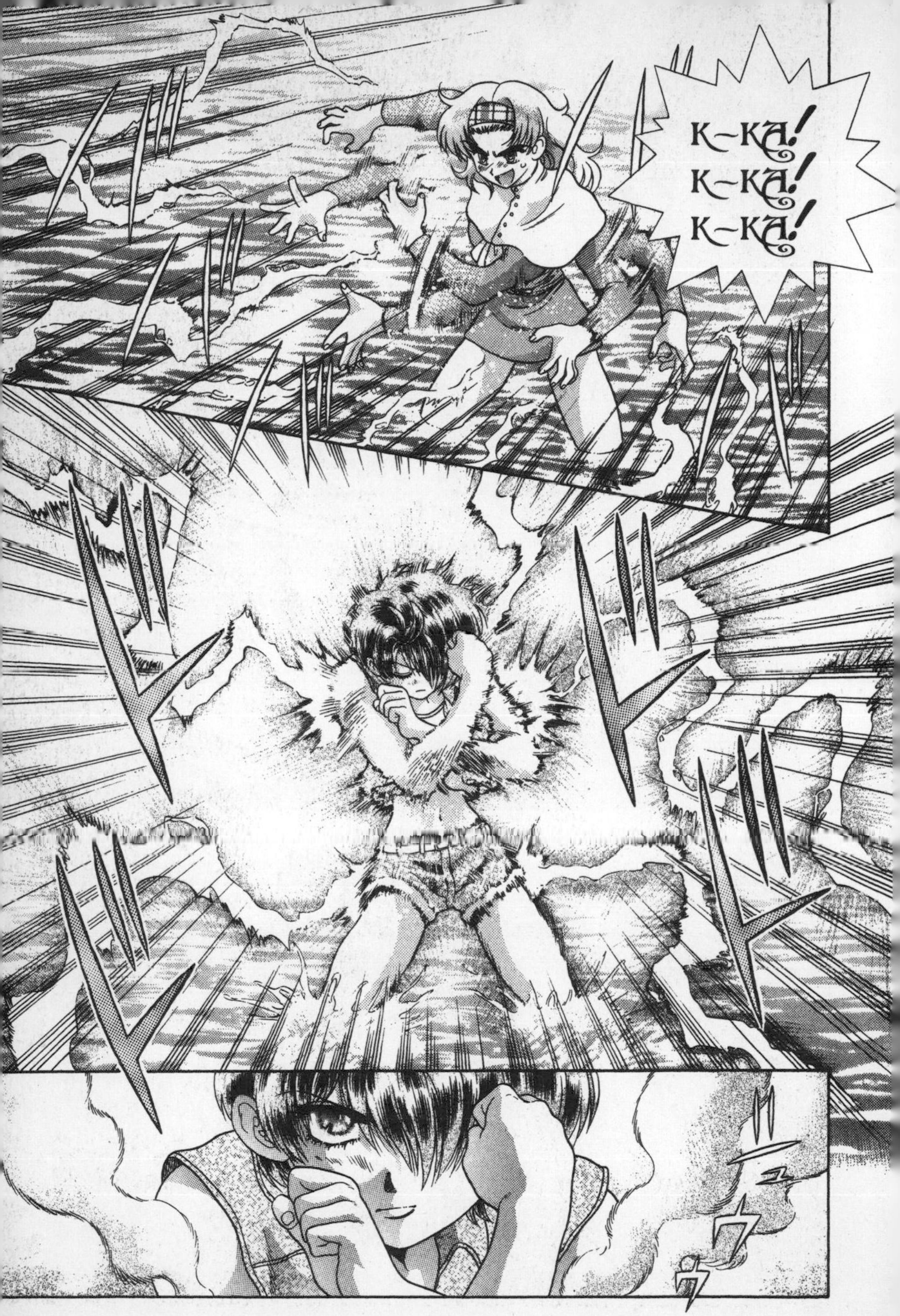
K-KA! K-KA! K-KA!

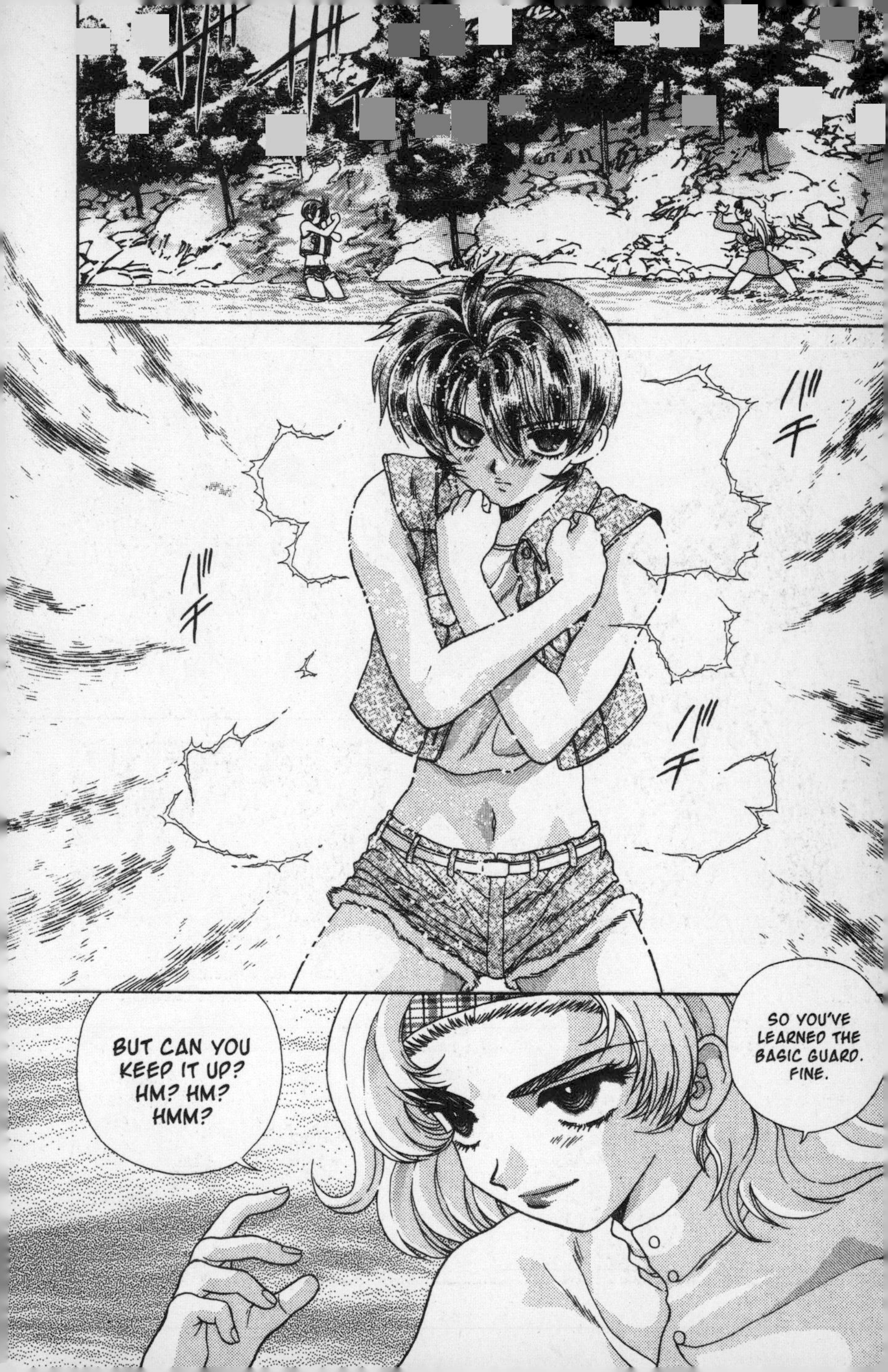
バチ
バチ
バチ
SO YOU'VE LEARNED THE BASIC GUARD. FINE.
BUT CAN YOU KEEP IT UP? HM? HM? HMM?

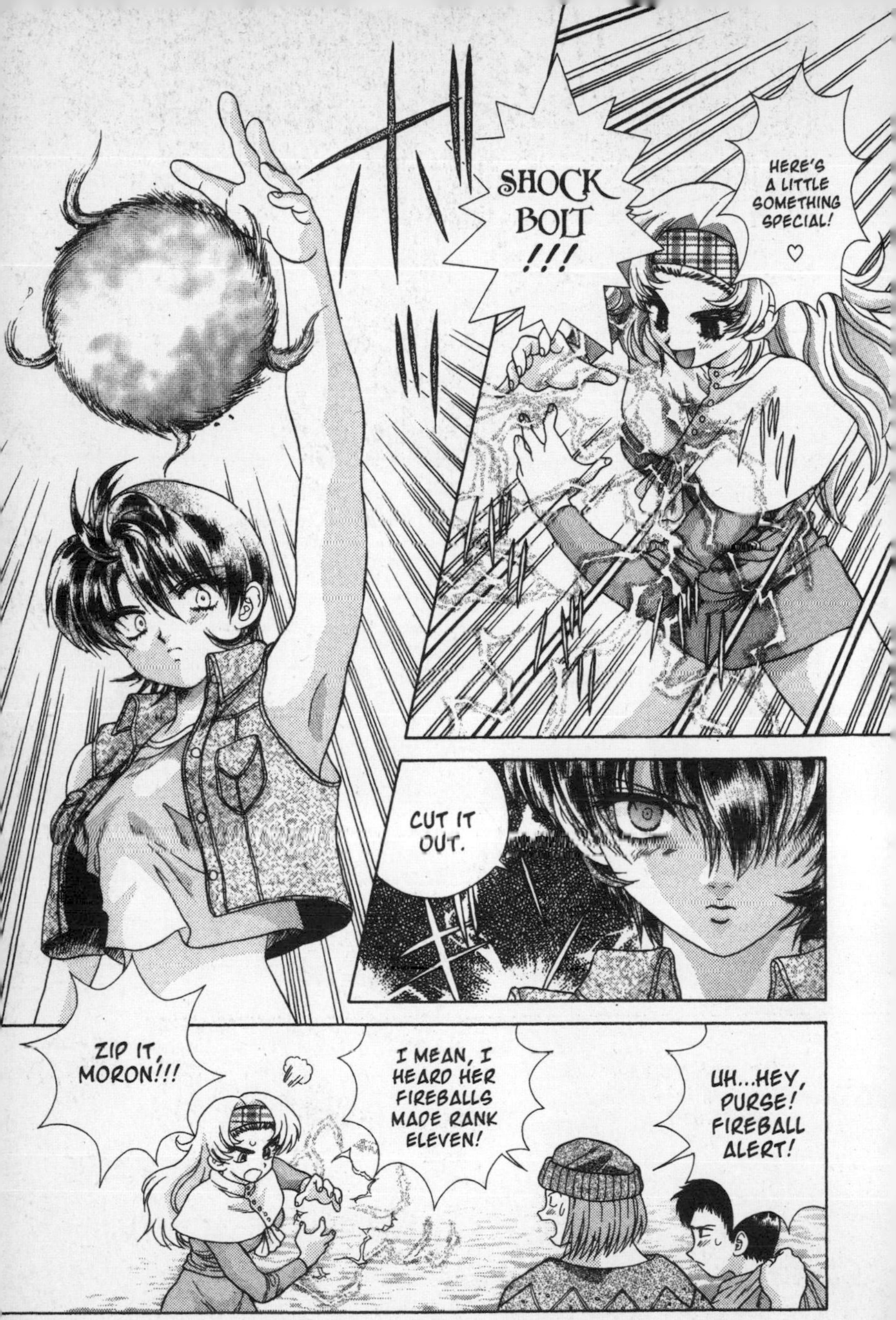
HERE'S A LITTLE SOMETHING SPECIAL! ♡
SHOCK BOLT!!!
CUT IT OUT.
UH...HEY, PURSE! FIREBALL ALERT!
I MEAN, I HEARD HER FIREBALLS MADE RANK ELEVEN!
ZIP IT, MORON!!!

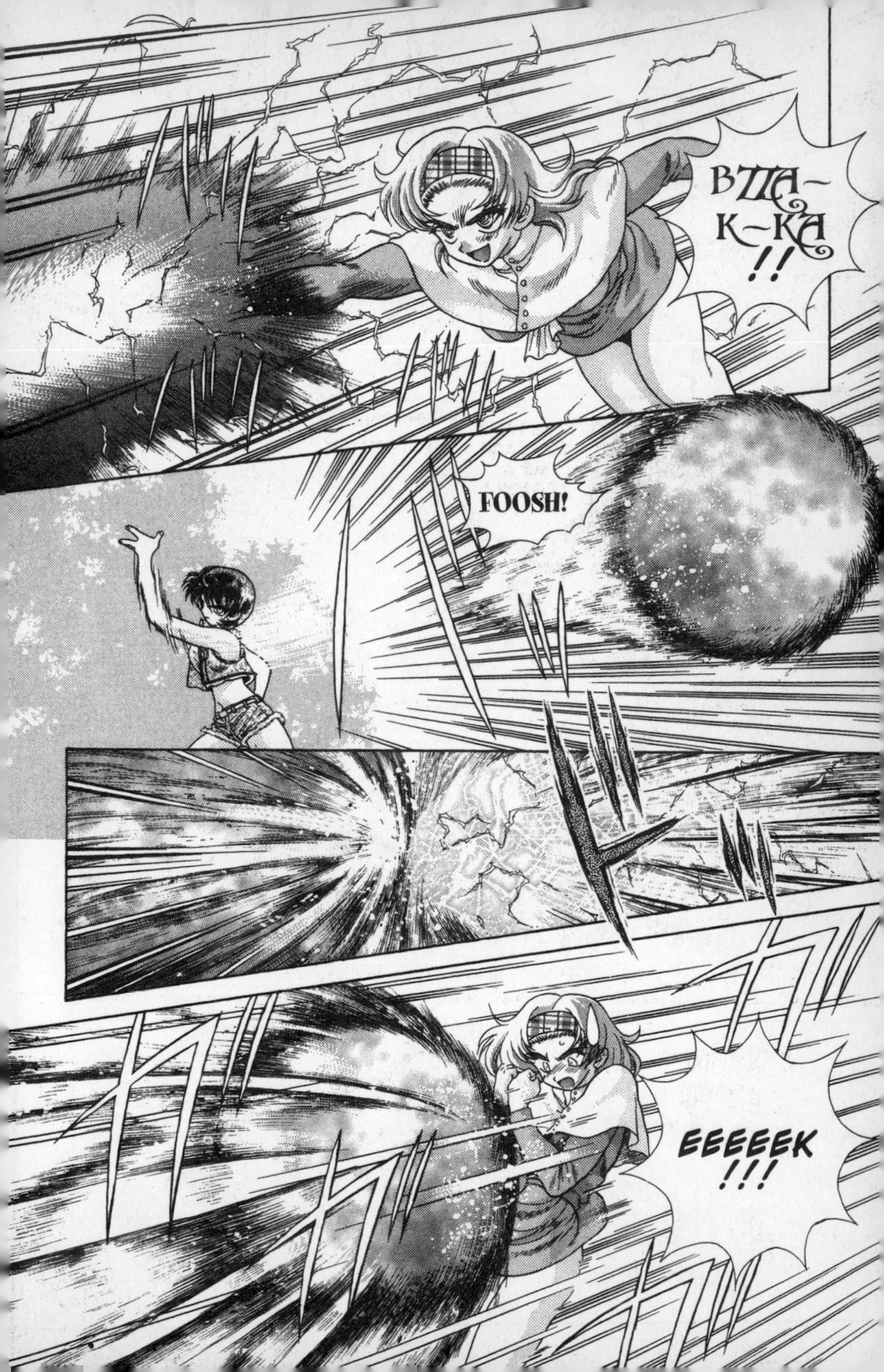
BZZA-K-KA!!
FOOSH!
EEEEEK!!!

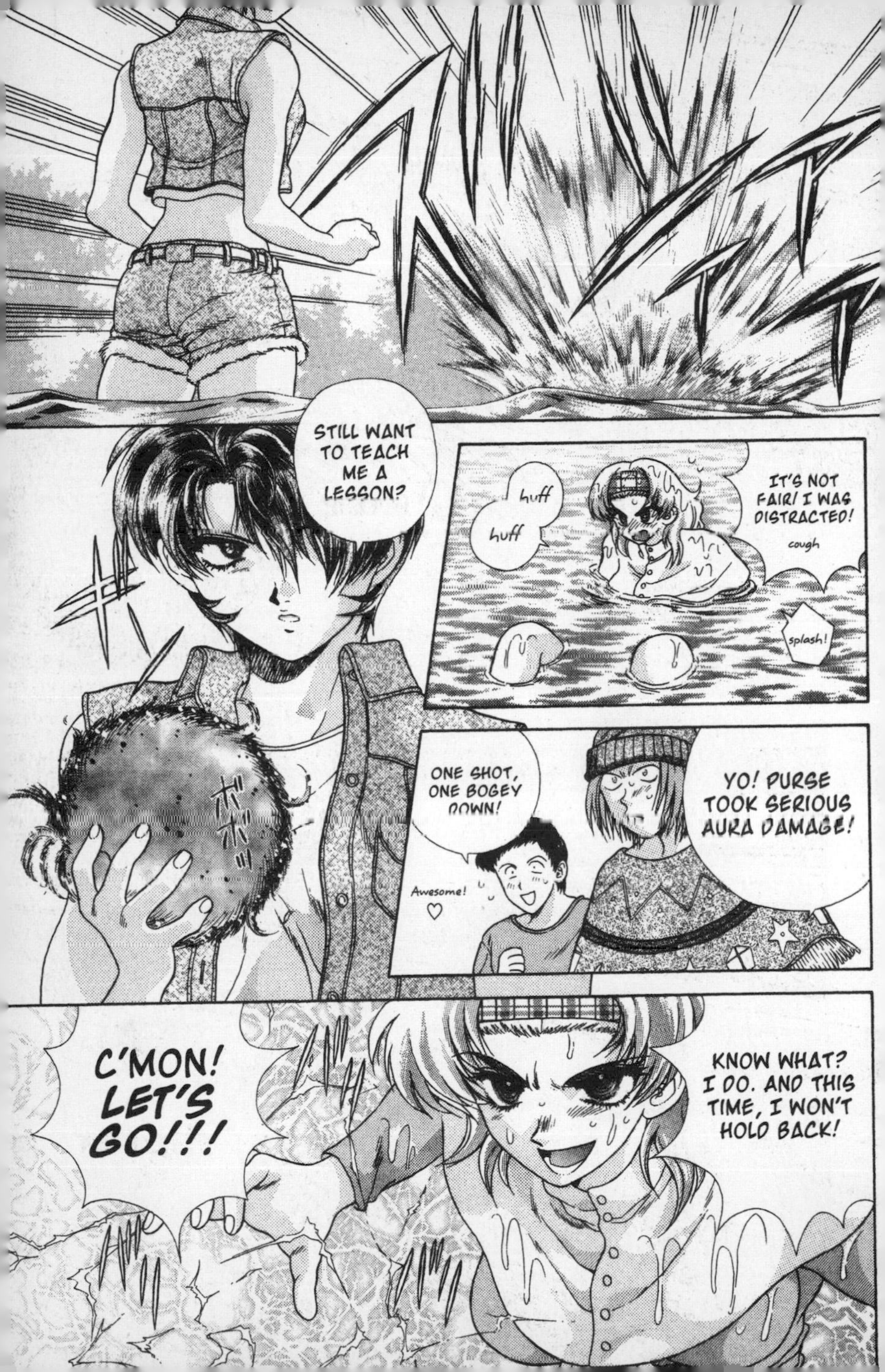
IT'S NOT FAIR! I WAS DISTRACTED!
cough
huff
huff
splash!
YO! PURSE TOOK SERIOUS AURA DAMAGE!
ONE SHOT, ONE BOGEY DOWN!
Awesome!
STILL WANT TO TEACH ME A LESSON?
KNOW WHAT? I DO. AND THIS TIME, I WON'T HOLD BACK!
C'MON! LET'S GO!!!

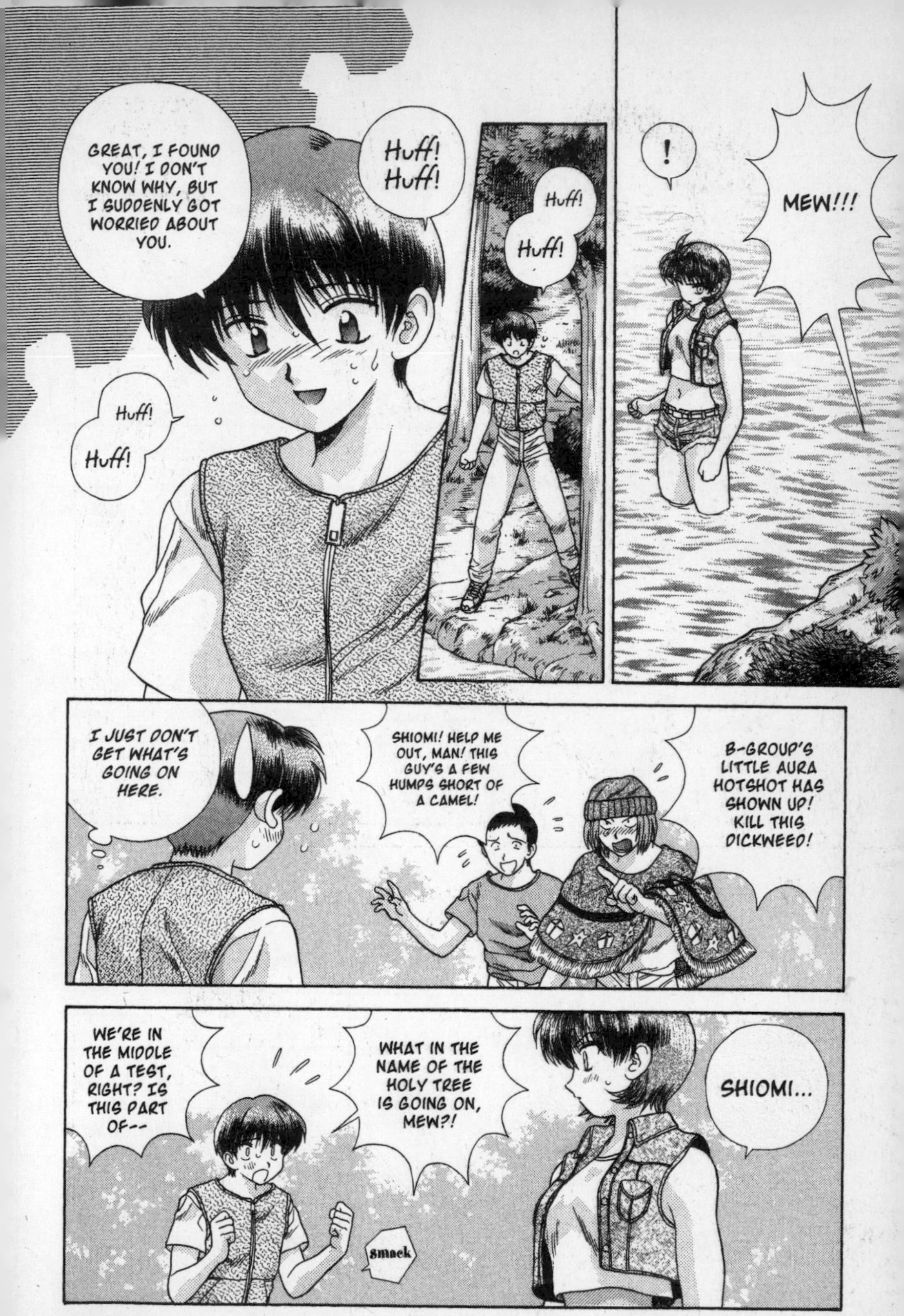
MEW!!!
!
Huff! Huff!
Huff! Huff!
GREAT, I FOUND YOU! I DON'T KNOW WHY, BUT I SUDDENLY GOT WORRIED ABOUT YOU.
Huff! Huff!
B-GROUP'S LITTLE AURA HOTSHOT HAS SHOWN UP! KILL THIS DICKWEED!
SHIOMI! HELP ME OUT, MAN! THIS GUY'S A FEW HUMPS SHORT OF A CAMEL!
I JUST DON'T GET WHAT'S GOING ON HERE.
SHIOMI...
WHAT IN THE NAME OF THE HOLY TREE IS GOING ON, MEW?!
WE'RE IN THE MIDDLE OF A TEST, RIGHT? IS THIS PART OF--
smack

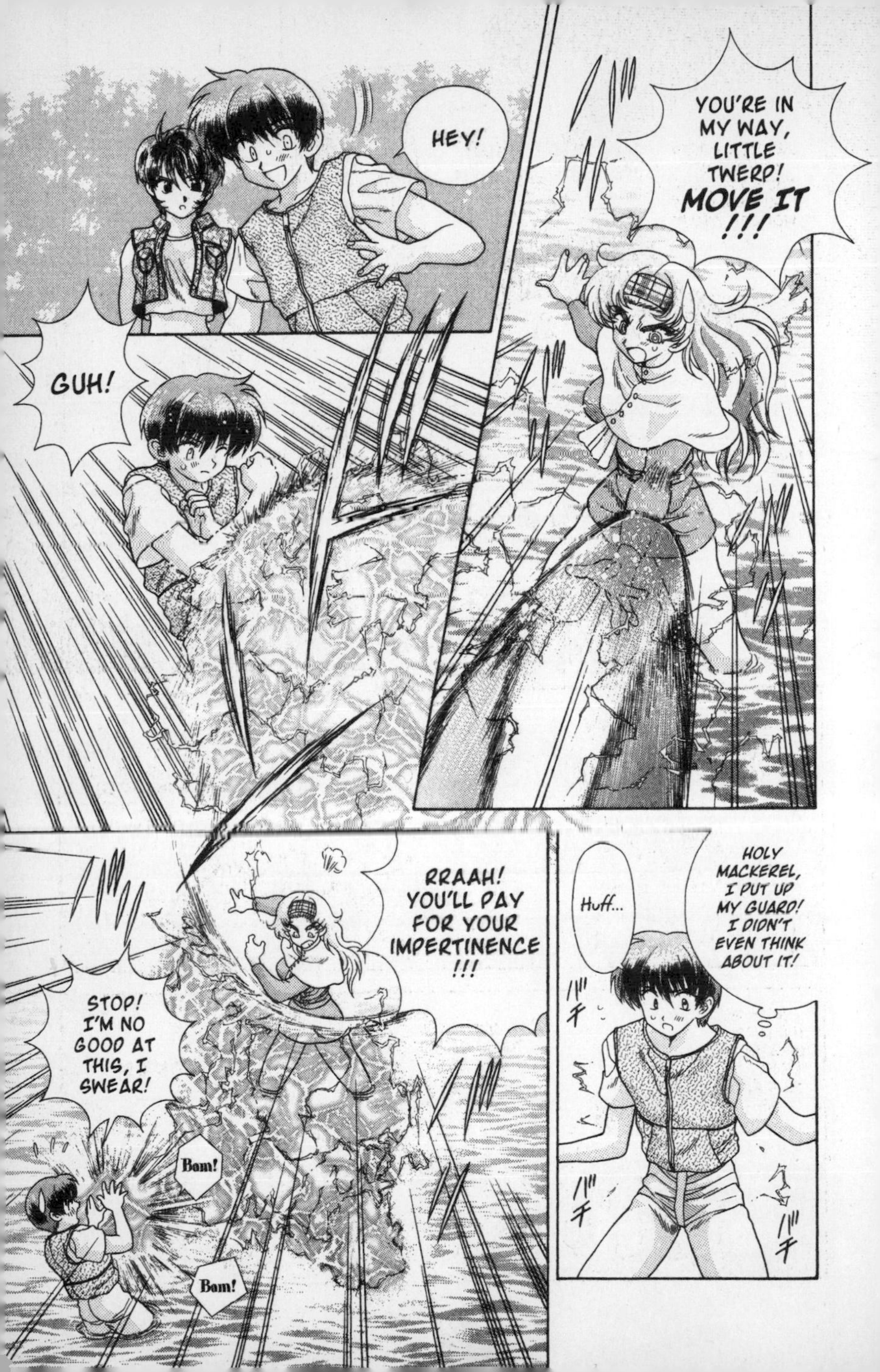

YOU'RE IN MY WAY, LITTLE TWERP! MOVE IT!!!
HEY!
GUH!
HOLY MACKEREL, I PUT UP MY GUARD! I DIDN'T EVEN THINK ABOUT IT!
Huff...
バチ
バチ
バチ
RRAAH! YOU'LL PAY FOR YOUR IMPERTINENCE!!!
STOP! I'M NO GOOD AT THIS, I SWEAR!
Bam!
Bam!

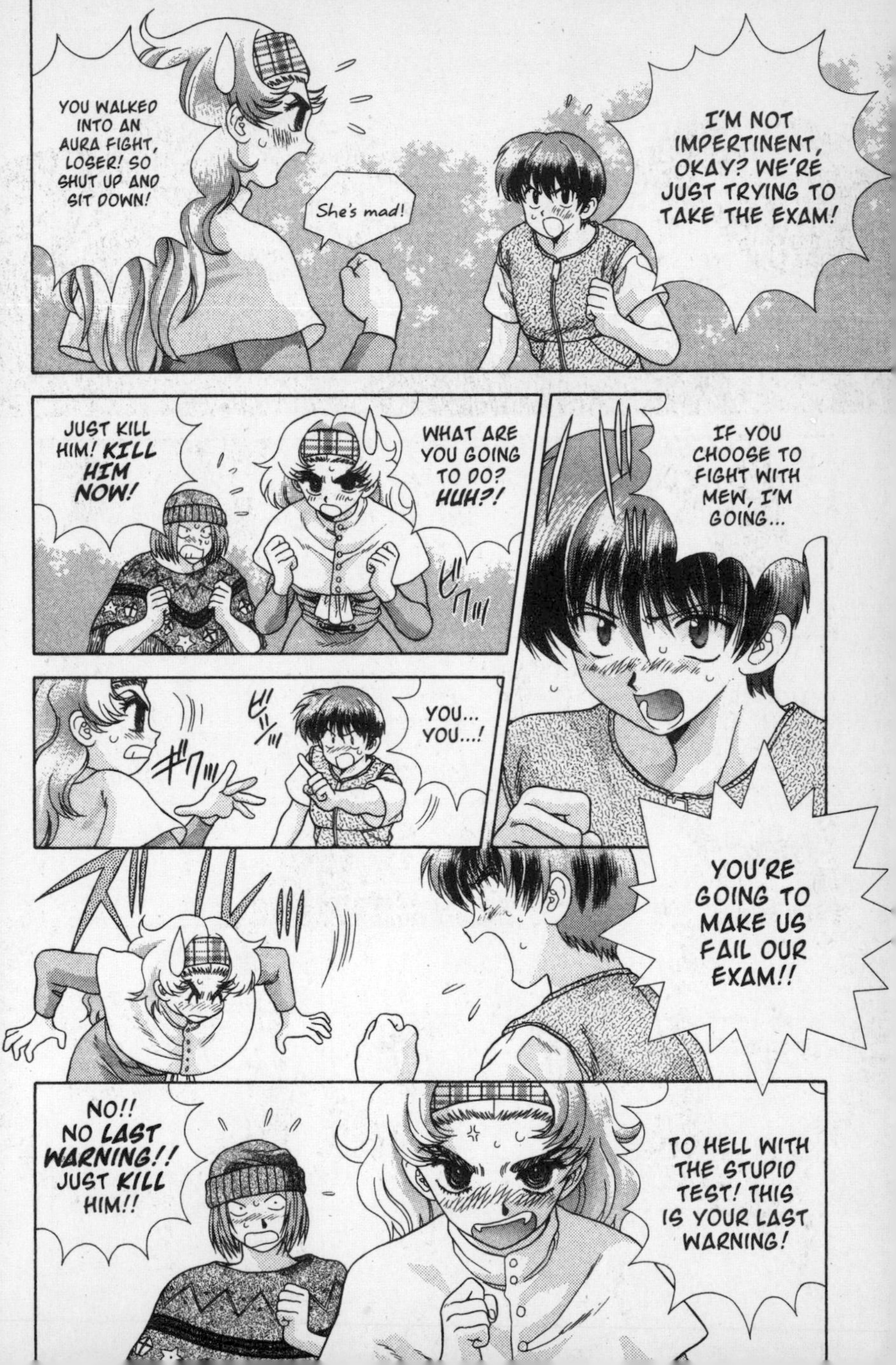
I'M NOT IMPERTINENT, OKAY? WE'RE JUST TRYING TO TAKE THE EXAM!
She's mad!
YOU WALKED INTO AN AURA FIGHT, LOSER! SO SHUT UP AND SIT DOWN!
IF YOU CHOOSE TO FIGHT WITH MEW, I'M GOING...
WHAT ARE YOU GOING TO DO? **HUH?!**
JUST KILL HIM! **KILL HIM NOW!**
YOU... YOU...!
YOU'RE GOING TO MAKE US FAIL OUR EXAM!!
TO HELL WITH THE STUPID TEST! THIS IS YOUR LAST WARNING!
NO!! NO **LAST WARNING!!** JUST **KILL** HIM!!

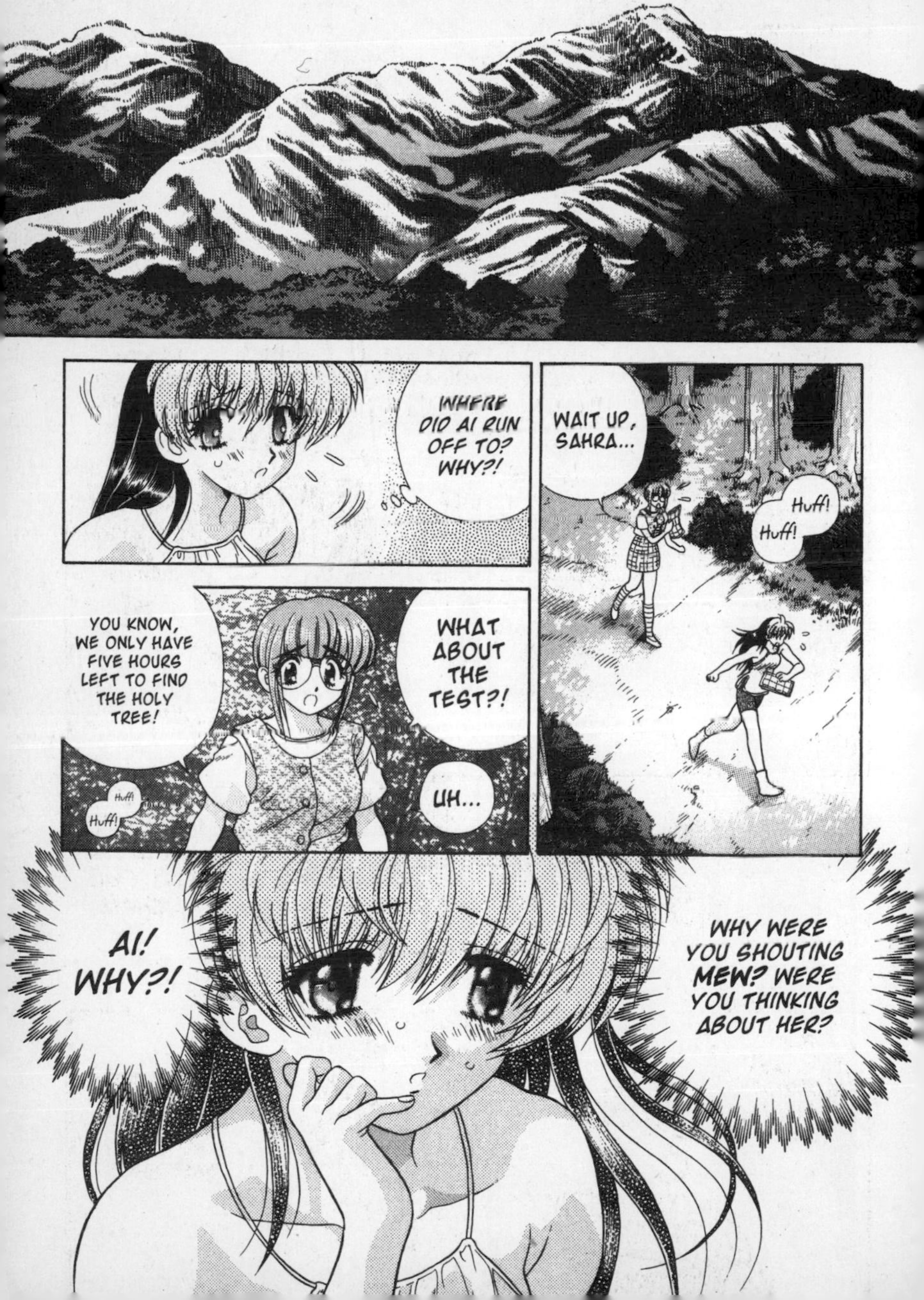
WAIT UP, SAHRA...
Huff! Huff!
WHERE DID AI RUN OFF TO? WHY?!
WHAT ABOUT THE TEST?!
YOU KNOW, WE ONLY HAVE FIVE HOURS LEFT TO FIND THE HOLY TREE!
UH...
Huff! Huff!
WHY WERE YOU SHOUTING MEW? WERE YOU THINKING ABOUT HER?
AI! WHY?!

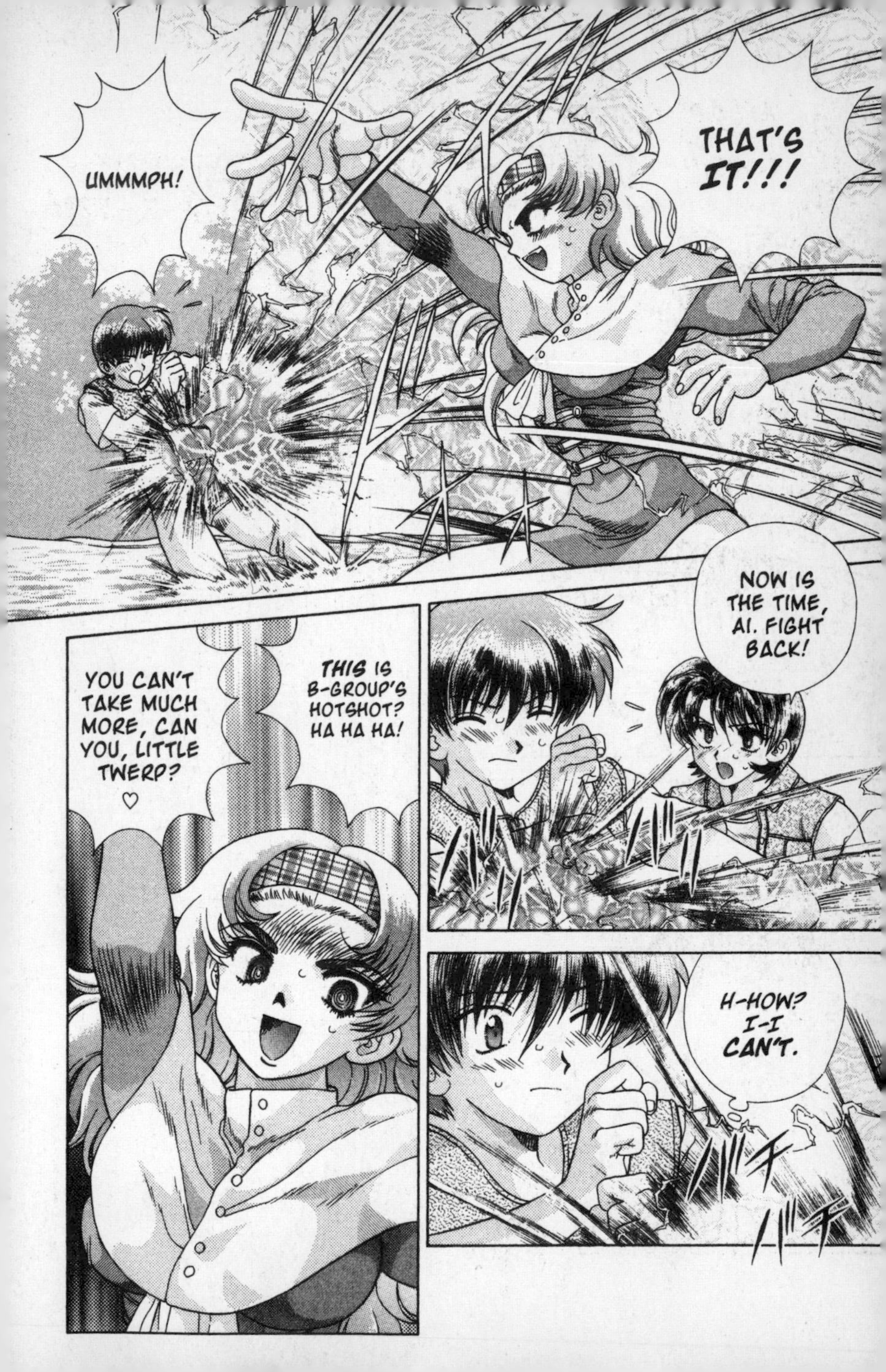
THAT'S IT!!!
UMMMPH!
NOW IS THE TIME, AI. FIGHT BACK!
H-HOW? I-I CAN'T.
バチ
バチ
THIS IS B-GROUP'S HOTSHOT? HA HA HA!
YOU CAN'T TAKE MUCH MORE, CAN YOU, LITTLE TWERP? ♡

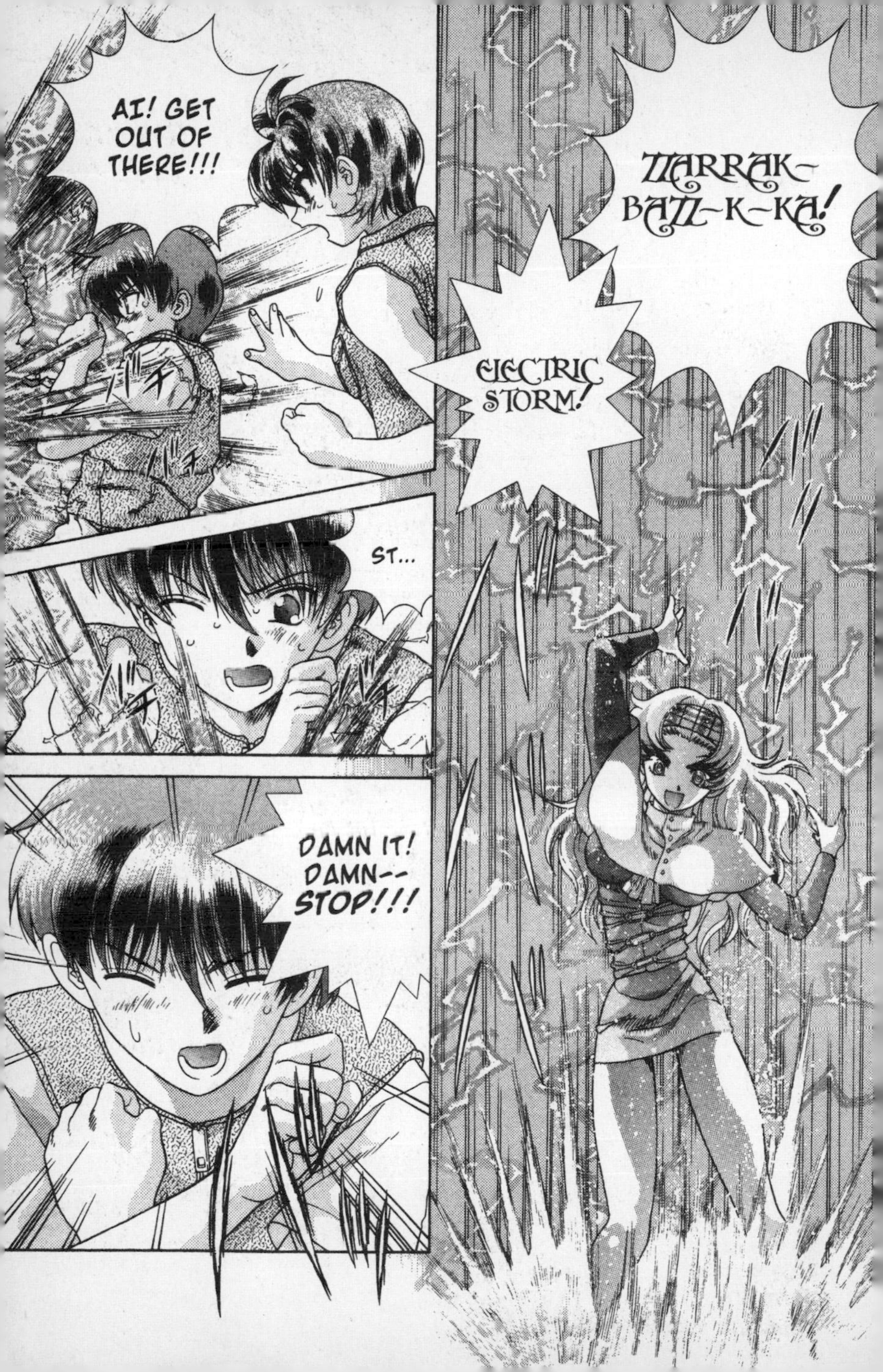
ZZARRAK-BAZZ-K-KA!
ELECTRIC STORM!
AI! GET OUT OF THERE!!!
ST...
DAMN IT! DAMN-- STOP!!!

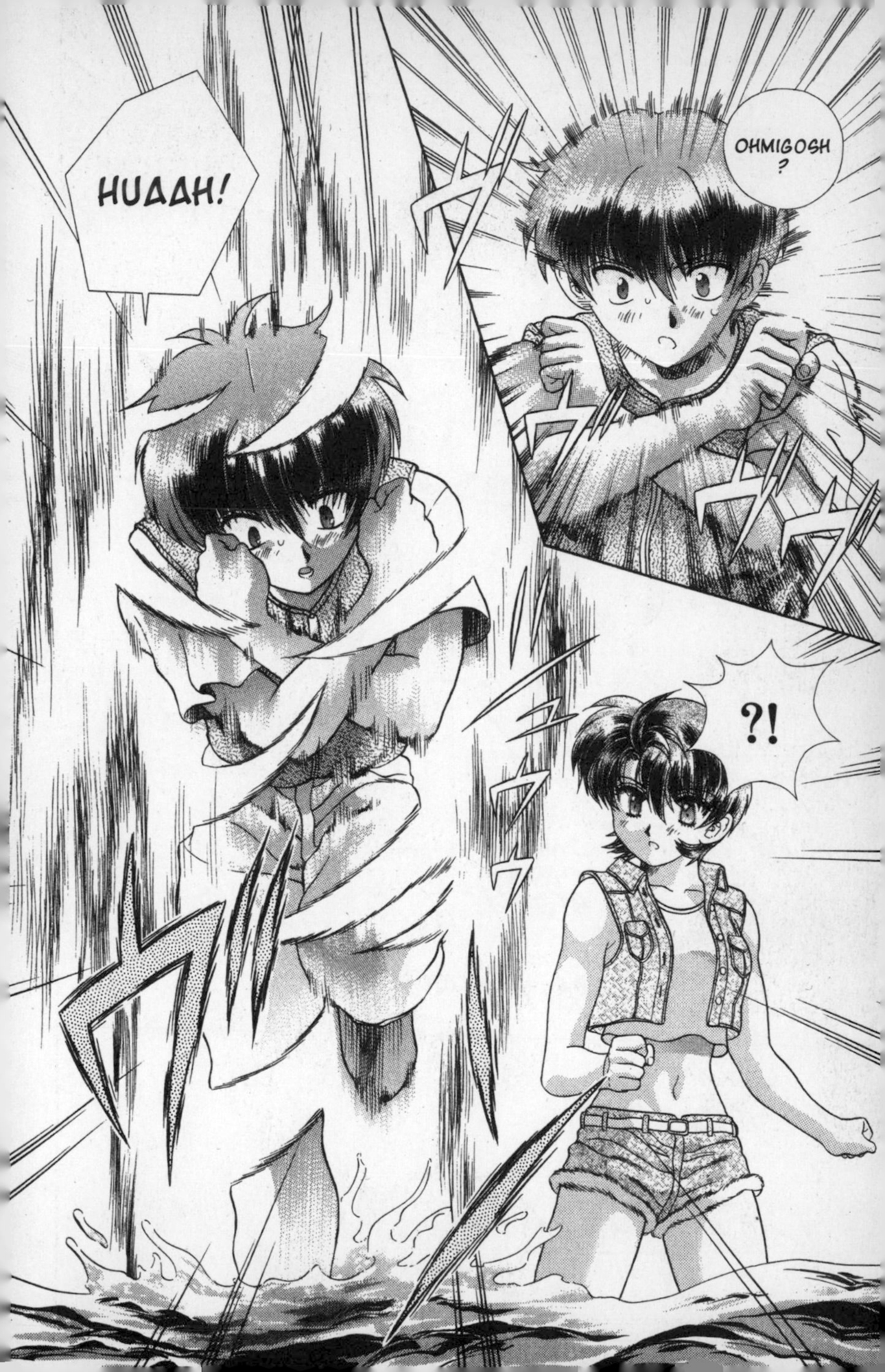
OHMIGOSH ?
?!
HUAAH!

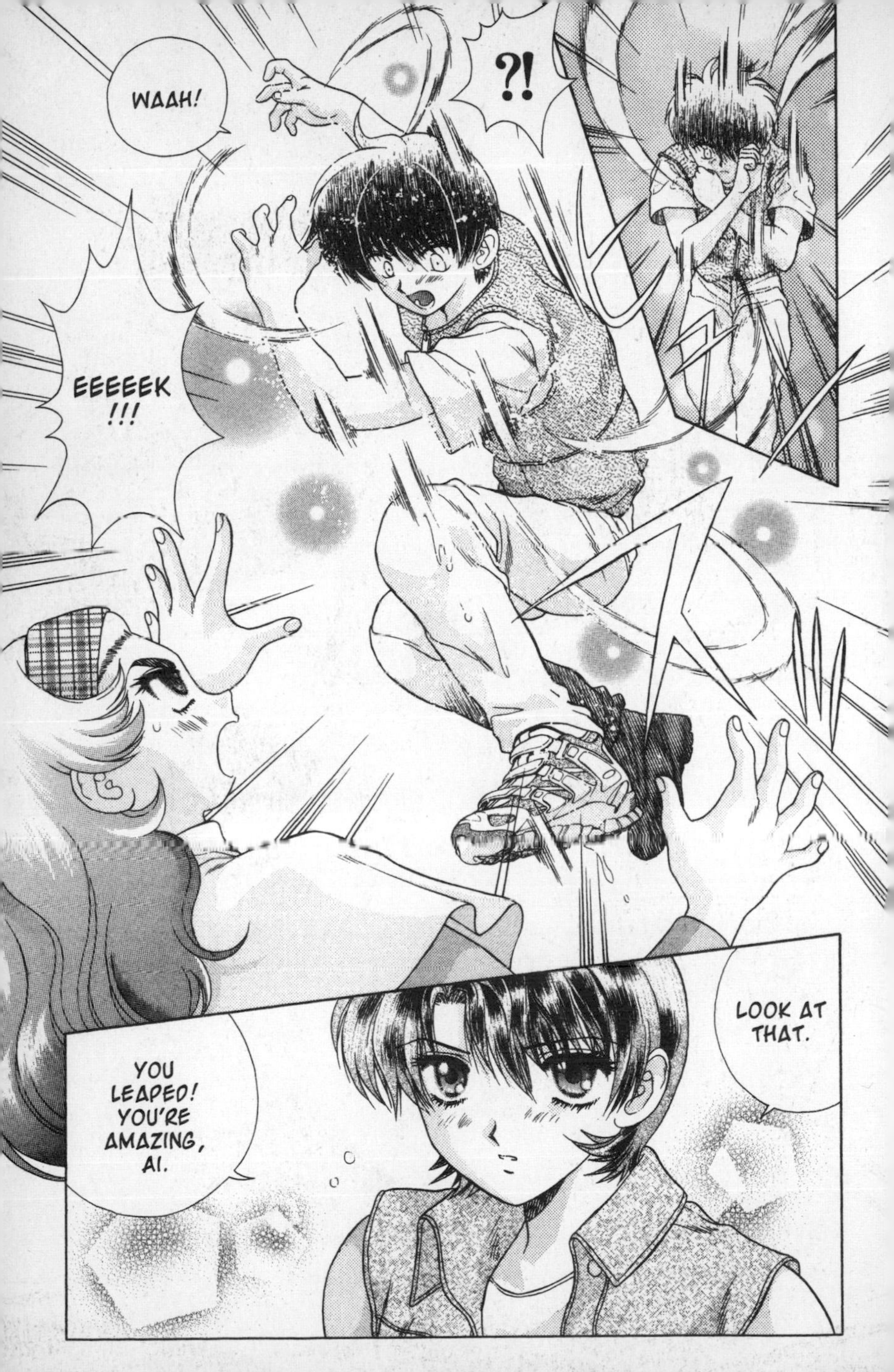
?!
WAAH!
EEEEEK !!!
LOOK AT THAT.
YOU LEAPED! YOU'RE AMAZING, AI.

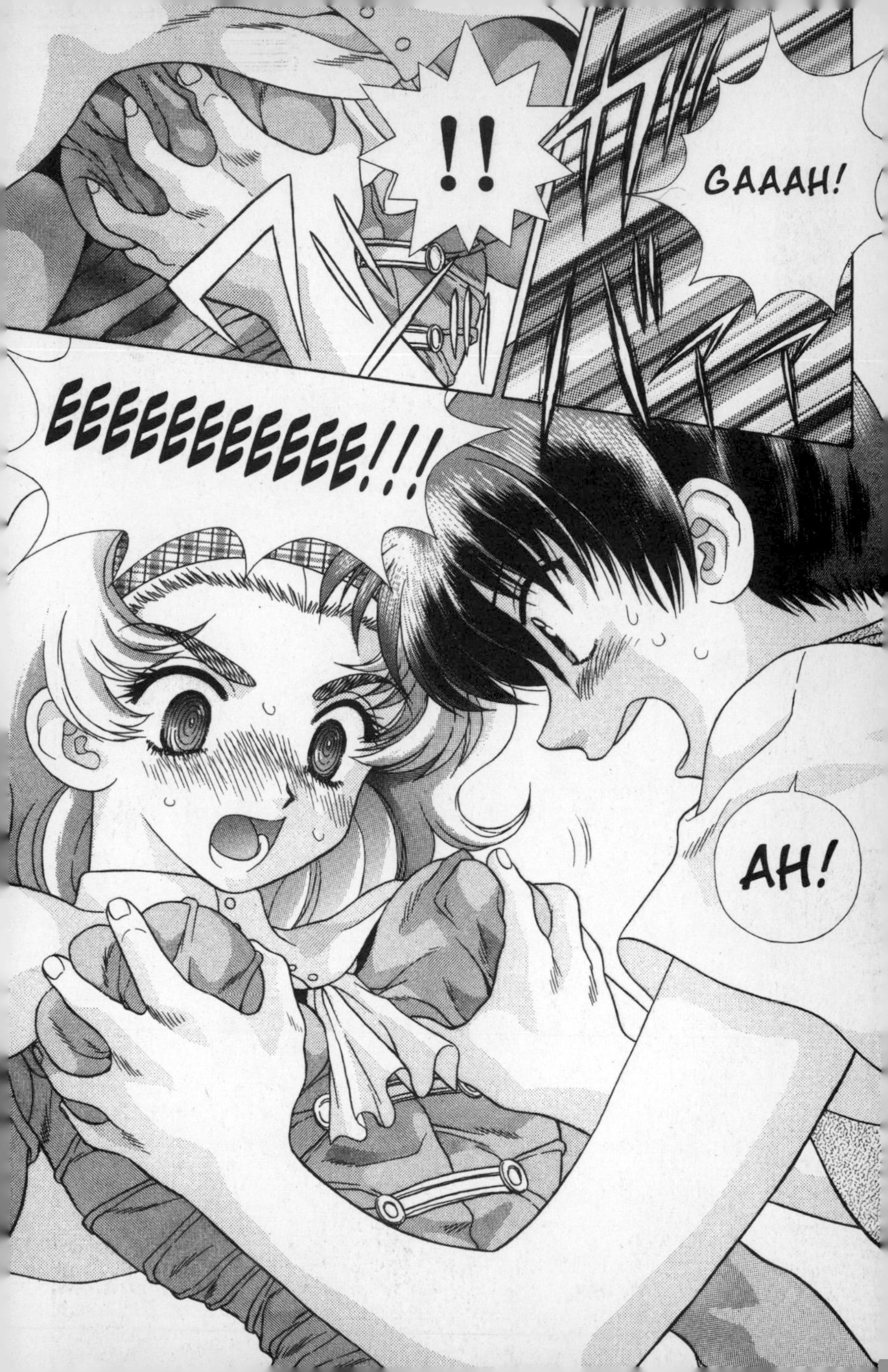
GAAAH!
!!
EEEEEEEEEEEEE!!!
AH!

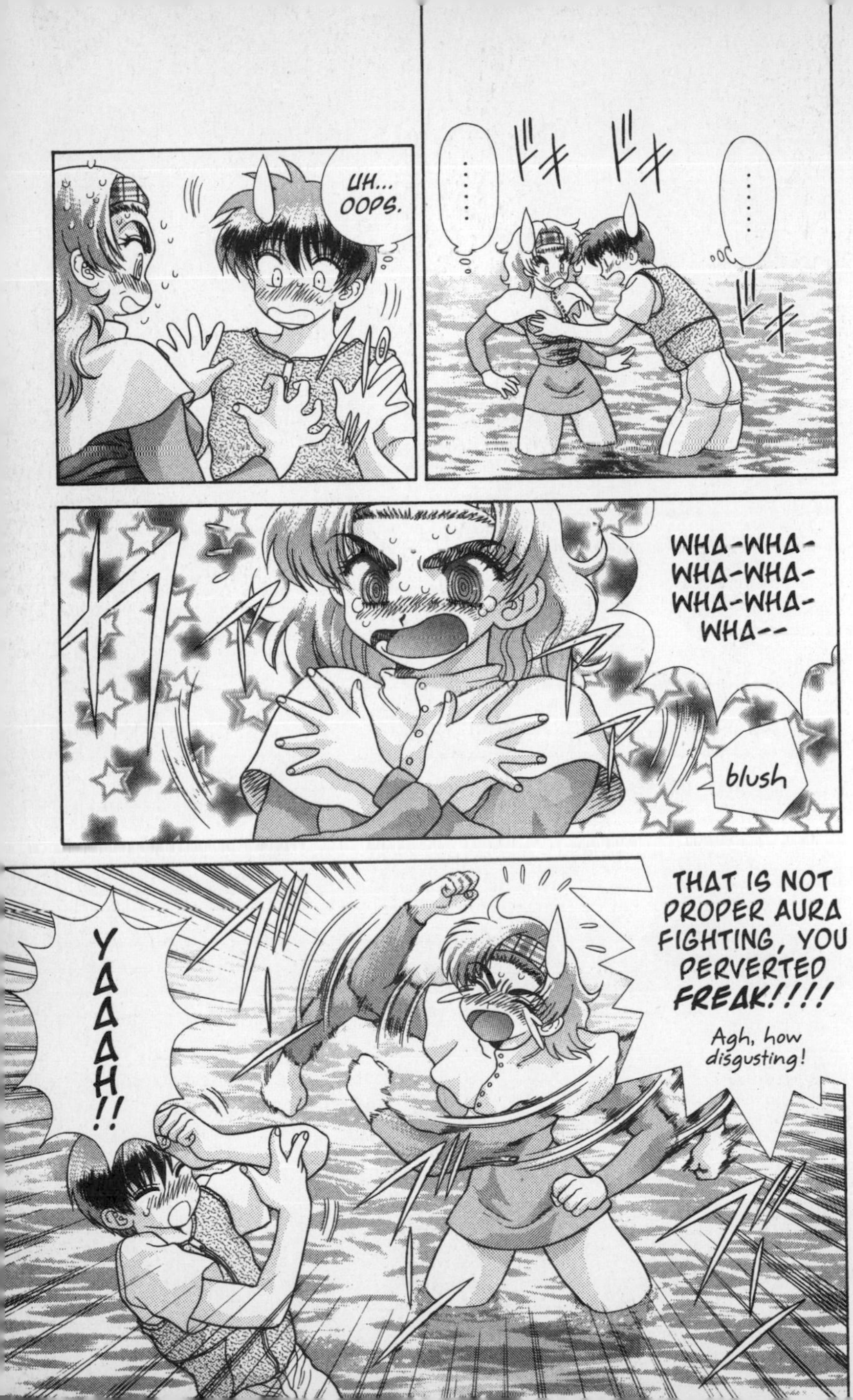
......
ドキ ドキ
......
ドキ
UH... OOPS.
WHA-WHA-WHA-WHA-WHA-WHA-WHA--
blush
THAT IS NOT PROPER AURA FIGHTING, YOU PERVERTED FREAK!!!!
Agh, how disgusting!
YAAAAH!!

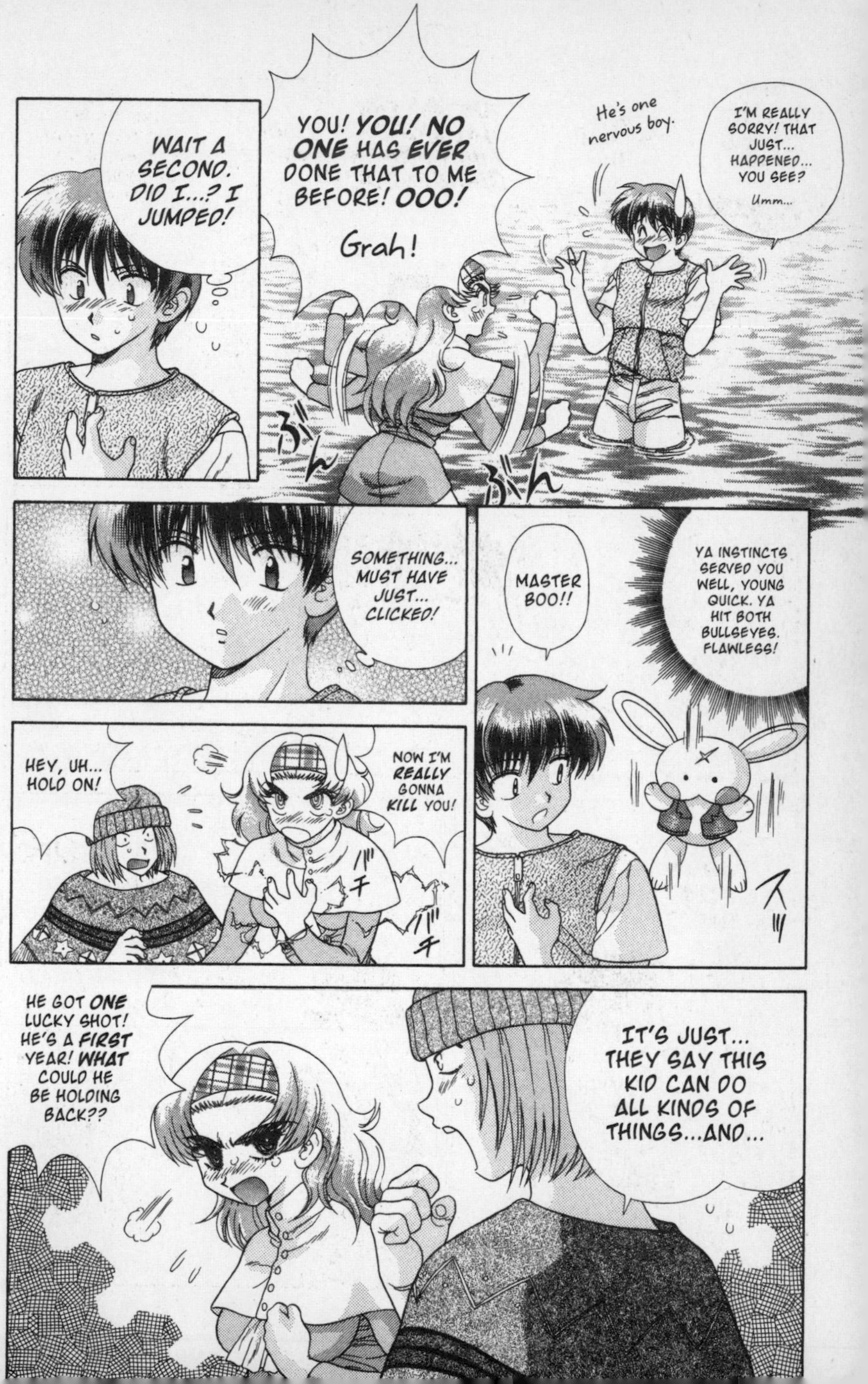
I'M REALLY SORRY! THAT JUST... HAPPENED... YOU SEE?
Umm...
He's one nervous boy.
YOU! YOU! NO ONE HAS EVER DONE THAT TO ME BEFORE! OOO!
Grah!
WAIT A SECOND. DID I...? I JUMPED!
YA INSTINCTS SERVED YOU WELL, YOUNG QUICK. YA HIT BOTH BULLSEYES. FLAWLESS!
MASTER BOO!!
SOMETHING... MUST HAVE JUST... CLICKED!
NOW I'M REALLY GONNA KILL YOU!
HEY, UH... HOLD ON!
IT'S JUST... THEY SAY THIS KID CAN DO ALL KINDS OF THINGS...AND...
HE GOT ONE LUCKY SHOT! HE'S A FIRST YEAR! WHAT COULD HE BE HOLDING BACK??

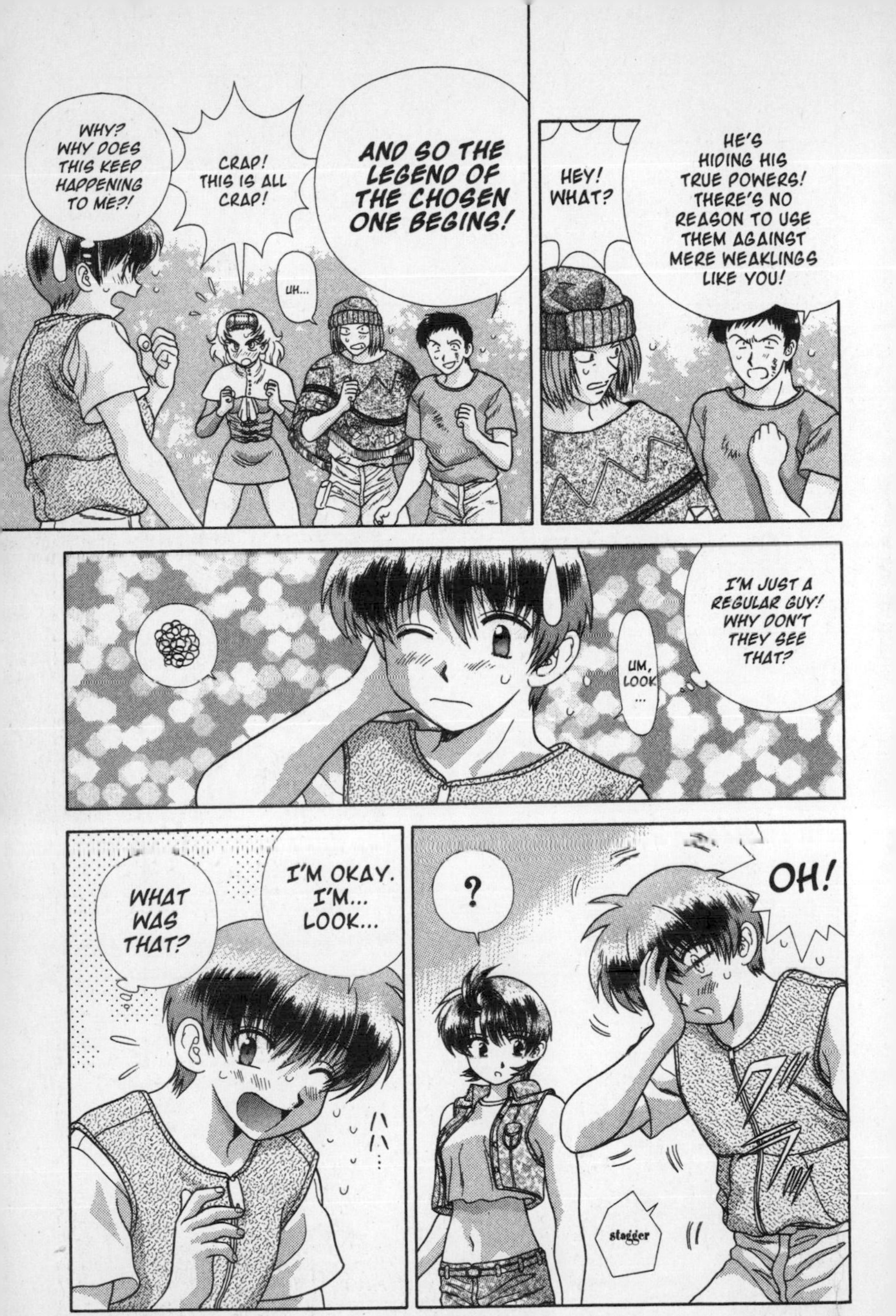
HE'S HIDING HIS TRUE POWERS! THERE'S NO REASON TO USE THEM AGAINST MERE WEAKLINGS LIKE YOU!
HEY! WHAT?
AND SO THE LEGEND OF THE CHOSEN ONE BEGINS!
CRAP! THIS IS ALL CRAP!
WHY? WHY DOES THIS KEEP HAPPENING TO ME?!
UH...
I'M JUST A REGULAR GUY! WHY DON'T THEY SEE THAT?
UM, LOOK ...
OH!
?
stagger
I'M OKAY. I'M... LOOK...
WHAT WAS THAT?

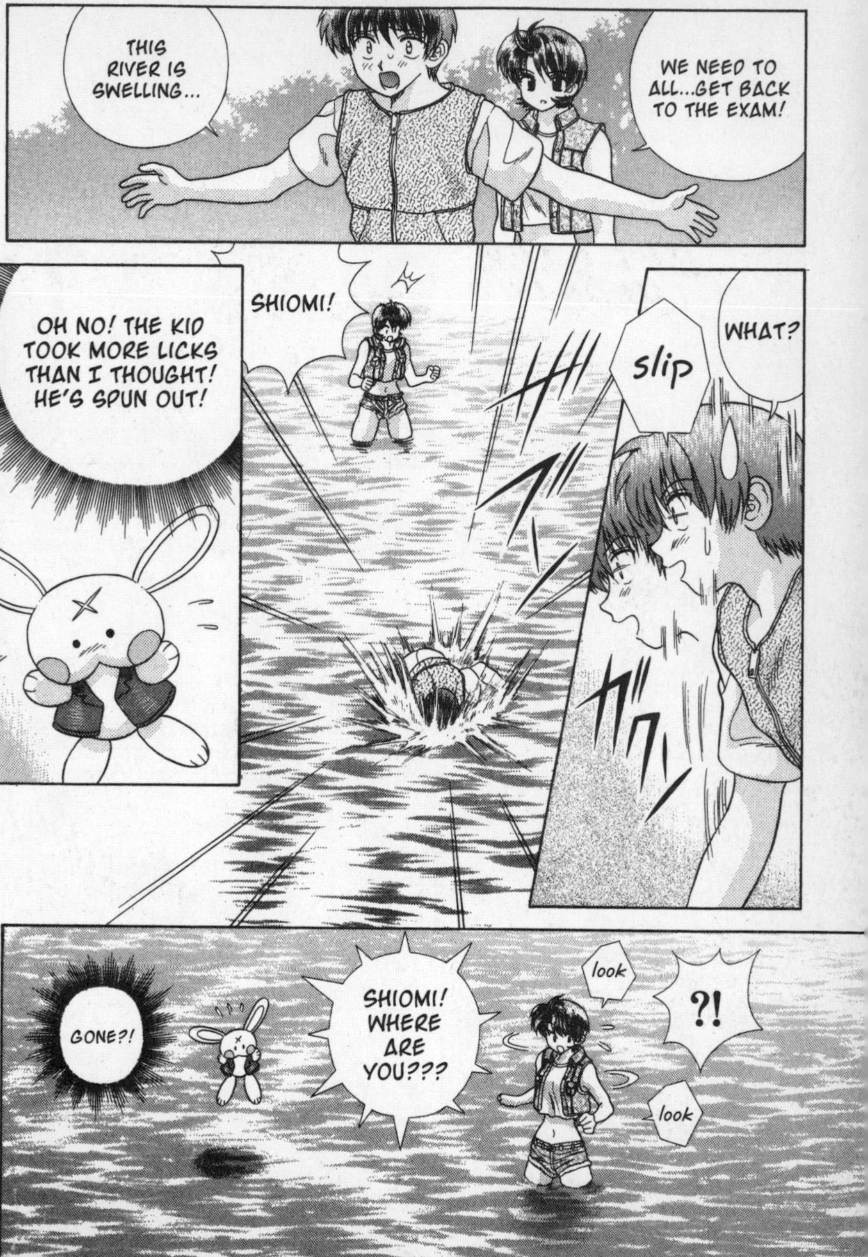
WE NEED TO ALL...GET BACK TO THE EXAM!
THIS RIVER IS SWELLING...
WHAT?
slip
SHIOMI!
OH NO! THE KID TOOK MORE LICKS THAN I THOUGHT! HE'S SPUN OUT!
?!
look
look
SHIOMI! WHERE ARE YOU???
GONE?!

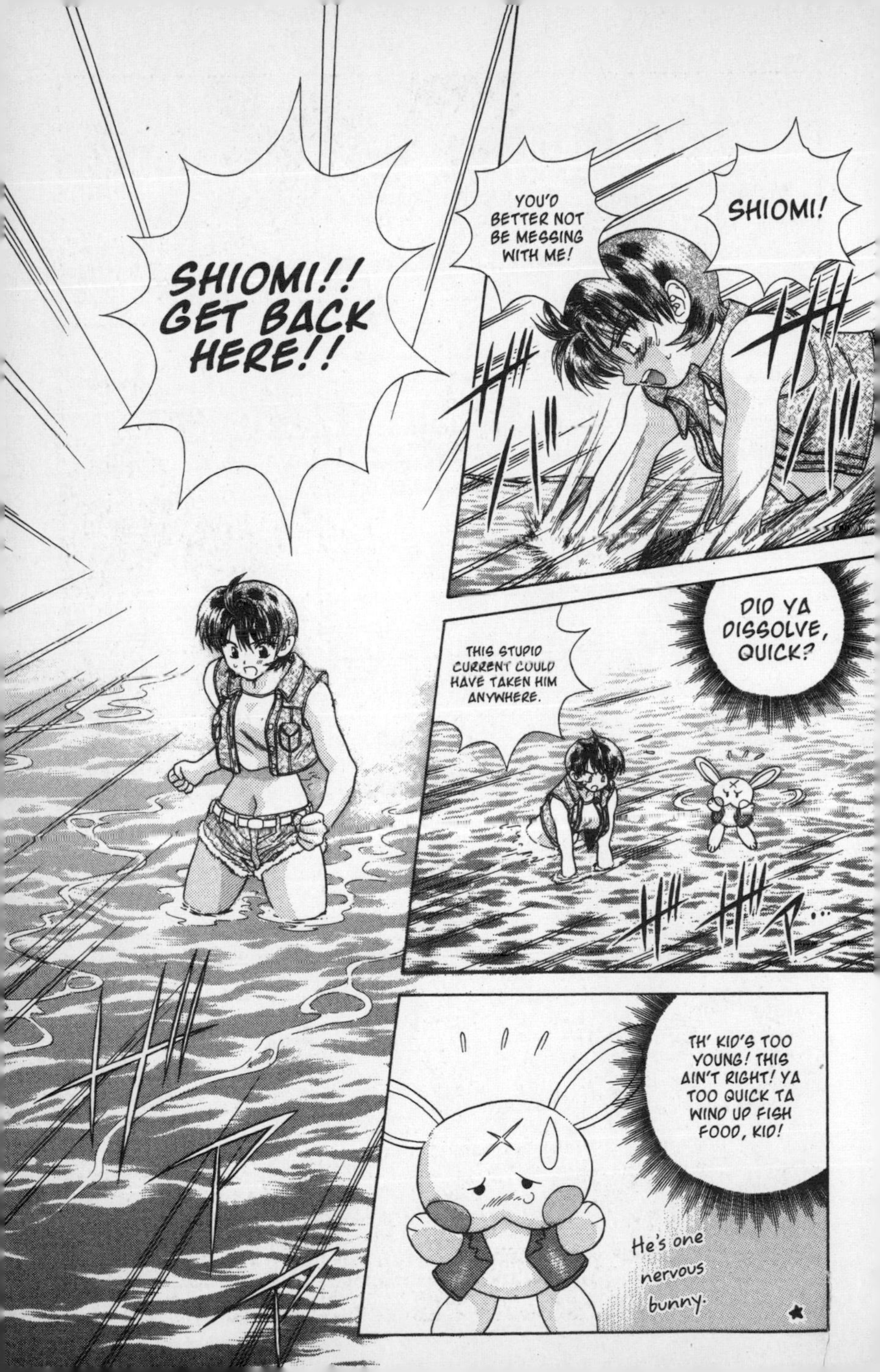
SHIOMI!
YOU'D BETTER NOT BE MESSING WITH ME!
DID YA DISSOLVE, QUICK?
THIS STUPID CURRENT COULD HAVE TAKEN HIM ANYWHERE.
TH' KID'S TOO YOUNG! THIS AIN'T RIGHT! YA TOO QUICK TA WIND UP FISH FOOD, KID!
He's one nervous bunny.
SHIOMI!! GET BACK HERE!!

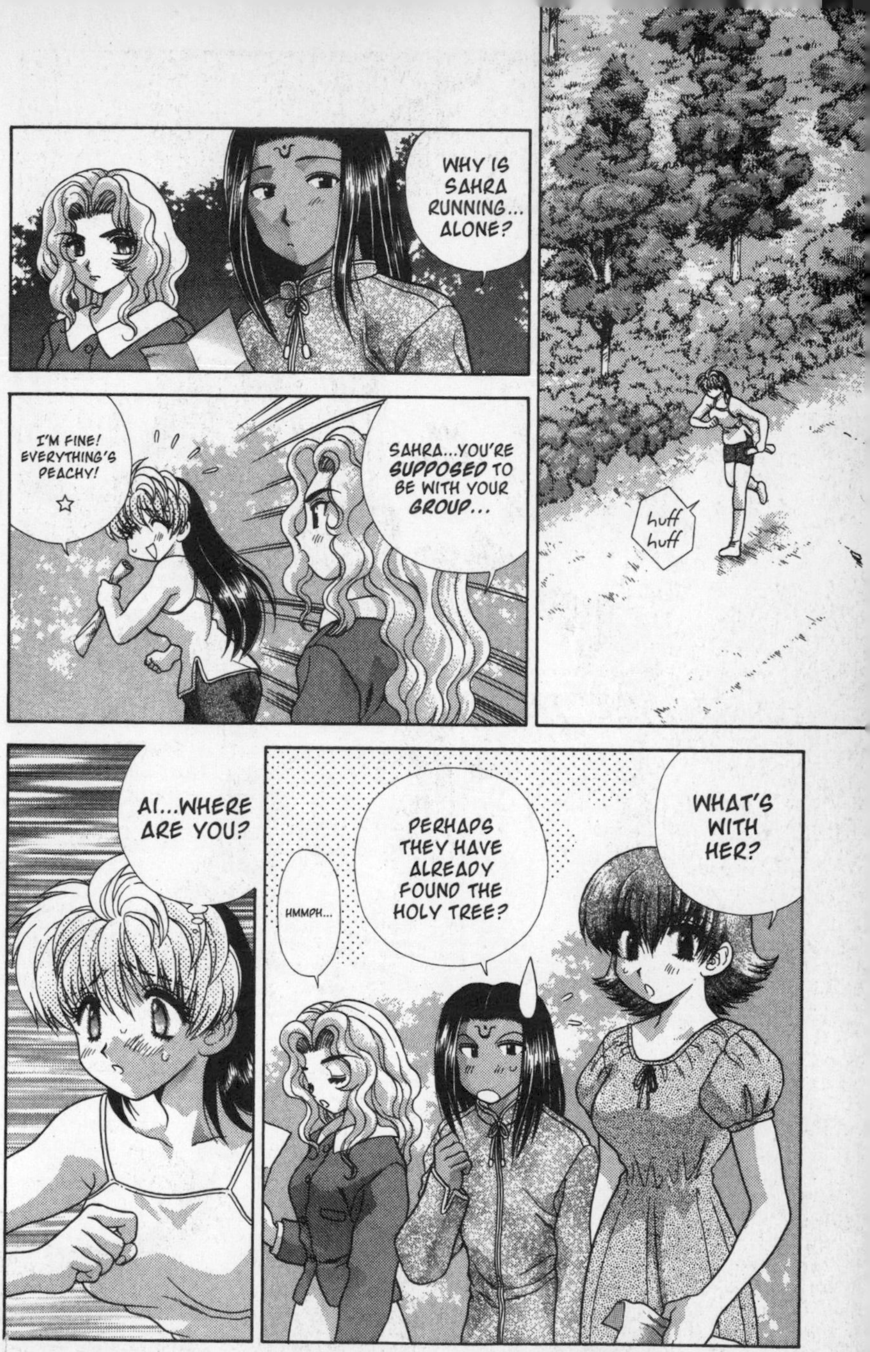
huff huff
WHY IS SAHRA RUNNING... ALONE?
SAHRA...YOU'RE SUPPOSED TO BE WITH YOUR GROUP...
I'M FINE! EVERYTHING'S PEACHY! ☆
WHAT'S WITH HER?
PERHAPS THEY HAVE ALREADY FOUND THE HOLY TREE?
HMMPH...
AI...WHERE ARE YOU?

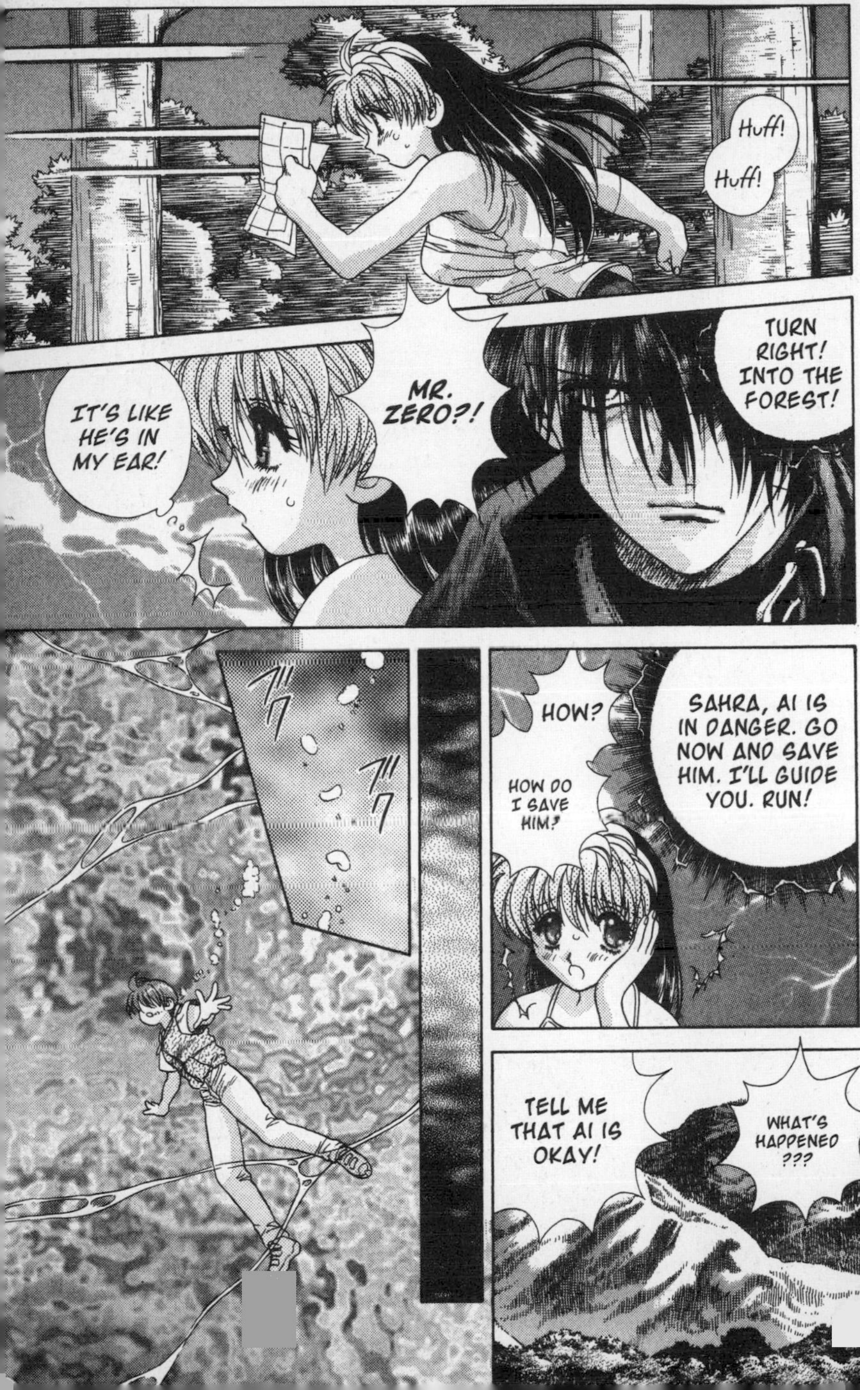
Huff!
Huff!
TURN RIGHT! INTO THE FOREST!
MR. ZERO?!
IT'S LIKE HE'S IN MY EAR!
SAHRA, AI IS IN DANGER. GO NOW AND SAVE HIM. I'LL GUIDE YOU. RUN!
HOW?
HOW DO I SAVE HIM?
WHAT'S HAPPENED ???
TELL ME THAT AI IS OKAY!

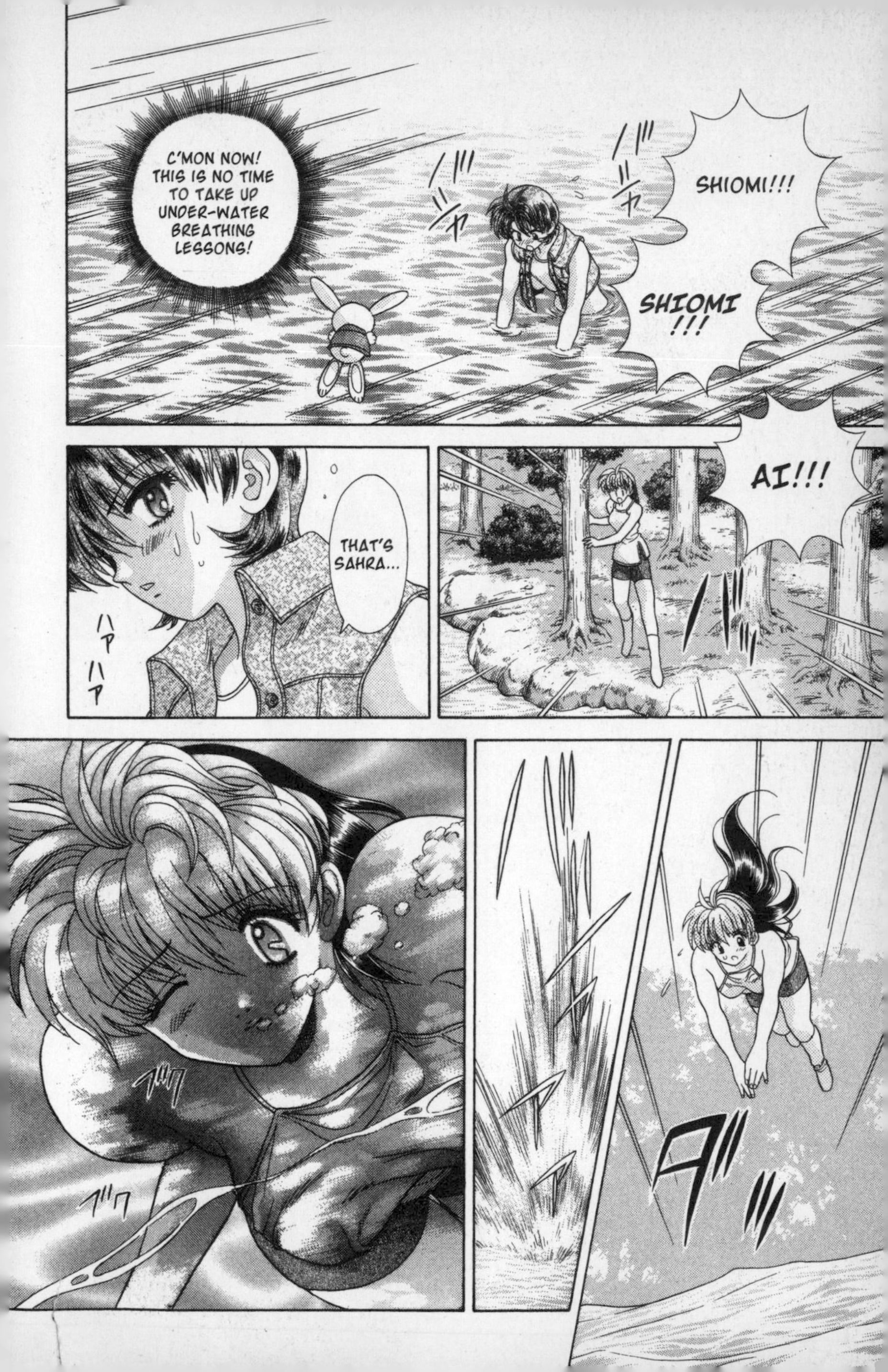
SHIOMI!!!
SHIOMI !!!
C'MON NOW! THIS IS NO TIME TO TAKE UP UNDER-WATER BREATHING LESSONS!
AI!!!
THAT'S SAHRA...
ハァ ハァ

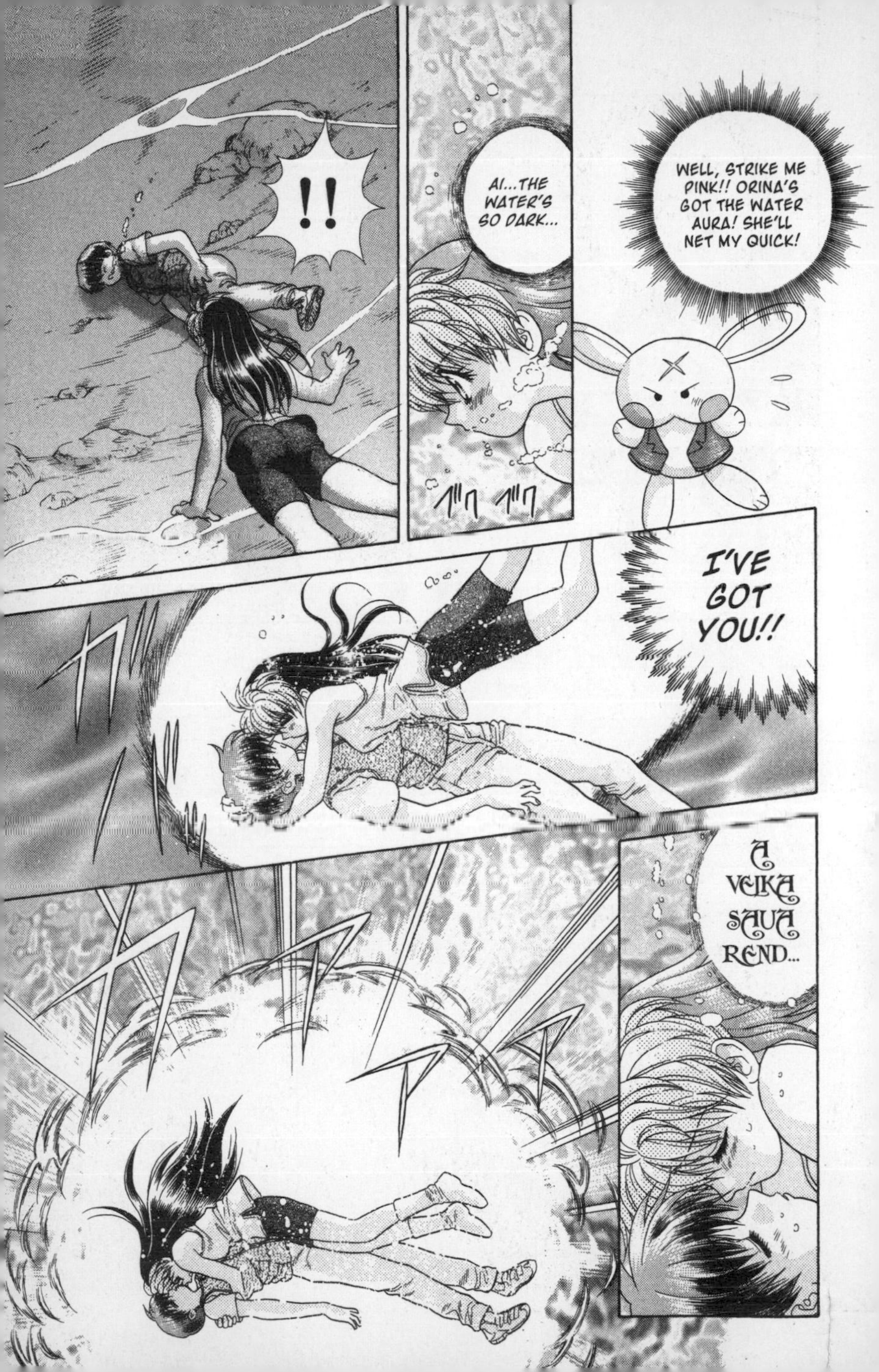
WELL, STRIKE ME PINK!! ORINA'S GOT THE WATER AURA! SHE'LL NET MY QUICK!
AI...THE WATER'S SO DARK...
ブク ブク
!!
I'VE GOT YOU!!
A VELKA SAUA REND...

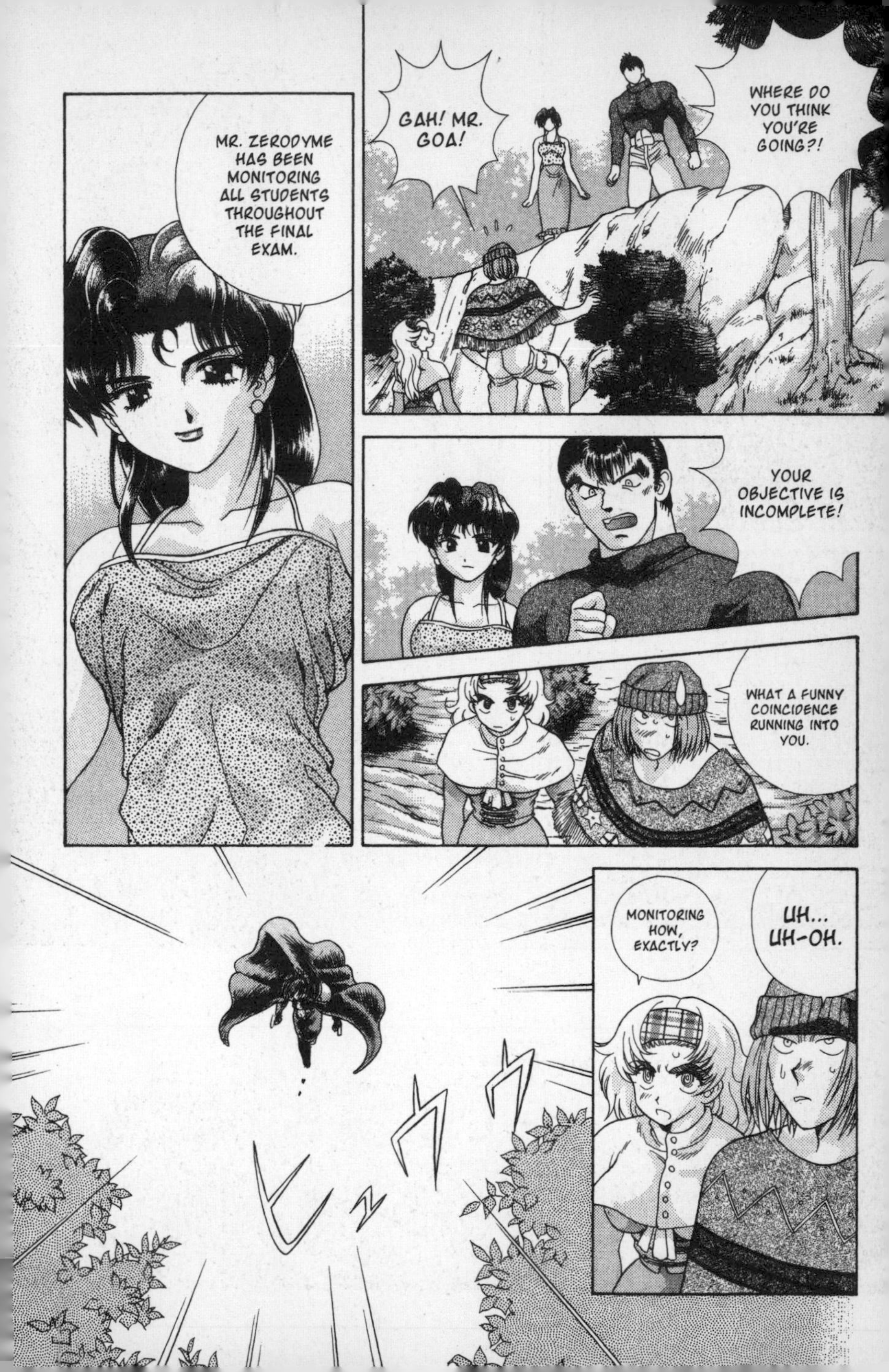
WHERE DO YOU THINK YOU'RE GOING?!
GAH! MR. GOA!
YOUR OBJECTIVE IS INCOMPLETE!
WHAT A FUNNY COINCIDENCE RUNNING INTO YOU.
MR. ZERODYME HAS BEEN MONITORING ALL STUDENTS THROUGHOUT THE FINAL EXAM.
UH... UH-OH.
MONITORING HOW, EXACTLY?

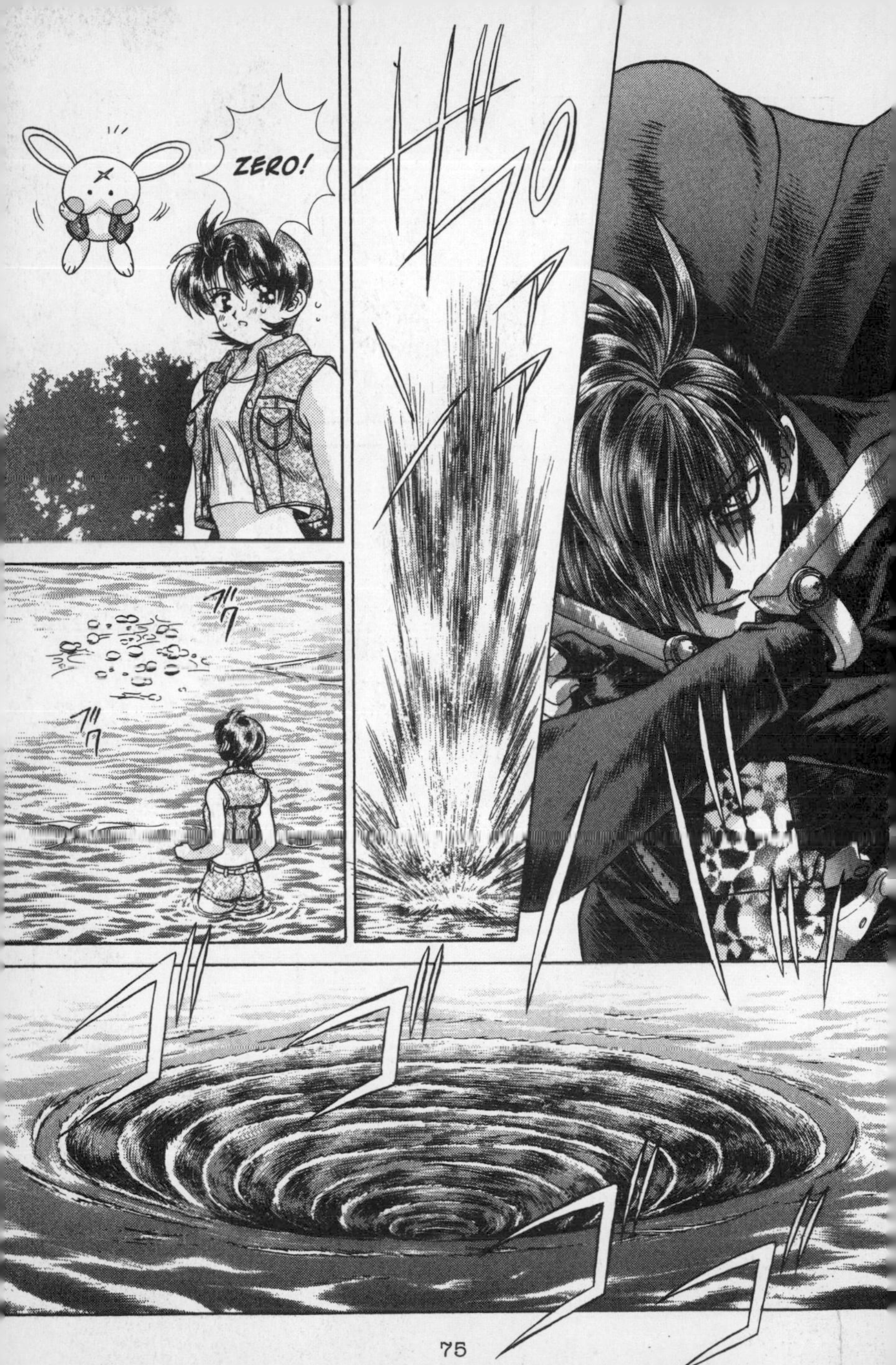
ZERO!

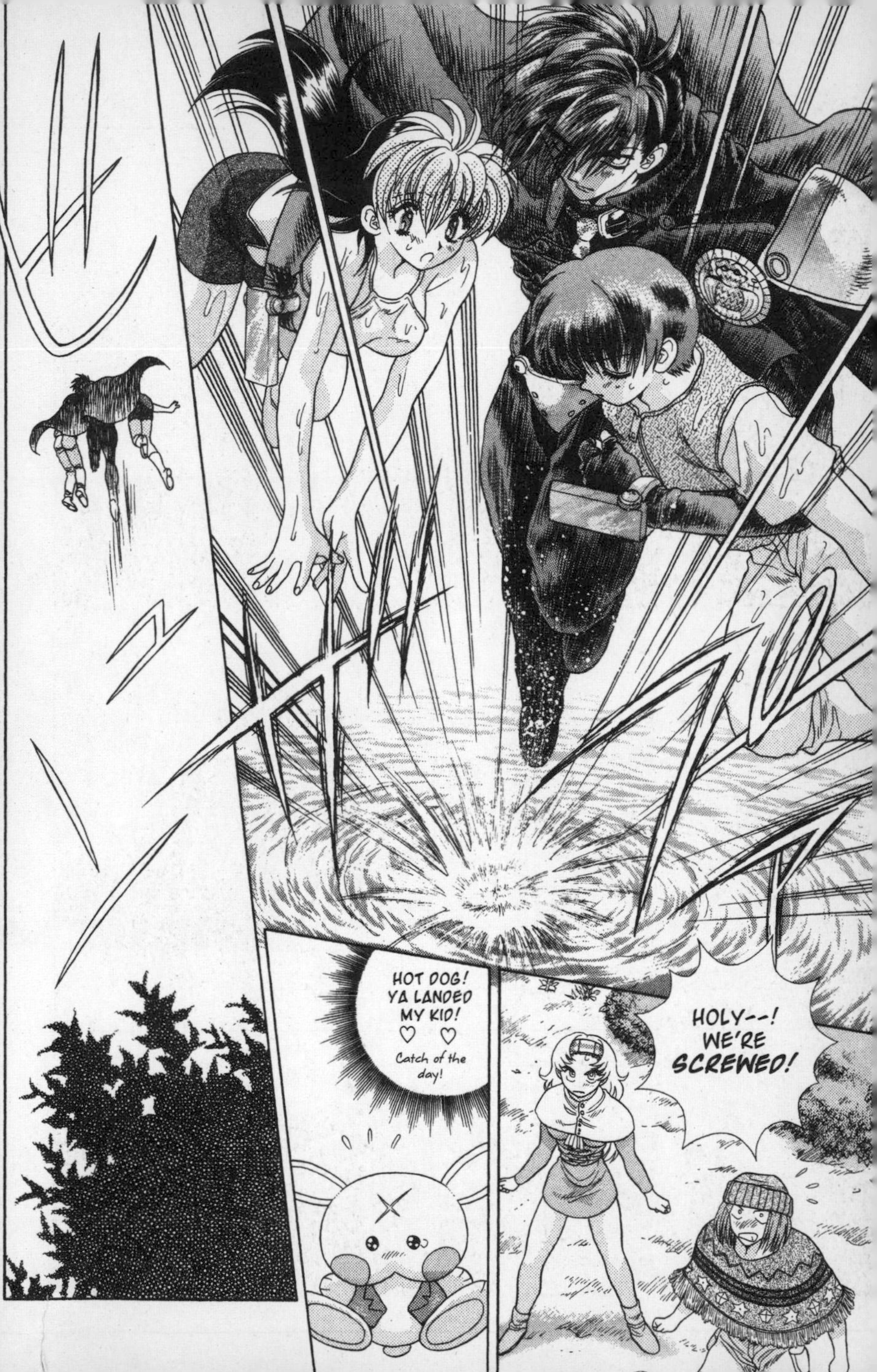
HOLY--! WE'RE SCREWED!
HOT DOG! YA LANDED MY KID! ♡ ♡
Catch of the day!

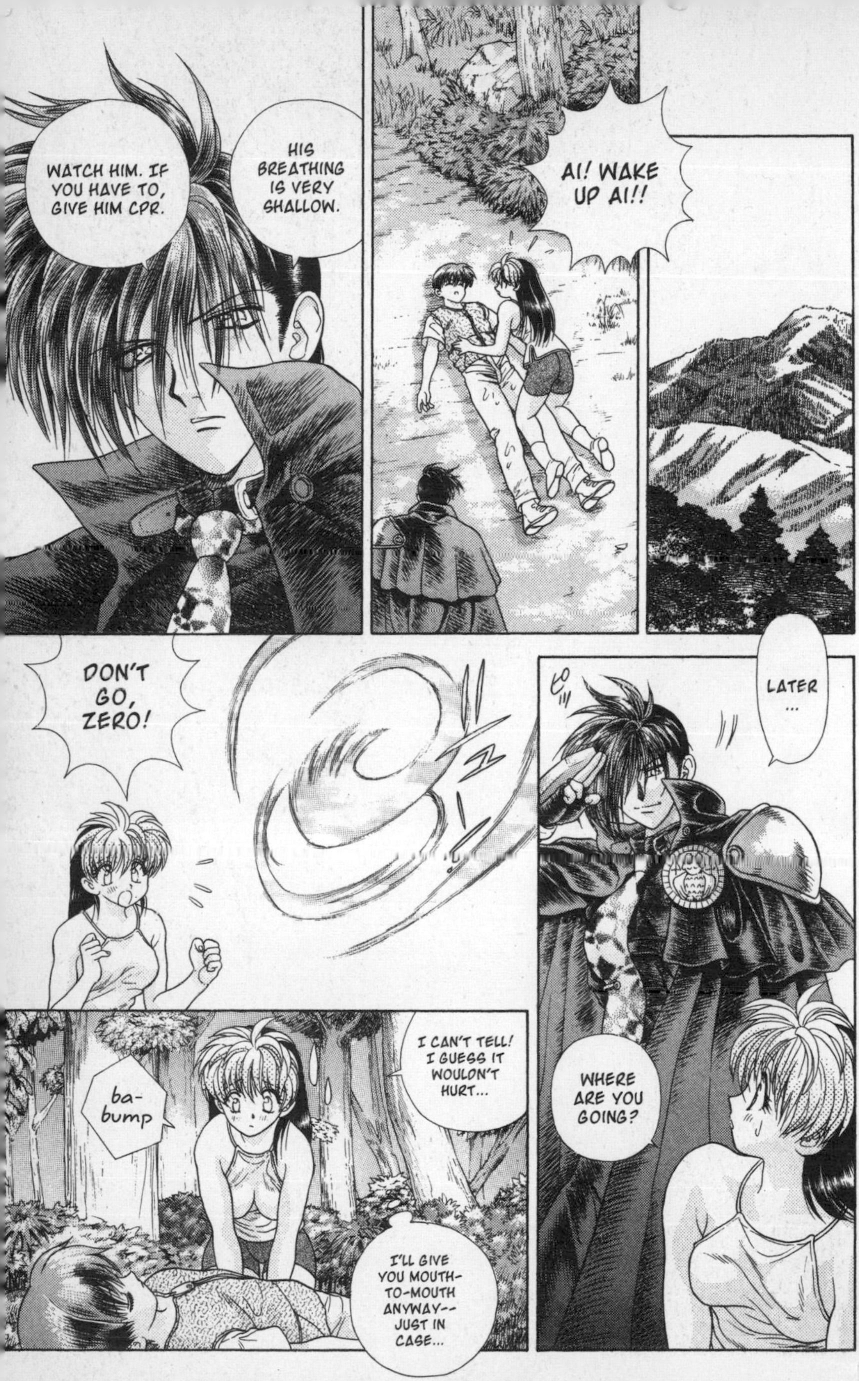
AI! WAKE UP AI!!
HIS BREATHING IS VERY SHALLOW.
WATCH HIM. IF YOU HAVE TO, GIVE HIM CPR.
LATER ...
WHERE ARE YOU GOING?
DON'T GO, ZERO!
I CAN'T TELL! I GUESS IT WOULDN'T HURT...
ba-bump
I'LL GIVE YOU MOUTH-TO-MOUTH ANYWAY--JUST IN CASE...

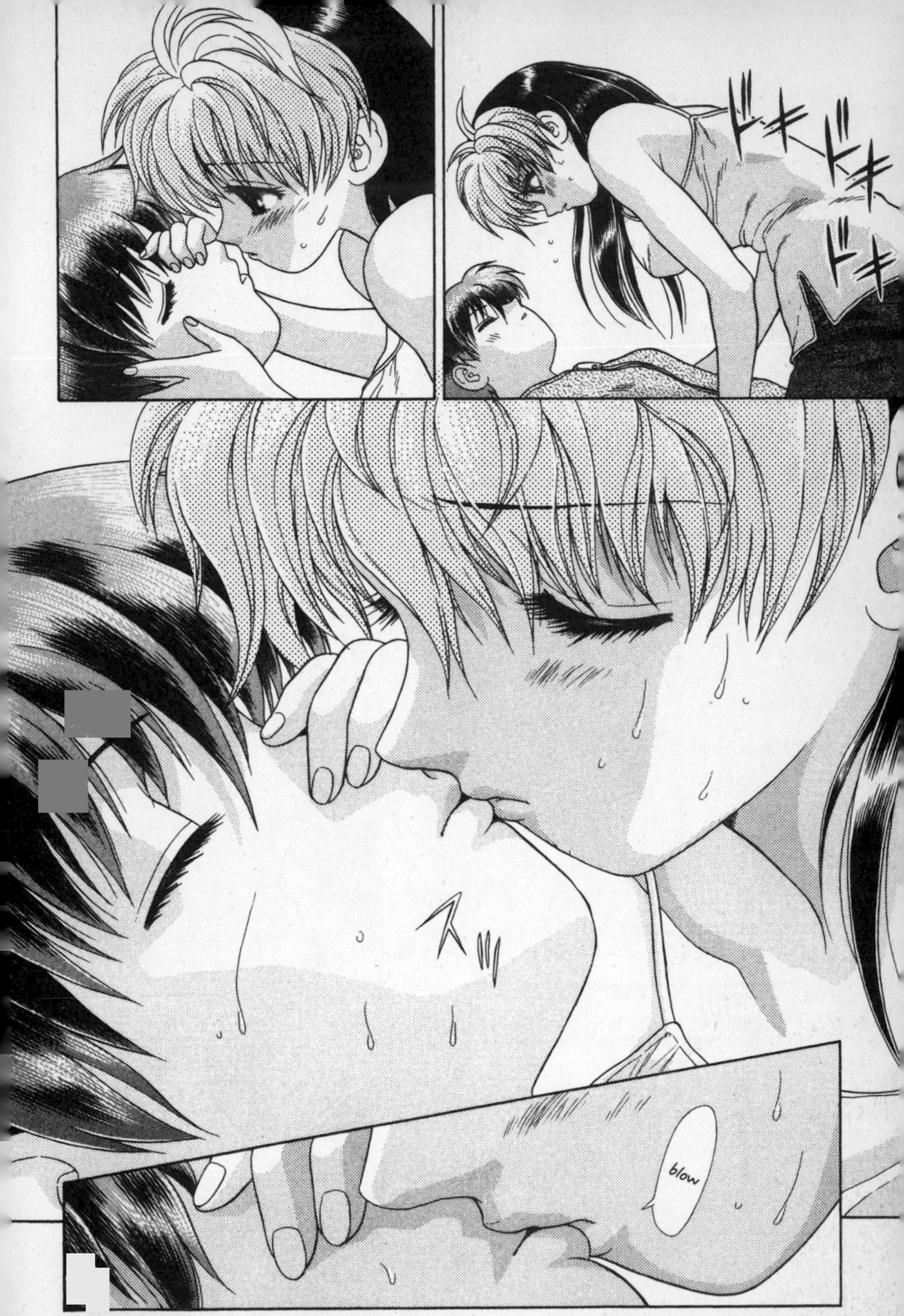

ドキドキドキ
ス
blow

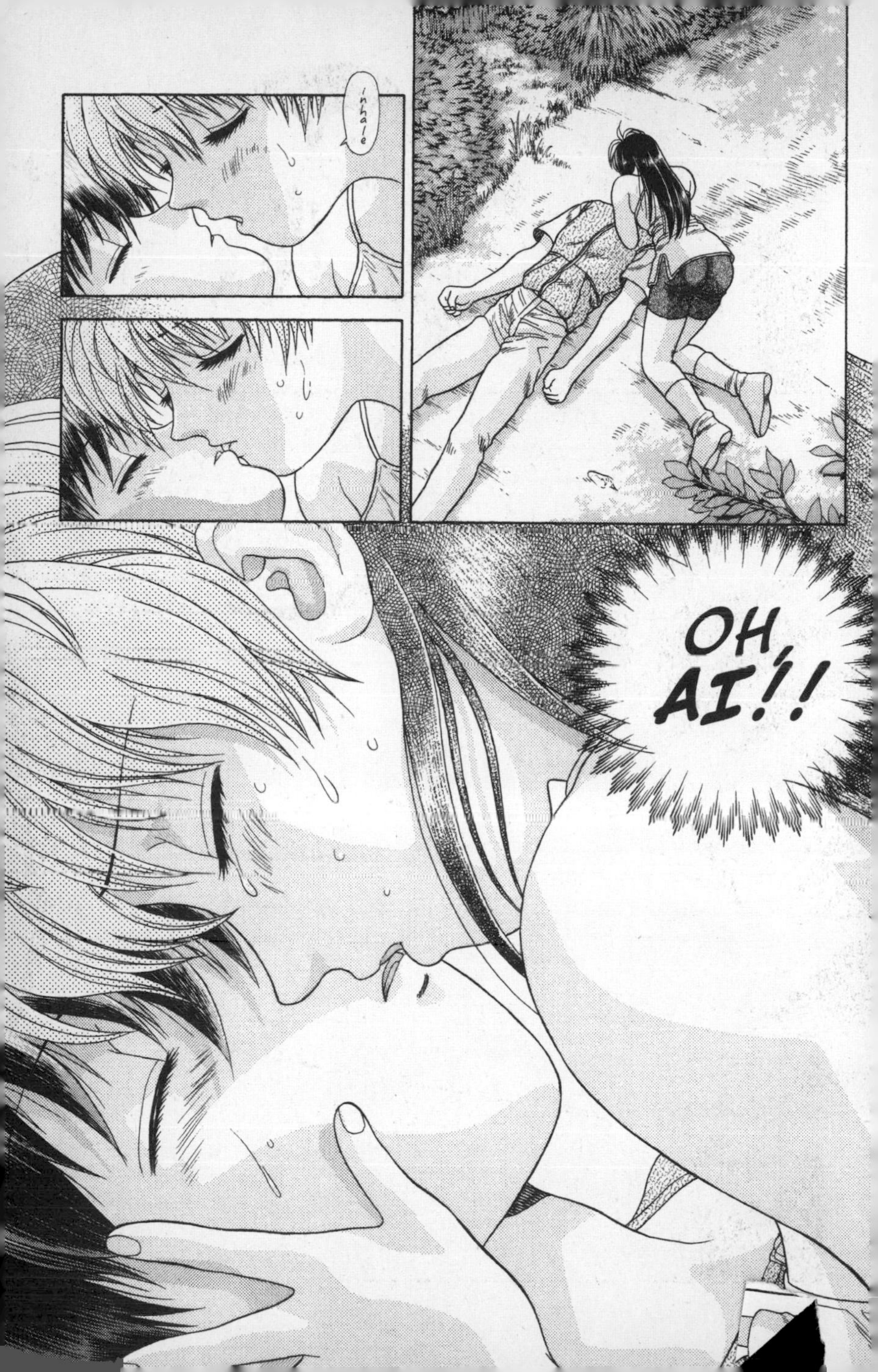
inhale
OH, AI!!

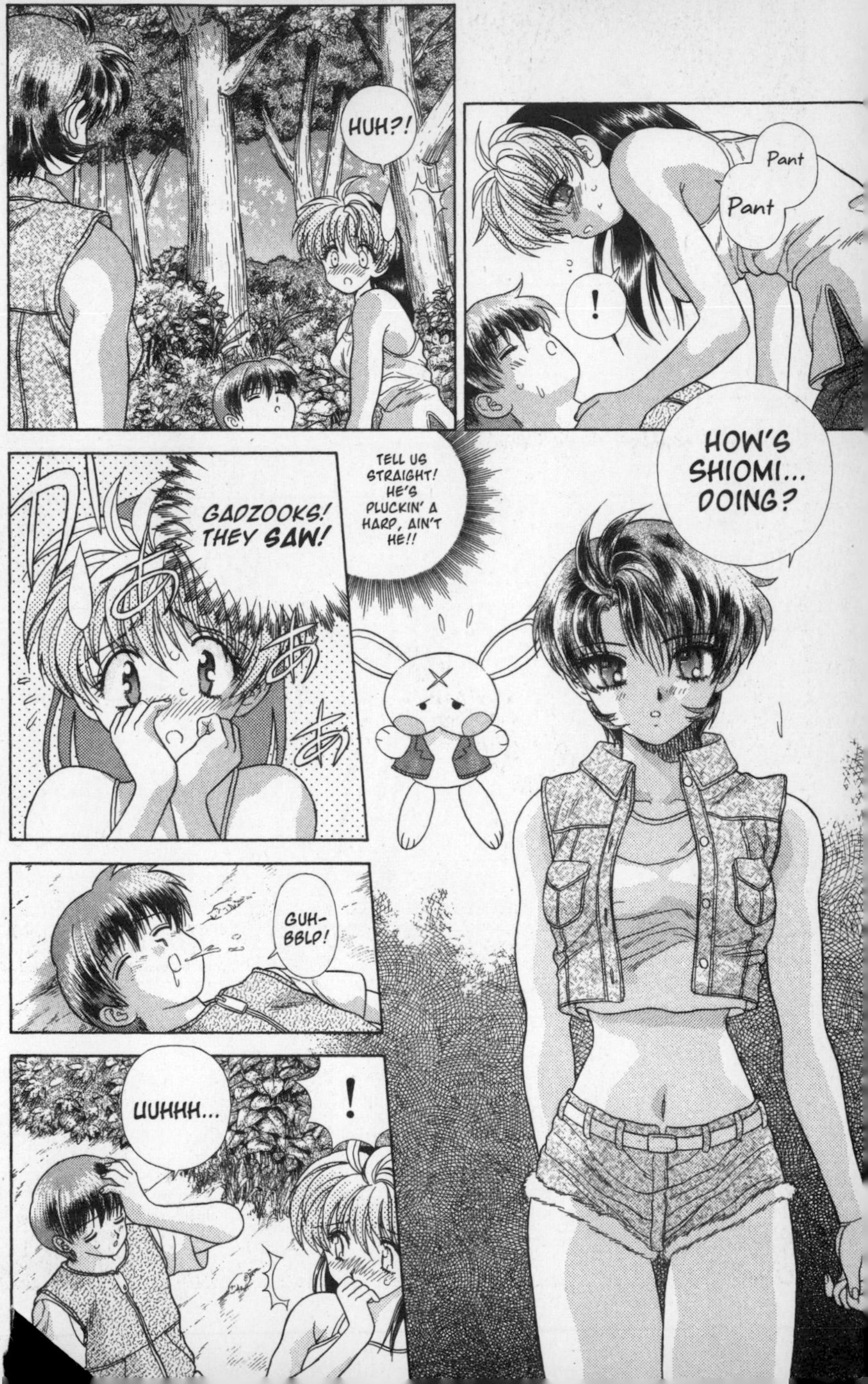
Pant
Pant
!
HUH?!
HOW'S SHIOMI... DOING?
TELL US STRAIGHT! HE'S PLUCKIN' A HARP, AIN'T HE!!
GADZOOKS! THEY SAW!
GUH-BBLP!
!
UUHHH...

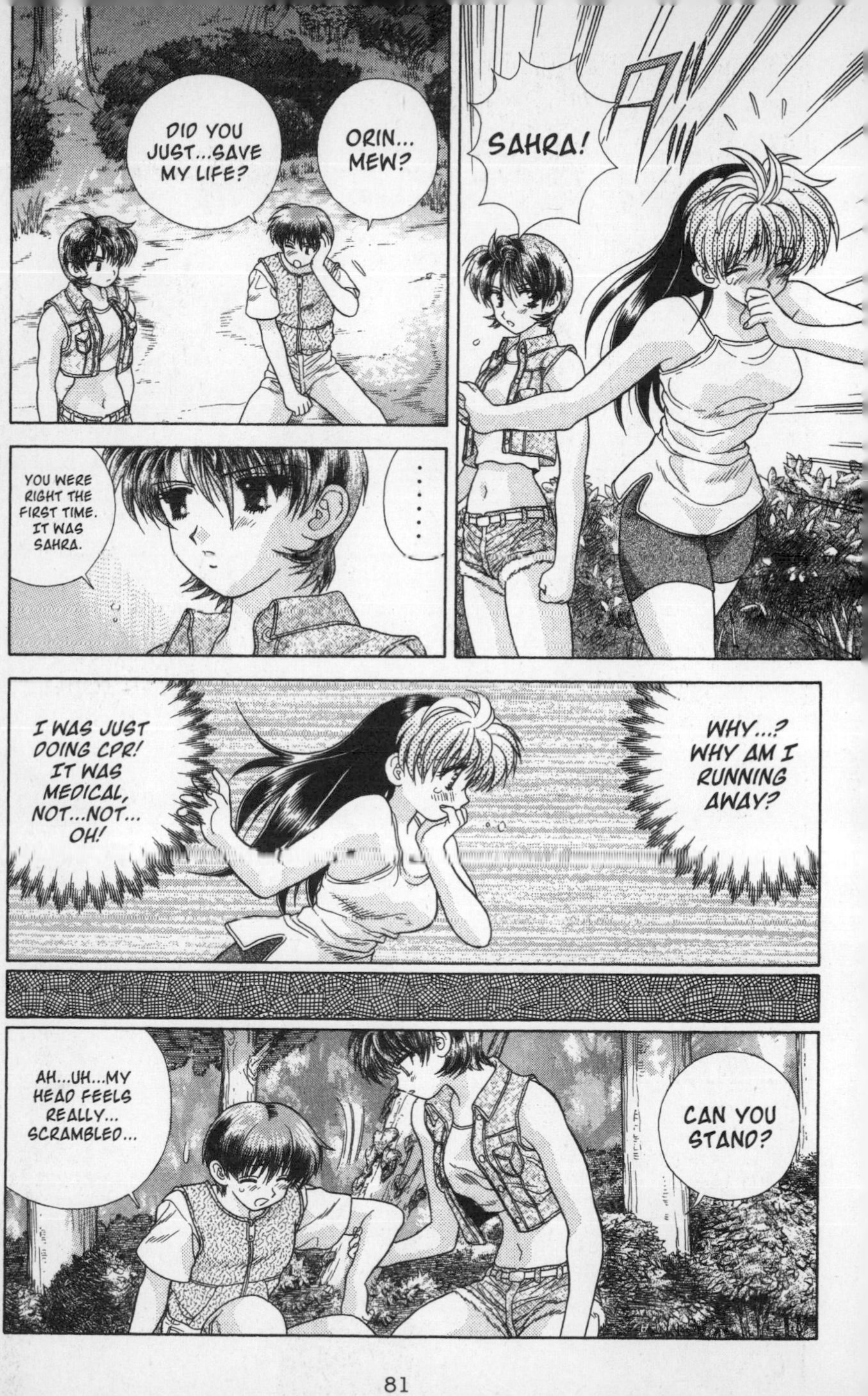
SAHRA!
ORIN... MEW?
DID YOU JUST...SAVE MY LIFE?
......
YOU WERE RIGHT THE FIRST TIME. IT WAS SAHRA.
WHY...? WHY AM I RUNNING AWAY?
I WAS JUST DOING CPR! IT WAS MEDICAL, NOT...NOT... OH!
CAN YOU STAND?
AH...UH...MY HEAD FEELS REALLY... SCRAMBLED...

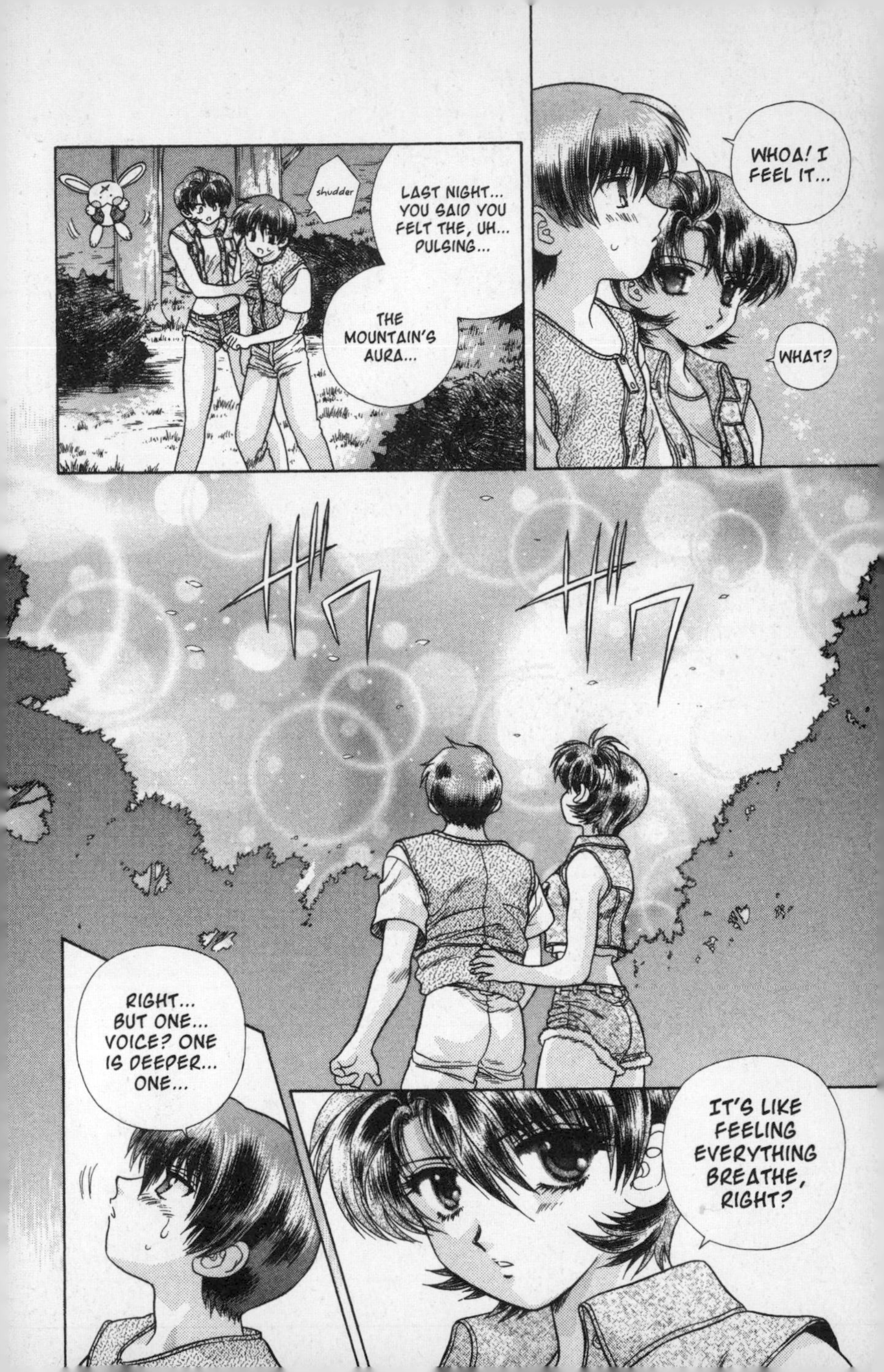
WHOA! I FEEL IT...
WHAT?
shudder
LAST NIGHT... YOU SAID YOU FELT THE, UH... PULSING...
THE MOUNTAIN'S AURA...
IT'S LIKE FEELING EVERYTHING BREATHE, RIGHT?
RIGHT... BUT ONE... VOICE? ONE IS DEEPER... ONE...

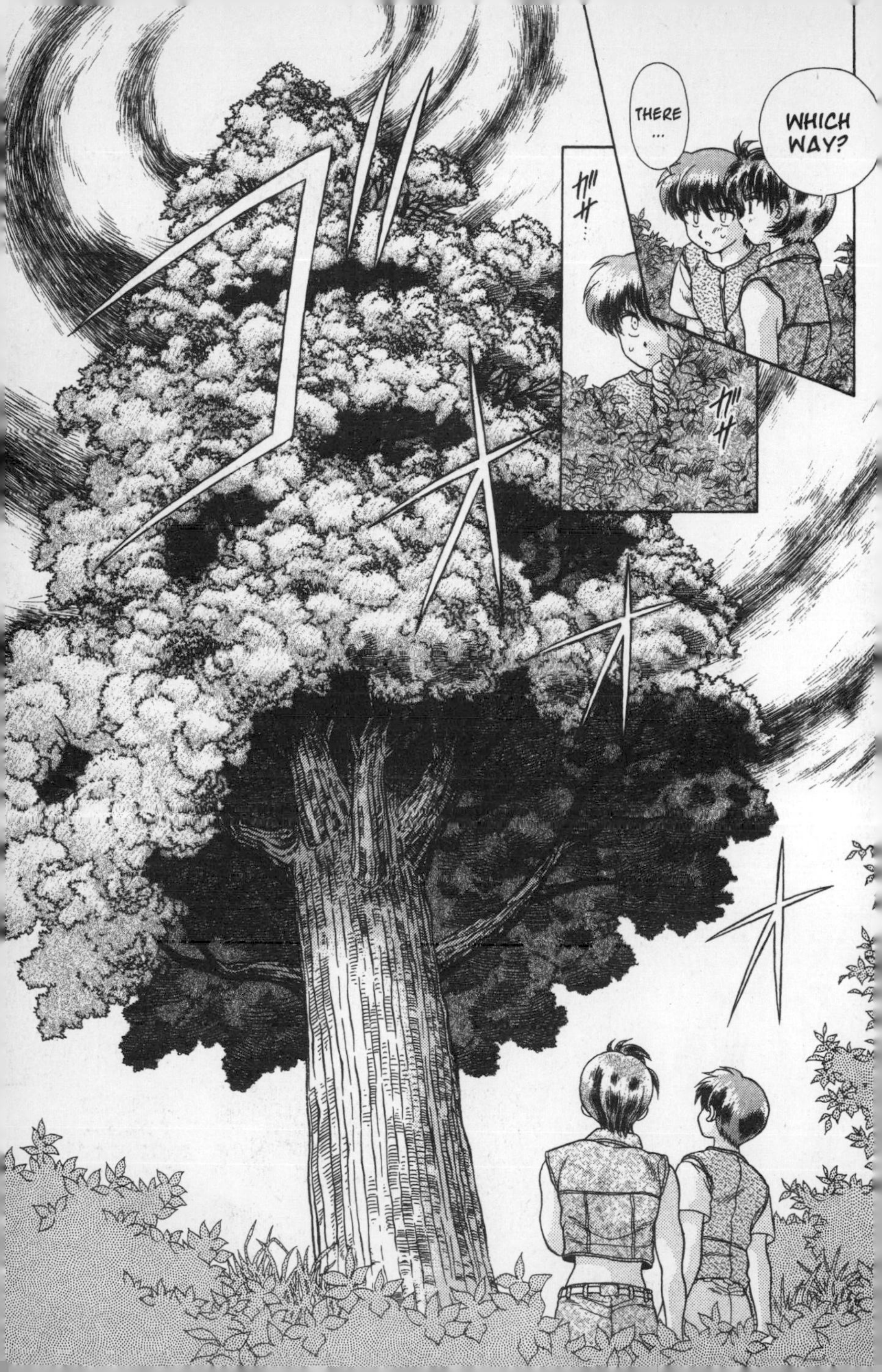
WHICH WAY?
THERE ...
ガサ…
ガサ

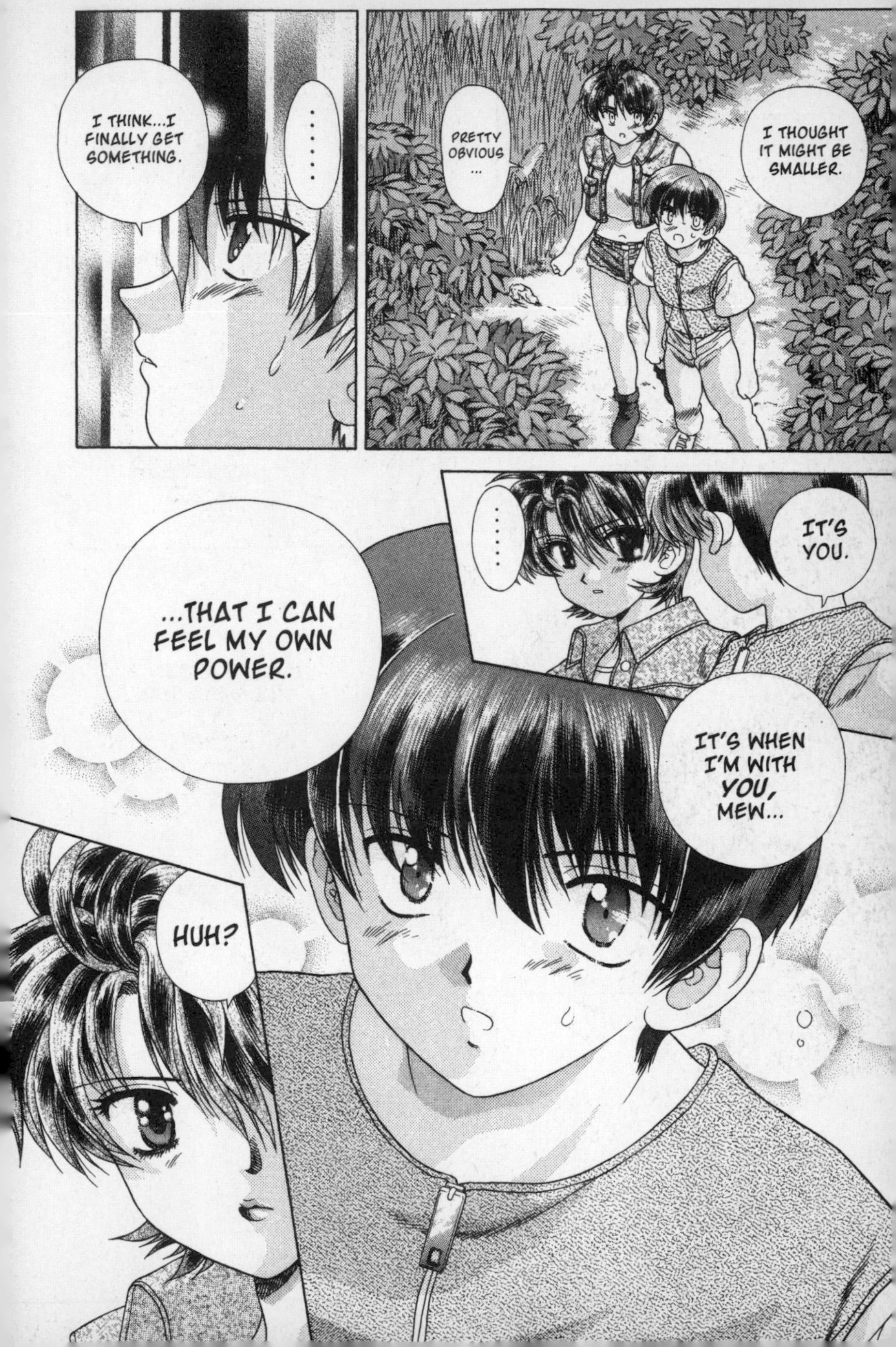
I THOUGHT IT MIGHT BE SMALLER.
PRETTY OBVIOUS ...
......
I THINK...I FINALLY GET SOMETHING.
IT'S YOU.
......
IT'S WHEN I'M WITH *YOU*, MEW...
...THAT I CAN FEEL MY OWN POWER.
HUH?

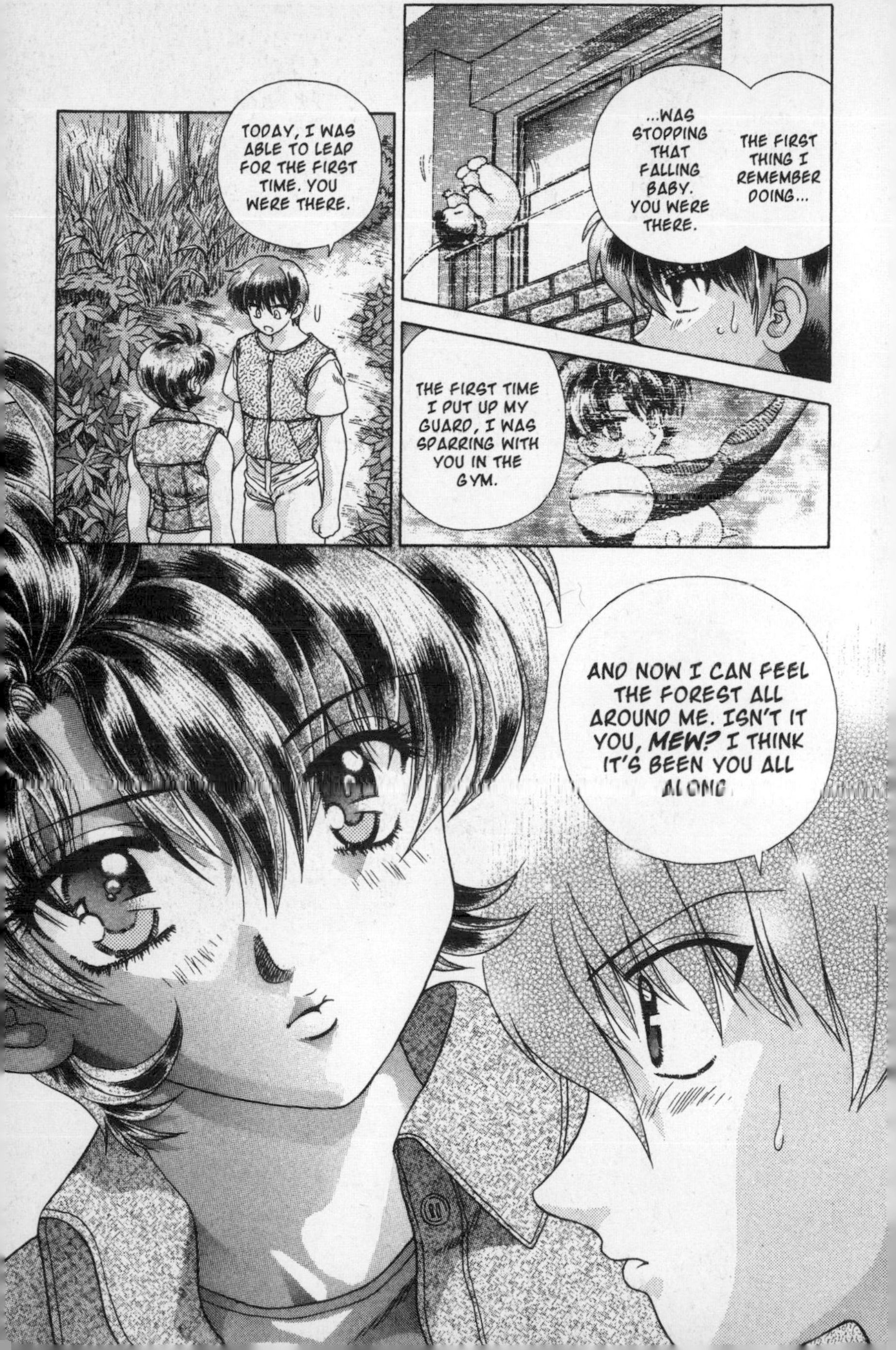
THE FIRST THING I REMEMBER DOING...
...WAS STOPPING THAT FALLING BABY. YOU WERE THERE.
THE FIRST TIME I PUT UP MY GUARD, I WAS SPARRING WITH YOU IN THE GYM.
TODAY, I WAS ABLE TO LEAP FOR THE FIRST TIME. YOU WERE THERE.
AND NOW I CAN FEEL THE FOREST ALL AROUND ME. ISN'T IT YOU, *MEW?* I THINK IT'S BEEN YOU ALL ALONG.

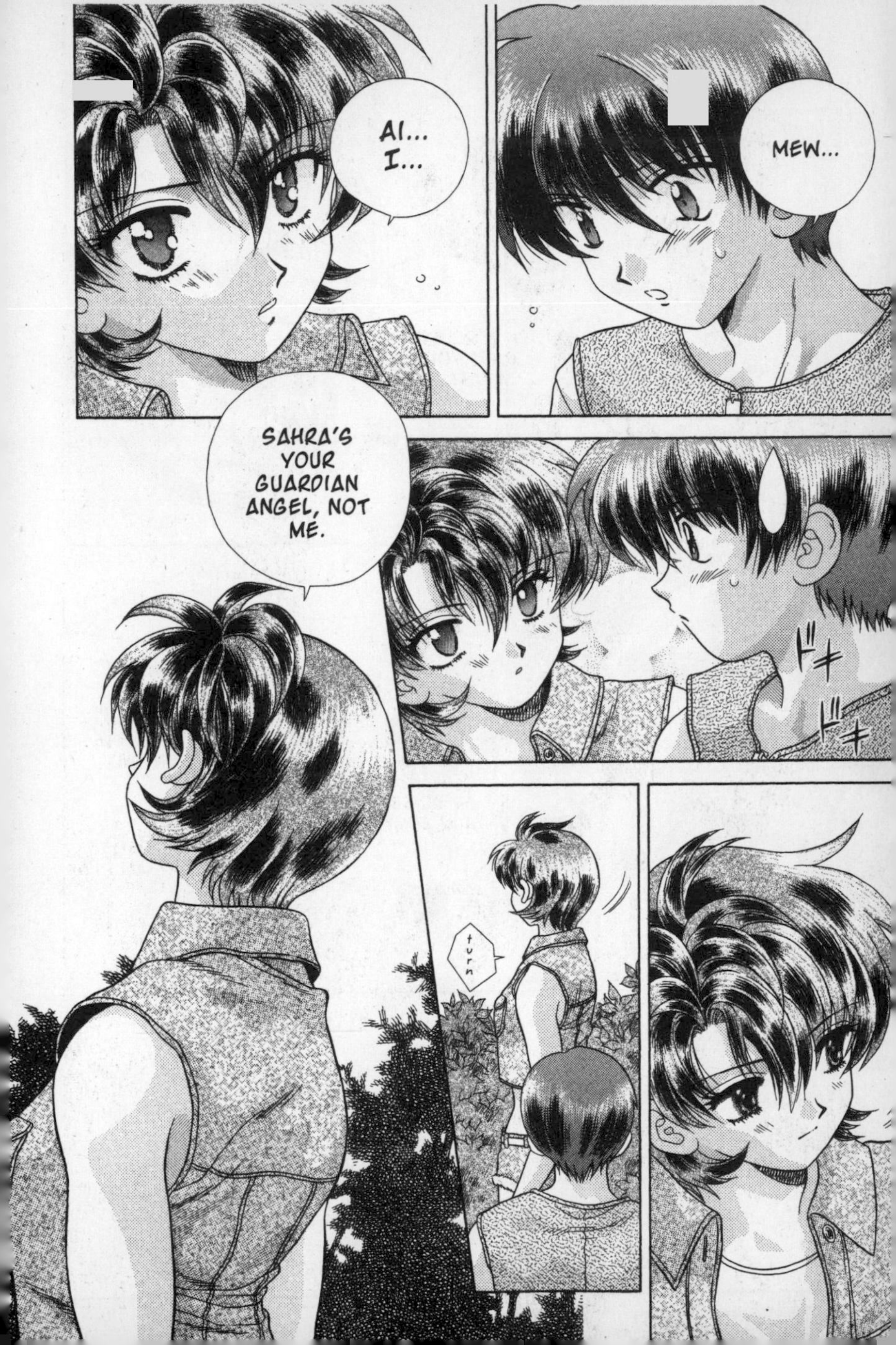
MEW...
AI...
I...
ドキ
ドキ
turn
SAHRA'S YOUR GUARDIAN ANGEL, NOT ME.

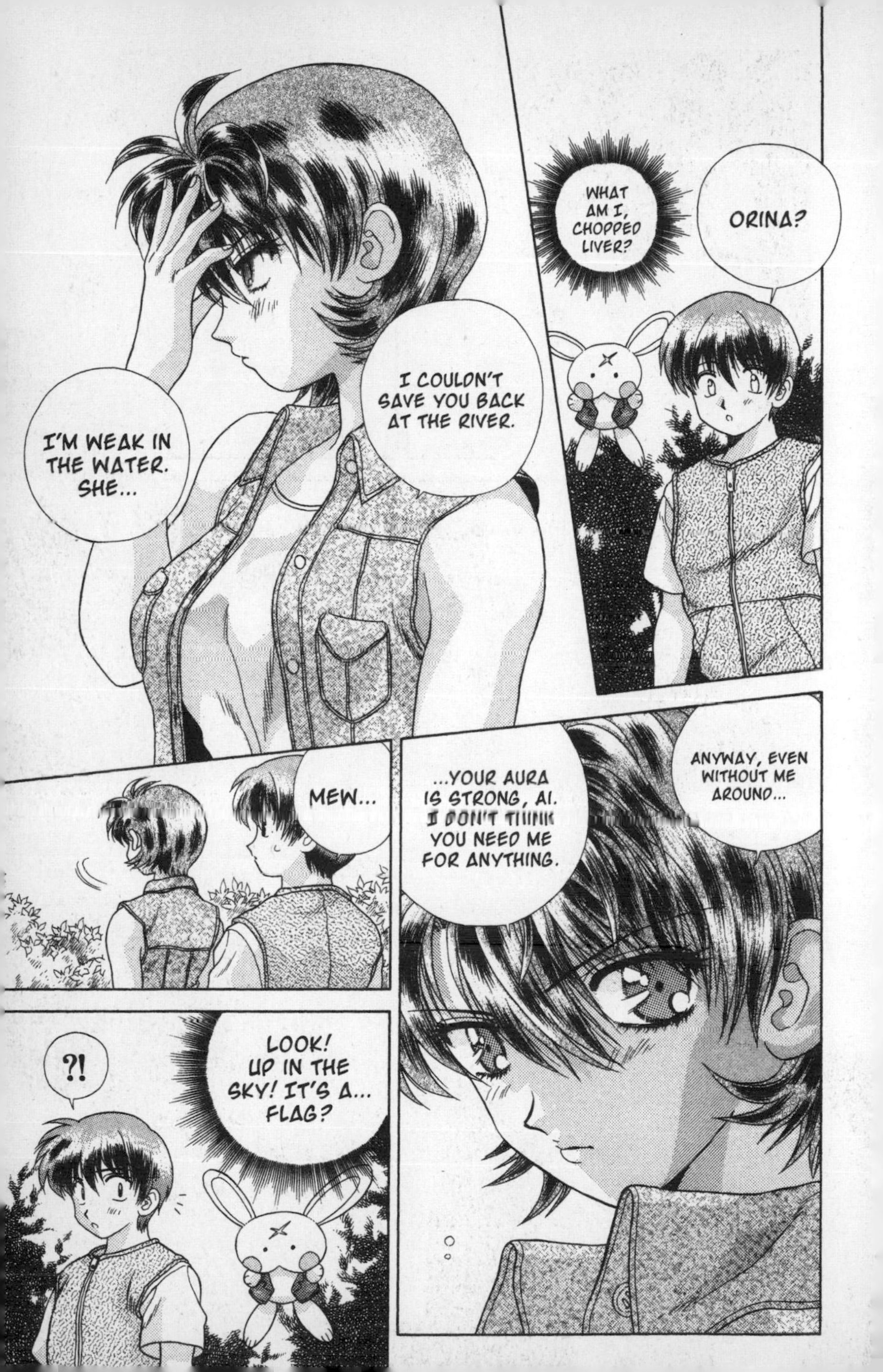
ORINA?
WHAT AM I, CHOPPED LIVER?
I COULDN'T SAVE YOU BACK AT THE RIVER.
I'M WEAK IN THE WATER. SHE...
ANYWAY, EVEN WITHOUT ME AROUND...
...YOUR AURA IS STRONG, AI. I DON'T THINK YOU NEED ME FOR ANYTHING.
MEW...
LOOK! UP IN THE SKY! IT'S A... FLAG?
?!

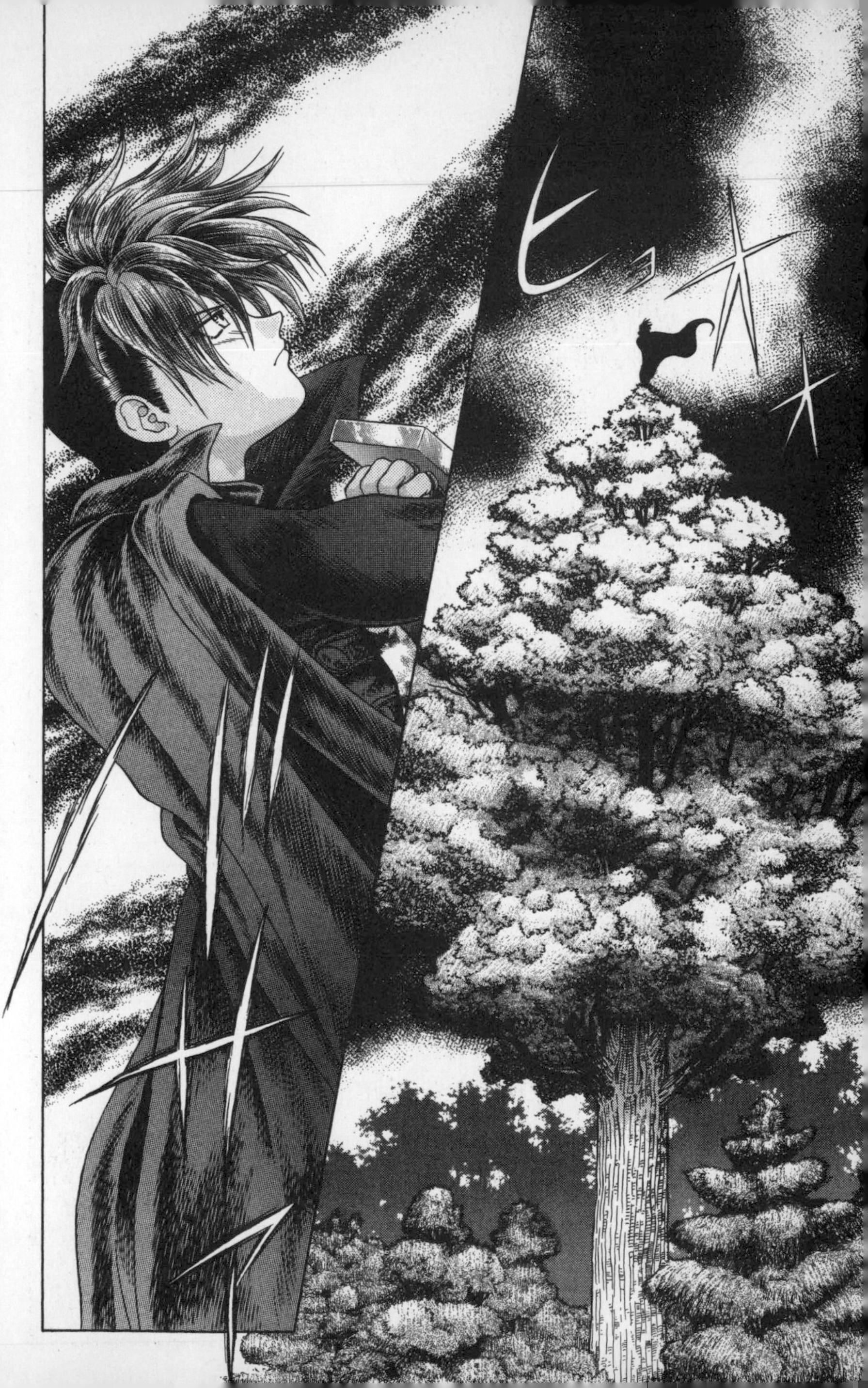
ヒョオ

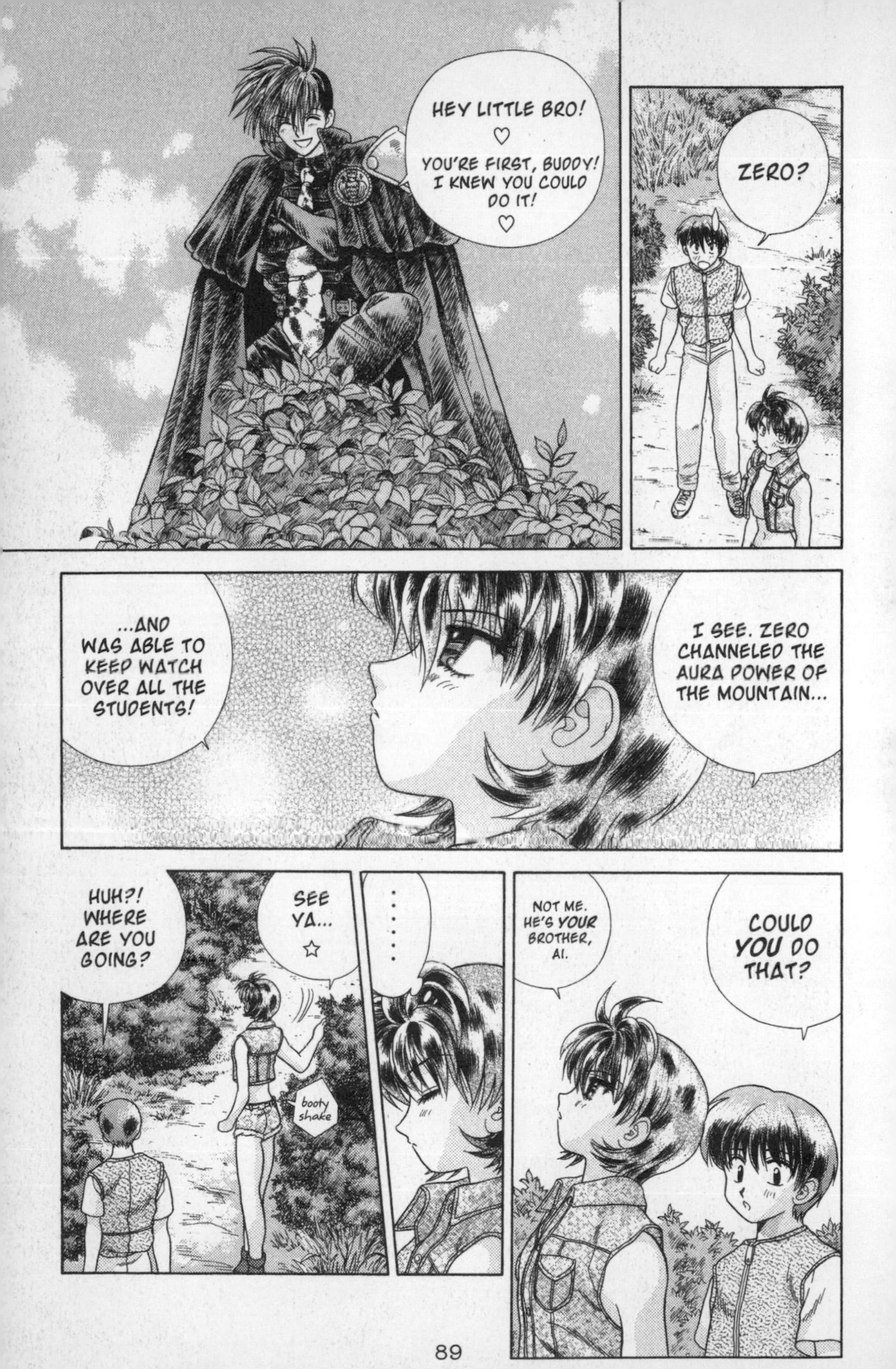
ZERO?
HEY LITTLE BRO! ♡ YOU'RE FIRST, BUDDY! I KNEW YOU COULD DO IT! ♡
I SEE. ZERO CHANNELED THE AURA POWER OF THE MOUNTAIN...
...AND WAS ABLE TO KEEP WATCH OVER ALL THE STUDENTS!
COULD *YOU* DO THAT?
NOT ME. HE'S *YOUR* BROTHER, AI.
......
SEE YA... ☆
HUH?! WHERE ARE YOU GOING?
booty shake

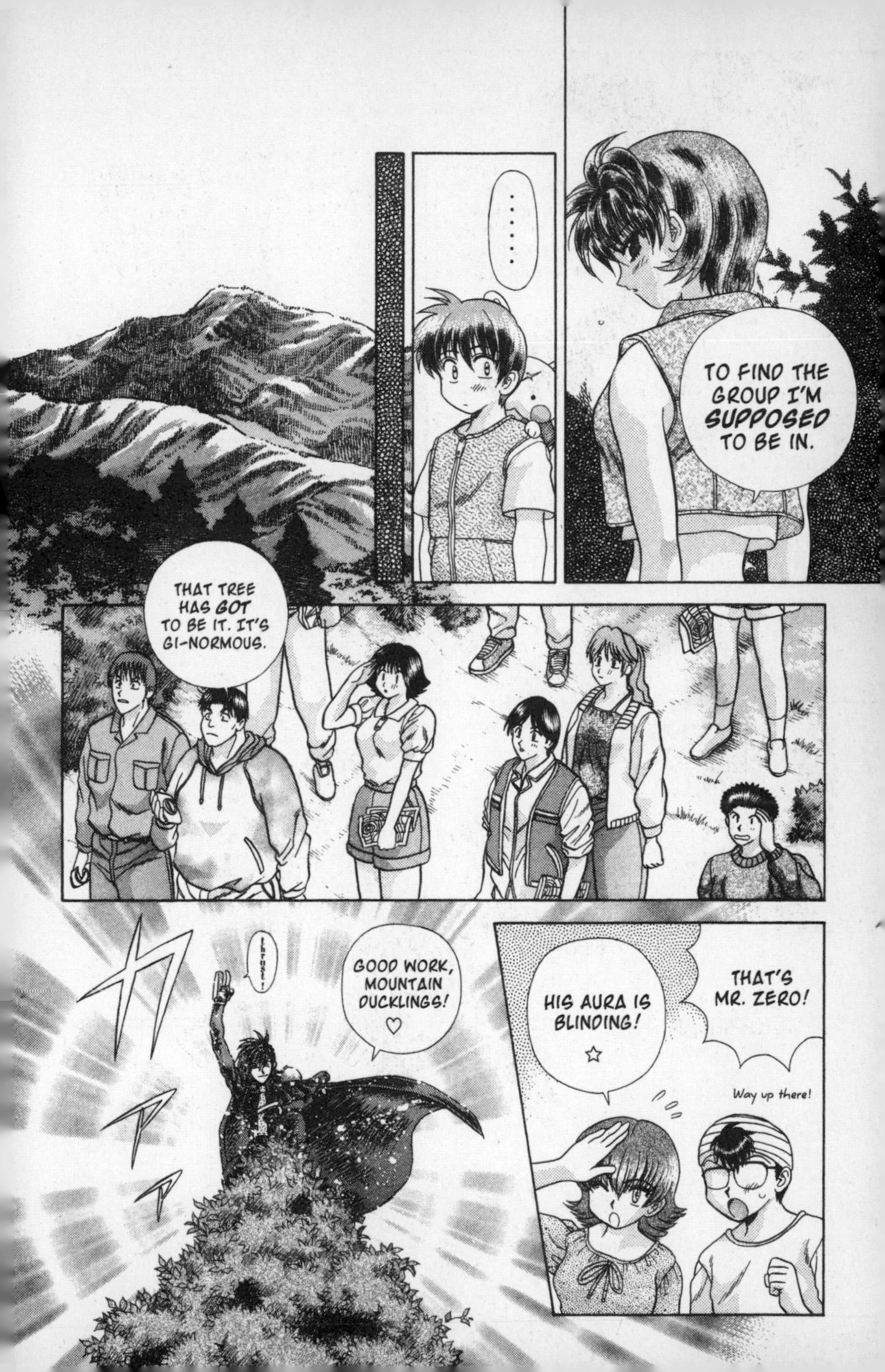
TO FIND THE GROUP I'M **SUPPOSED** TO BE IN.
......
THAT TREE HAS **GOT** TO BE IT. IT'S GI-NORMOUS.
THAT'S MR. ZERO!
HIS AURA IS BLINDING! ☆
Way up there!
GOOD WORK, MOUNTAIN DUCKLINGS! ♡

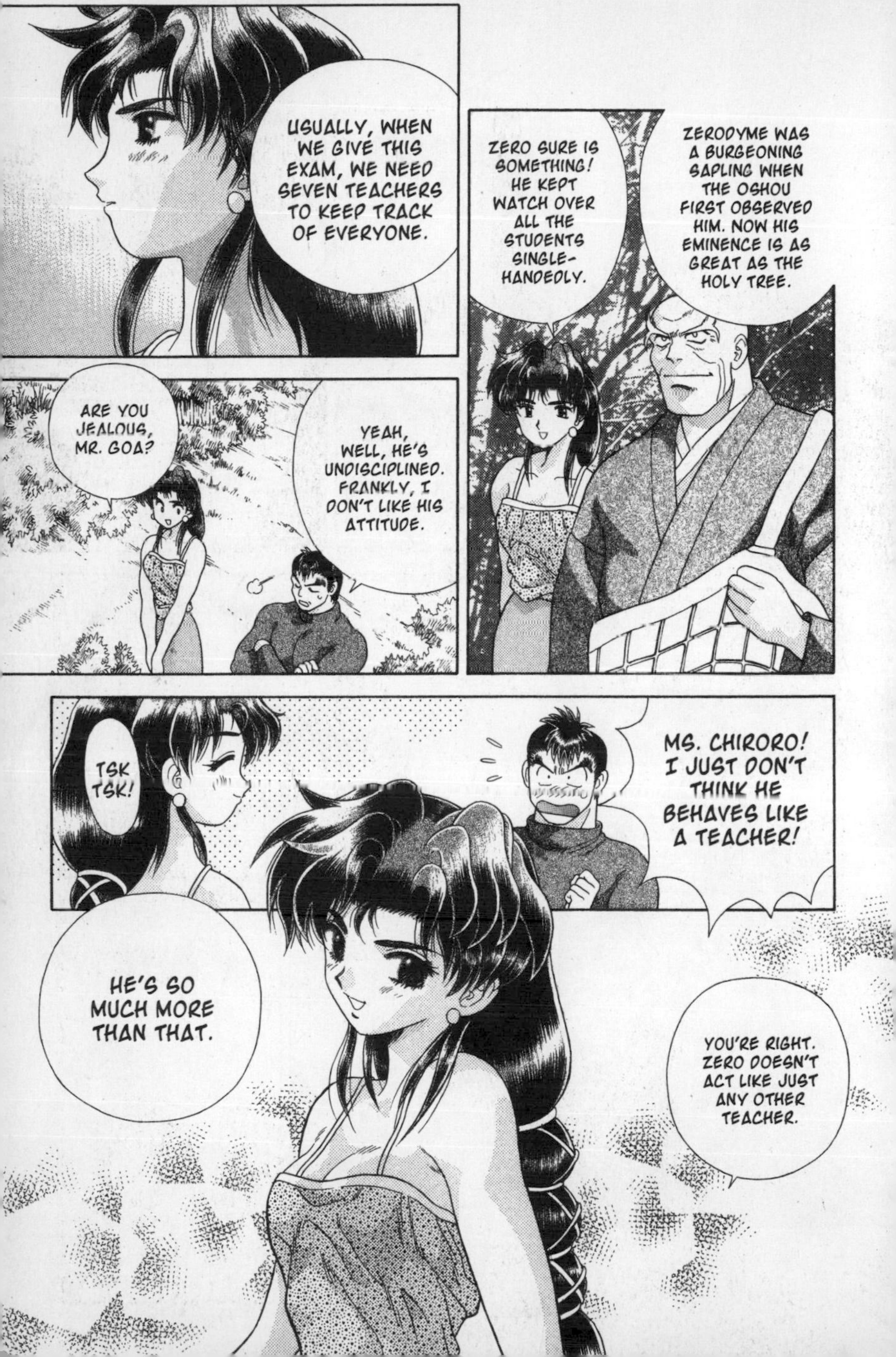
ZERODYME WAS A BURGEONING SAPLING WHEN THE OSHOU FIRST OBSERVED HIM. NOW HIS EMINENCE IS AS GREAT AS THE HOLY TREE.
ZERO SURE IS SOMETHING! HE KEPT WATCH OVER ALL THE STUDENTS SINGLE-HANDEDLY.
USUALLY, WHEN WE GIVE THIS EXAM, WE NEED SEVEN TEACHERS TO KEEP TRACK OF EVERYONE.
ARE YOU JEALOUS, MR. GOA?
YEAH, WELL, HE'S UNDISCIPLINED. FRANKLY, I DON'T LIKE HIS ATTITUDE.
MS. CHIRORO! I JUST DON'T THINK HE BEHAVES LIKE A TEACHER!
TSK TSK!
YOU'RE RIGHT. ZERO DOESN'T ACT LIKE JUST ANY OTHER TEACHER.
HE'S SO MUCH MORE THAN THAT.

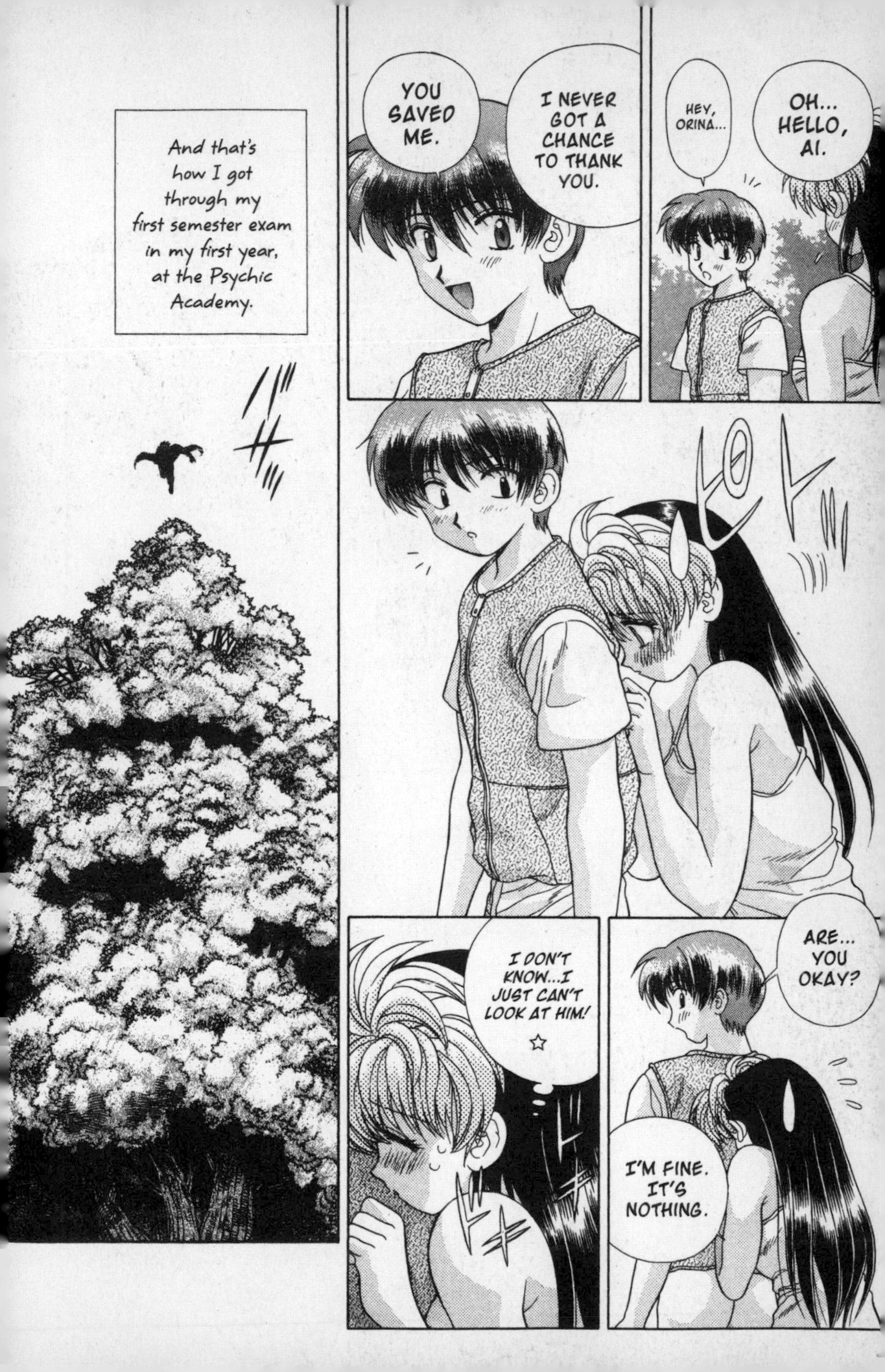
OH... HELLO, AI.
HEY, ORINA...
I NEVER GOT A CHANCE TO THANK YOU.
YOU SAVED ME.
ARE... YOU OKAY?
I'M FINE. IT'S NOTHING.
I DON'T KNOW...I JUST CAN'T LOOK AT HIM! ☆
And that's how I got through my first semester exam in my first year, at the Psychic Academy.

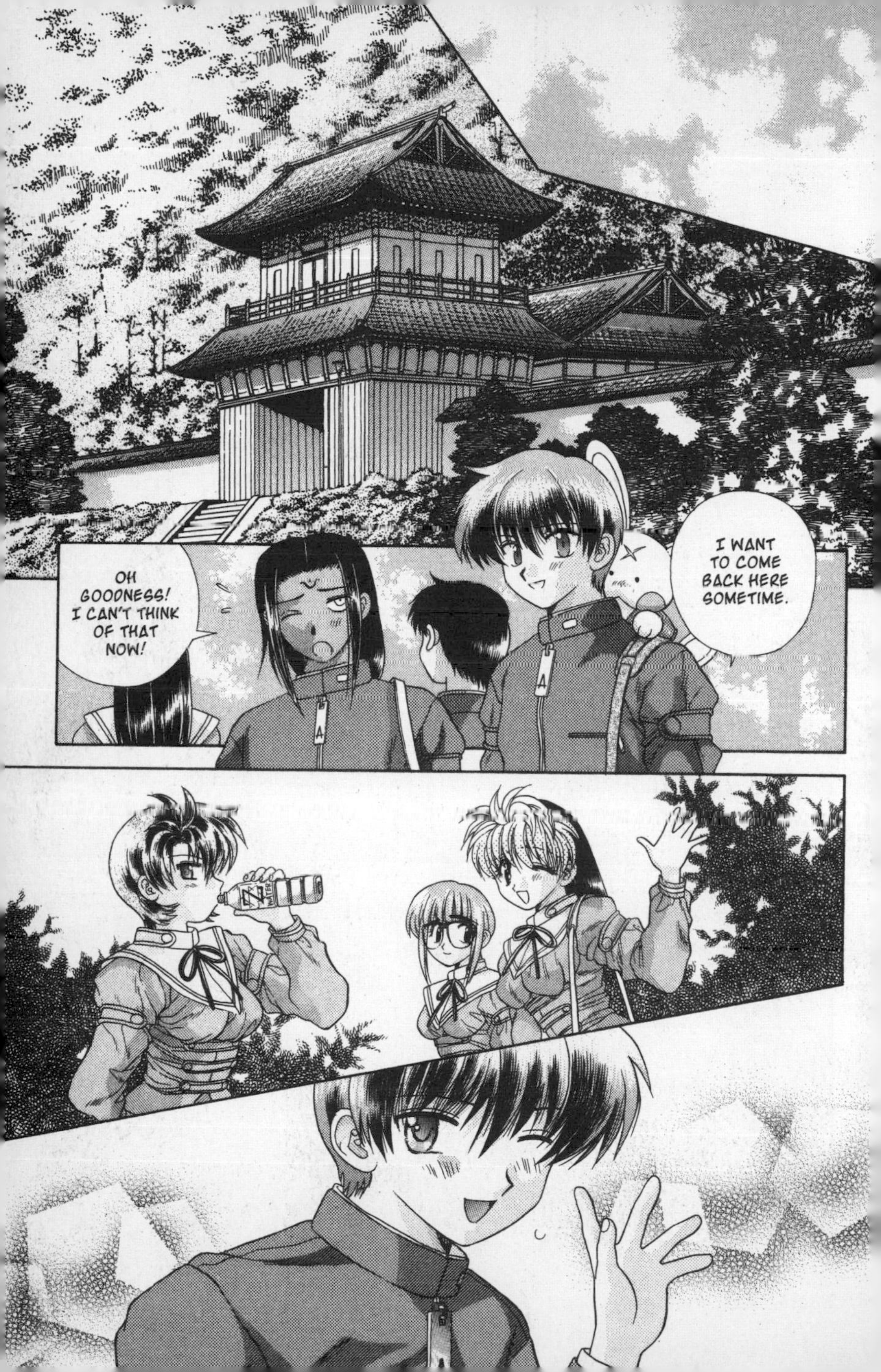
I WANT TO COME BACK HERE SOMETIME.
OH GOODNESS! I CAN'T THINK OF THAT NOW!

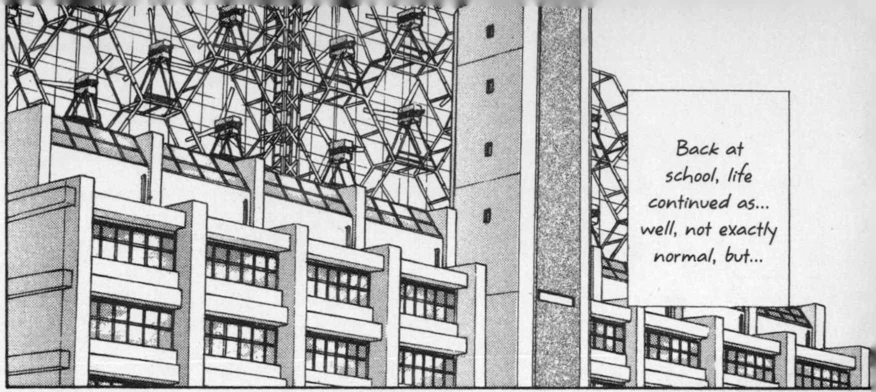
Back at school, life continued as... well, not exactly normal, but...

In oval: Ai Shiomi Sign: First Semester Examination, Passing Students

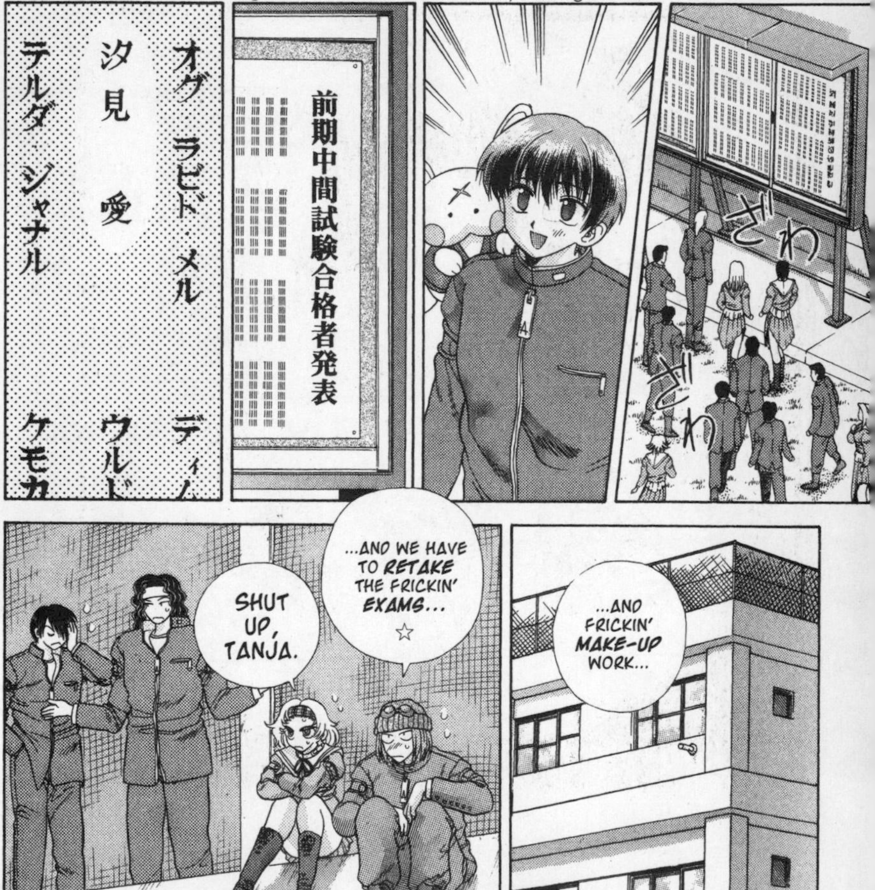
ざわ
ざわ
前期中間試験合格者発表
オグ ラビド・メル
汐見 愛
テルダ ジャナル
...AND FRICKIN' MAKE-UP WORK...
...AND WE HAVE TO RETAKE THE FRICKIN' EXAMS... ☆
SHUT UP, TANJA.

Exam END

ψchic aca

サイキック アカデミー

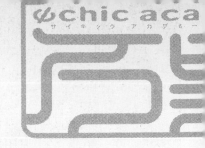

Chapter 6: Love Geometry

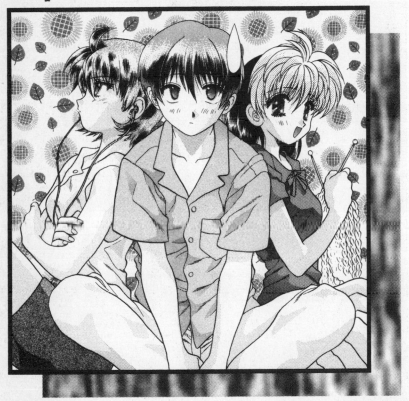

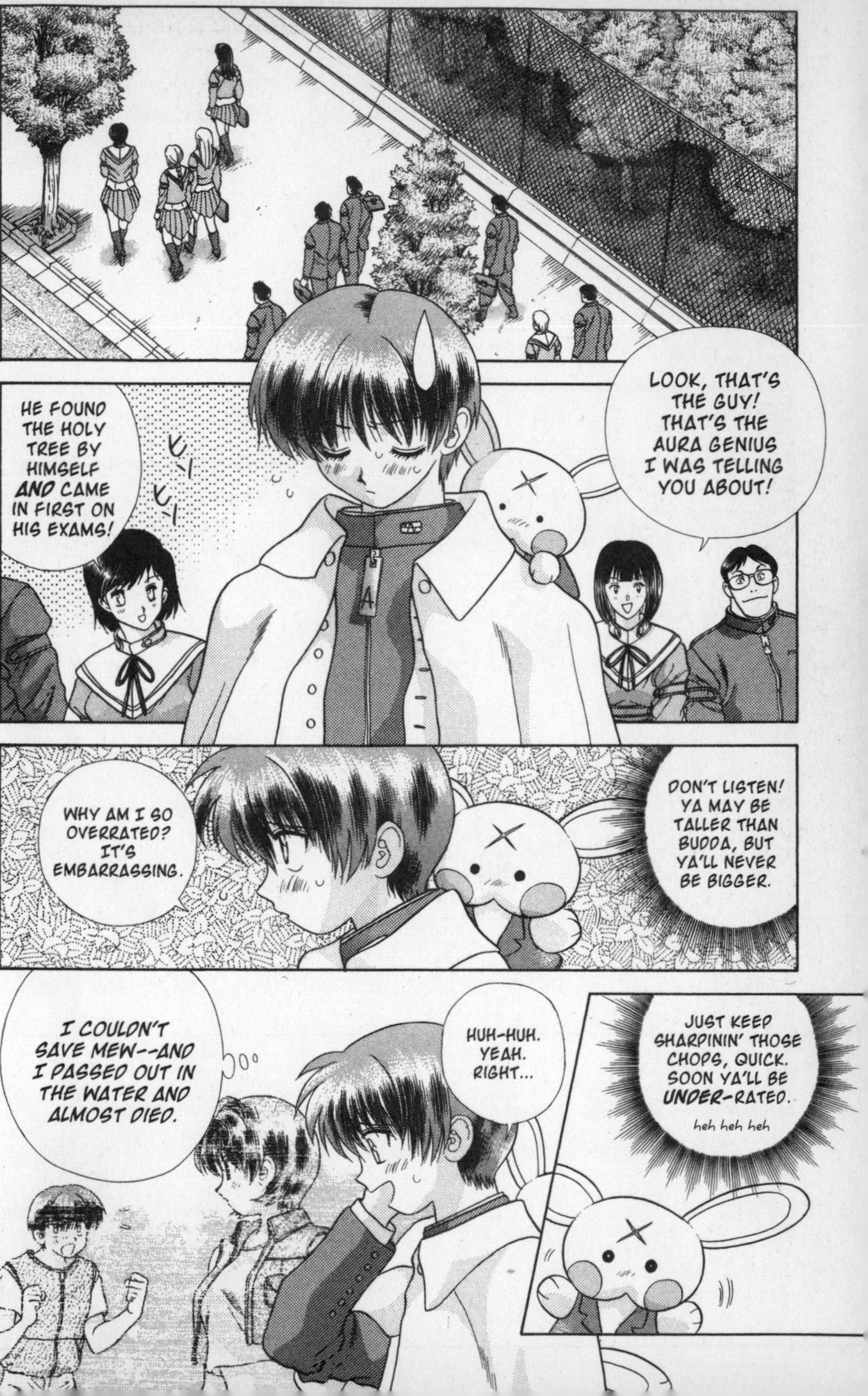
LOOK, THAT'S THE GUY! THAT'S THE AURA GENIUS I WAS TELLING YOU ABOUT!
HE FOUND THE HOLY TREE BY HIMSELF AND CAME IN FIRST ON HIS EXAMS!
DON'T LISTEN! YA MAY BE TALLER THAN BUDDA, BUT YA'LL NEVER BE BIGGER.
WHY AM I SO OVERRATED? IT'S EMBARRASSING.
JUST KEEP SHARPININ' THOSE CHOPS, QUICK. SOON YA'LL BE UNDER-RATED.
heh heh heh
HUH-HUH. YEAH. RIGHT...
I COULDN'T SAVE MEW--AND I PASSED OUT IN THE WATER AND ALMOST DIED.

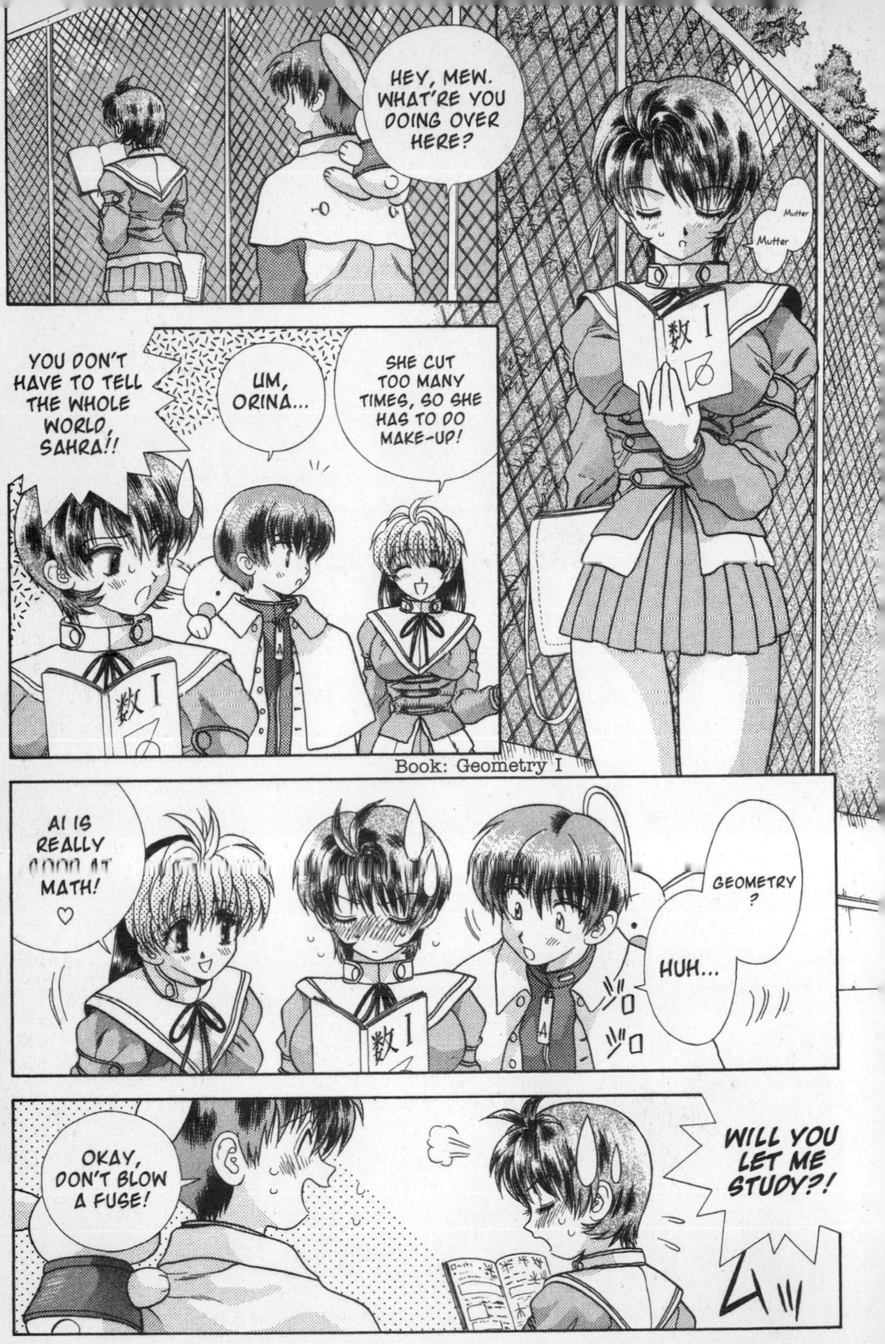
Mutter
Mutter
HEY, MEW. WHAT'RE YOU DOING OVER HERE?
数 I
SHE CUT TOO MANY TIMES, SO SHE HAS TO DO MAKE-UP!
UM, ORINA...
YOU DON'T HAVE TO TELL THE WHOLE WORLD, SAHRA!!
数 I
Book: Geometry I
GEOMETRY ?
HUH...
ジロ
ジロ
数 I
AI IS REALLY GOOD AT MATH! ♡
WILL YOU LET ME STUDY?!
OKAY, DON'T BLOW A FUSE!

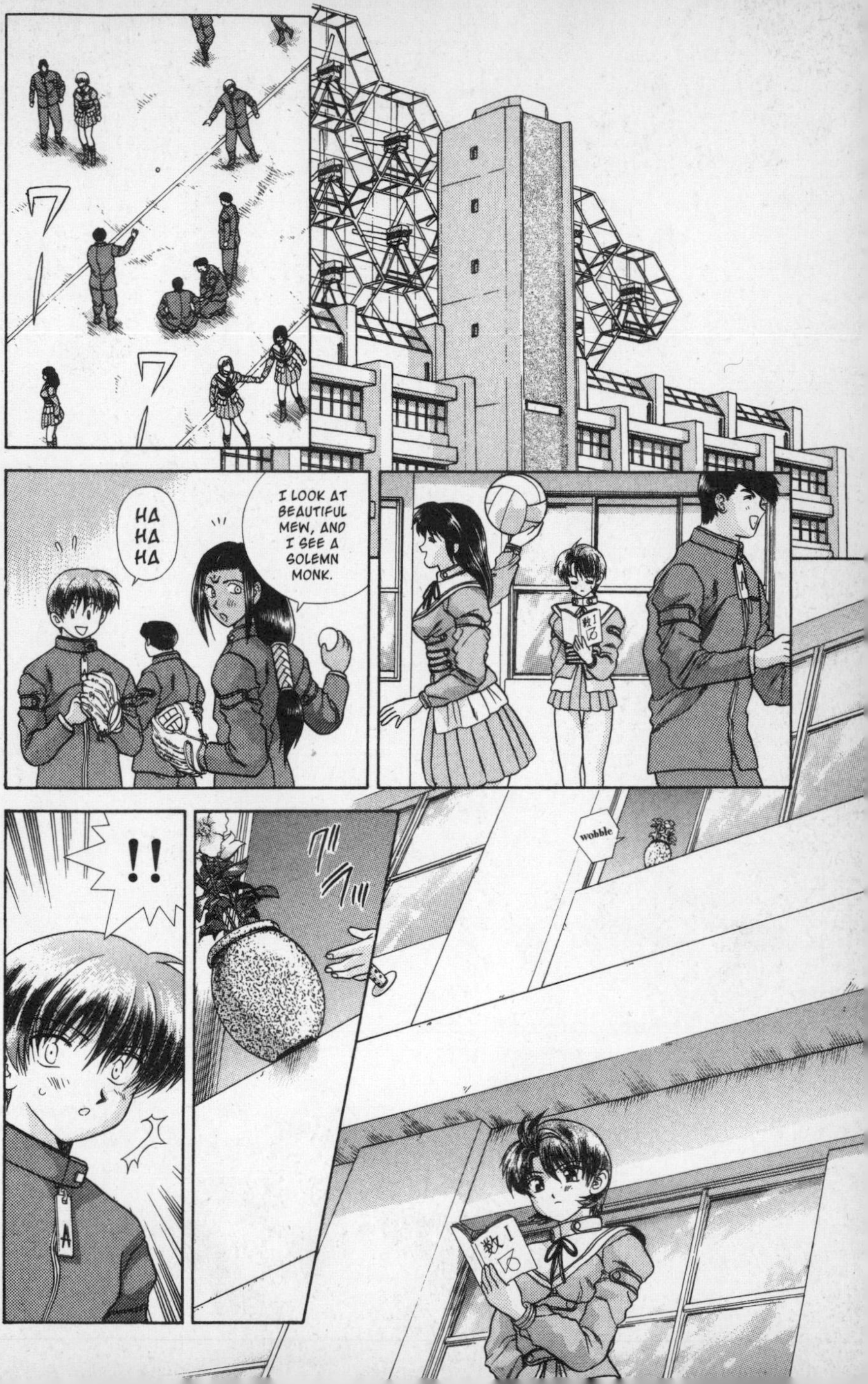
I LOOK AT BEAUTIFUL MEW, AND I SEE A SOLEMN MONK.
HA HA HA
wobble
!!

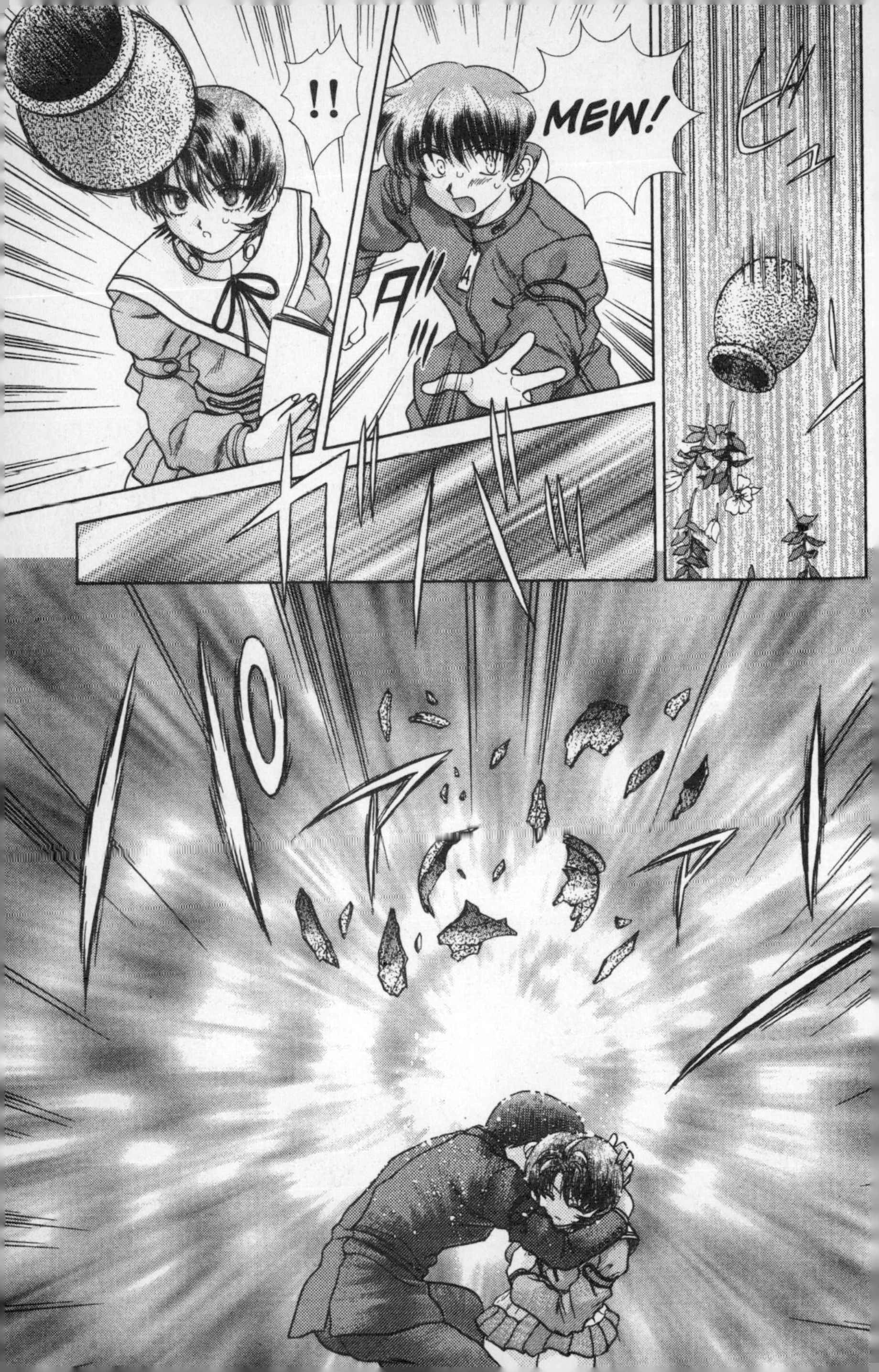
MEW!
!!

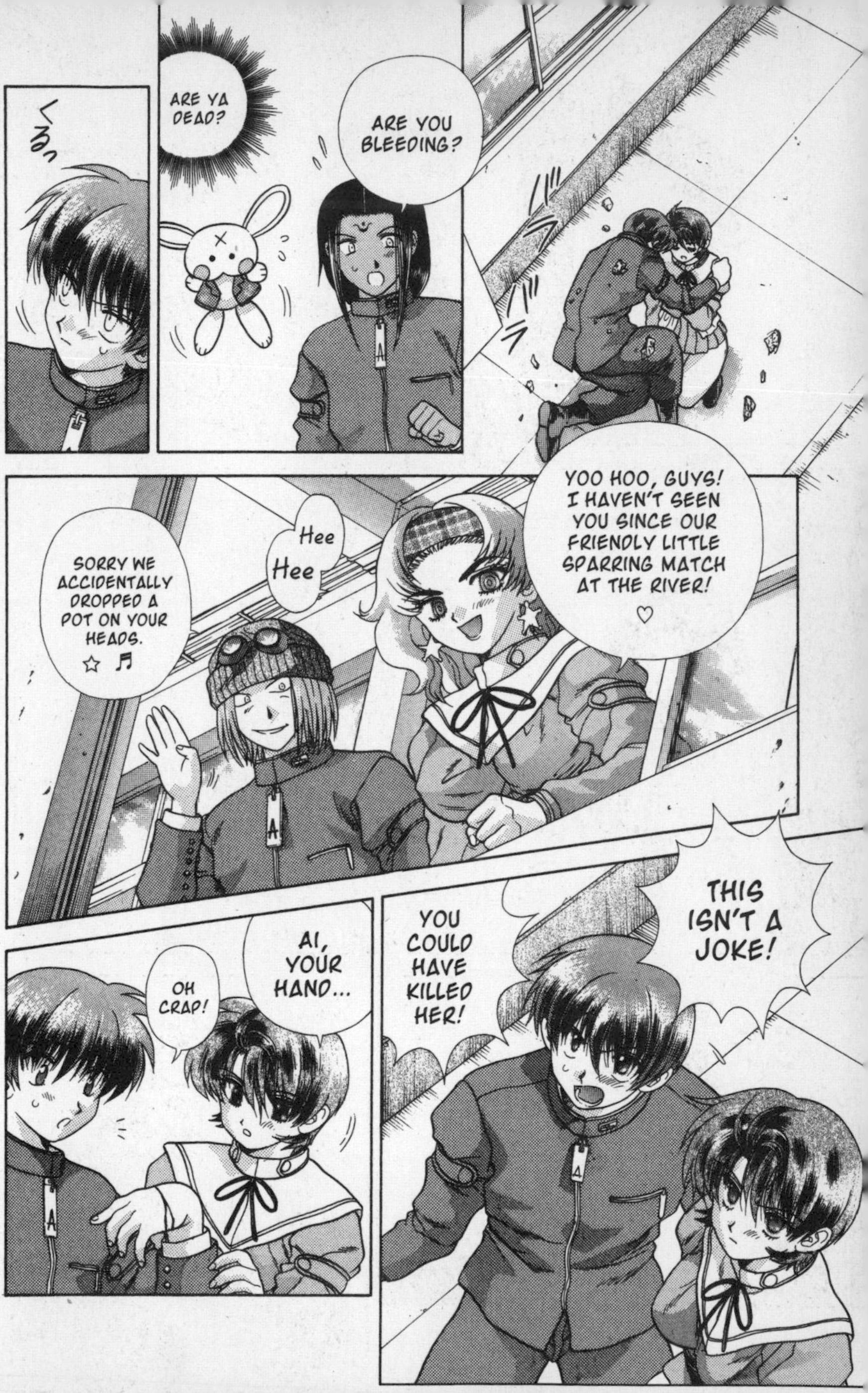
ARE YOU BLEEDING?
ARE YA DEAD?
くるっ
YOO HOO, GUYS! I HAVEN'T SEEN YOU SINCE OUR FRIENDLY LITTLE SPARRING MATCH AT THE RIVER! ♡
Hee Hee
SORRY WE ACCIDENTALLY DROPPED A POT ON YOUR HEADS. ☆ ♬
THIS ISN'T A JOKE!
YOU COULD HAVE KILLED HER!
AI, YOUR HAND...
OH CRAP!

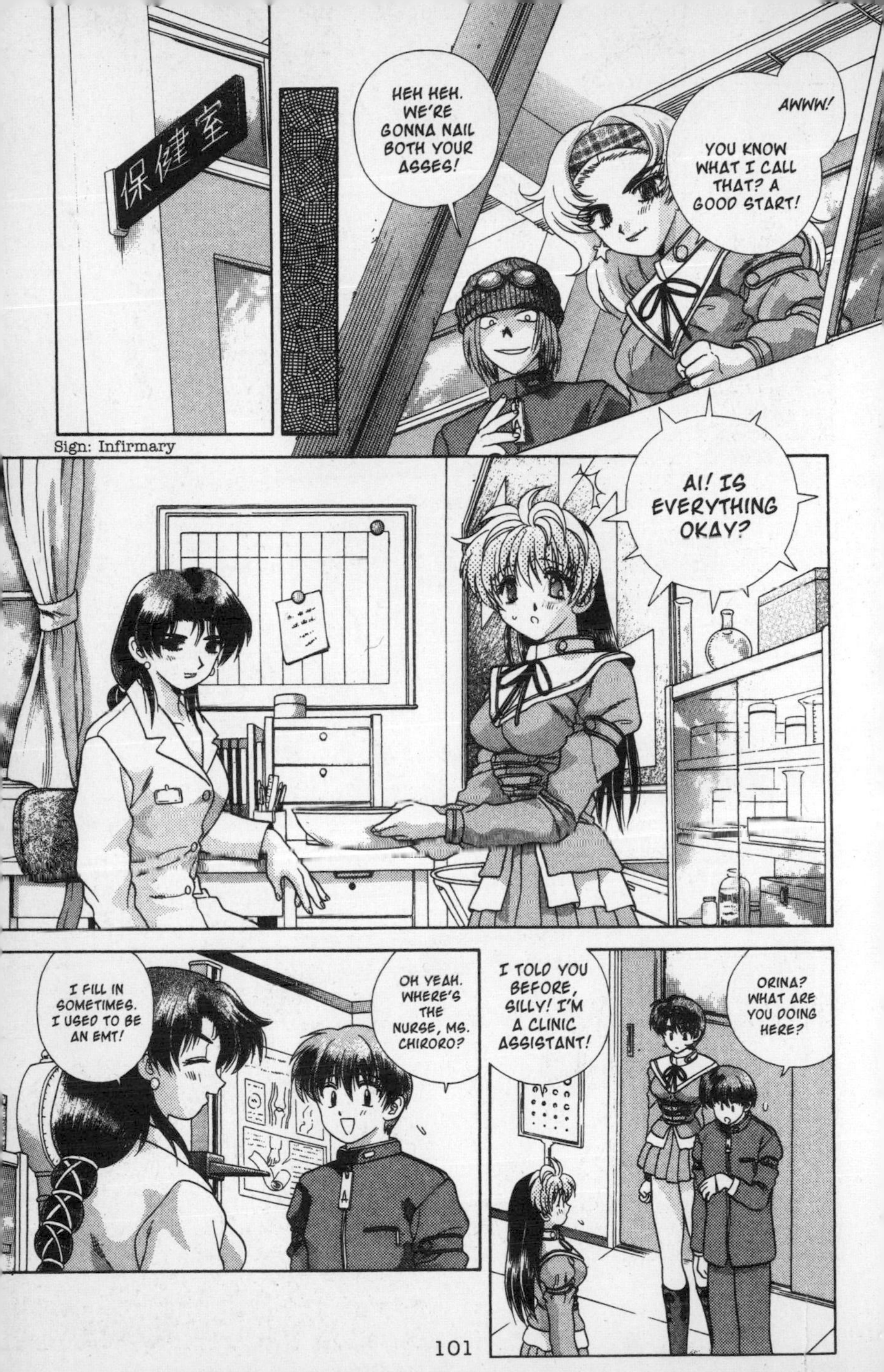
AWWW!
YOU KNOW WHAT I CALL THAT? A GOOD START!
HEH HEH. WE'RE GONNA NAIL BOTH YOUR ASSES!
保健室
Sign: Infirmary
AI! IS EVERYTHING OKAY?
ORINA? WHAT ARE YOU DOING HERE?
I TOLD YOU BEFORE, SILLY! I'M A CLINIC ASSISTANT!
OH YEAH. WHERE'S THE NURSE, MS. CHIRORO?
I FILL IN SOMETIMES. I USED TO BE AN EMT!

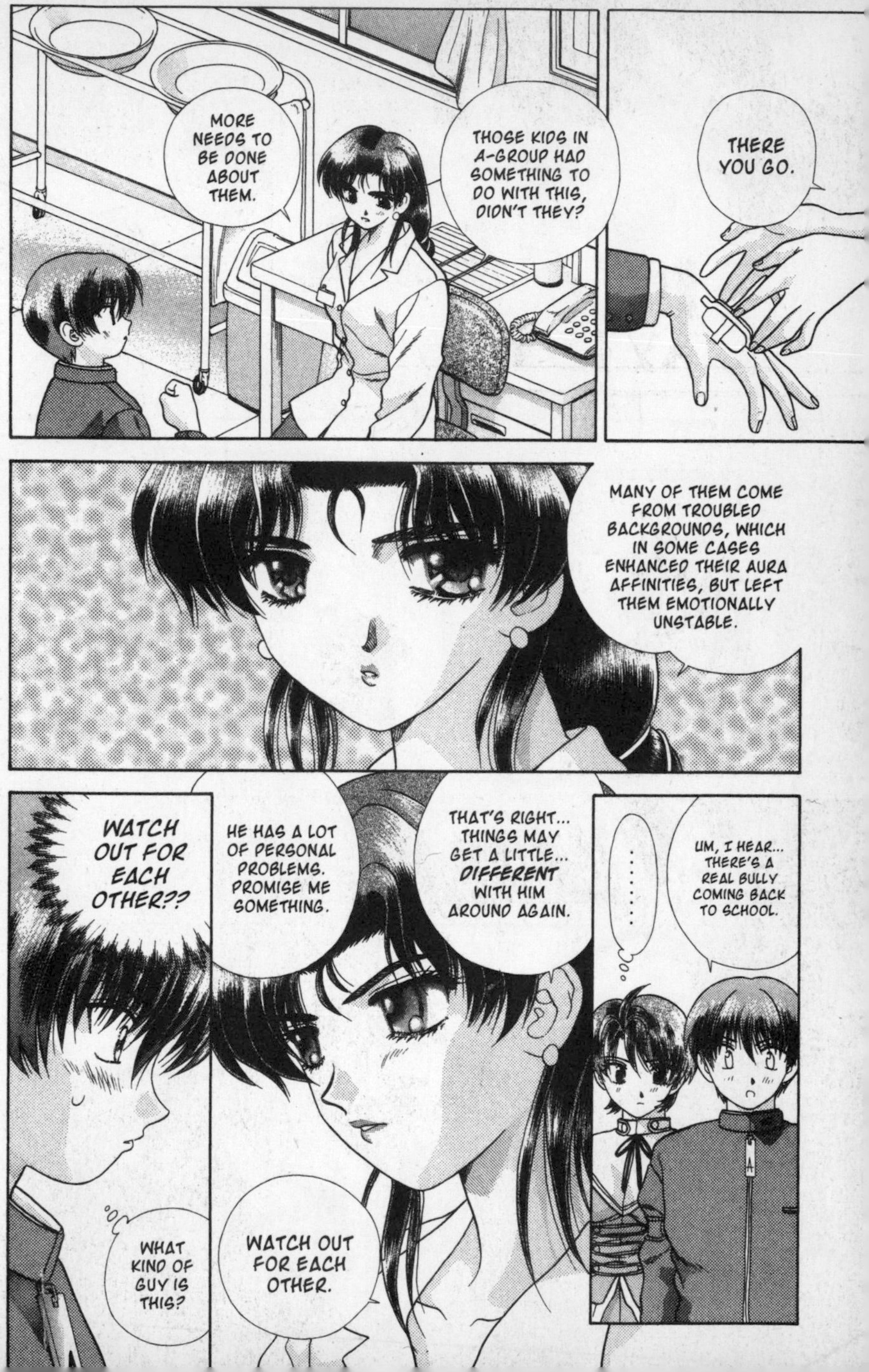
THERE YOU GO.
THOSE KIDS IN A-GROUP HAD SOMETHING TO DO WITH THIS, DIDN'T THEY?
MORE NEEDS TO BE DONE ABOUT THEM.
MANY OF THEM COME FROM TROUBLED BACKGROUNDS, WHICH IN SOME CASES ENHANCED THEIR AURA AFFINITIES, BUT LEFT THEM EMOTIONALLY UNSTABLE.
UM, I HEAR... THERE'S A REAL BULLY COMING BACK TO SCHOOL.
......
THAT'S RIGHT... THINGS MAY GET A LITTLE... *DIFFERENT* WITH HIM AROUND AGAIN.
HE HAS A LOT OF PERSONAL PROBLEMS. PROMISE ME SOMETHING.
WATCH OUT FOR EACH OTHER.
WATCH OUT FOR EACH OTHER??
WHAT KIND OF GUY IS THIS?

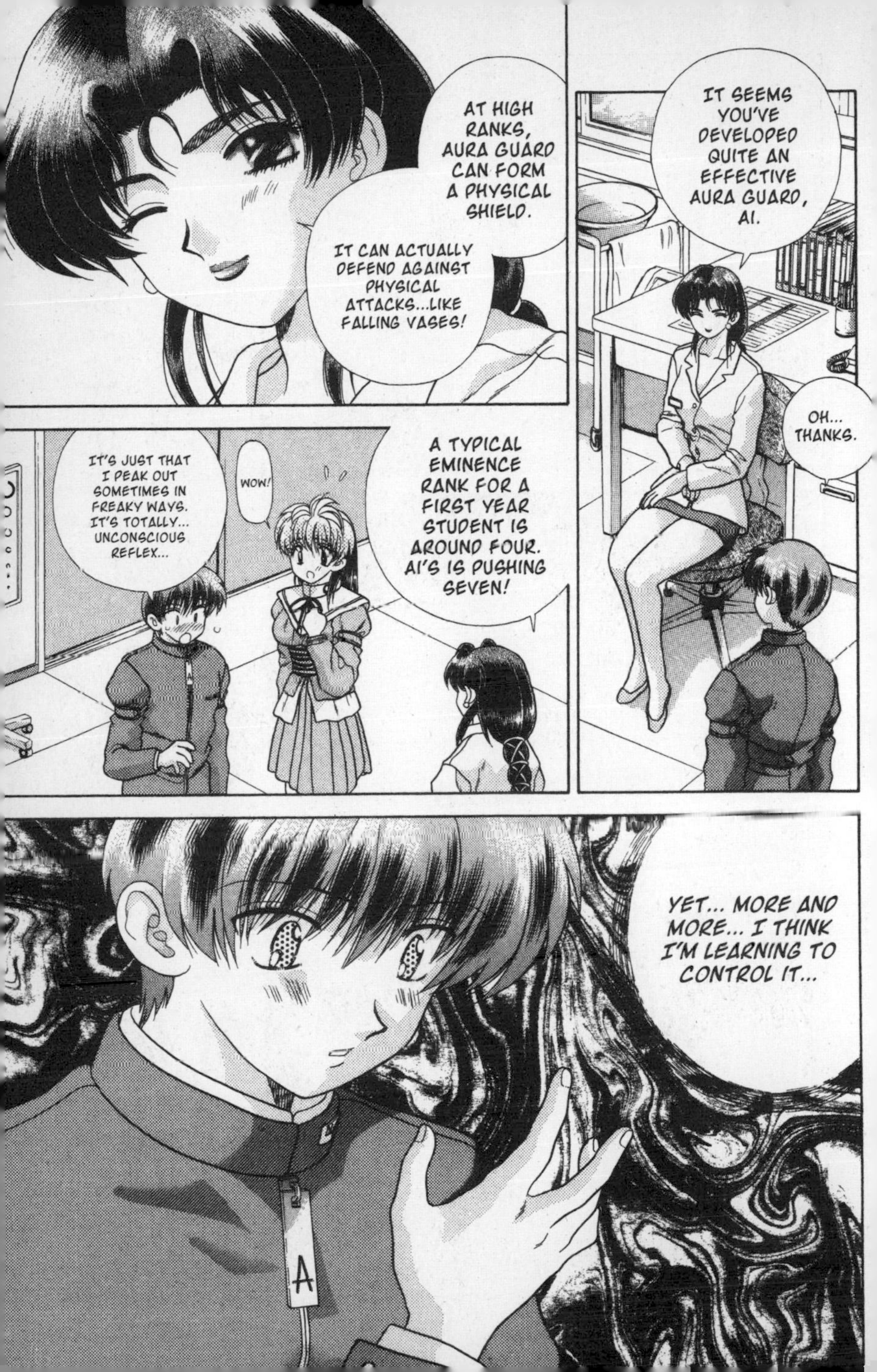
IT SEEMS YOU'VE DEVELOPED QUITE AN EFFECTIVE AURA GUARD, AI.
OH... THANKS.
AT HIGH RANKS, AURA GUARD CAN FORM A PHYSICAL SHIELD.
IT CAN ACTUALLY DEFEND AGAINST PHYSICAL ATTACKS...LIKE FALLING VASES!
A TYPICAL EMINENCE RANK FOR A FIRST YEAR STUDENT IS AROUND FOUR. AI'S IS PUSHING SEVEN!
WOW!
IT'S JUST THAT I PEAK OUT SOMETIMES IN FREAKY WAYS. IT'S TOTALLY... UNCONSCIOUS REFLEX...
YET... MORE AND MORE... I THINK I'M LEARNING TO CONTROL IT...

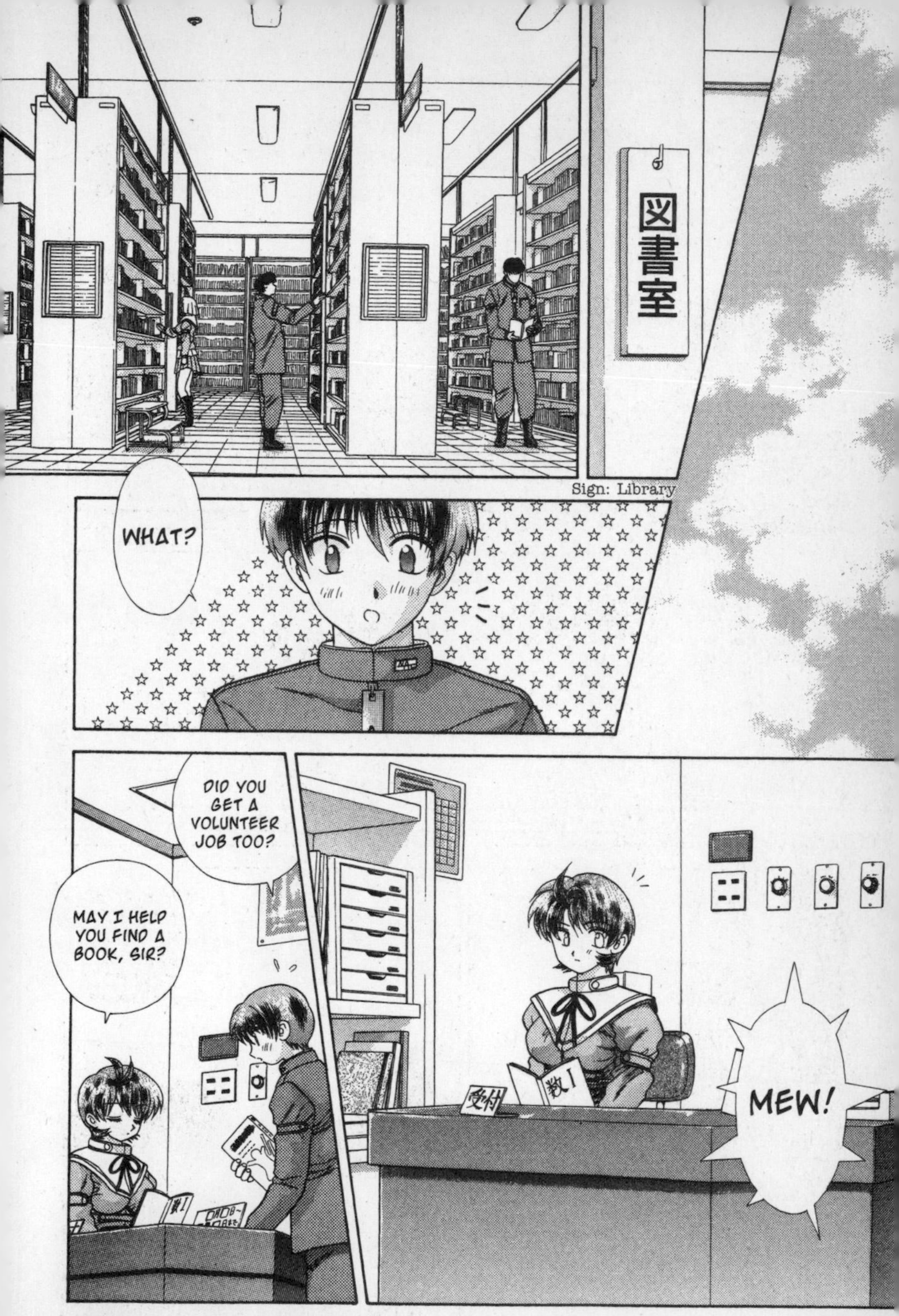
図書室
Sign: Library
WHAT?
受付
数I
MEW!
DID YOU GET A VOLUNTEER JOB TOO?
MAY I HELP YOU FIND A BOOK, SIR?

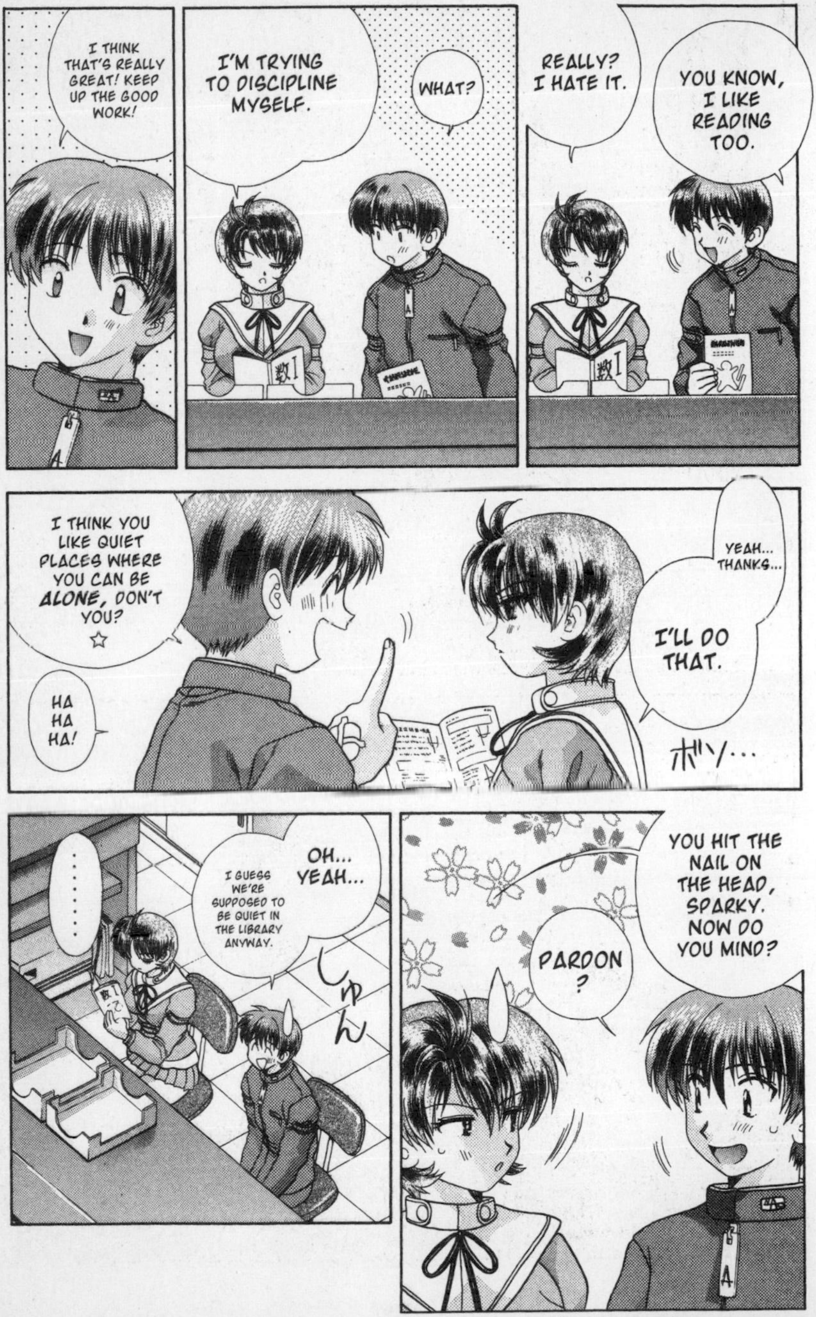
YOU KNOW, I LIKE READING TOO.
REALLY? I HATE IT.
WHAT?
I'M TRYING TO DISCIPLINE MYSELF.
I THINK THAT'S REALLY GREAT! KEEP UP THE GOOD WORK!
YEAH... THANKS...
I'LL DO THAT.
ボソ…
I THINK YOU LIKE QUIET PLACES WHERE YOU CAN BE ALONE, DON'T YOU? ☆
HA HA HA!
YOU HIT THE NAIL ON THE HEAD, SPARKY. NOW DO YOU MIND?
PARDON?
OH... YEAH...
I GUESS WE'RE SUPPOSED TO BE QUIET IN THE LIBRARY ANYWAY.
しゅん
....

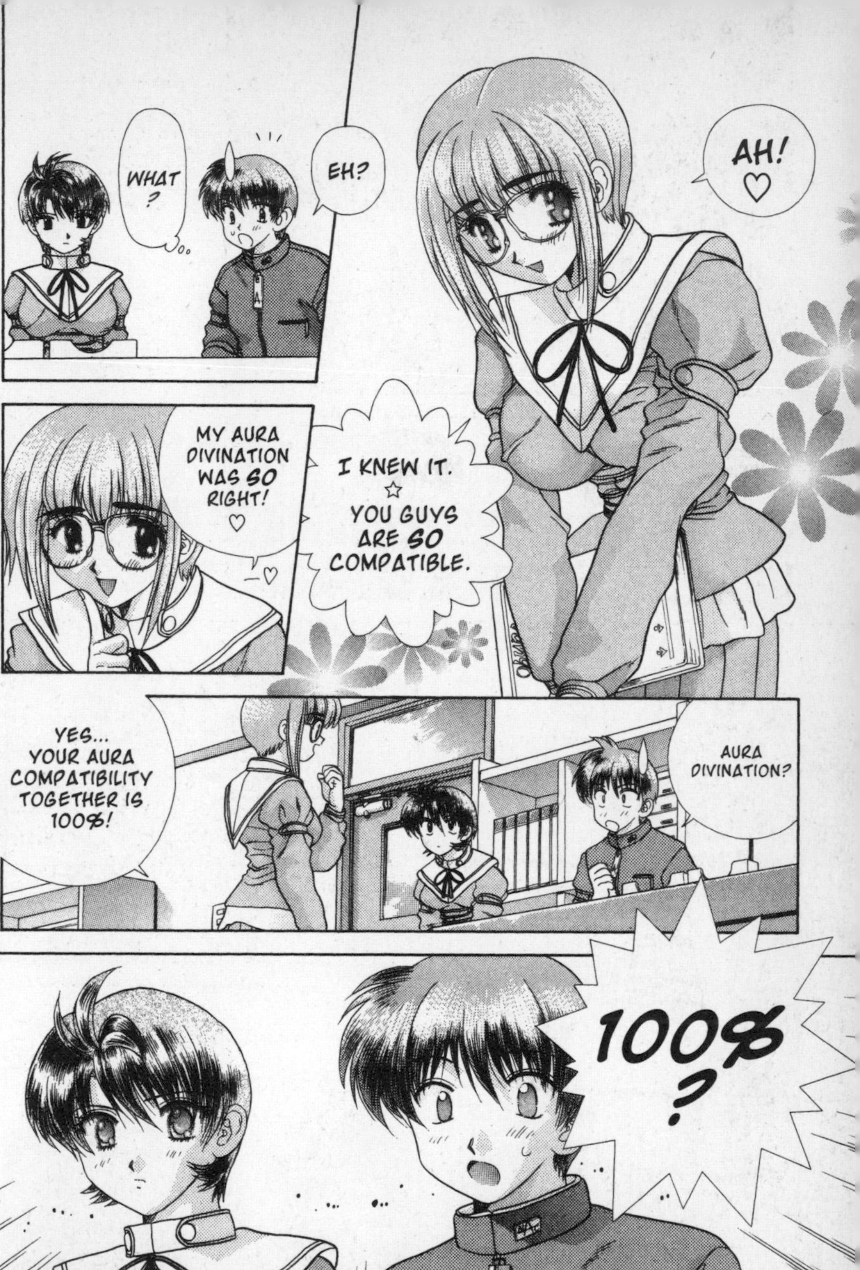
AH! ♡
I KNEW IT. ☆ YOU GUYS ARE SO COMPATIBLE.
EH?
WHAT ?
MY AURA DIVINATION WAS SO RIGHT! ♡
AURA DIVINATION?
YES... YOUR AURA COMPATIBILITY TOGETHER IS 100%!
100% ?

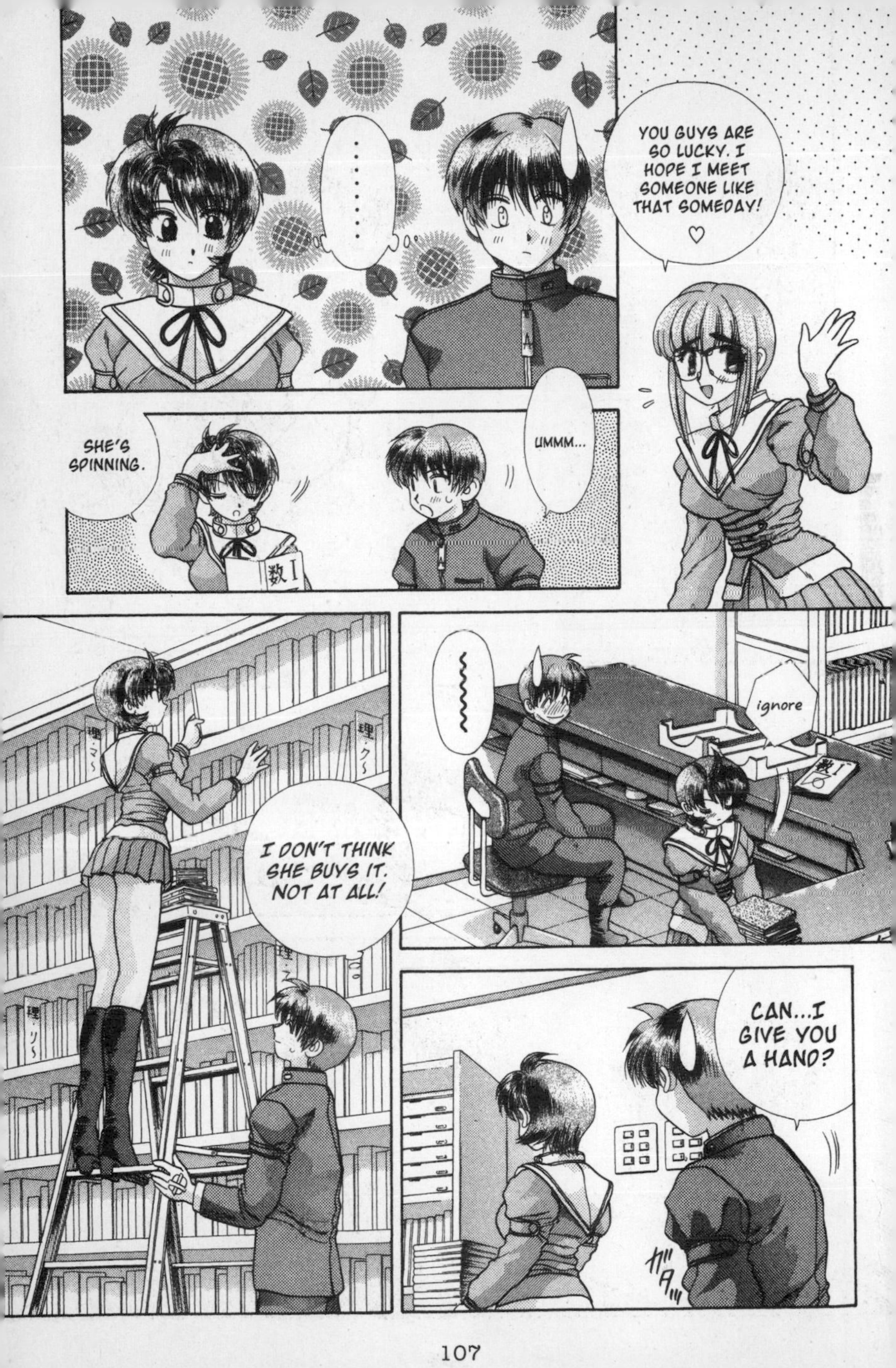
YOU GUYS ARE SO LUCKY. I HOPE I MEET SOMEONE LIKE THAT SOMEDAY! ♡
....
UMMM...
SHE'S SPINNING.
ignore
CAN...I GIVE YOU A HAND?
I DON'T THINK SHE BUYS IT. NOT AT ALL!

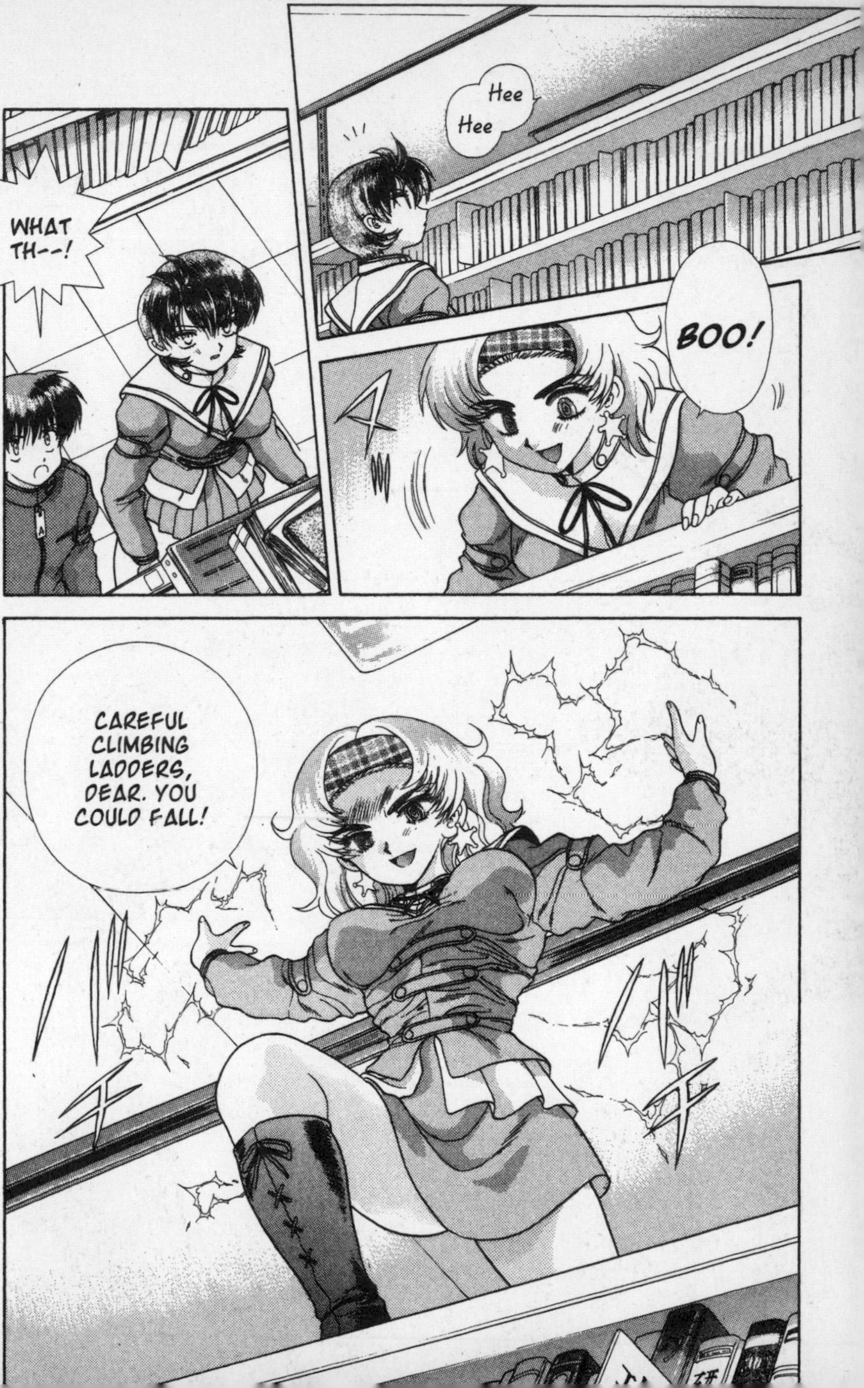
Hee Hee
BOO!
WHAT TH--!
CAREFUL CLIMBING LADDERS, DEAR. YOU COULD FALL!

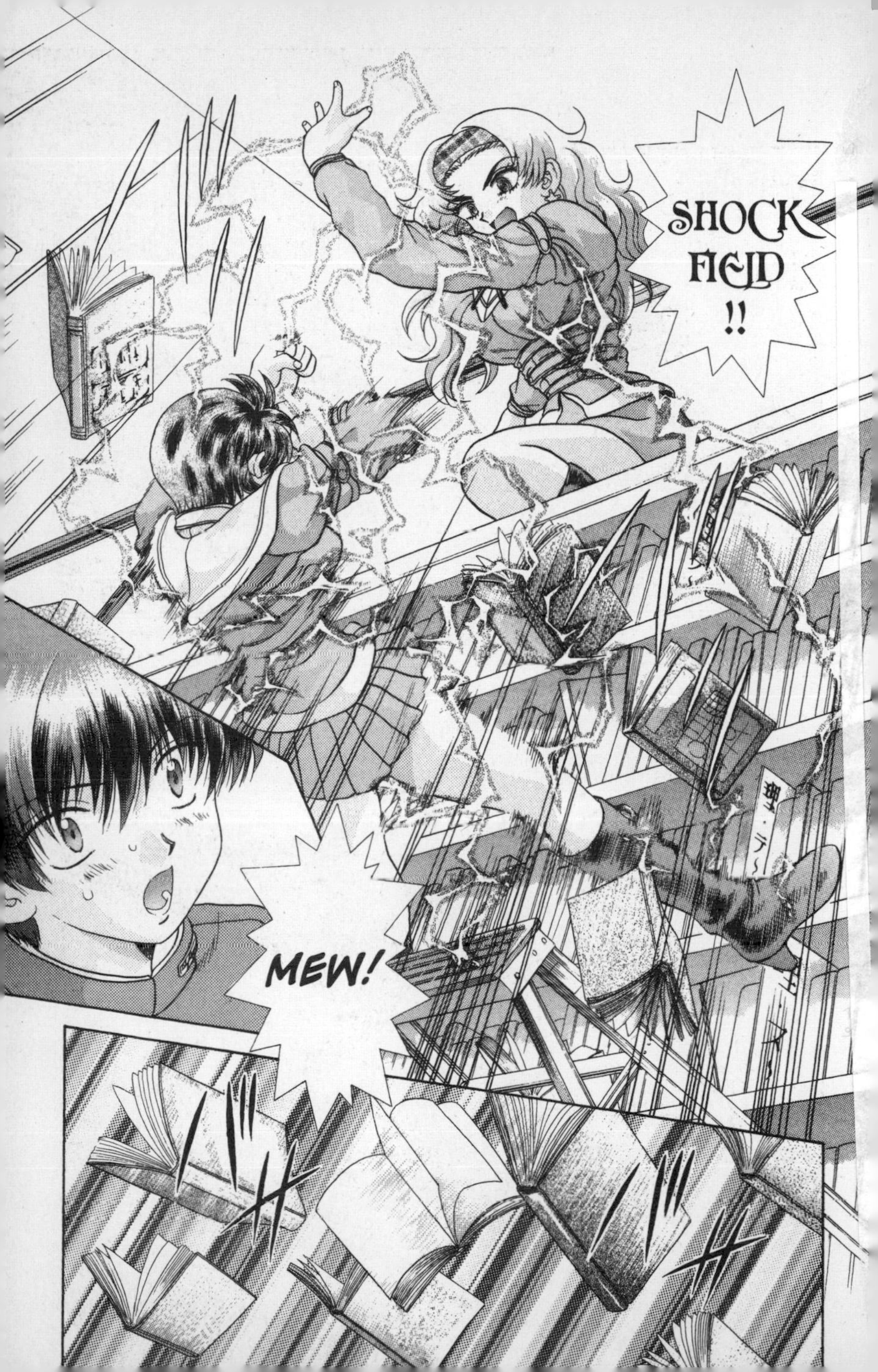
SHOCK FIELD !!
MEW!

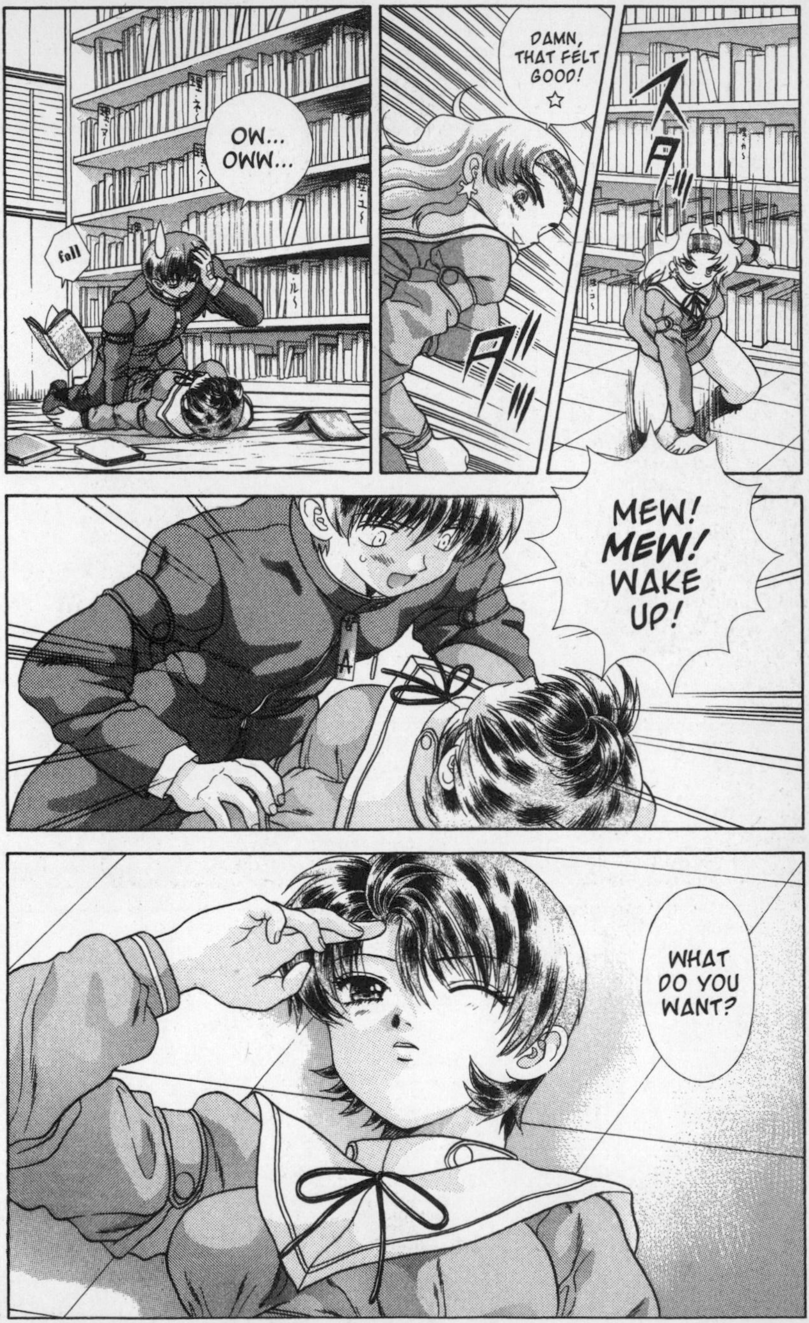
DAMN, THAT FELT GOOD! ☆
OW... OWW...
fall
MEW! MEW! WAKE UP!
WHAT DO YOU WANT?

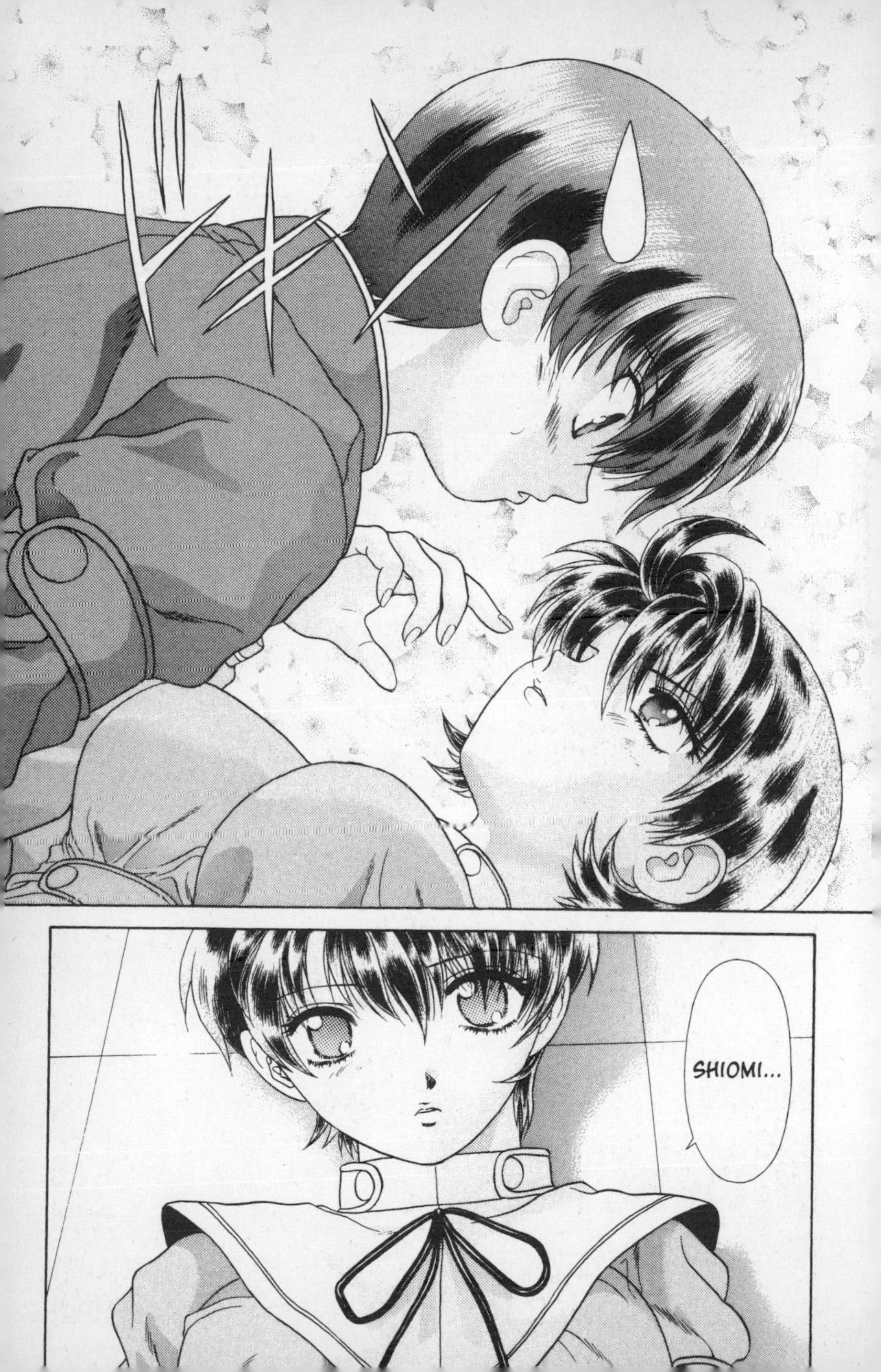
SHIOMI...

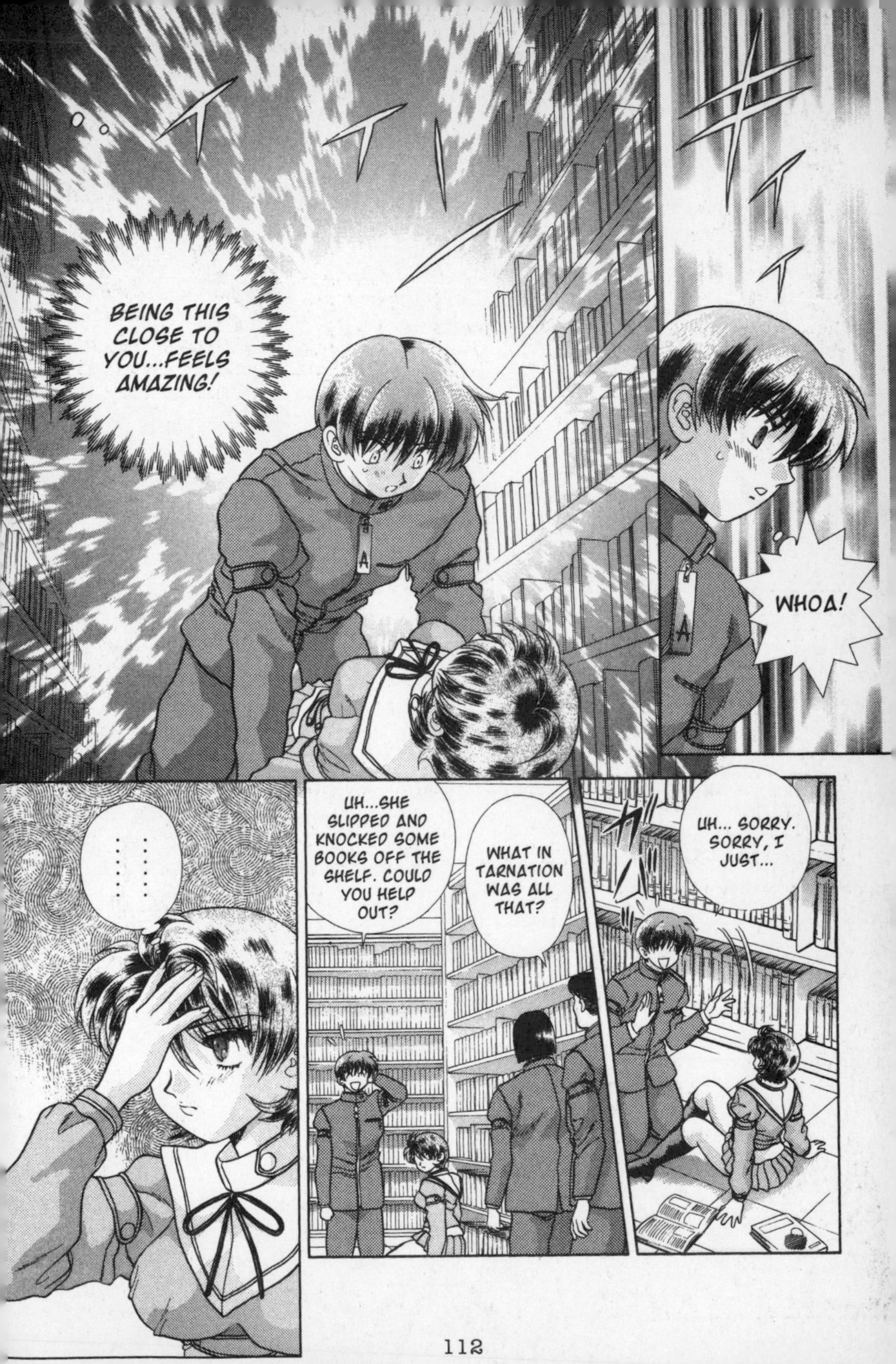
WHOA!
BEING THIS CLOSE TO YOU...FEELS AMAZING!
UH... SORRY. SORRY, I JUST...
WHAT IN TARNATION WAS ALL THAT?
UH...SHE SLIPPED AND KNOCKED SOME BOOKS OFF THE SHELF. COULD YOU HELP OUT?
......

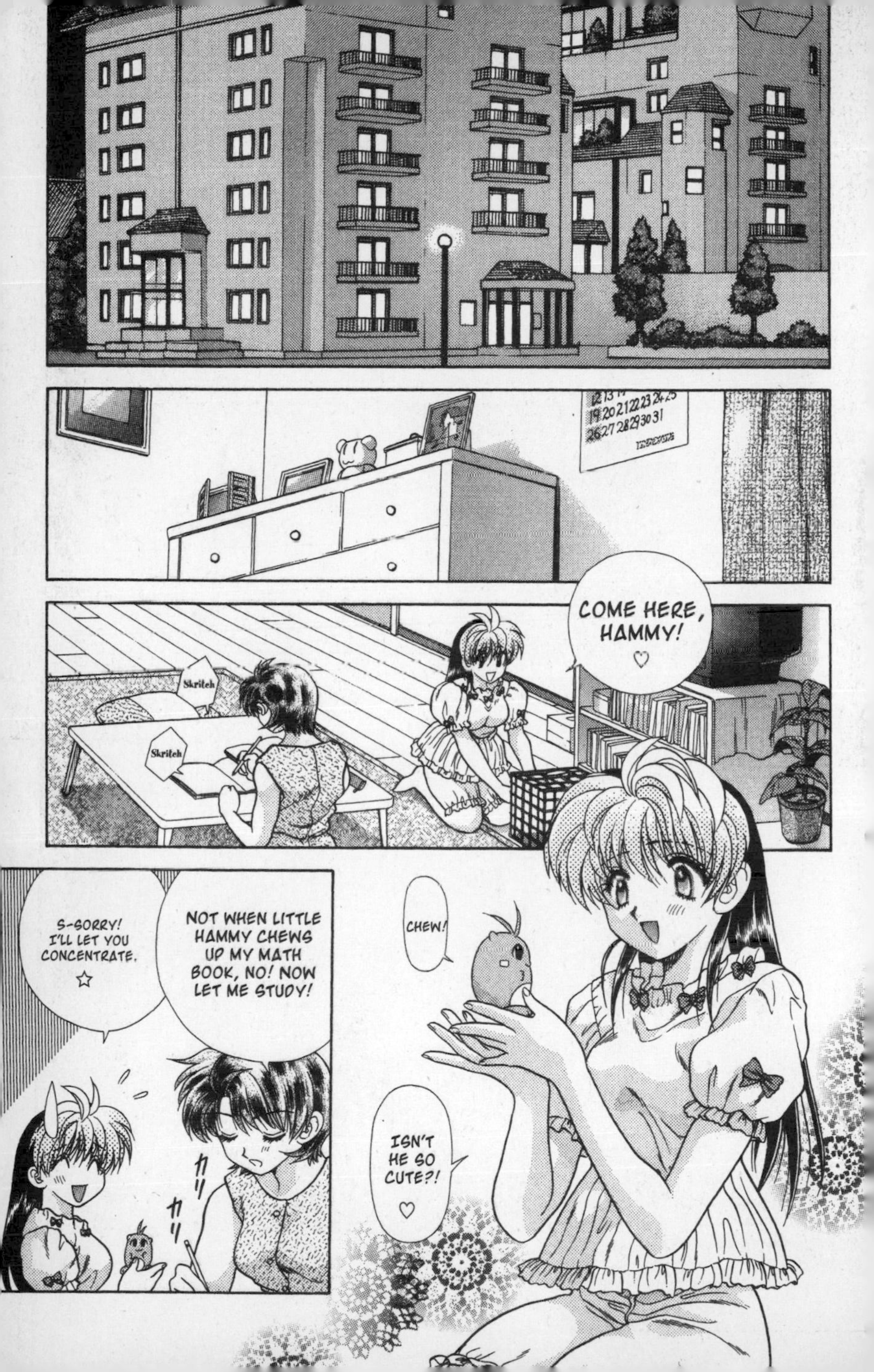
COME HERE, HAMMY! ♡
Skritch
Skritch
CHEW!
ISN'T HE SO CUTE?! ♡
NOT WHEN LITTLE HAMMY CHEWS UP MY MATH BOOK, NO! NOW LET ME STUDY!
S-SORRY! I'LL LET YOU CONCENTRATE. ☆
カリ
カリ

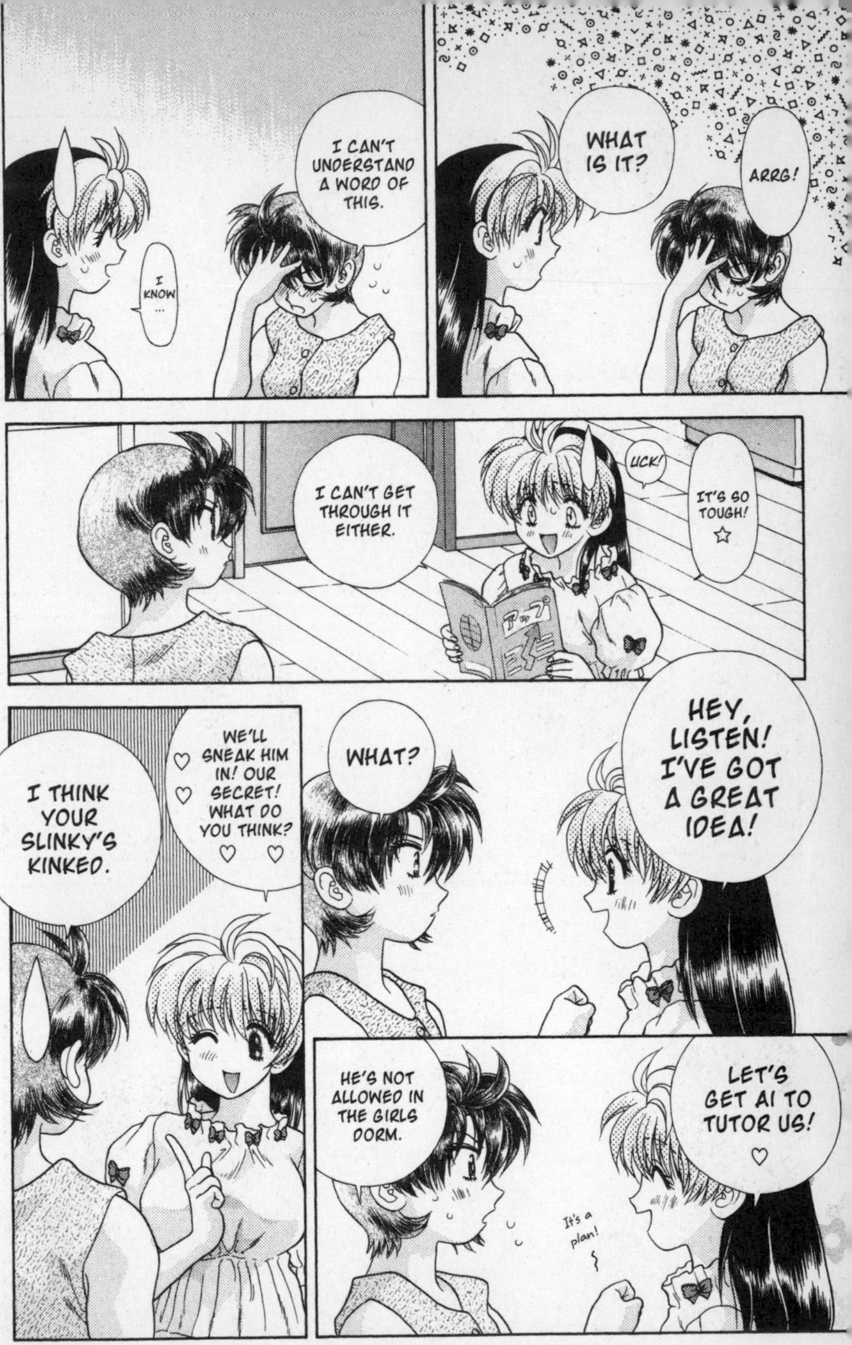
ARRG!
WHAT IS IT?
I CAN'T UNDERSTAND A WORD OF THIS.
I KNOW...
UCK!
IT'S SO TOUGH! ☆
I CAN'T GET THROUGH IT EITHER.
HEY, LISTEN! I'VE GOT A GREAT IDEA!
WHAT?
LET'S GET AI TO TUTOR US! ♡
It's a plan!
HE'S NOT ALLOWED IN THE GIRLS DORM.
♡ WE'LL SNEAK HIM IN! OUR SECRET! WHAT DO YOU THINK? ♡ ♡
I THINK YOUR SLINKY'S KINKED.

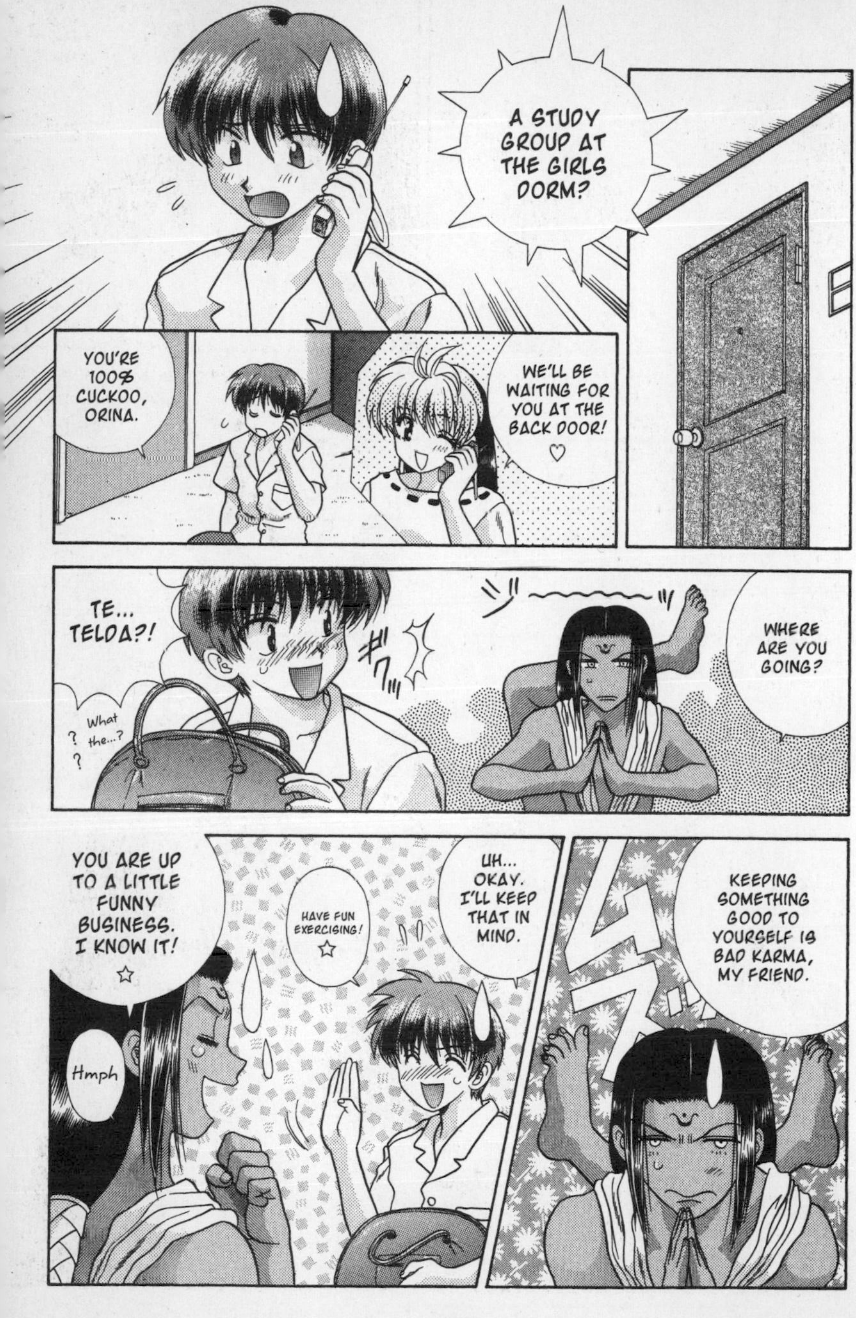

A STUDY GROUP AT THE GIRLS DORM?
WE'LL BE WAITING FOR YOU AT THE BACK DOOR! ♡
YOU'RE 100% CUCKOO, ORINA.
WHERE ARE YOU GOING?
TE... TELDA?!
What the...? ? ?
KEEPING SOMETHING GOOD TO YOURSELF IS BAD KARMA, MY FRIEND.
UH... OKAY. I'LL KEEP THAT IN MIND.
HAVE FUN EXERCISING! ☆
YOU ARE UP TO A LITTLE FUNNY BUSINESS. I KNOW IT! ☆
Hmph

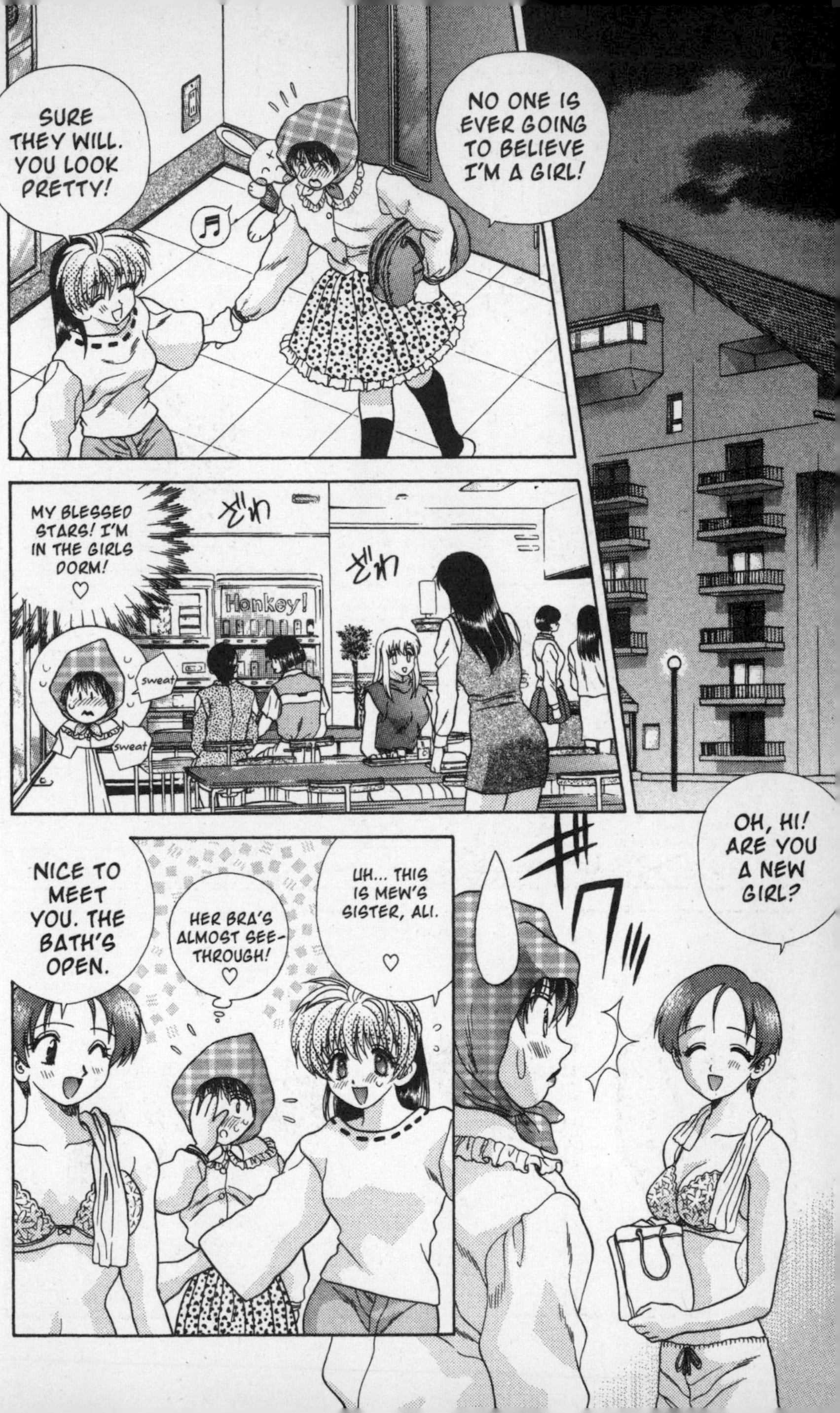
NO ONE IS EVER GOING TO BELIEVE I'M A GIRL!
SURE THEY WILL. YOU LOOK PRETTY!
MY BLESSED STARS! I'M IN THE GIRLS DORM! ♡
ざわ
ざわ
Honkey!
sweat
sweat
OH, HI! ARE YOU A NEW GIRL?
UH... THIS IS MEW'S SISTER, ALI. ♡
HER BRA'S ALMOST SEE-THROUGH! ♡
NICE TO MEET YOU. THE BATH'S OPEN.

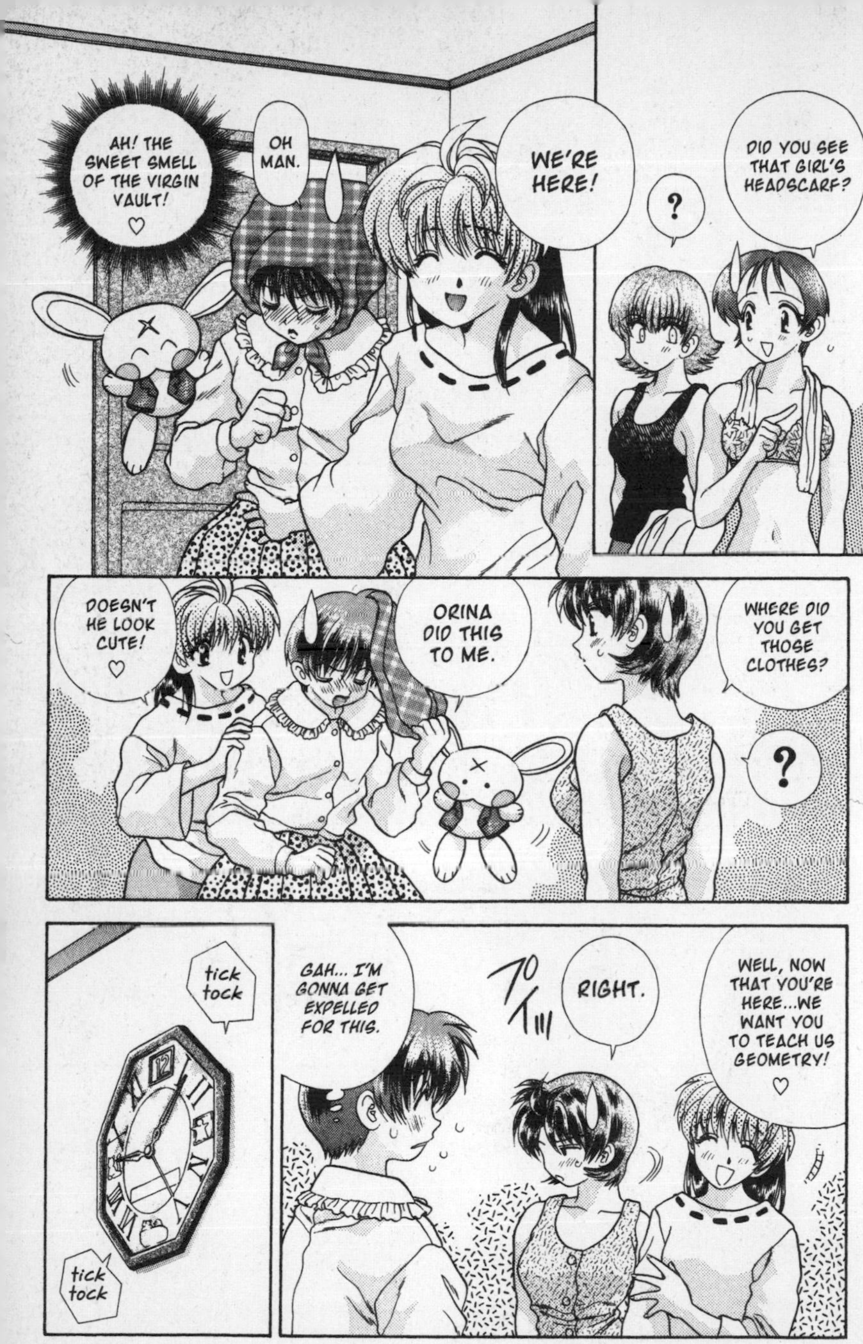
DID YOU SEE THAT GIRL'S HEADSCARF?
?
WE'RE HERE!
OH MAN.
AH! THE SWEET SMELL OF THE VIRGIN VAULT! ♡
WHERE DID YOU GET THOSE CLOTHES?
?
ORINA DID THIS TO ME.
DOESN'T HE LOOK CUTE! ♡
WELL, NOW THAT YOU'RE HERE...WE WANT YOU TO TEACH US GEOMETRY! ♡
RIGHT.
プイ
GAH... I'M GONNA GET EXPELLED FOR THIS.
tick tock
tick tock

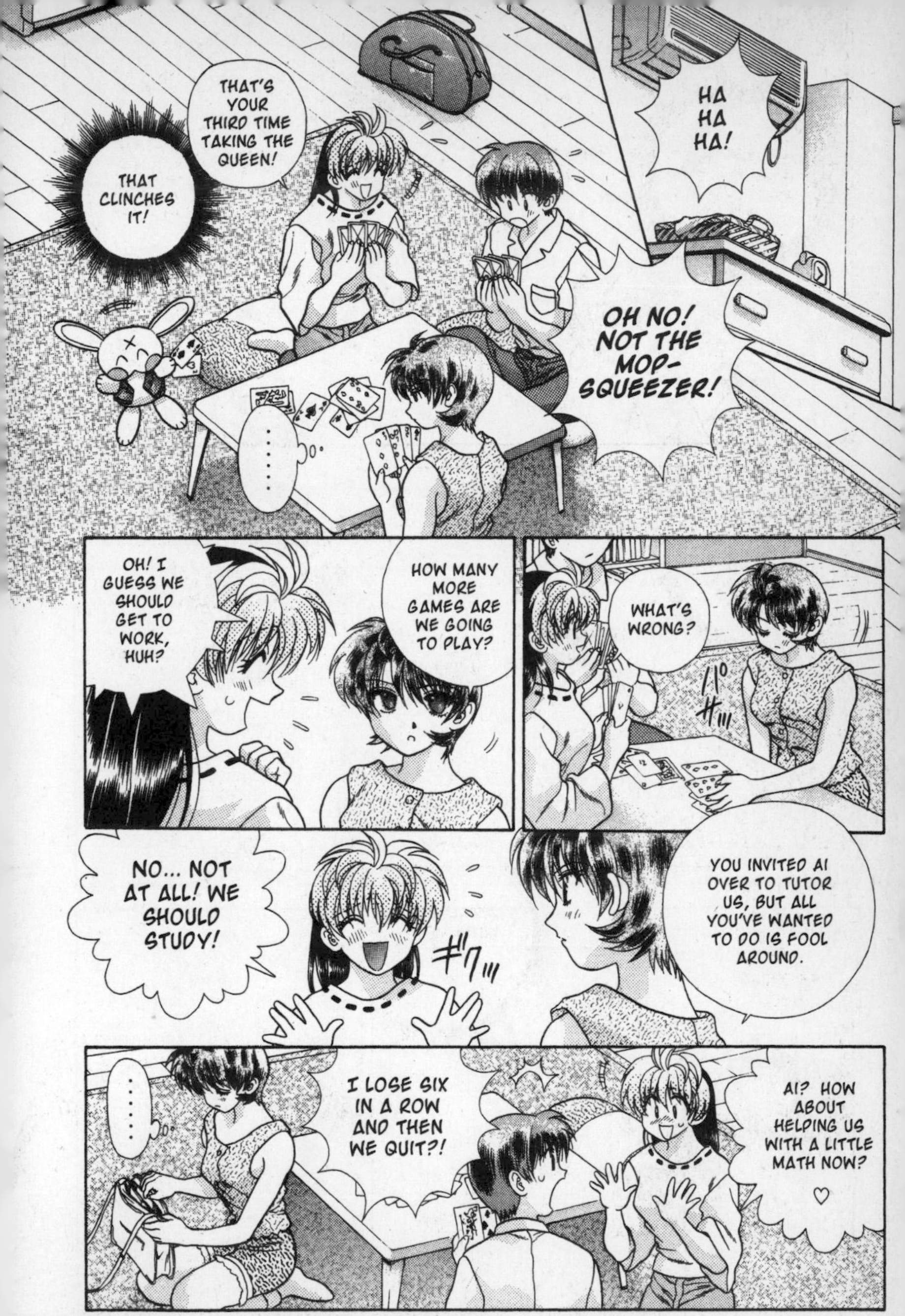
HA HA HA!
THAT'S YOUR THIRD TIME TAKING THE QUEEN!
THAT CLINCHES IT!
OH NO! NOT THE MOP-SQUEEZER!
......
WHAT'S WRONG?
HOW MANY MORE GAMES ARE WE GOING TO PLAY?
OH! I GUESS WE SHOULD GET TO WORK, HUH?
YOU INVITED AI OVER TO TUTOR US, BUT ALL YOU'VE WANTED TO DO IS FOOL AROUND.
NO... NOT AT ALL! WE SHOULD STUDY!
AI? HOW ABOUT HELPING US WITH A LITTLE MATH NOW?
I LOSE SIX IN A ROW AND THEN WE QUIT?!
......

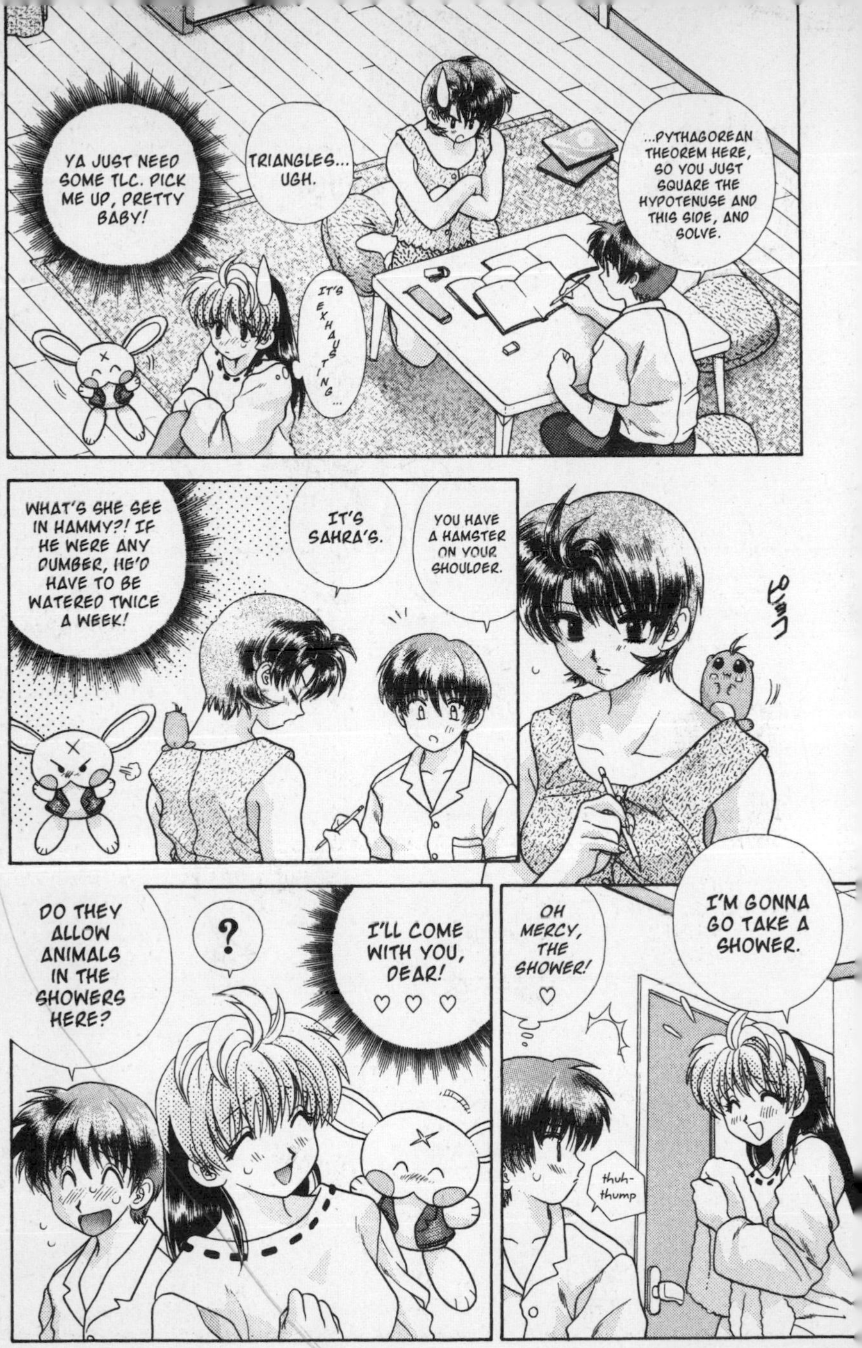
...PYTHAGOREAN THEOREM HERE, SO YOU JUST SQUARE THE HYPOTENUSE AND THIS SIDE, AND SOLVE.
TRIANGLES... UGH.
IT'S EXHAUSTING...
YA JUST NEED SOME TLC. PICK ME UP, PRETTY BABY!
YOU HAVE A HAMSTER ON YOUR SHOULDER.
IT'S SAHRA'S.
WHAT'S SHE SEE IN HAMMY?! IF HE WERE ANY DUMBER, HE'D HAVE TO BE WATERED TWICE A WEEK!
I'M GONNA GO TAKE A SHOWER.
OH MERCY, THE SHOWER! ♡
thuh-thump
I'LL COME WITH YOU, DEAR! ♡ ♡ ♡
?
DO THEY ALLOW ANIMALS IN THE SHOWERS HERE?

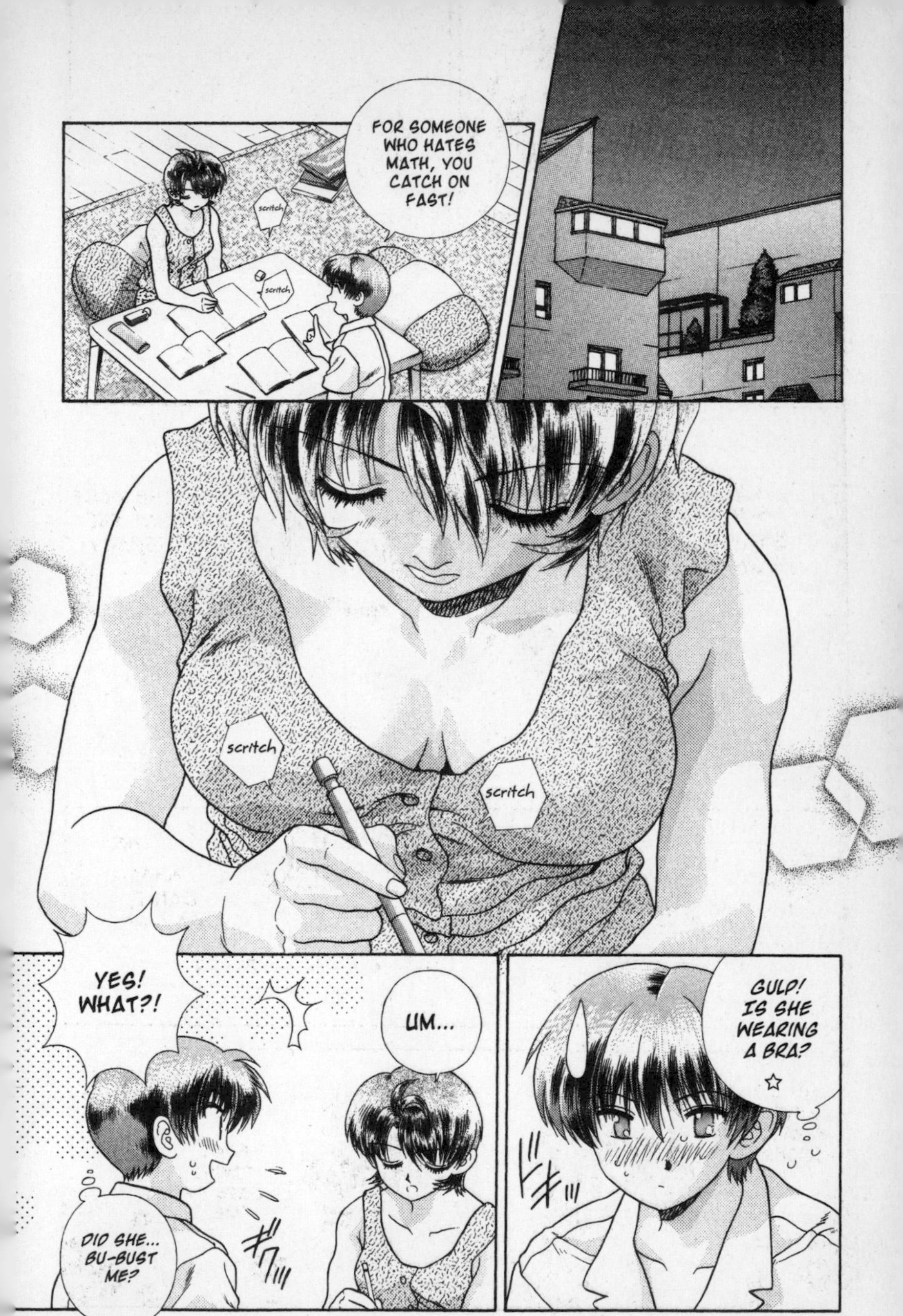
FOR SOMEONE WHO HATES MATH, YOU CATCH ON FAST!
scritch
scritch
scritch
scritch
GULP! IS SHE WEARING A BRA? ☆
UM...
YES! WHAT?!
DID SHE... BU-BUST ME?

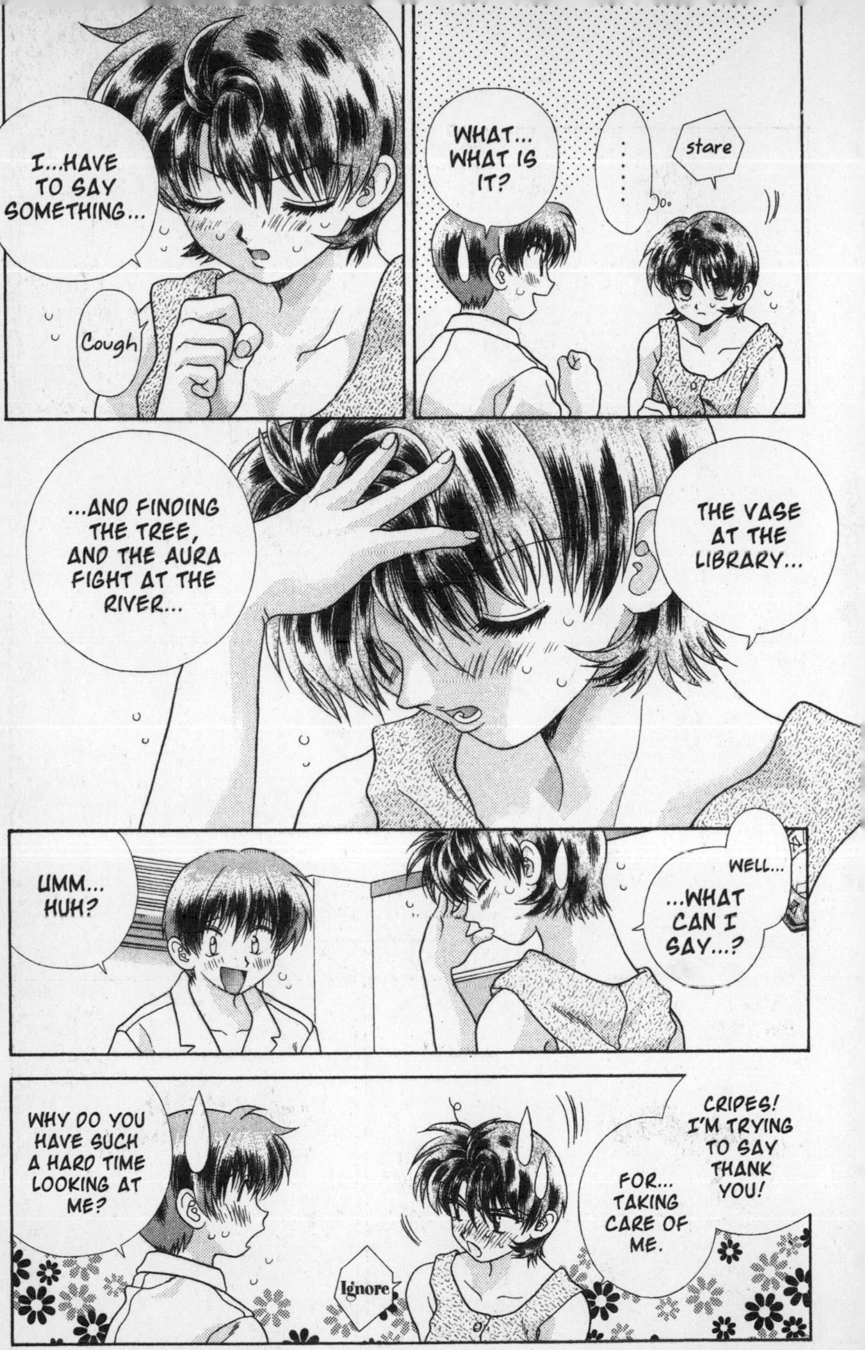
stare
......
WHAT... WHAT IS IT?
I...HAVE TO SAY SOMETHING...
Cough
THE VASE AT THE LIBRARY...
...AND FINDING THE TREE, AND THE AURA FIGHT AT THE RIVER...
WELL... ...WHAT CAN I SAY...?
UMM... HUH?
CRIPES! I'M TRYING TO SAY THANK YOU!
FOR... TAKING CARE OF ME.
Ignore
WHY DO YOU HAVE SUCH A HARD TIME LOOKING AT ME?

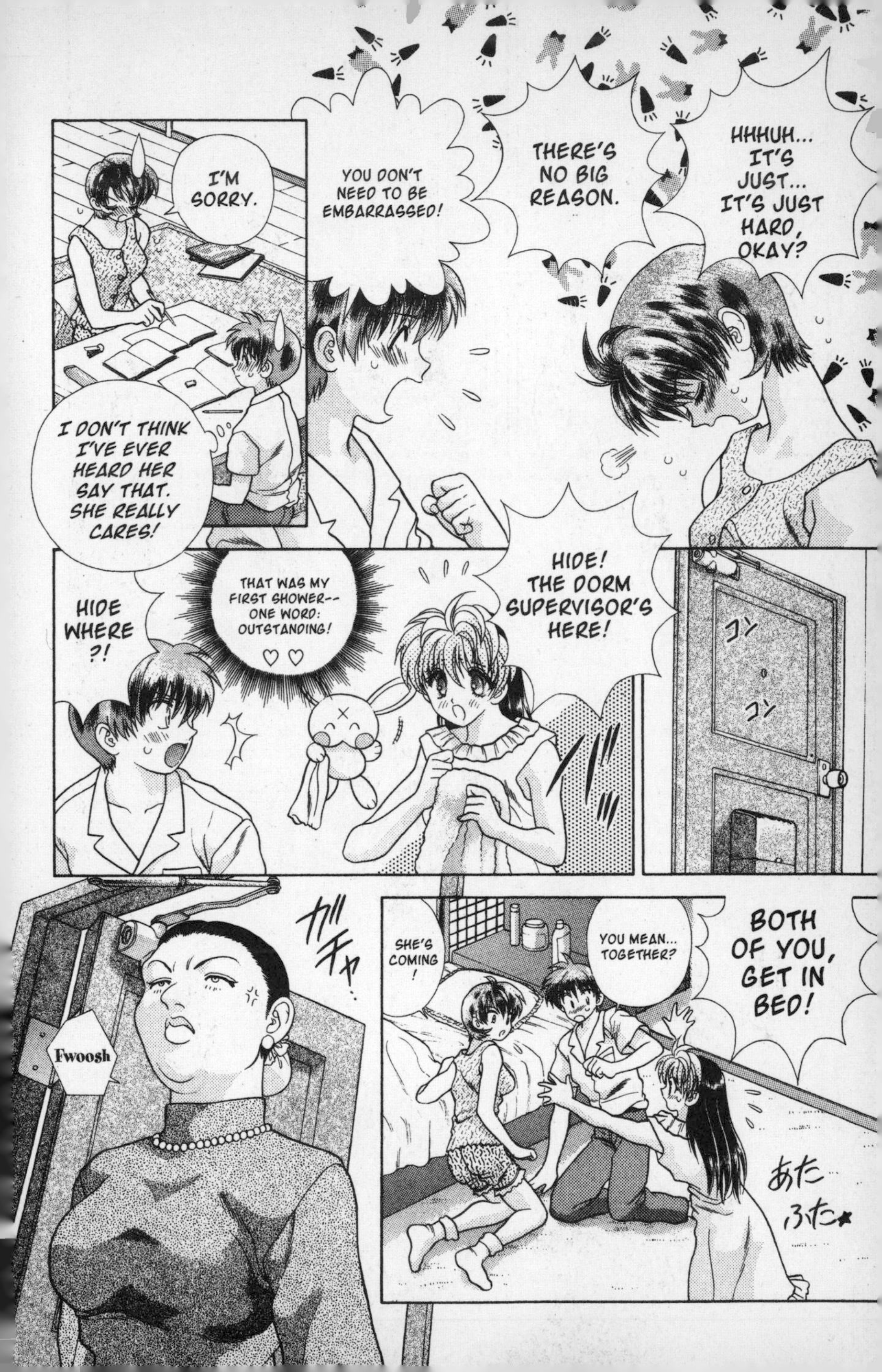
HHHUH... IT'S JUST... IT'S JUST HARD, OKAY?
THERE'S NO BIG REASON.
YOU DON'T NEED TO BE EMBARRASSED!
I'M SORRY.
I DON'T THINK I'VE EVER HEARD HER SAY THAT. SHE REALLY CARES!
コン
コン
HIDE! THE DORM SUPERVISOR'S HERE!
THAT WAS MY FIRST SHOWER-- ONE WORD: OUTSTANDING! ♡ ♡
HIDE WHERE?!
BOTH OF YOU, GET IN BED!
YOU MEAN... TOGETHER?
SHE'S COMING!
あたふた
ガチャ
Fwoosh

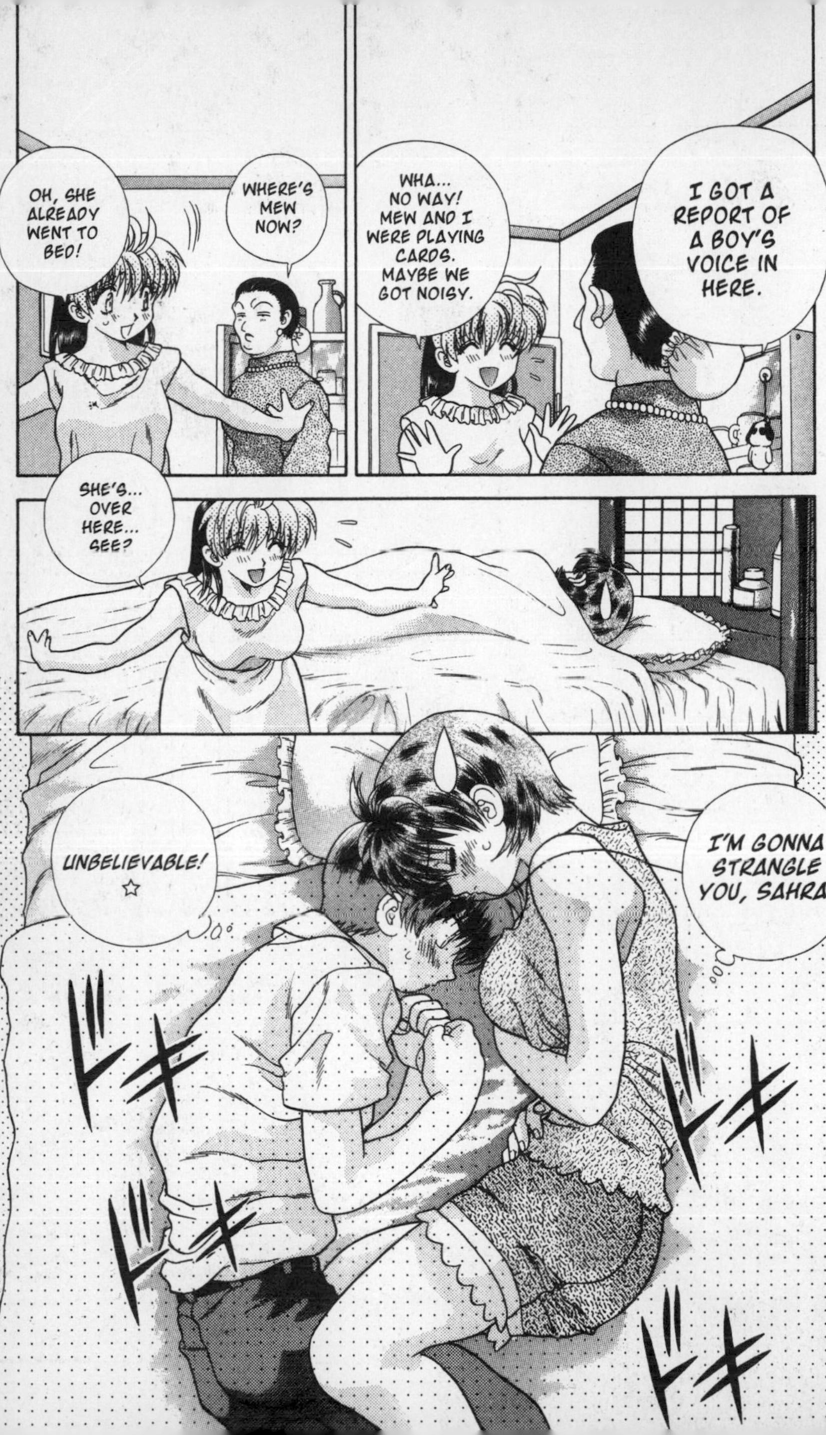
I GOT A REPORT OF A BOY'S VOICE IN HERE.
WHA... NO WAY! MEW AND I WERE PLAYING CARDS. MAYBE WE GOT NOISY.
WHERE'S MEW NOW?
OH, SHE ALREADY WENT TO BED!
SHE'S... OVER HERE... SEE?
I'M GONNA STRANGLE YOU, SAHRA!
UNBELIEVABLE! ☆
ドキ
ドキ
ドキ
ドキ

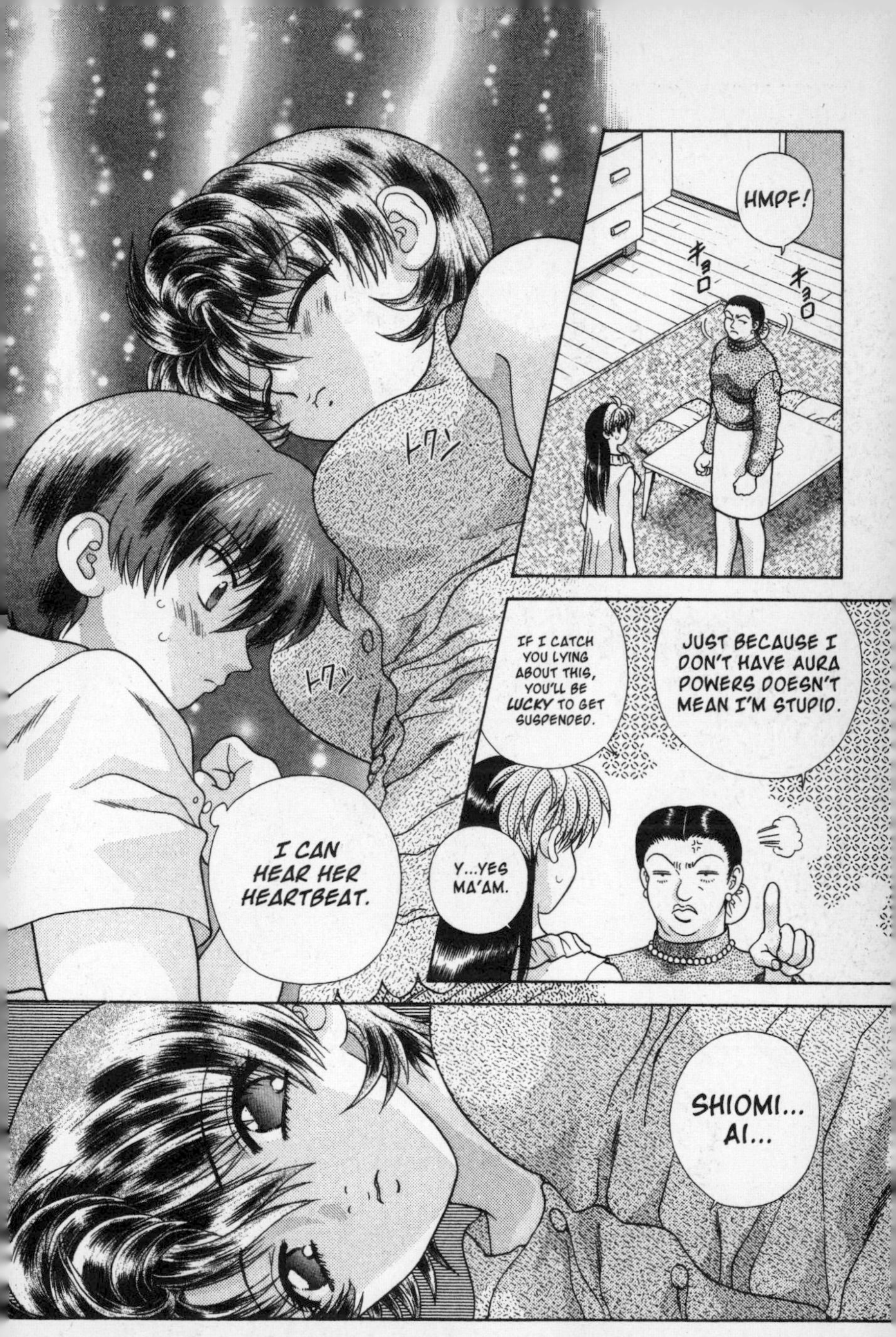
HMPF!
キョロ
キョロ
JUST BECAUSE I DON'T HAVE AURA POWERS DOESN'T MEAN I'M STUPID.
IF I CATCH YOU LYING ABOUT THIS, YOU'LL BE **LUCKY** TO GET SUSPENDED.
Y...YES MA'AM.
トクン
トクン
I CAN HEAR HER HEARTBEAT.
SHIOMI... AI...

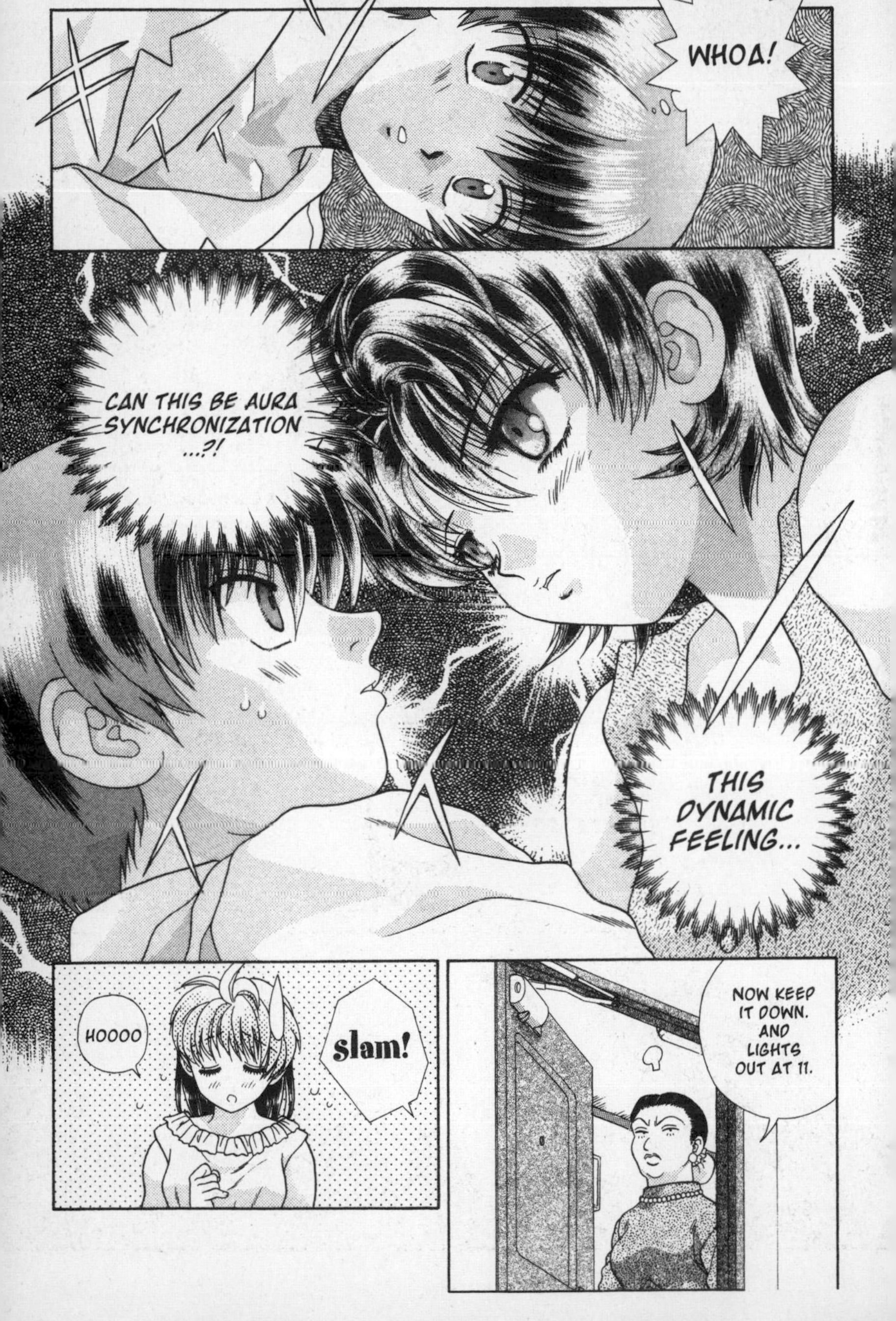
WHOA!
CAN THIS BE AURA SYNCHRONIZATION ...?!
THIS DYNAMIC FEELING...
NOW KEEP IT DOWN. AND LIGHTS OUT AT 11.
slam!
HOOOO

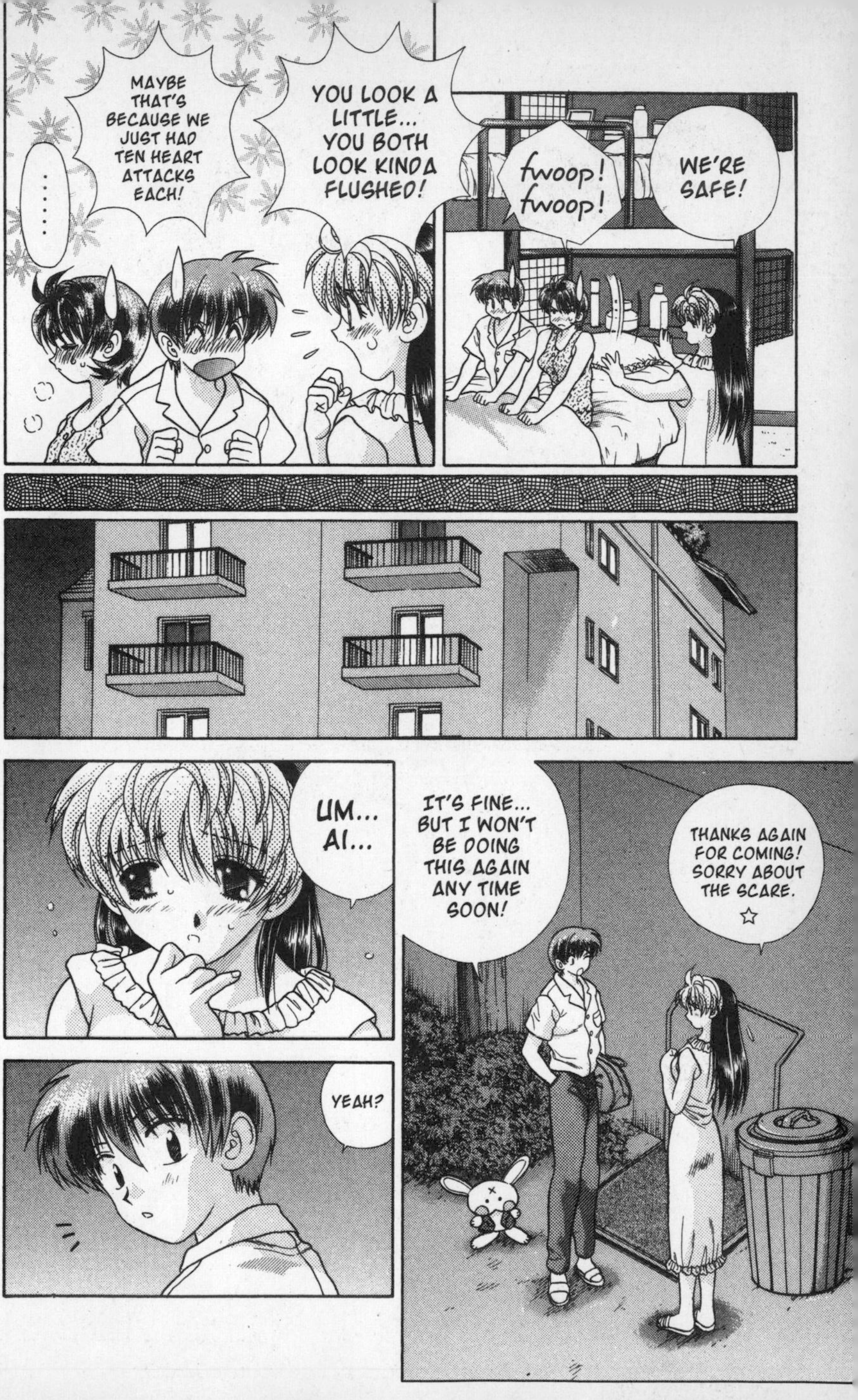
WE'RE SAFE!
fwoop! fwoop!
YOU LOOK A LITTLE... YOU BOTH LOOK KINDA FLUSHED!
MAYBE THAT'S BECAUSE WE JUST HAD TEN HEART ATTACKS EACH!
......
THANKS AGAIN FOR COMING! SORRY ABOUT THE SCARE. ☆
IT'S FINE... BUT I WON'T BE DOING THIS AGAIN ANY TIME SOON!
UM... AI...
YEAH?

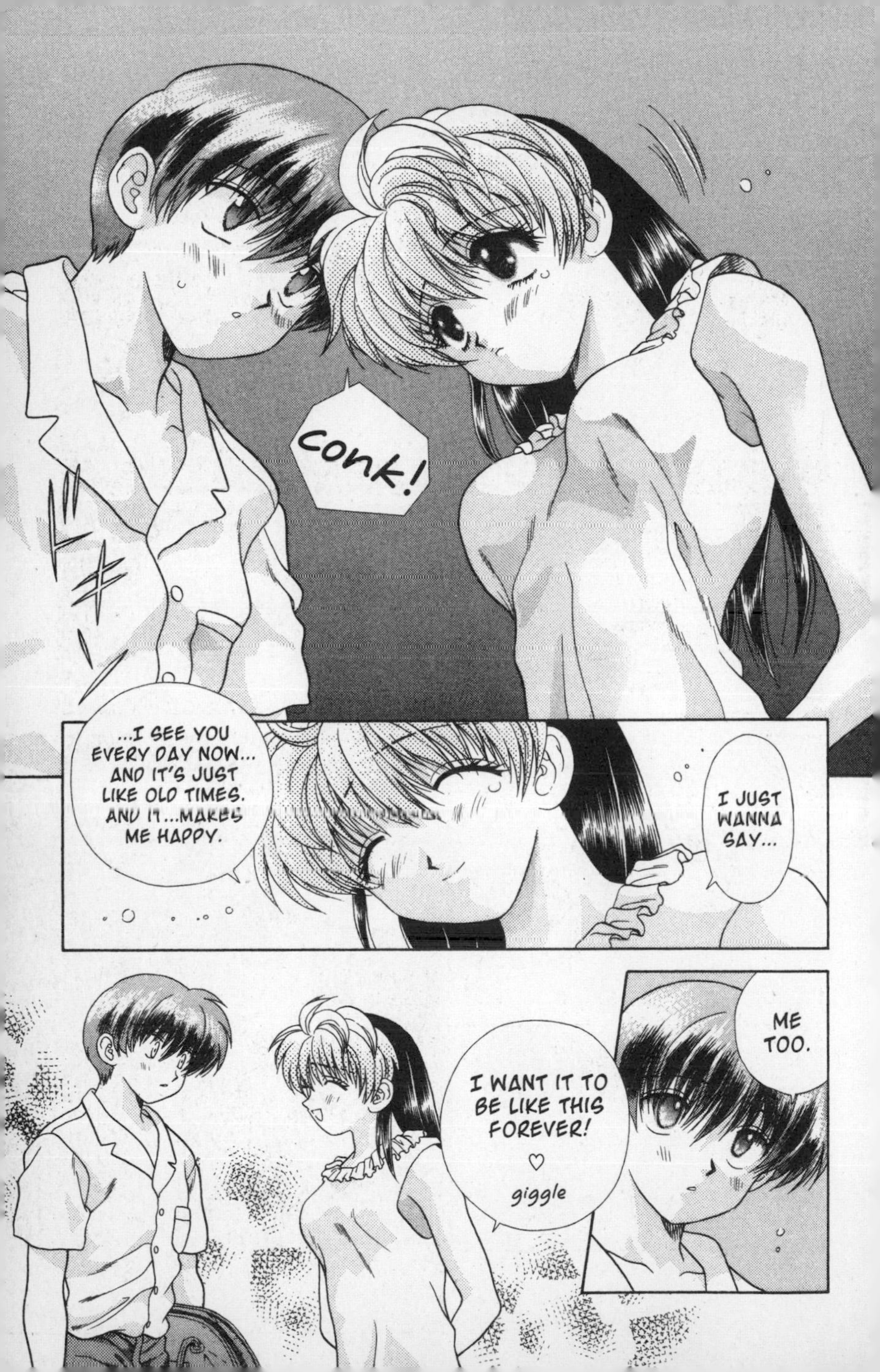
conk!
I JUST WANNA SAY...
...I SEE YOU EVERY DAY NOW... AND IT'S JUST LIKE OLD TIMES. AND IT...MAKES ME HAPPY.
I WANT IT TO BE LIKE THIS FOREVER! ♡
giggle
ME TOO.

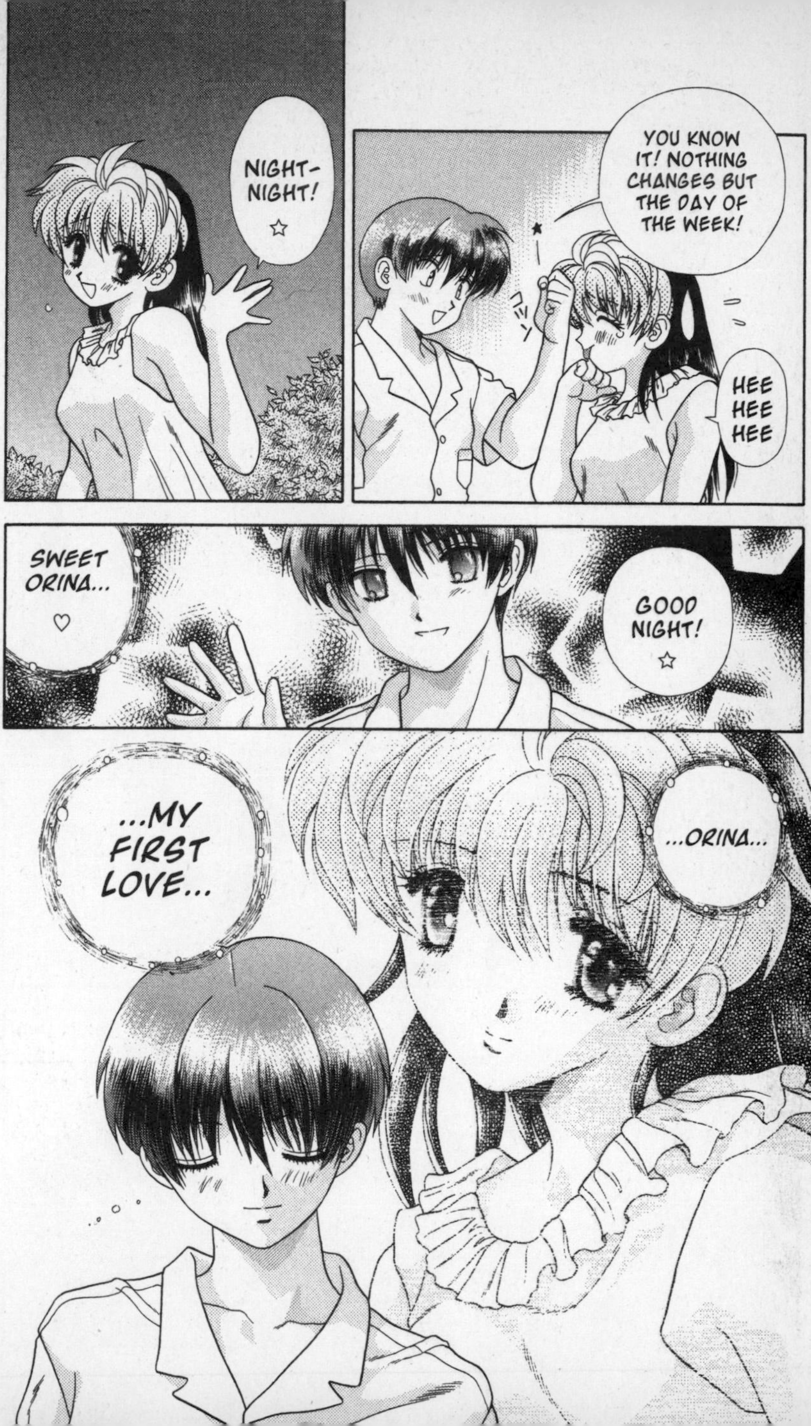
YOU KNOW IT! NOTHING CHANGES BUT THE DAY OF THE WEEK!
HEE HEE HEE
NIGHT-NIGHT! ☆
GOOD NIGHT! ☆
SWEET ORINA... ♡
...ORINA...
...MY FIRST LOVE...

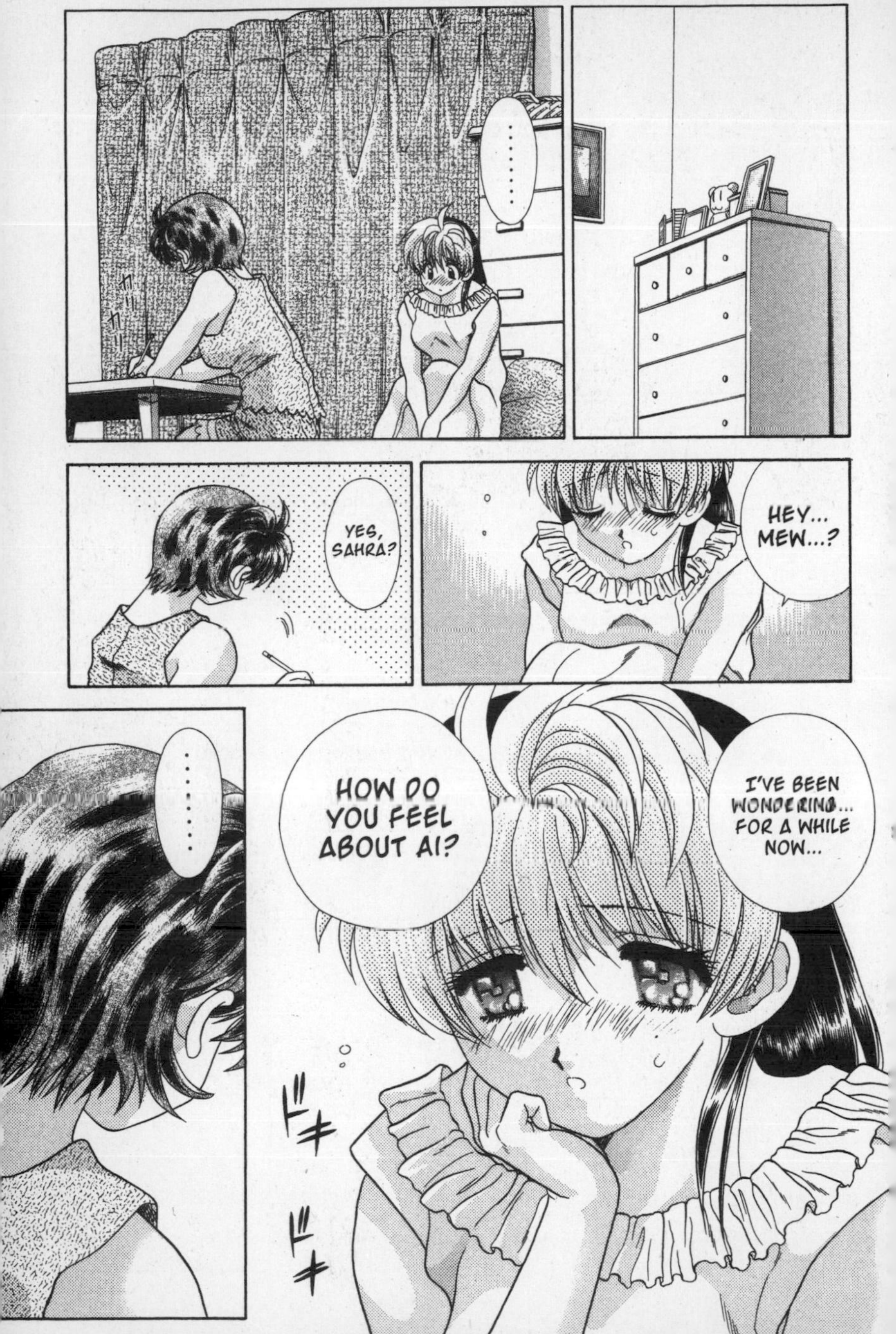
......
HEY... MEW...?
YES, SAHRA?
I'VE BEEN WONDERING... FOR A WHILE NOW...
HOW DO YOU FEEL ABOUT AI?
ドキ ドキ
......

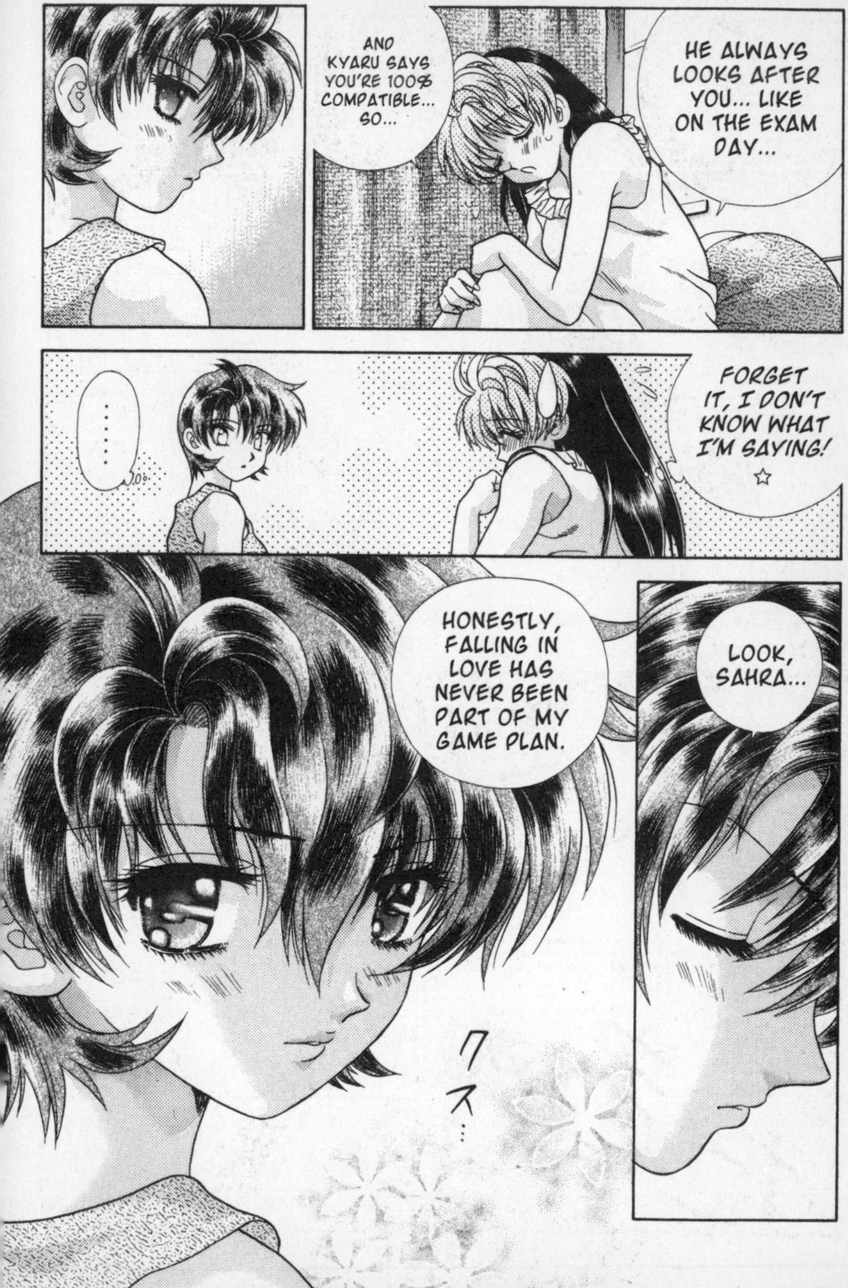
HE ALWAYS LOOKS AFTER YOU... LIKE ON THE EXAM DAY...
AND KYARU SAYS YOU'RE 100% COMPATIBLE... SO...
FORGET IT, I DON'T KNOW WHAT I'M SAYING! ☆
......
LOOK, SAHRA...
HONESTLY, FALLING IN LOVE HAS NEVER BEEN PART OF MY GAME PLAN.
クス…

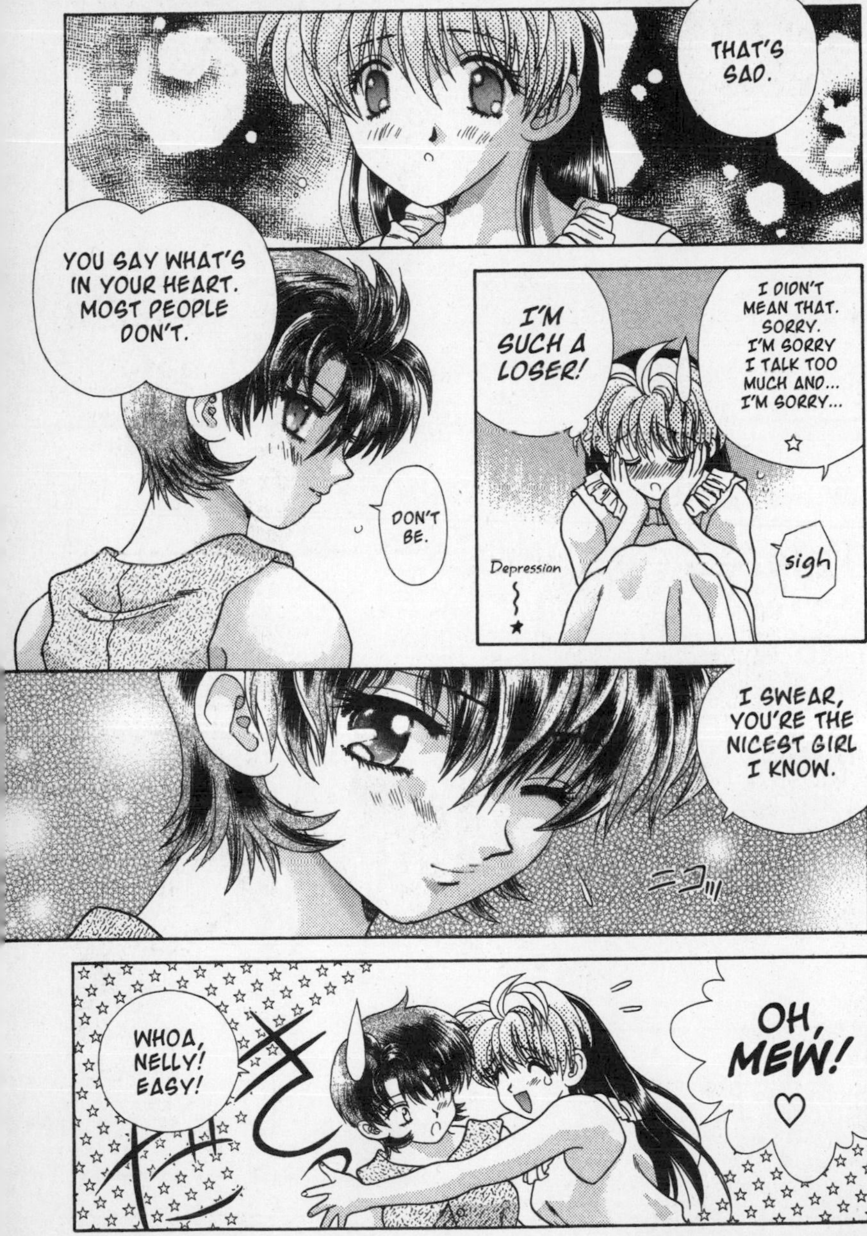
THAT'S SAD.
I DIDN'T MEAN THAT. SORRY. I'M SORRY I TALK TOO MUCH AND... I'M SORRY... ☆
I'M SUCH A LOSER!
sigh
Depression ★
DON'T BE.
YOU SAY WHAT'S IN YOUR HEART. MOST PEOPLE DON'T.
I SWEAR, YOU'RE THE NICEST GIRL I KNOW.
ニコッ
OH, MEW! ♡
WHOA, NELLY! EASY!

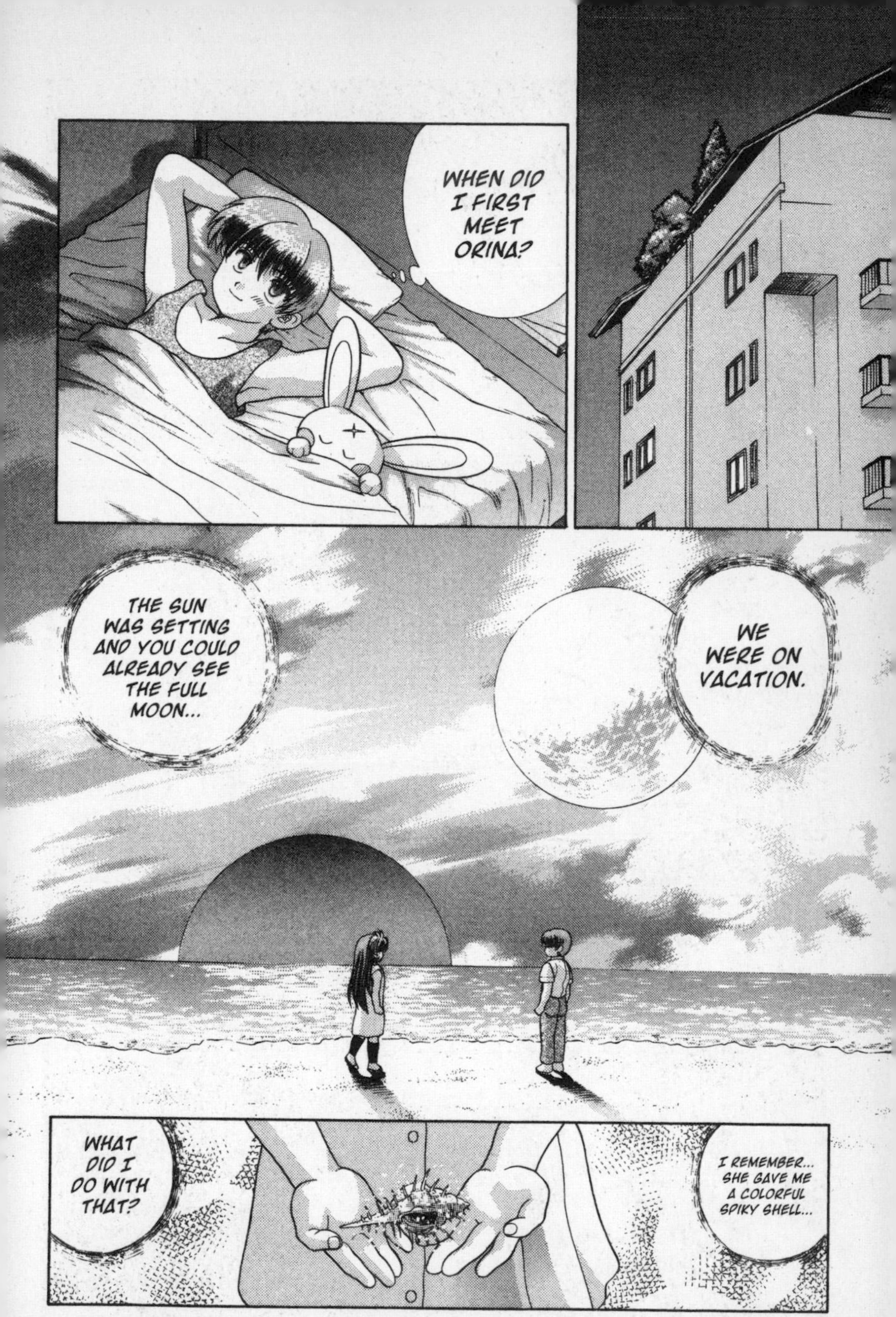
WHEN DID I FIRST MEET ORINA?
WE WERE ON VACATION.
THE SUN WAS SETTING AND YOU COULD ALREADY SEE THE FULL MOON...
I REMEMBER... SHE GAVE ME A COLORFUL SPIKY SHELL...
WHAT DID I DO WITH THAT?

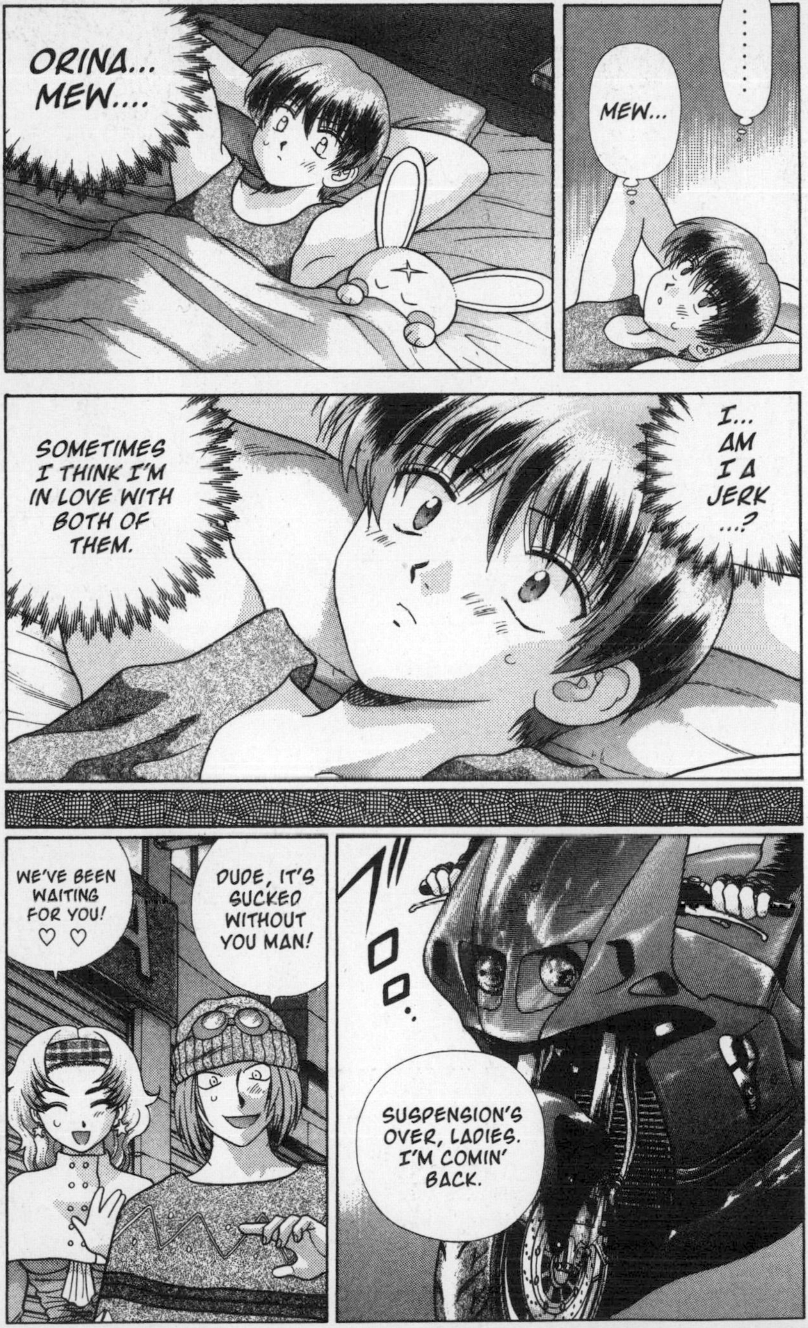
......
MEW...
ORINA... MEW....
I... AM I A JERK ...?
SOMETIMES I THINK I'M IN LOVE WITH BOTH OF THEM.
SUSPENSION'S OVER, LADIES. I'M COMIN' BACK.
DUDE, IT'S SUCKED WITHOUT YOU MAN!
WE'VE BEEN WAITING FOR YOU! ♡ ♡

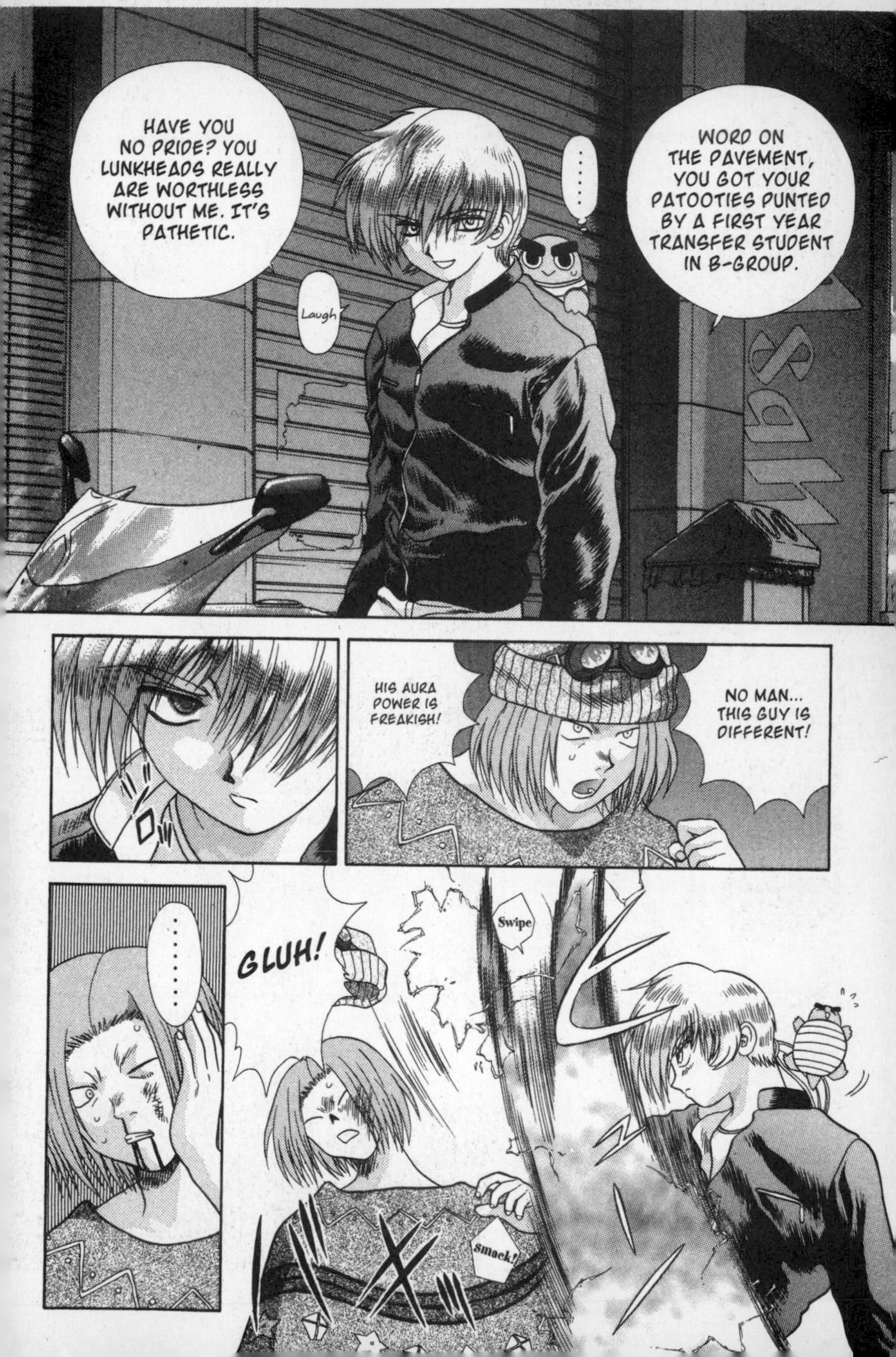
WORD ON THE PAVEMENT, YOU GOT YOUR PATOOTIES PUNTED BY A FIRST YEAR TRANSFER STUDENT IN B-GROUP.
......
HAVE YOU NO PRIDE? YOU LUNKHEADS REALLY ARE WORTHLESS WITHOUT ME. IT'S PATHETIC.
Laugh
NO MAN... THIS GUY IS DIFFERENT!
HIS AURA POWER IS FREAKISH!
Swipe
GLUH!
Smack!
......

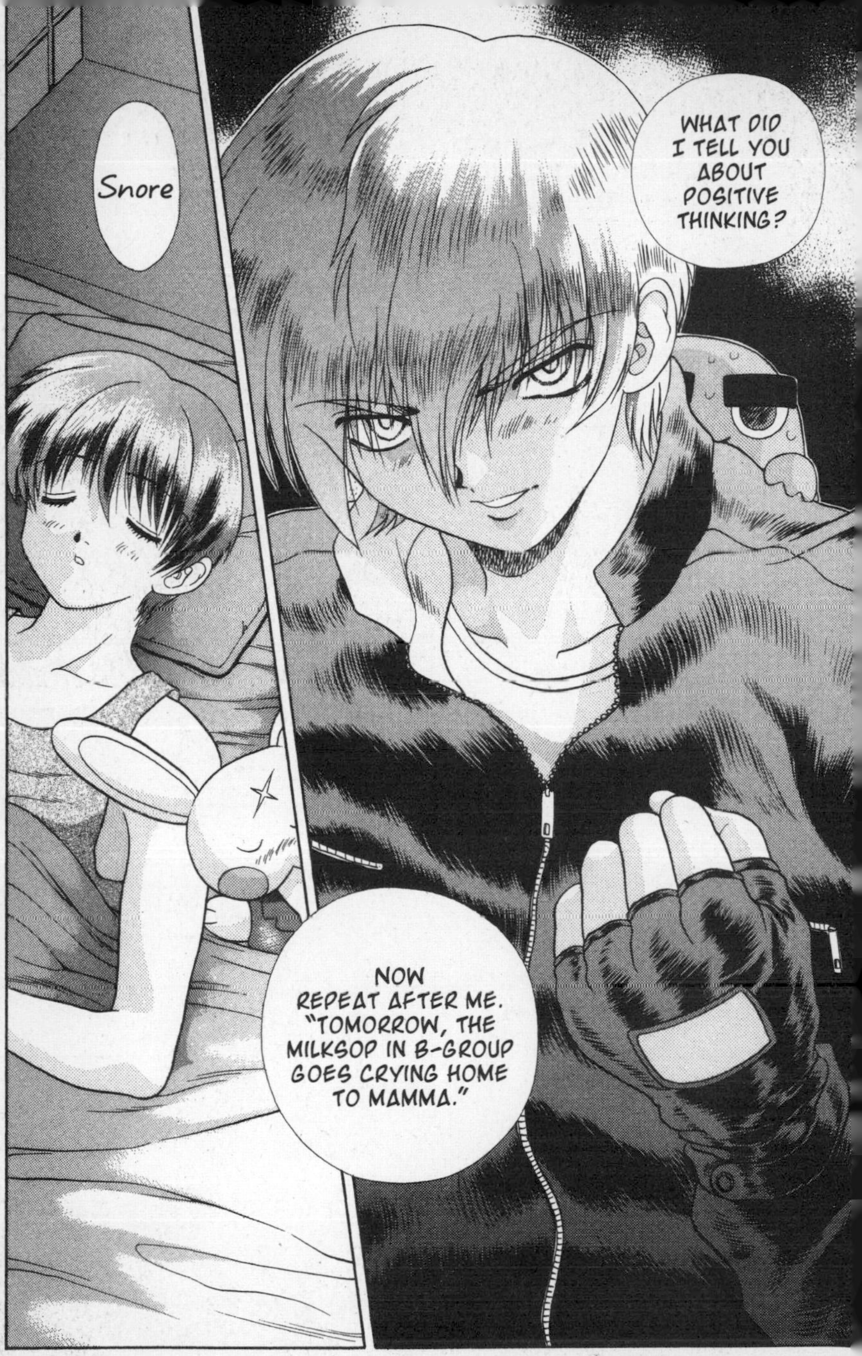
WHAT DID I TELL YOU ABOUT POSITIVE THINKING?
NOW REPEAT AFTER ME. "TOMORROW, THE MILKSOP IN B-GROUP GOES CRYING HOME TO MAMMA."
Snore

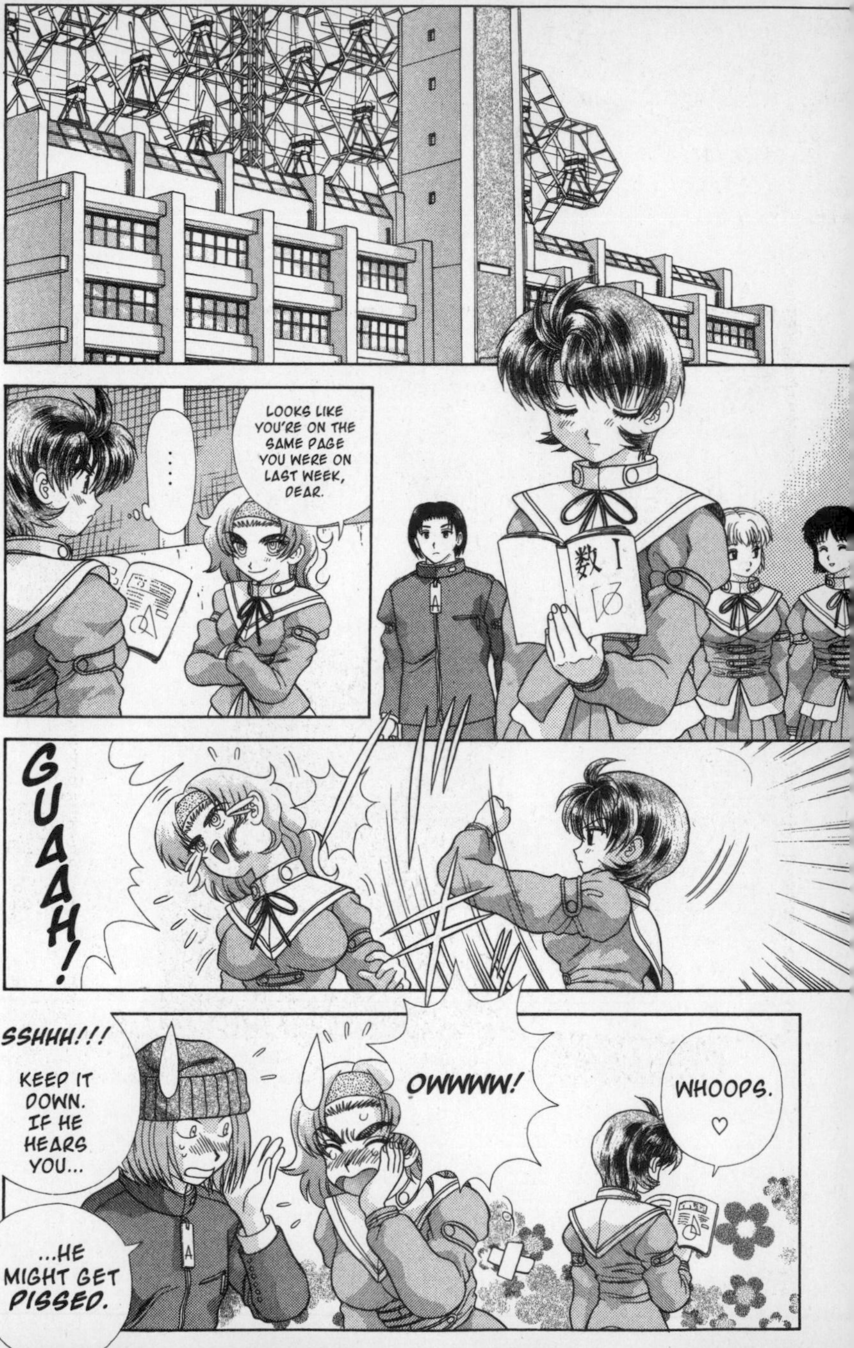
数 I
LOOKS LIKE YOU'RE ON THE SAME PAGE YOU WERE ON LAST WEEK, DEAR.
.....
GUAAAH!
WHOOPS. ♡
OWWWW!
SSHHH!!!
KEEP IT DOWN. IF HE HEARS YOU...
...HE MIGHT GET PISSED.

academy

Chapter 7: The Lady and the Punk

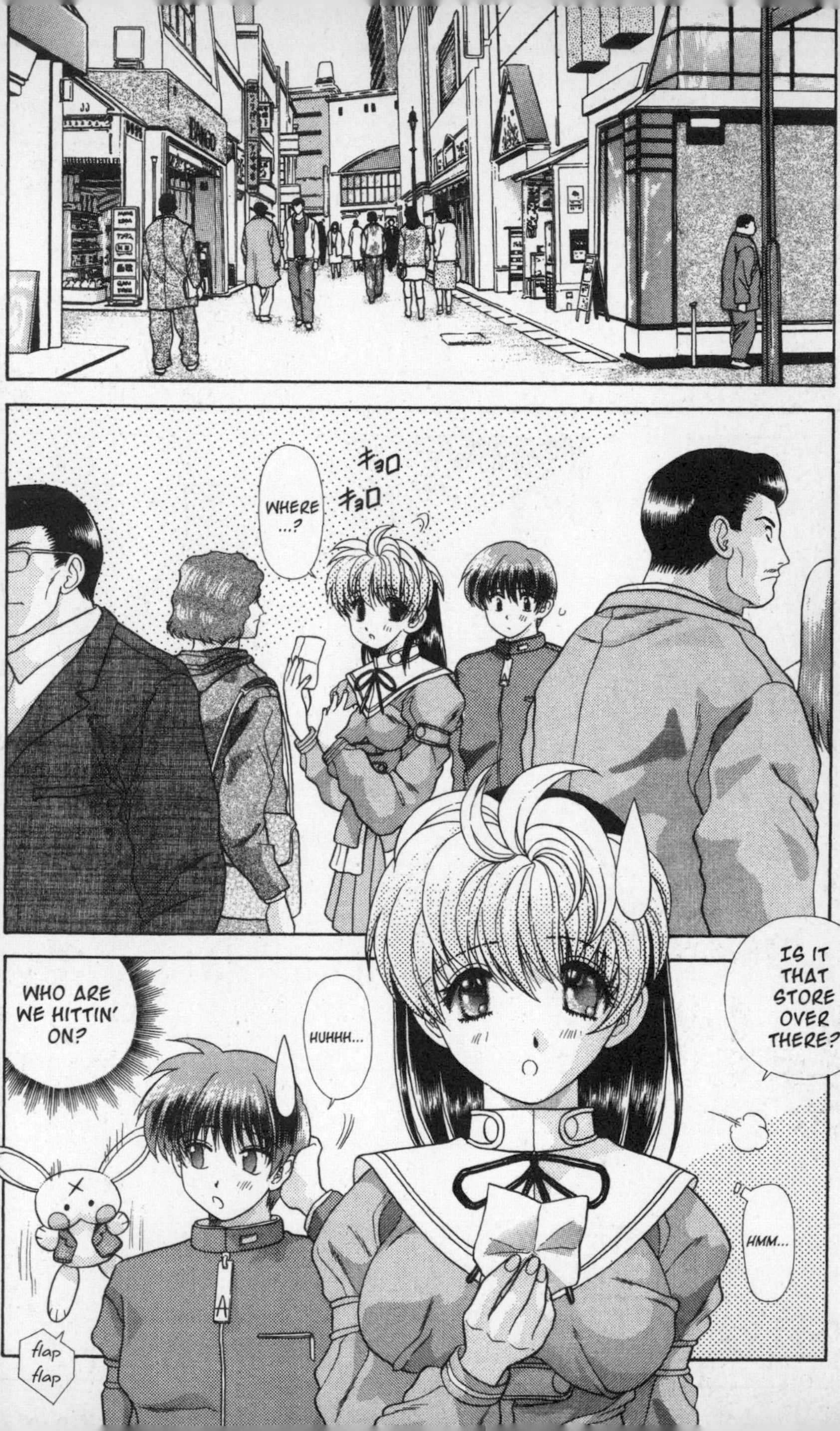
キョロ
キョロ
WHERE ...?
IS IT THAT STORE OVER THERE?
HMM...
HUHHH...
WHO ARE WE HITTIN' ON?
flap flap

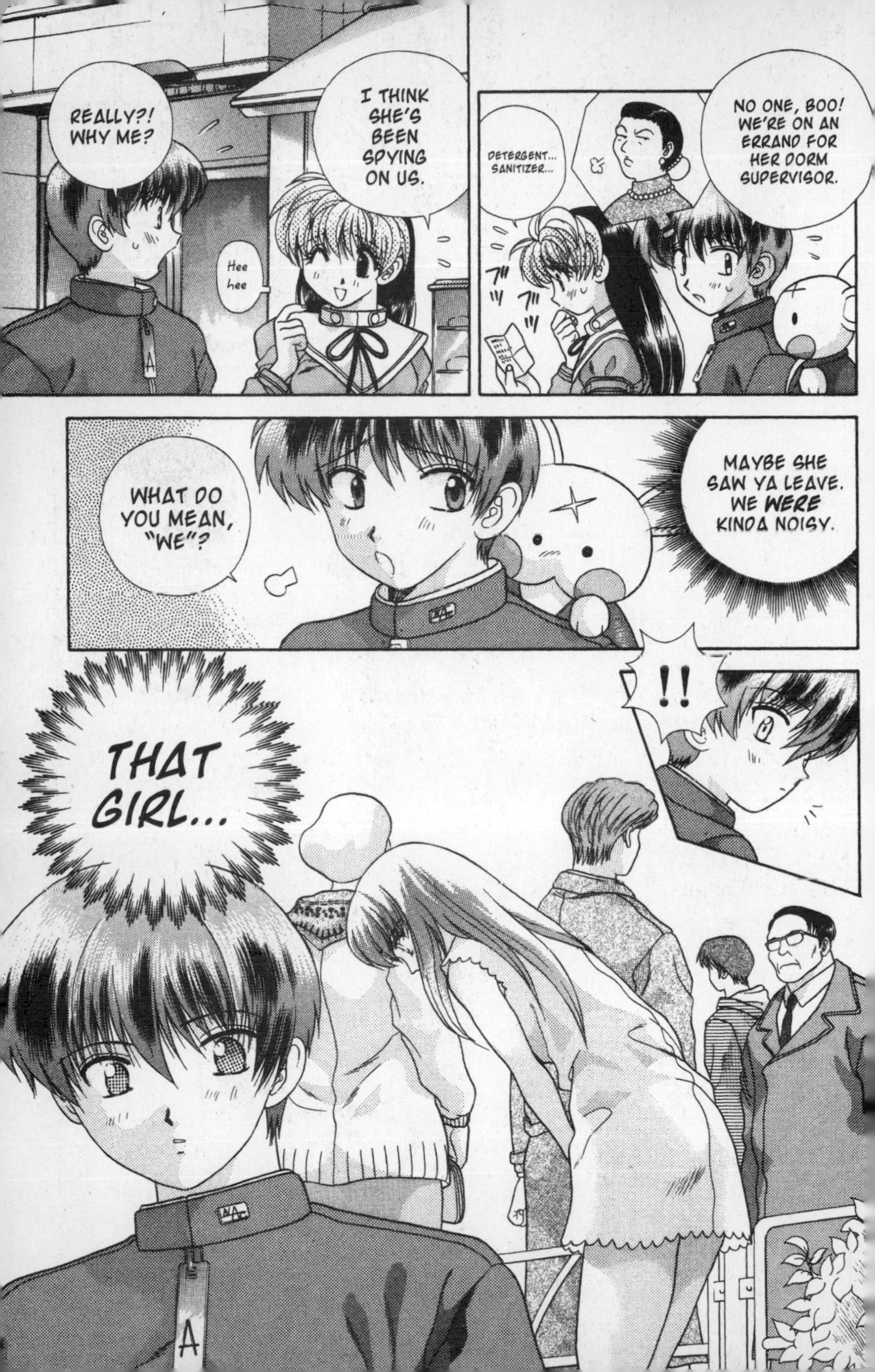
NO ONE, BOO! WE'RE ON AN ERRAND FOR HER DORM SUPERVISOR.
DETERGENT... SANITIZER...
I THINK SHE'S BEEN SPYING ON US.
REALLY?! WHY ME?
Hee hee
MAYBE SHE SAW YA LEAVE. WE *WERE* KINDA NOISY.
WHAT DO YOU MEAN, "WE"?
!!
THAT GIRL...

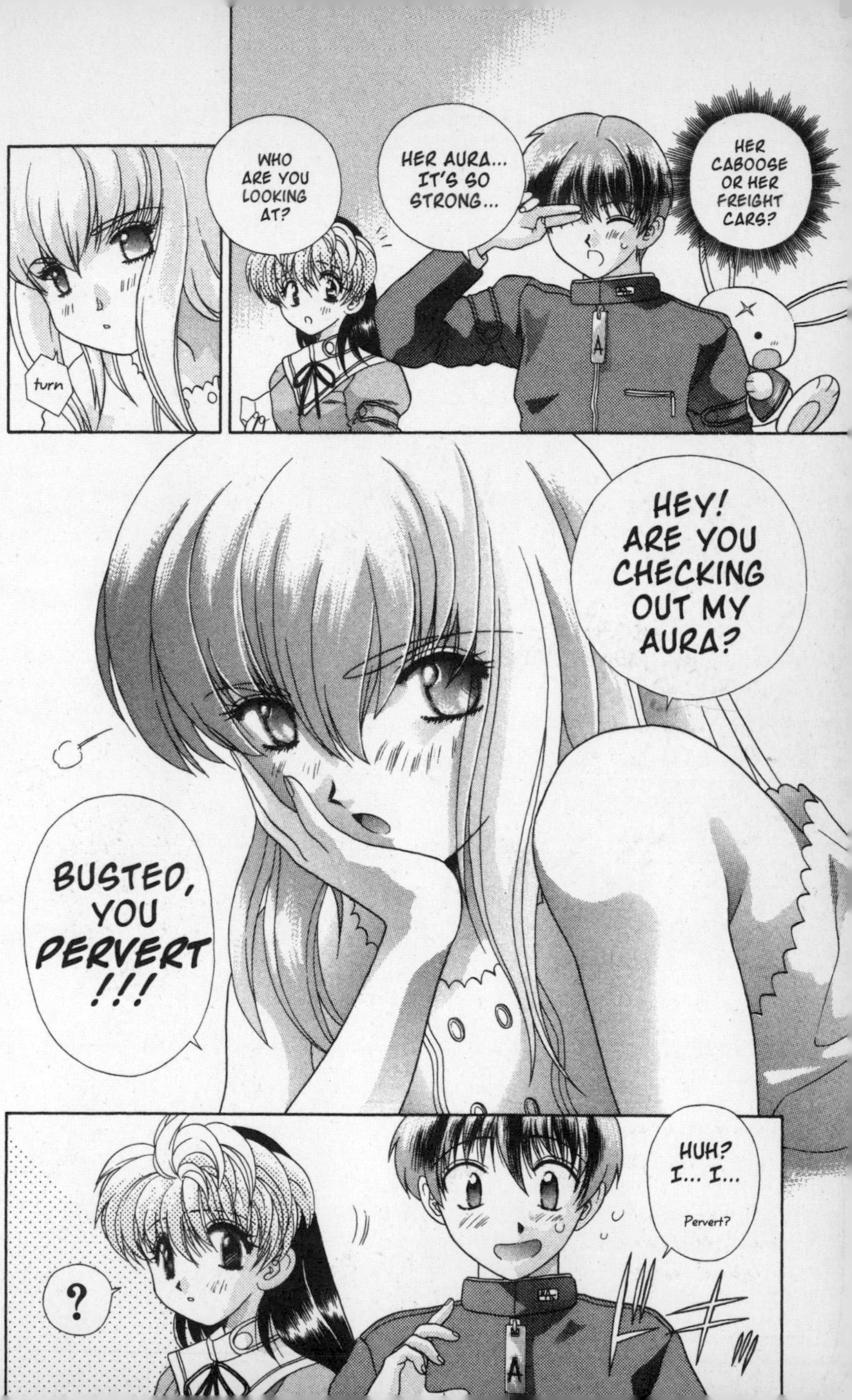
HER CABOOSE OR HER FREIGHT CARS?
HER AURA... IT'S SO STRONG...
WHO ARE YOU LOOKING AT?
turn
HEY! ARE YOU CHECKING OUT MY AURA?
BUSTED, YOU PERVERT!!!
HUH? I... I...
Pervert?
?

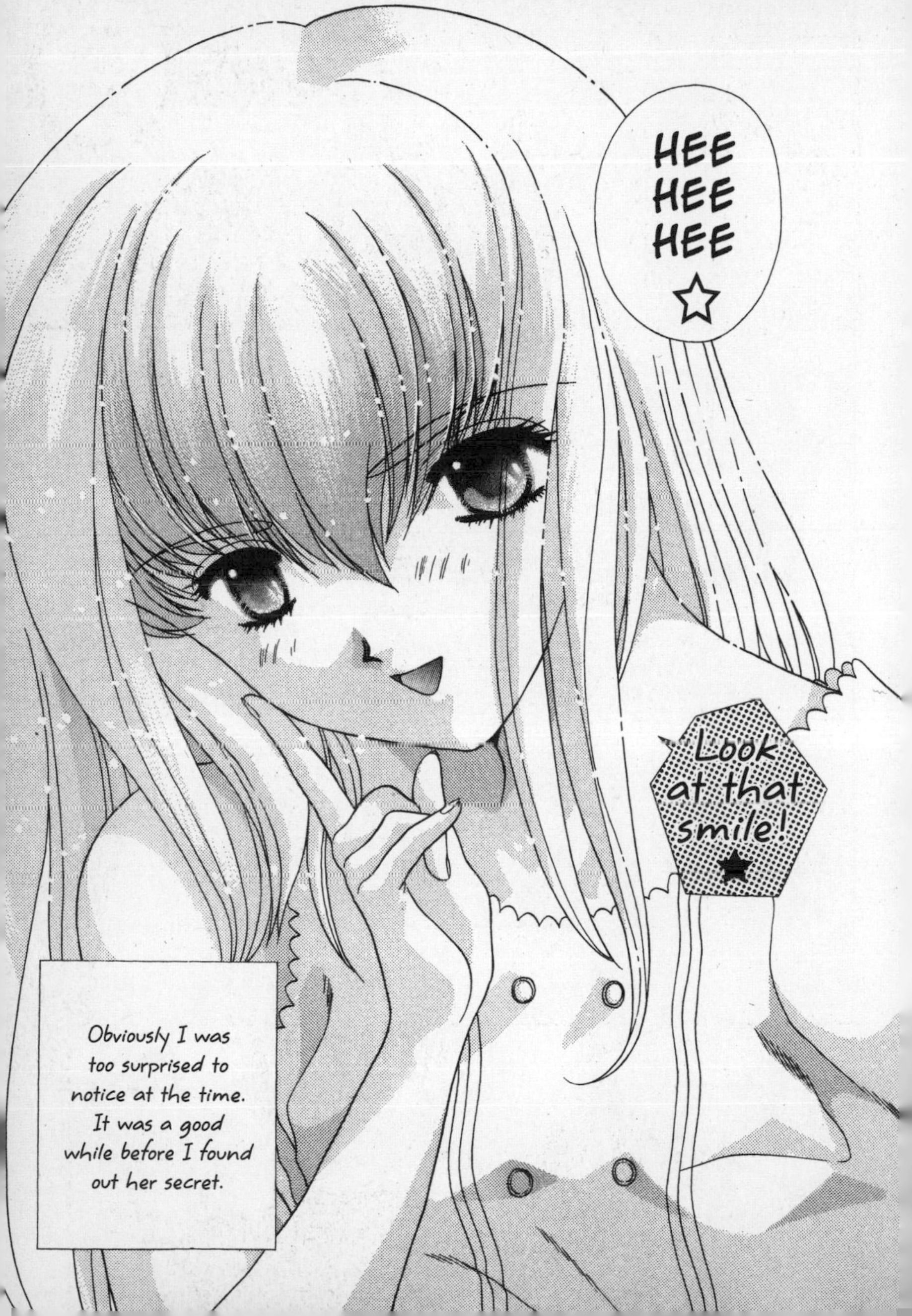
HEE HEE HEE ☆
Look at that smile! ★
Obviously I was too surprised to notice at the time. It was a good while before I found out her secret.

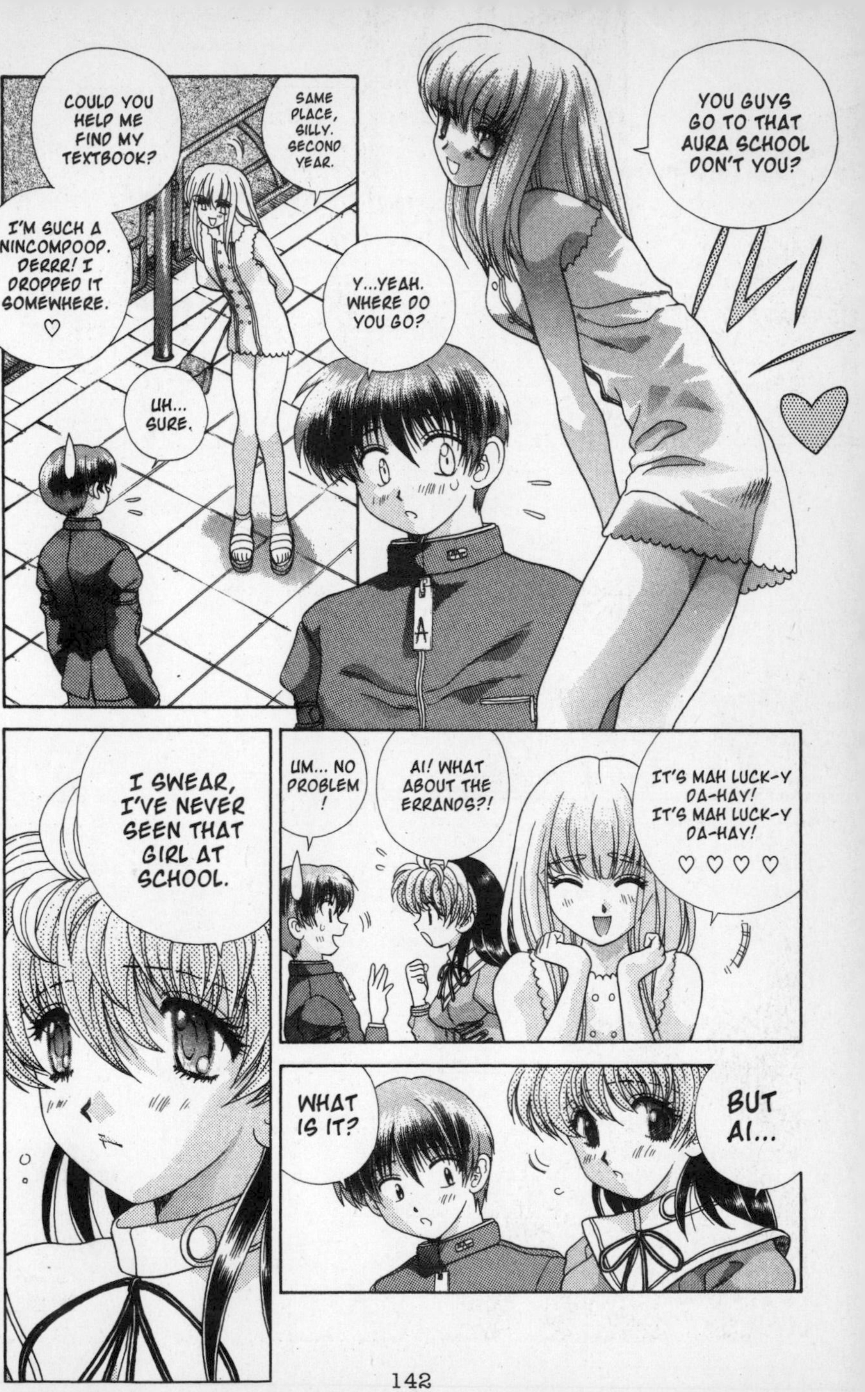
YOU GUYS GO TO THAT AURA SCHOOL DON'T YOU?
Y...YEAH. WHERE DO YOU GO?
SAME PLACE, SILLY. SECOND YEAR.
COULD YOU HELP ME FIND MY TEXTBOOK?
I'M SUCH A NINCOMPOOP. DERRR! I DROPPED IT SOMEWHERE. ♡
UH... SURE.
IT'S MAH LUCK-Y DA-HAY! IT'S MAH LUCK-Y DA-HAY! ♡ ♡ ♡ ♡
AI! WHAT ABOUT THE ERRANDS?!
UM... NO PROBLEM!
BUT AI...
WHAT IS IT?
I SWEAR, I'VE NEVER SEEN THAT GIRL AT SCHOOL.

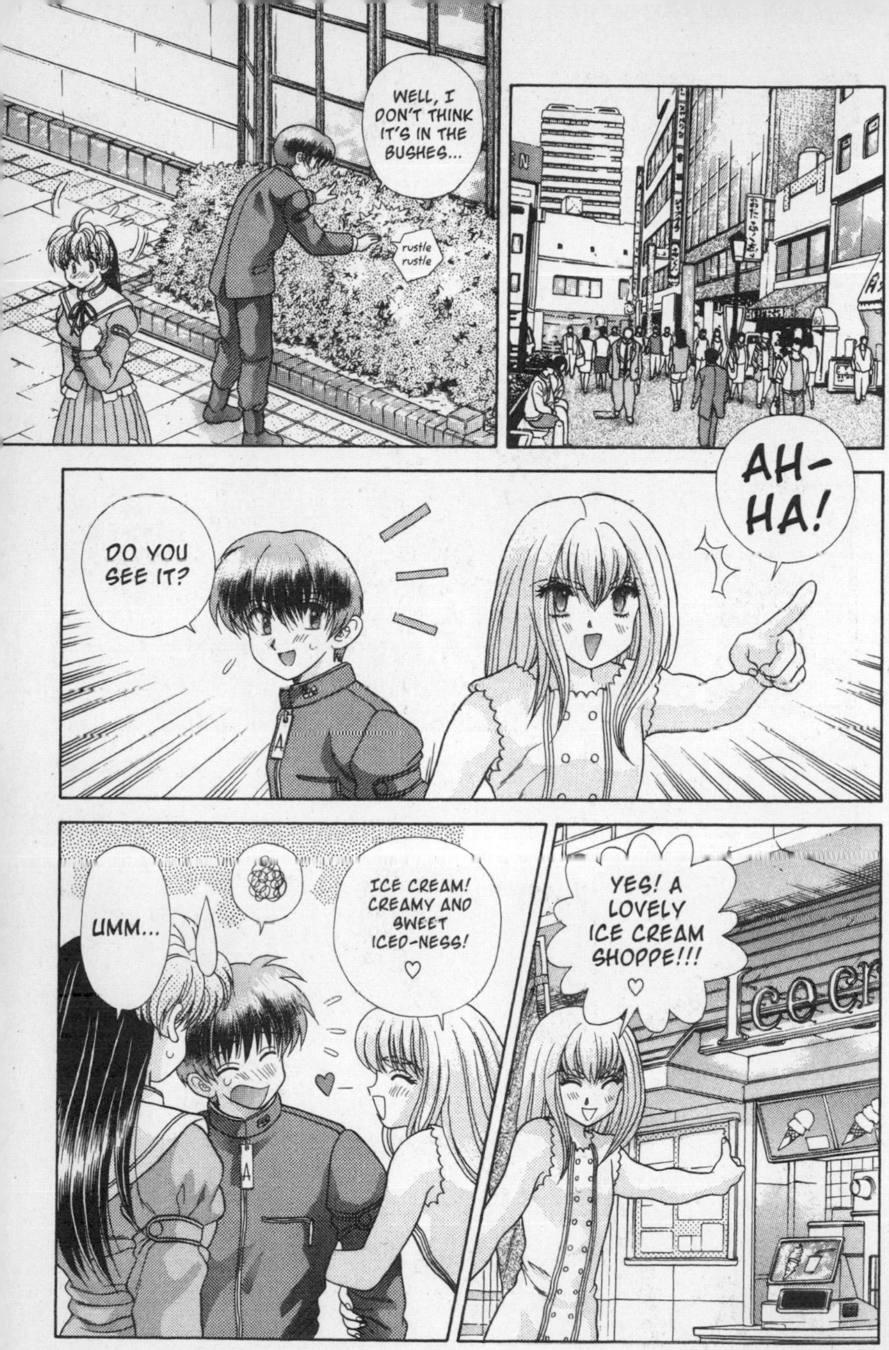
WELL, I DON'T THINK IT'S IN THE BUSHES...
rustle rustle
AH-HA!
DO YOU SEE IT?
YES! A LOVELY ICE CREAM SHOPPE!!! ♡
ICE CREAM! CREAMY AND SWEET ICED-NESS! ♡
UMM...

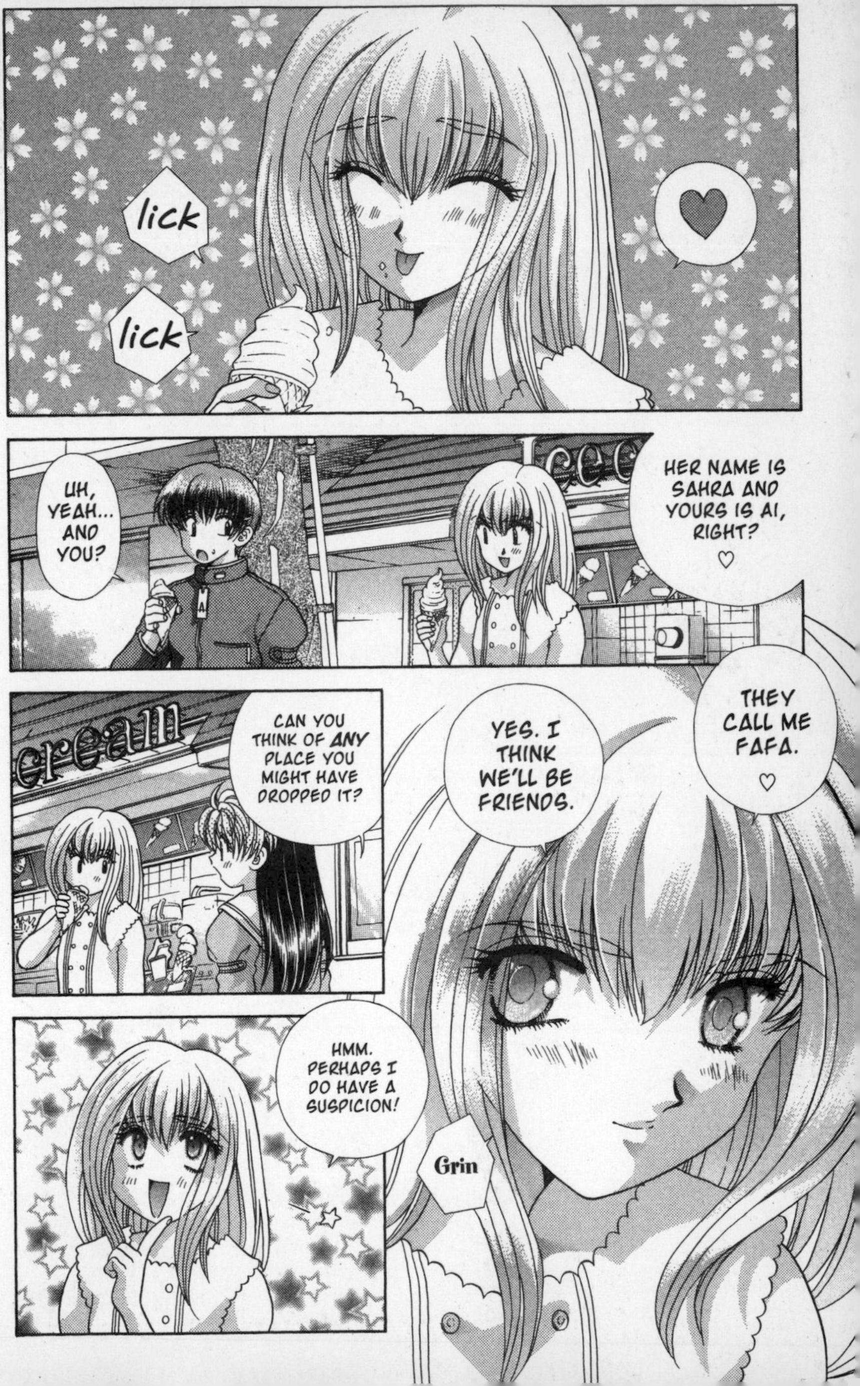
lick
lick
♥
HER NAME IS SAHRA AND YOURS IS AI, RIGHT? ♡
UH, YEAH... AND YOU?
THEY CALL ME FAFA. ♡
YES. I THINK WE'LL BE FRIENDS.
Grin
CAN YOU THINK OF ANY PLACE YOU MIGHT HAVE DROPPED IT?
HMM. PERHAPS I DO HAVE A SUSPICION!

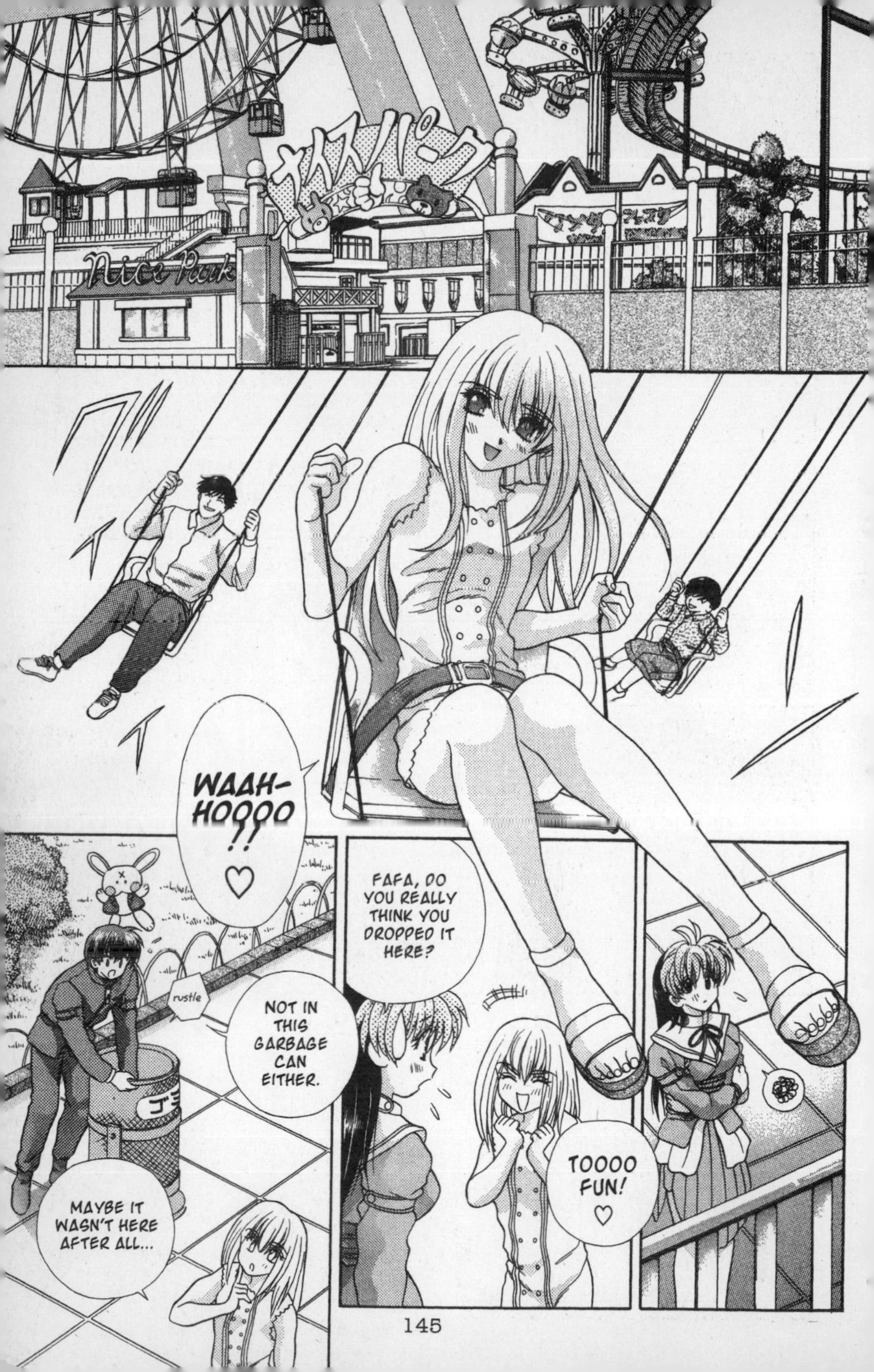
Nice Park
WAAH-HOOOO!! ♡
FAFA, DO YOU REALLY THINK YOU DROPPED IT HERE?
TOOOO FUN! ♡
rustle
NOT IN THIS GARBAGE CAN EITHER.
MAYBE IT WASN'T HERE AFTER ALL...

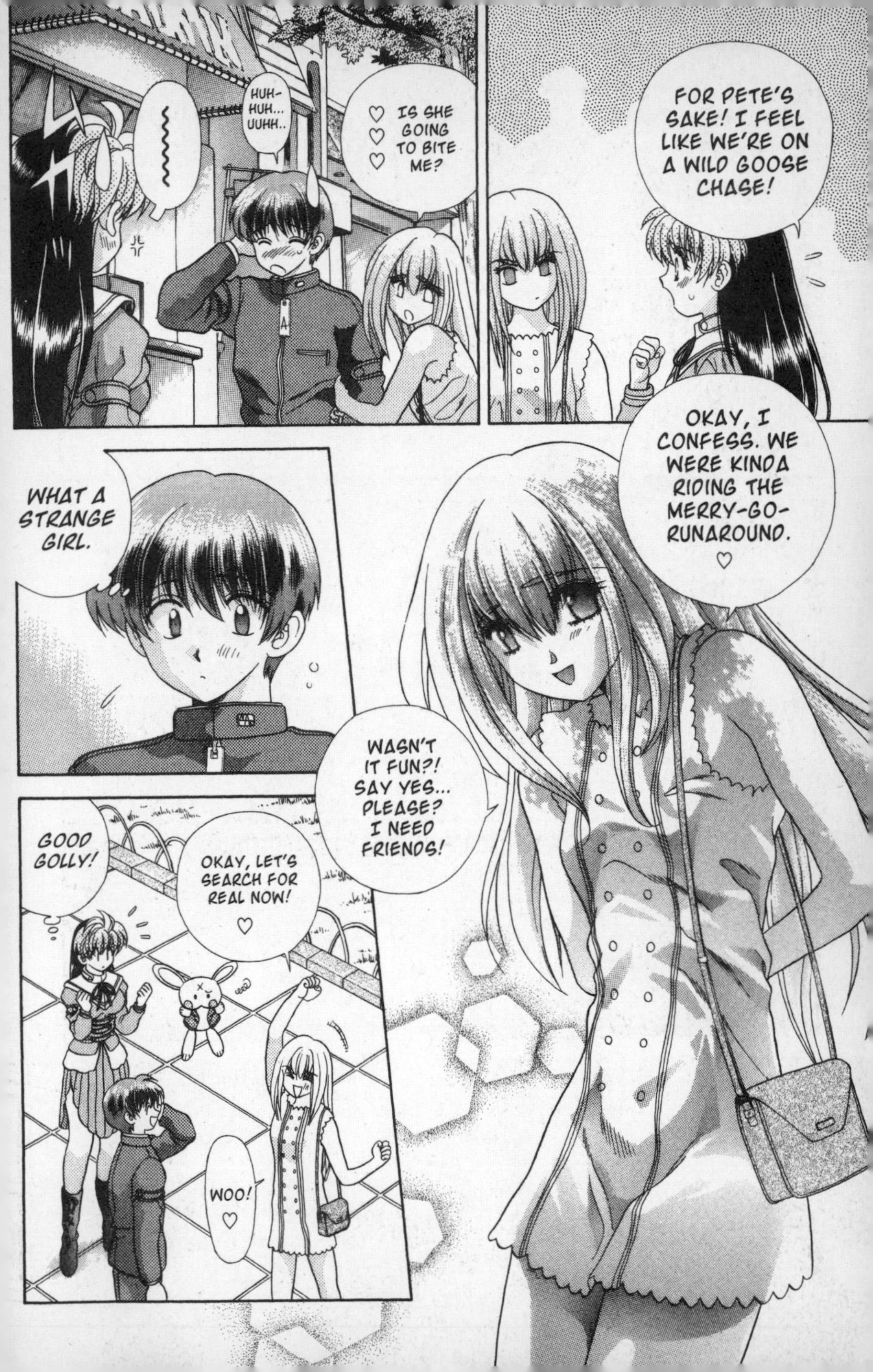
FOR PETE'S SAKE! I FEEL LIKE WE'RE ON A WILD GOOSE CHASE!
♡ IS SHE ♡ GOING ♡ TO BITE ME?
HUH-HUH... UUHH..
OKAY, I CONFESS. WE WERE KINDA RIDING THE MERRY-GO-RUNAROUND. ♡
WASN'T IT FUN?! SAY YES... PLEASE? I NEED FRIENDS!
WHAT A STRANGE GIRL.
OKAY, LET'S SEARCH FOR REAL NOW! ♡
GOOD GOLLY!
WOO! ♡

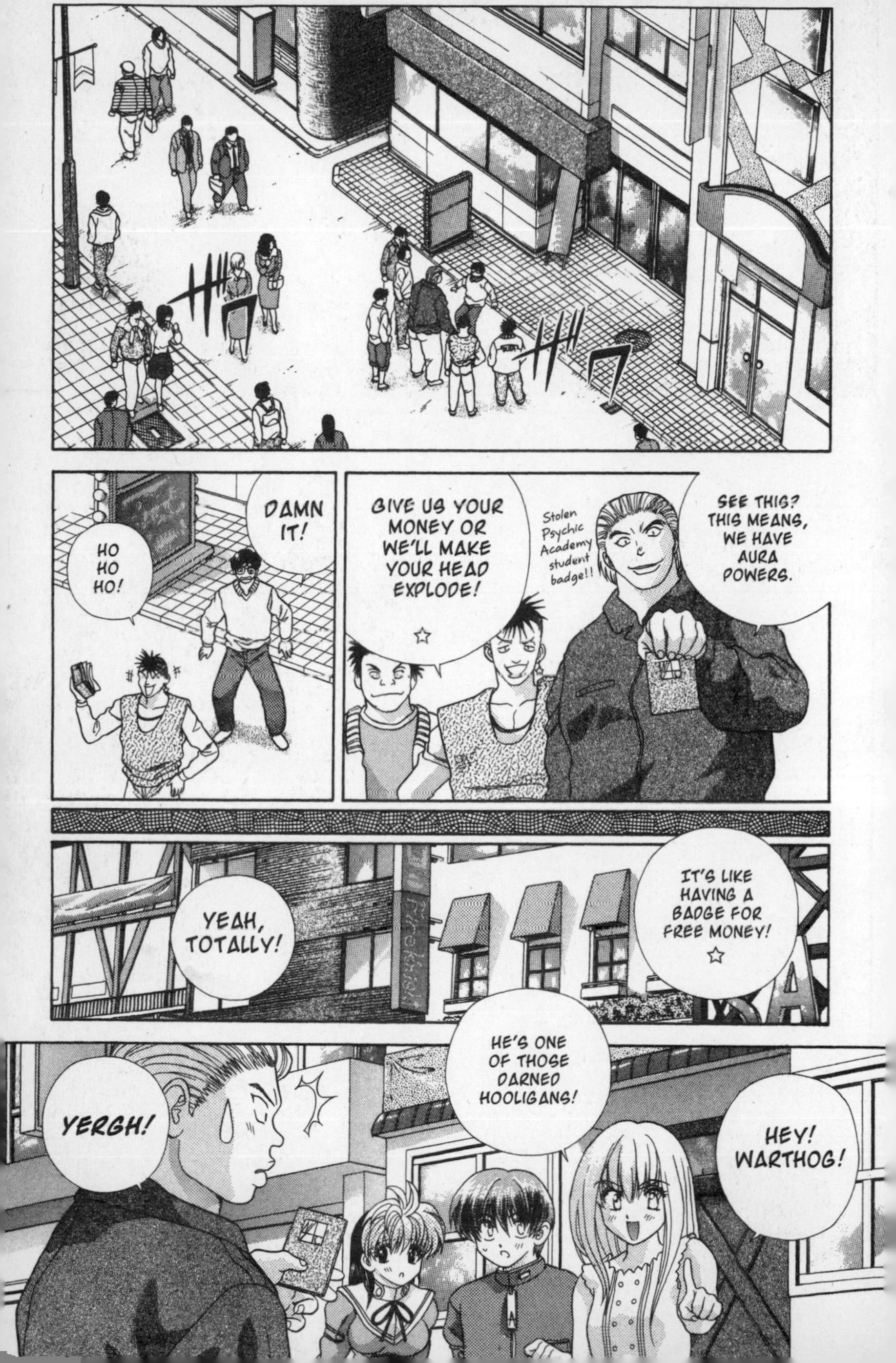
SEE THIS? THIS MEANS, WE HAVE AURA POWERS.
Stolen Psychic Academy student badge!!
GIVE US YOUR MONEY OR WE'LL MAKE YOUR HEAD EXPLODE! ☆
DAMN IT!
HO HO HO!
IT'S LIKE HAVING A BADGE FOR FREE MONEY! ☆
YEAH, TOTALLY!
HEY! WARTHOG!
HE'S ONE OF THOSE DARNED HOOLIGANS!
YERGH!

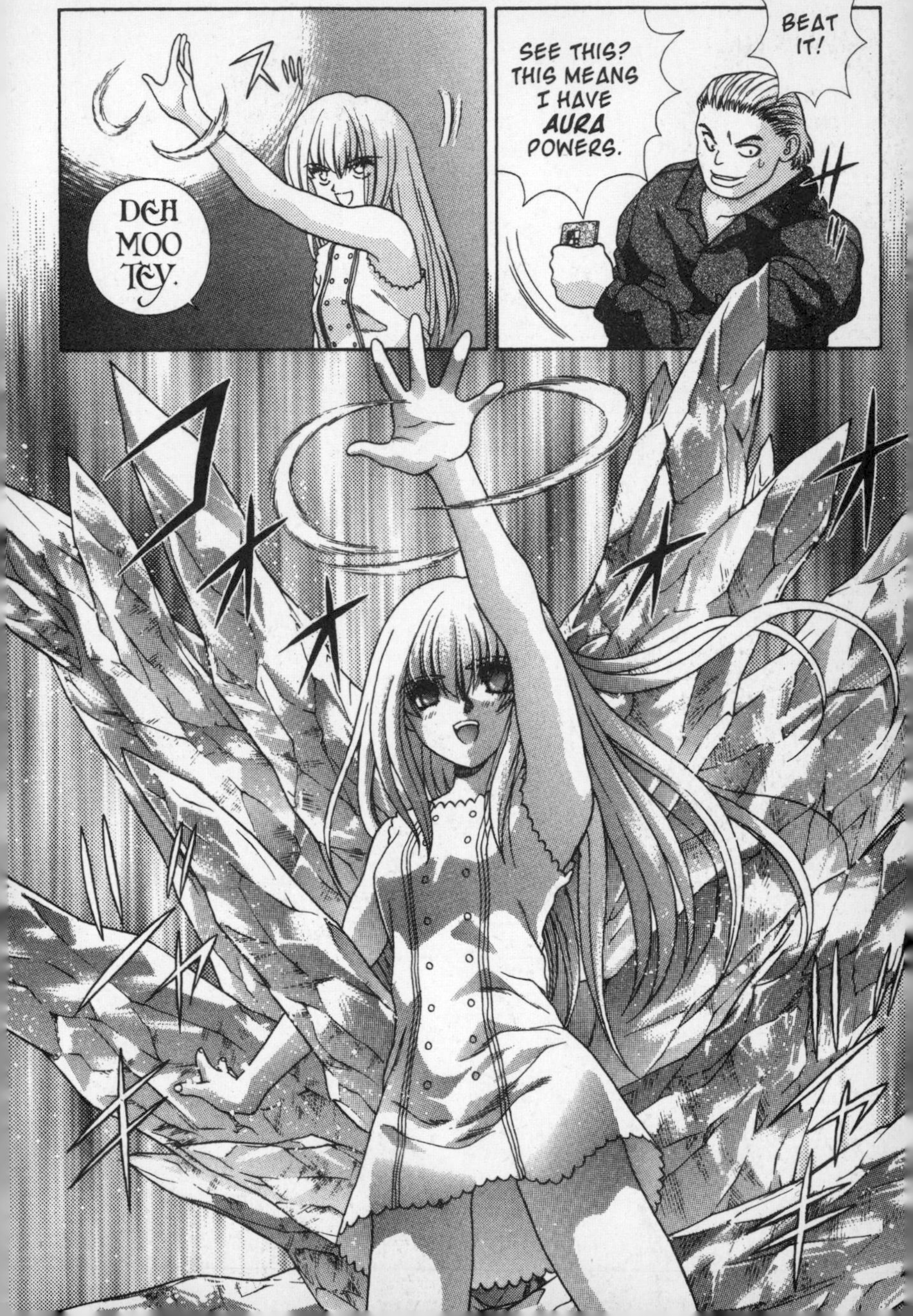
BEAT IT!
SEE THIS? THIS MEANS I HAVE **AURA** POWERS.
DEH MOO TEY.

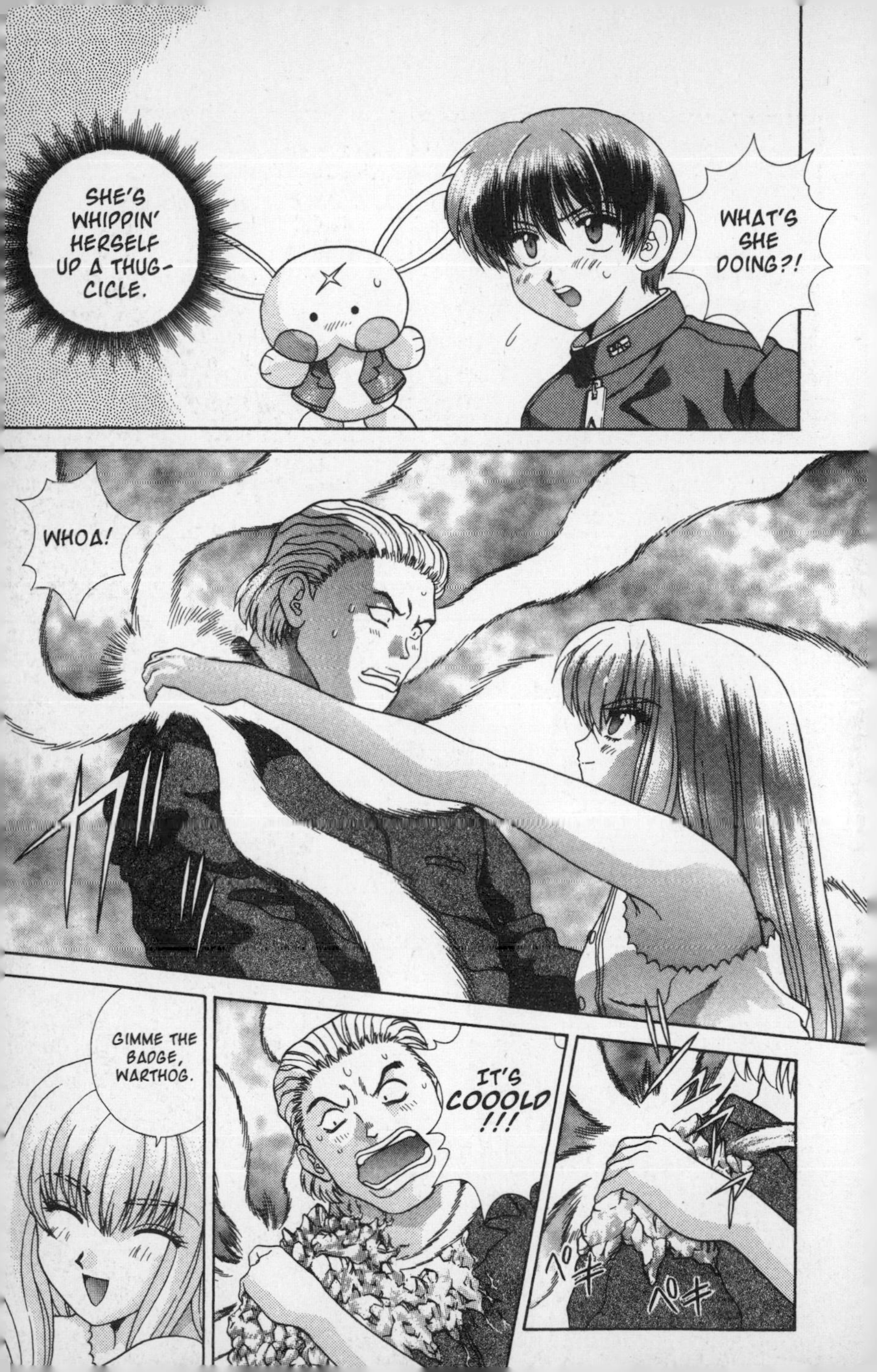
WHAT'S SHE DOING?!
SHE'S WHIPPIN' HERSELF UP A THUG-CICLE.
WHOA!
パキ
パキ
IT'S COOOLD!!!
GIMME THE BADGE, WARTHOG.

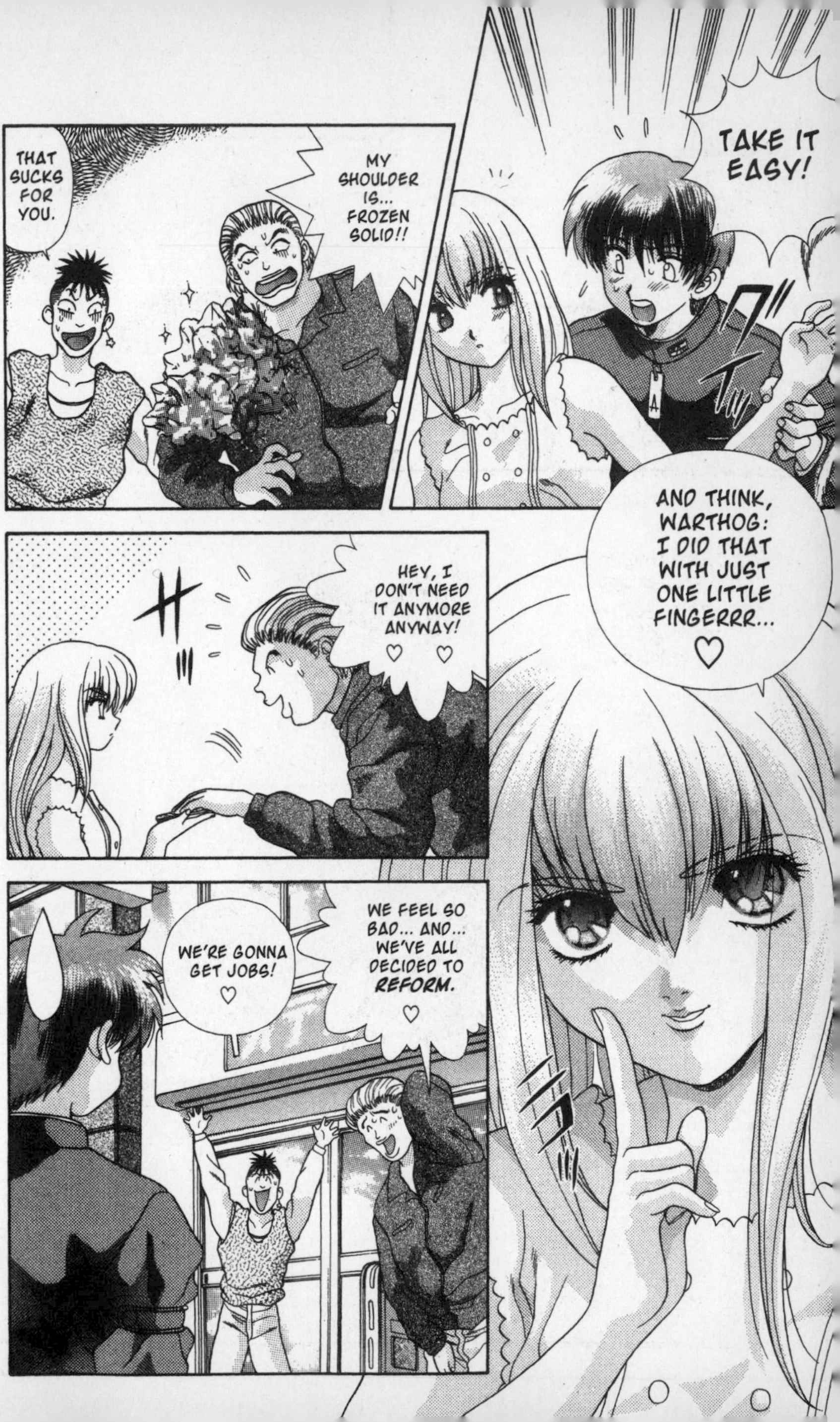
TAKE IT EASY!
MY SHOULDER IS... FROZEN SOLID!!
THAT SUCKS FOR YOU.
AND THINK, WARTHOG: I DID THAT WITH JUST ONE LITTLE FINGERRR... ♡
HEY, I DON'T NEED IT ANYMORE ANYWAY! ♡ ♡
WE FEEL SO BAD... AND... WE'VE ALL DECIDED TO **REFORM.** ♡
WE'RE GONNA GET JOBS! ♡

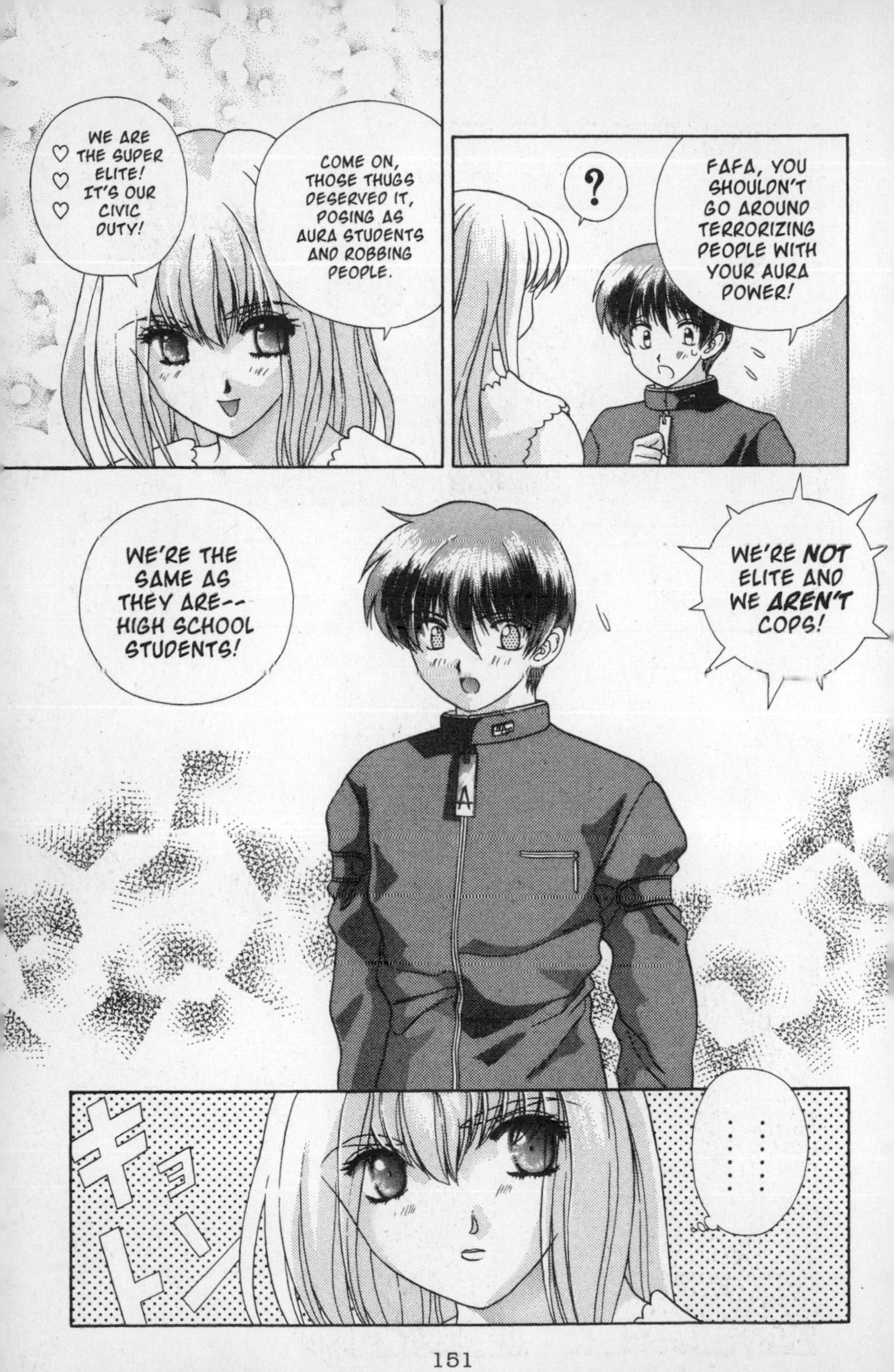
FAFA, YOU SHOULDN'T GO AROUND TERRORIZING PEOPLE WITH YOUR AURA POWER!
?
COME ON, THOSE THUGS DESERVED IT, POSING AS AURA STUDENTS AND ROBBING PEOPLE.
♡ ♡ ♡ WE ARE THE SUPER ELITE! IT'S OUR CIVIC DUTY!
WE'RE NOT ELITE AND WE AREN'T COPS!
WE'RE THE SAME AS THEY ARE--HIGH SCHOOL STUDENTS!
...
キョ

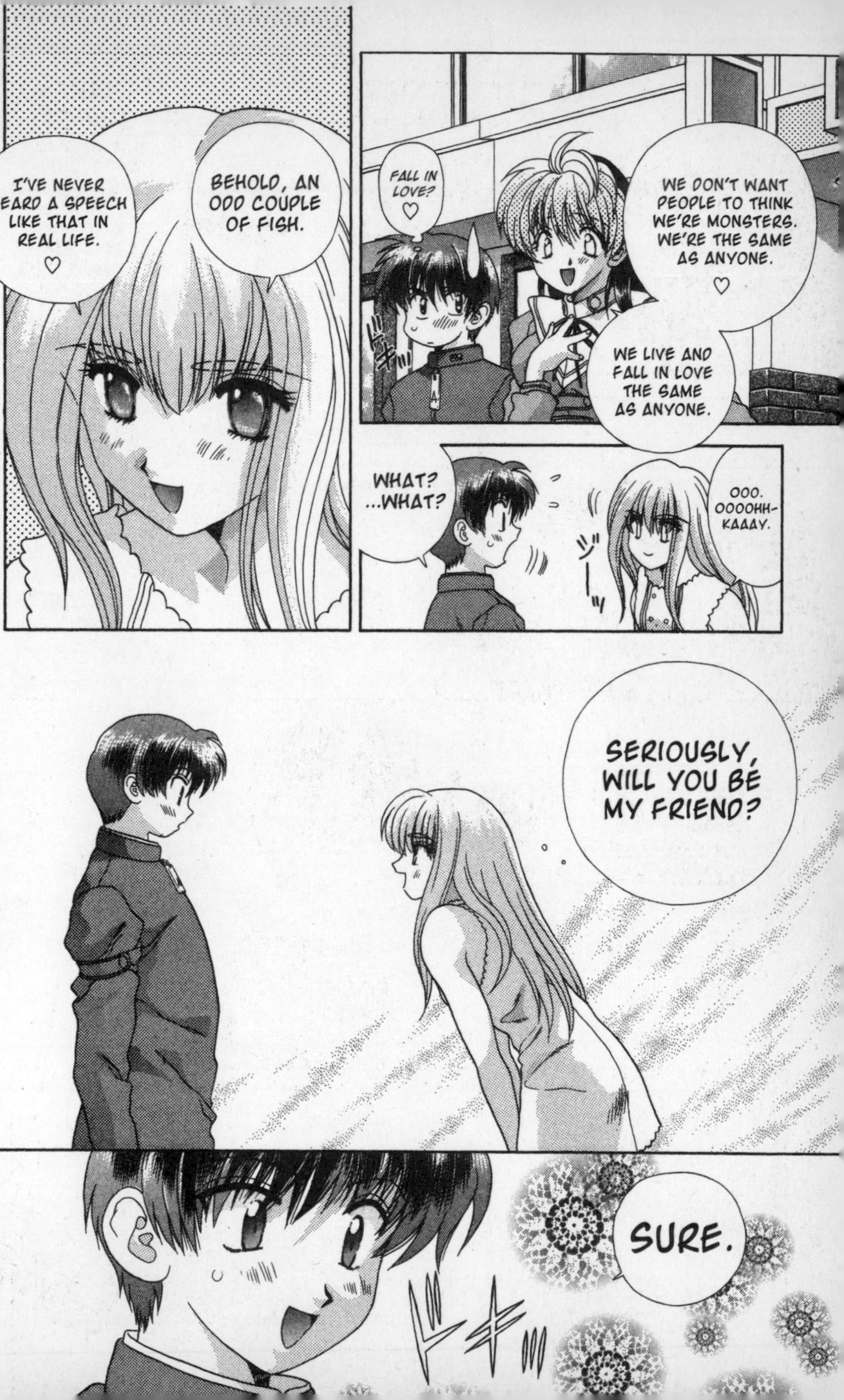
WE DON'T WANT PEOPLE TO THINK WE'RE MONSTERS. WE'RE THE SAME AS ANYONE. ♡
WE LIVE AND FALL IN LOVE THE SAME AS ANYONE.
FALL IN LOVE? ♡
OOO. OOOOHH-KAAAY.
WHAT? ...WHAT?
BEHOLD, AN ODD COUPLE OF FISH.
I'VE NEVER HEARD A SPEECH LIKE THAT IN REAL LIFE. ♡
SERIOUSLY, WILL YOU BE MY FRIEND?
SURE.

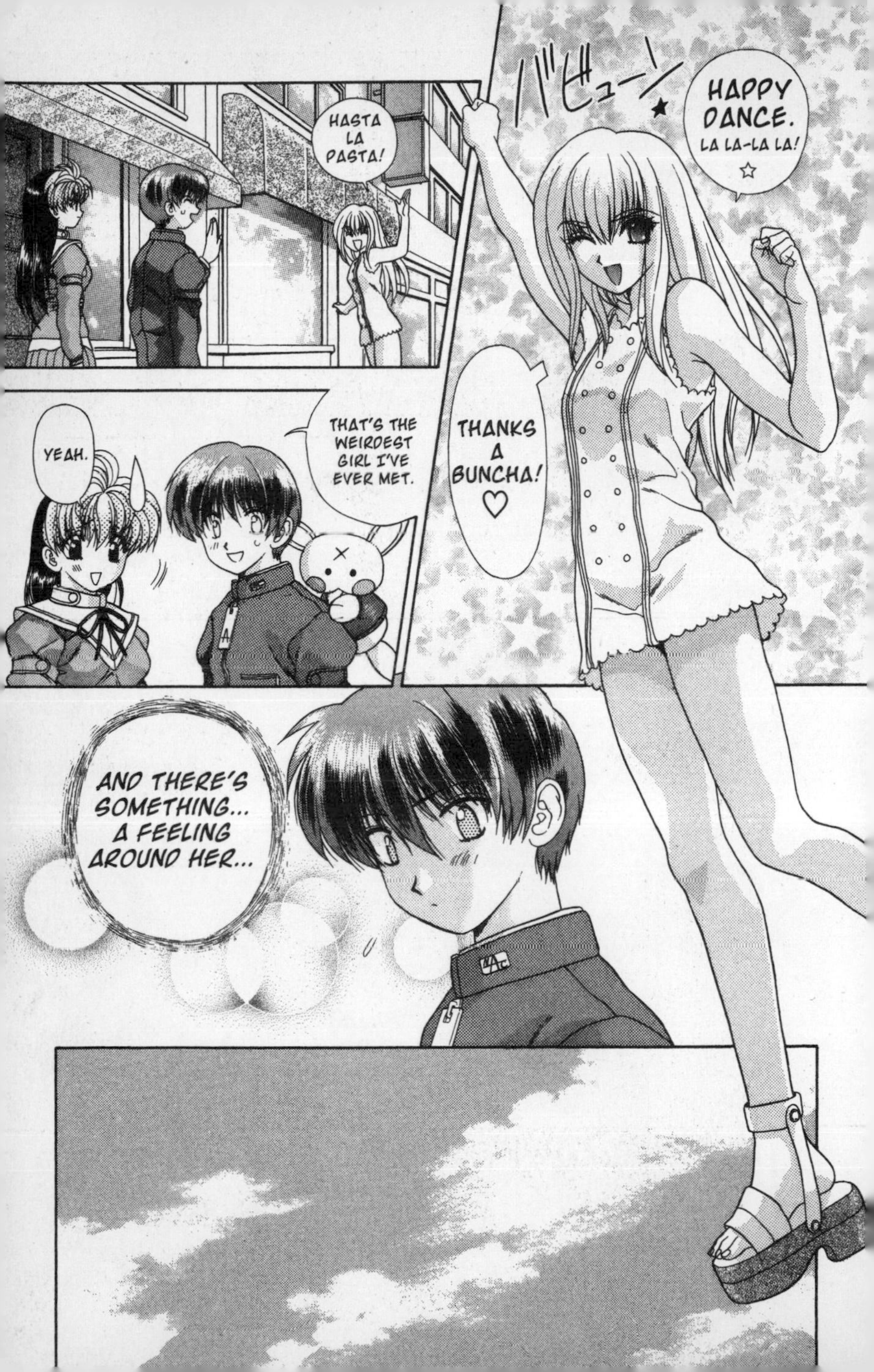
HAPPY DANCE. LA LA-LA LA! ☆
THANKS A BUNCHA! ♡
HASTA LA PASTA!
THAT'S THE WEIRDEST GIRL I'VE EVER MET.
YEAH.
AND THERE'S SOMETHING... A FEELING AROUND HER...

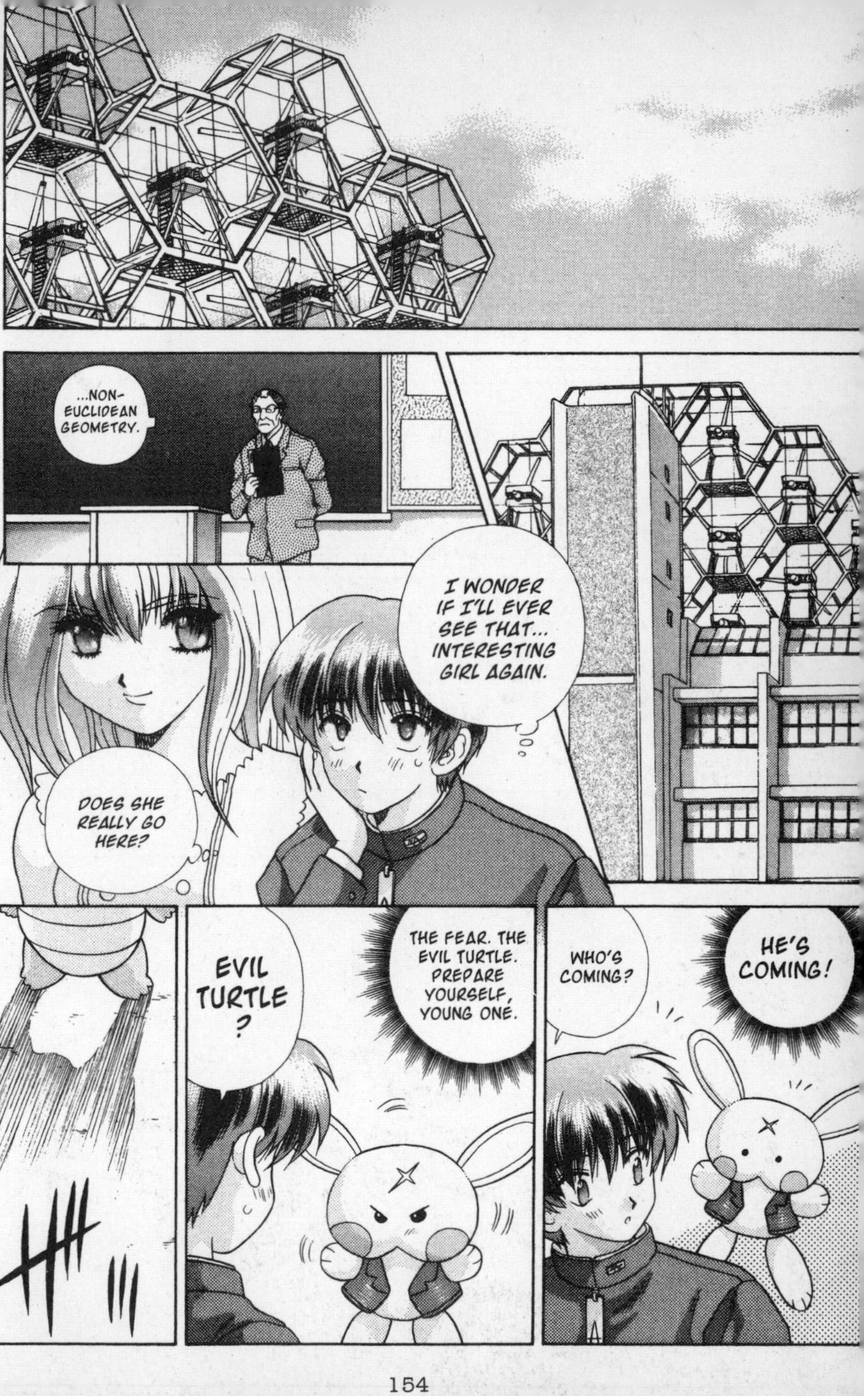
...NON-EUCLIDEAN GEOMETRY.
I WONDER IF I'LL EVER SEE THAT... INTERESTING GIRL AGAIN.
DOES SHE REALLY GO HERE?
HE'S COMING!
WHO'S COMING?
THE FEAR. THE EVIL TURTLE. PREPARE YOURSELF, YOUNG ONE.
EVIL TURTLE?

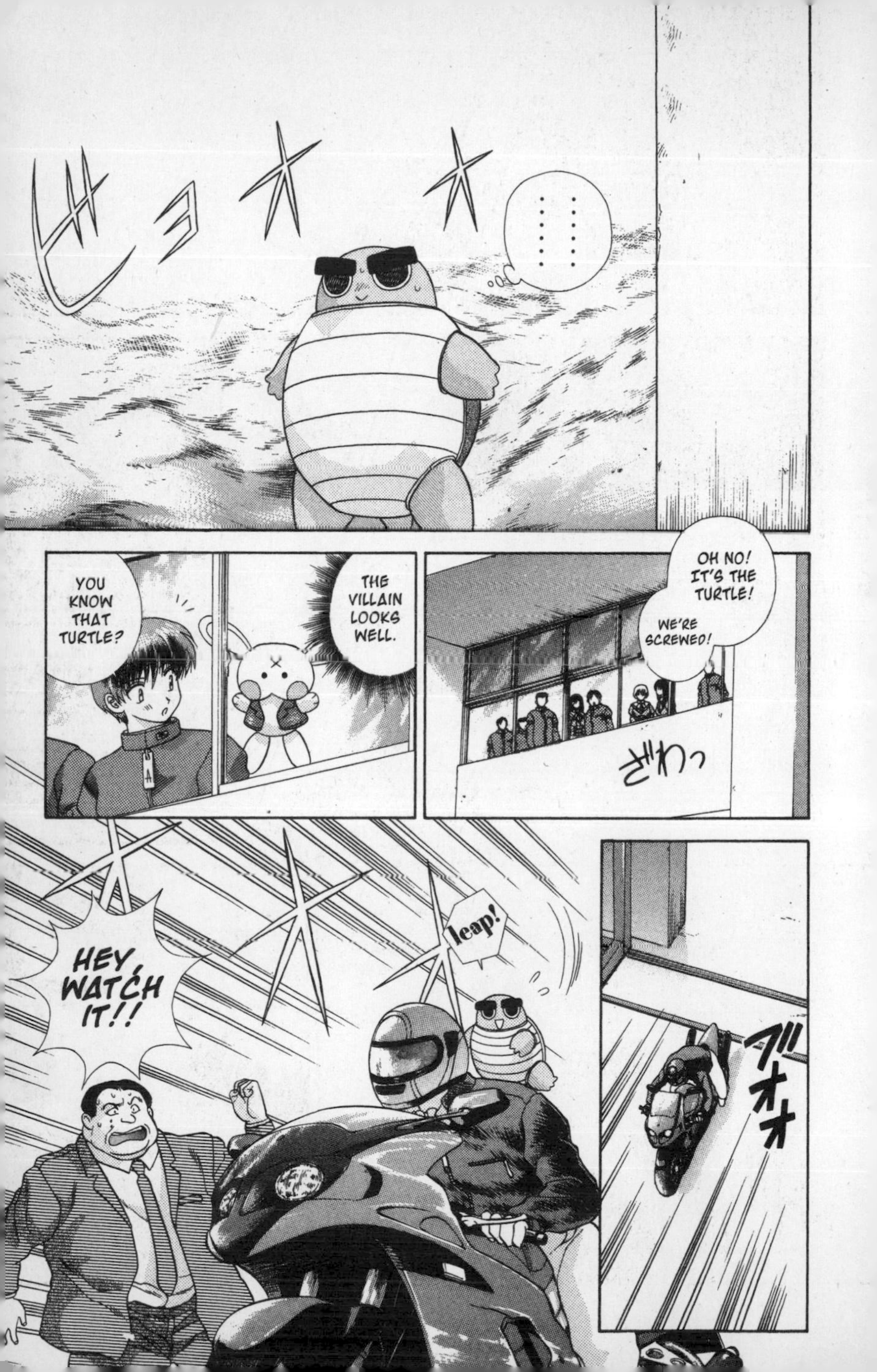
ビョオオ
......
OH NO! IT'S THE TURTLE!
WE'RE SCREWED!
ざわっ
THE VILLAIN LOOKS WELL.
YOU KNOW THAT TURTLE?
ブオオ
leap!
HEY, WATCH IT!!

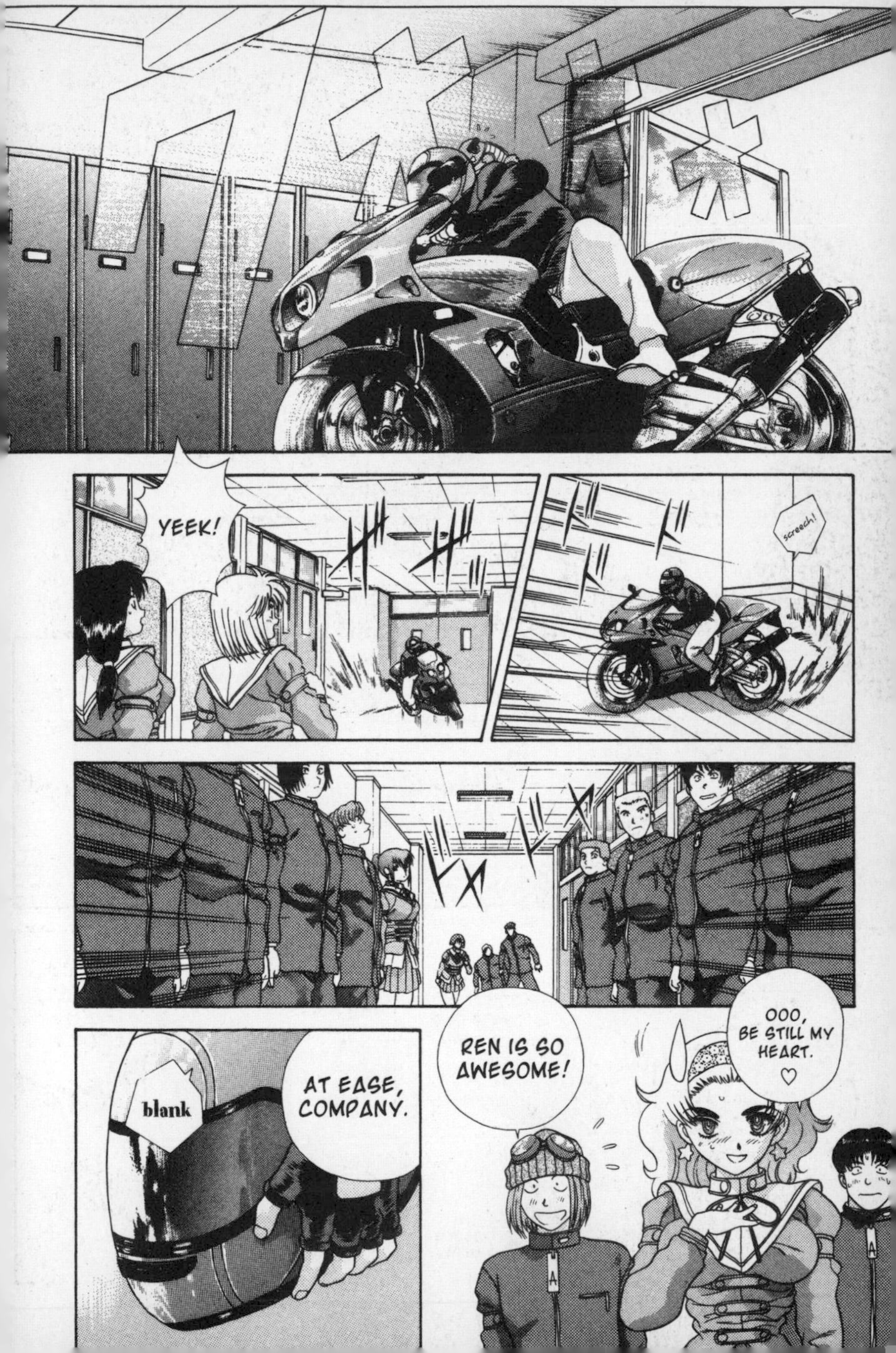
screech!
YEEK!
OOO, BE STILL MY HEART. ♡
REN IS SO AWESOME!
AT EASE, COMPANY.
blank

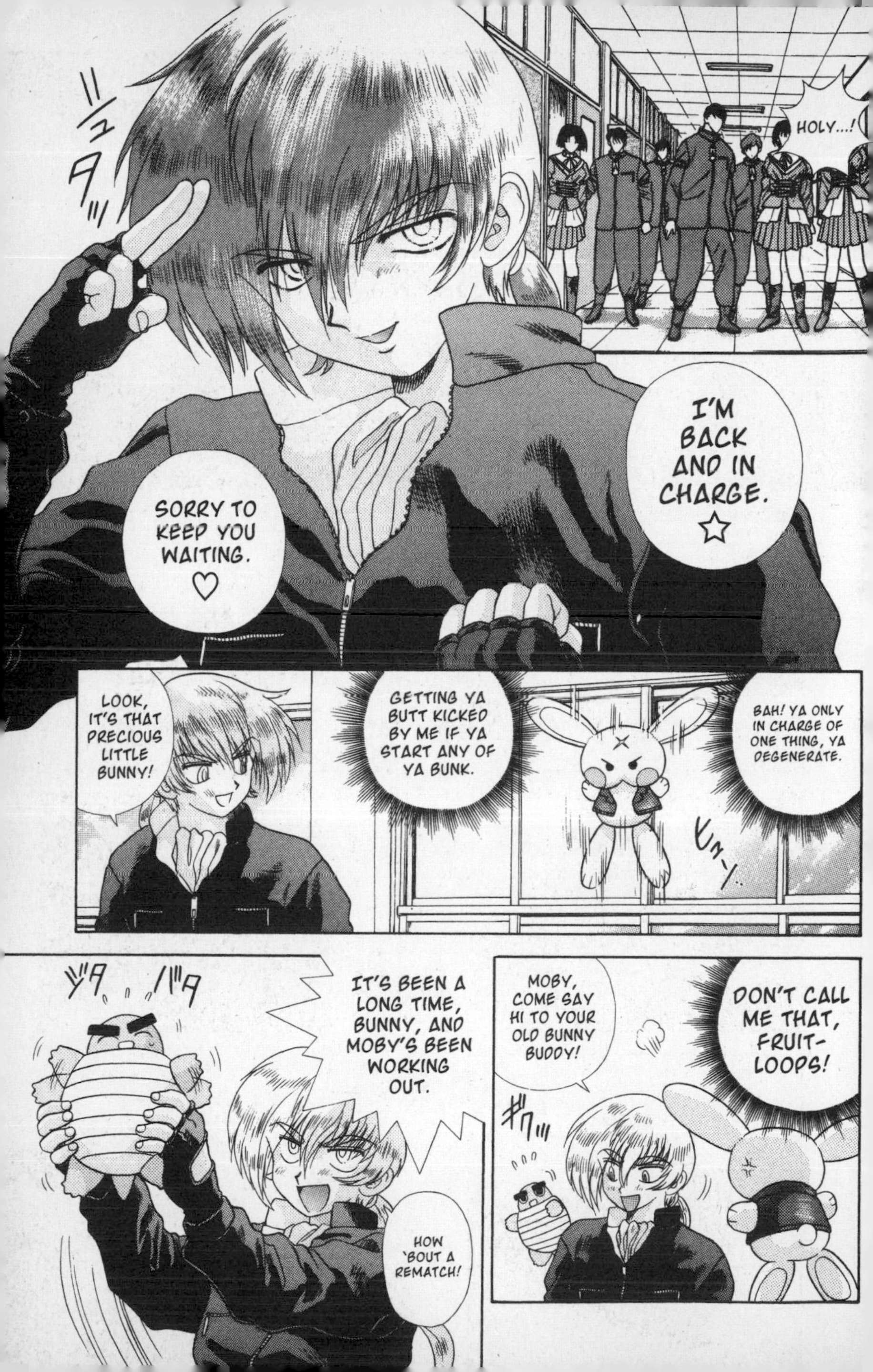
HOLY...!
I'M BACK AND IN CHARGE. ☆
SORRY TO KEEP YOU WAITING. ♡
BAH! YA ONLY IN CHARGE OF ONE THING, YA DEGENERATE.
GETTING YA BUTT KICKED BY ME IF YA START ANY OF YA BUNK.
LOOK, IT'S THAT PRECIOUS LITTLE BUNNY!
DON'T CALL ME THAT, FRUIT-LOOPS!
MOBY, COME SAY HI TO YOUR OLD BUNNY BUDDY!
IT'S BEEN A LONG TIME, BUNNY, AND MOBY'S BEEN WORKING OUT.
HOW 'BOUT A REMATCH!

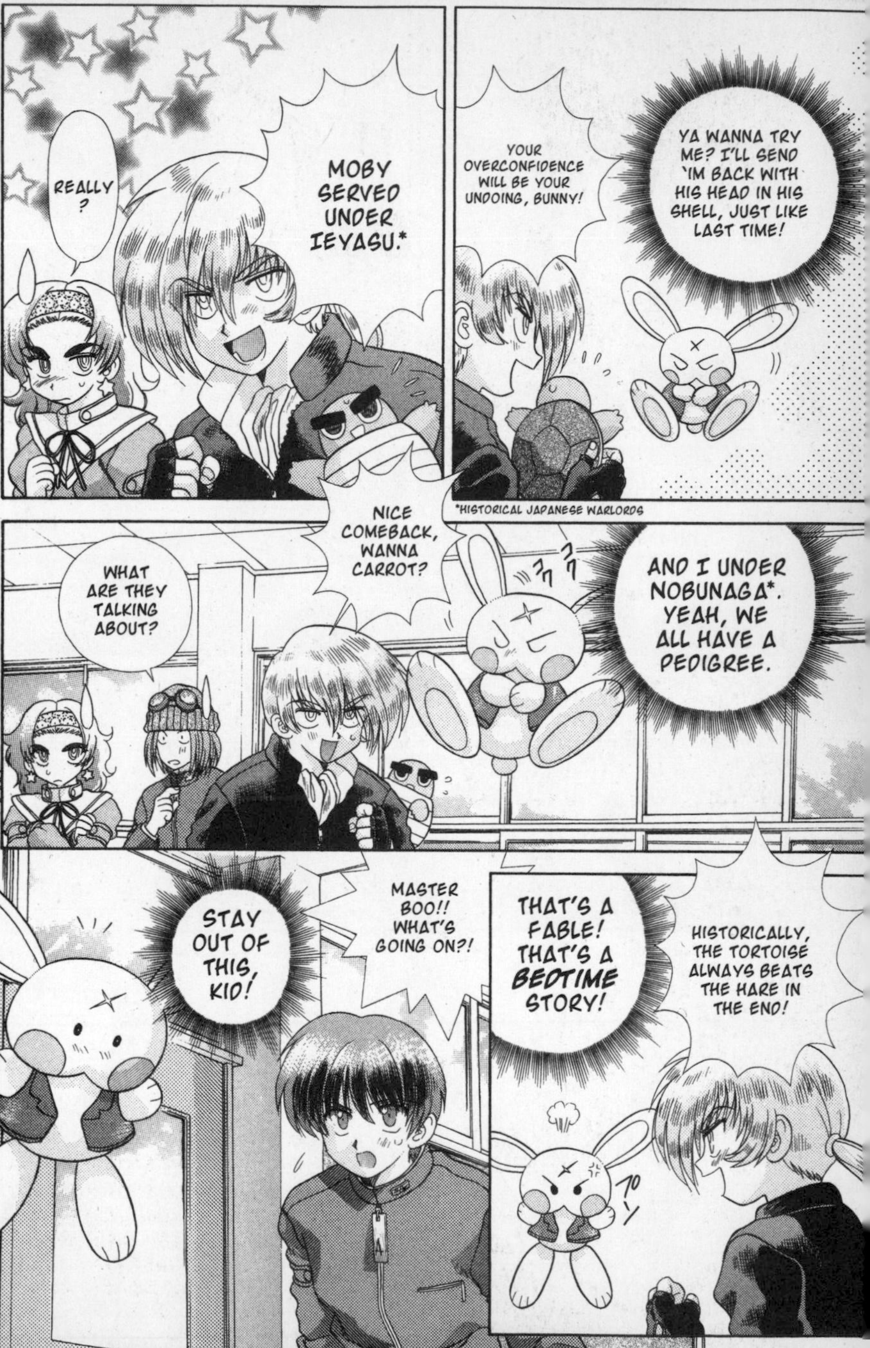
YA WANNA TRY ME? I'LL SEND 'IM BACK WITH HIS HEAD IN HIS SHELL, JUST LIKE LAST TIME!
YOUR OVERCONFIDENCE WILL BE YOUR UNDOING, BUNNY!
MOBY SERVED UNDER IEYASU.*
REALLY?
*HISTORICAL JAPANESE WARLORDS
AND I UNDER NOBUNAGA*. YEAH, WE ALL HAVE A PEDIGREE.
NICE COMEBACK, WANNA CARROT?
WHAT ARE THEY TALKING ABOUT?
HISTORICALLY, THE TORTOISE ALWAYS BEATS THE HARE IN THE END!
THAT'S A FABLE! THAT'S A BEDTIME STORY!
MASTER BOO!! WHAT'S GOING ON?!
STAY OUT OF THIS, KID!

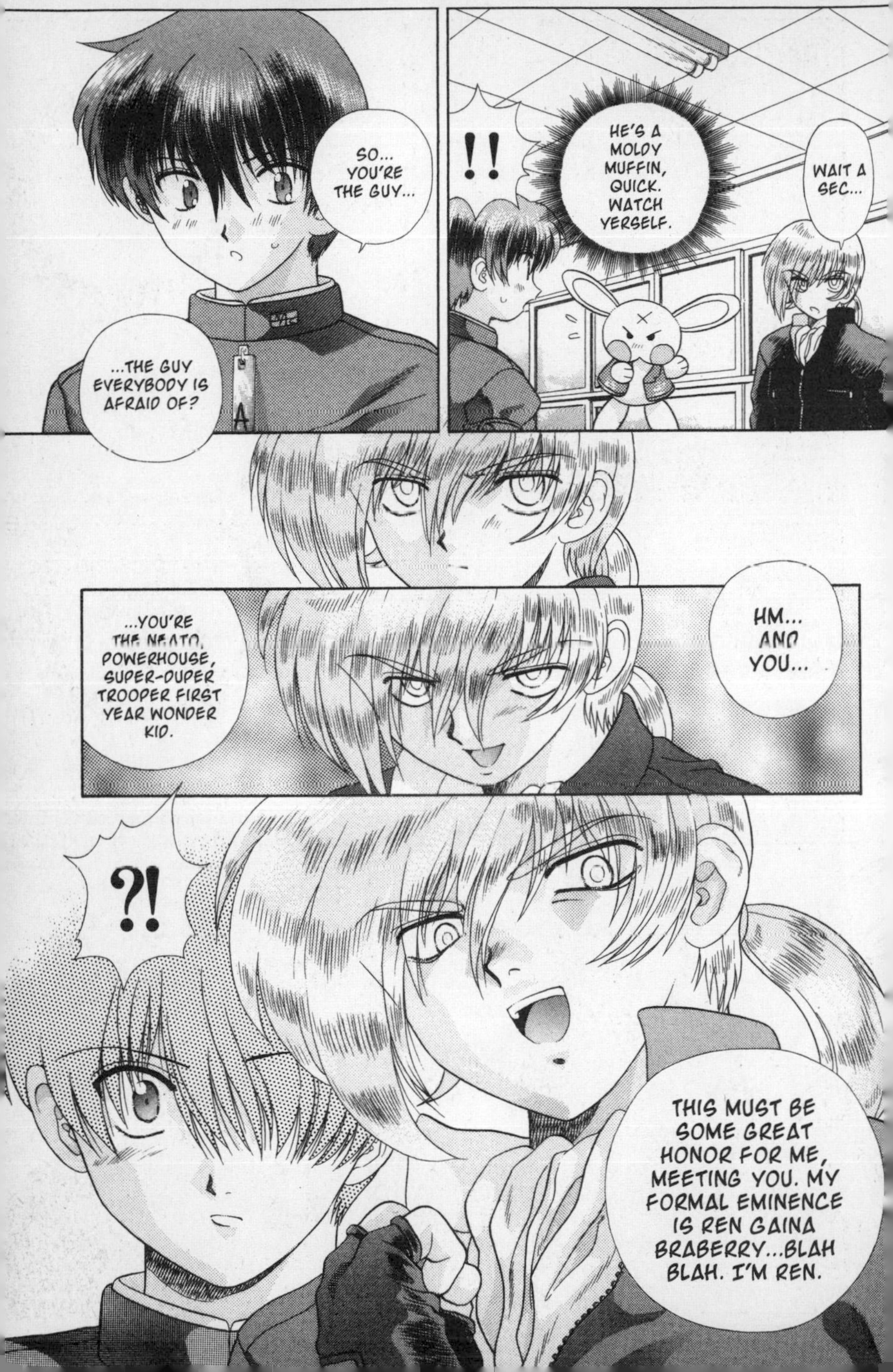
WAIT A SEC...
HE'S A MOLDY MUFFIN, QUICK. WATCH YERSELF.
!!
SO... YOU'RE THE GUY...
...THE GUY EVERYBODY IS AFRAID OF?
HM... AND YOU...
...YOU'RE THE NEATO, POWERHOUSE, SUPER-DUPER TROOPER FIRST YEAR WONDER KID.
?!
THIS MUST BE SOME GREAT HONOR FOR ME, MEETING YOU. MY FORMAL EMINENCE IS REN GAINA BRABERRY...BLAH BLAH. I'M REN.

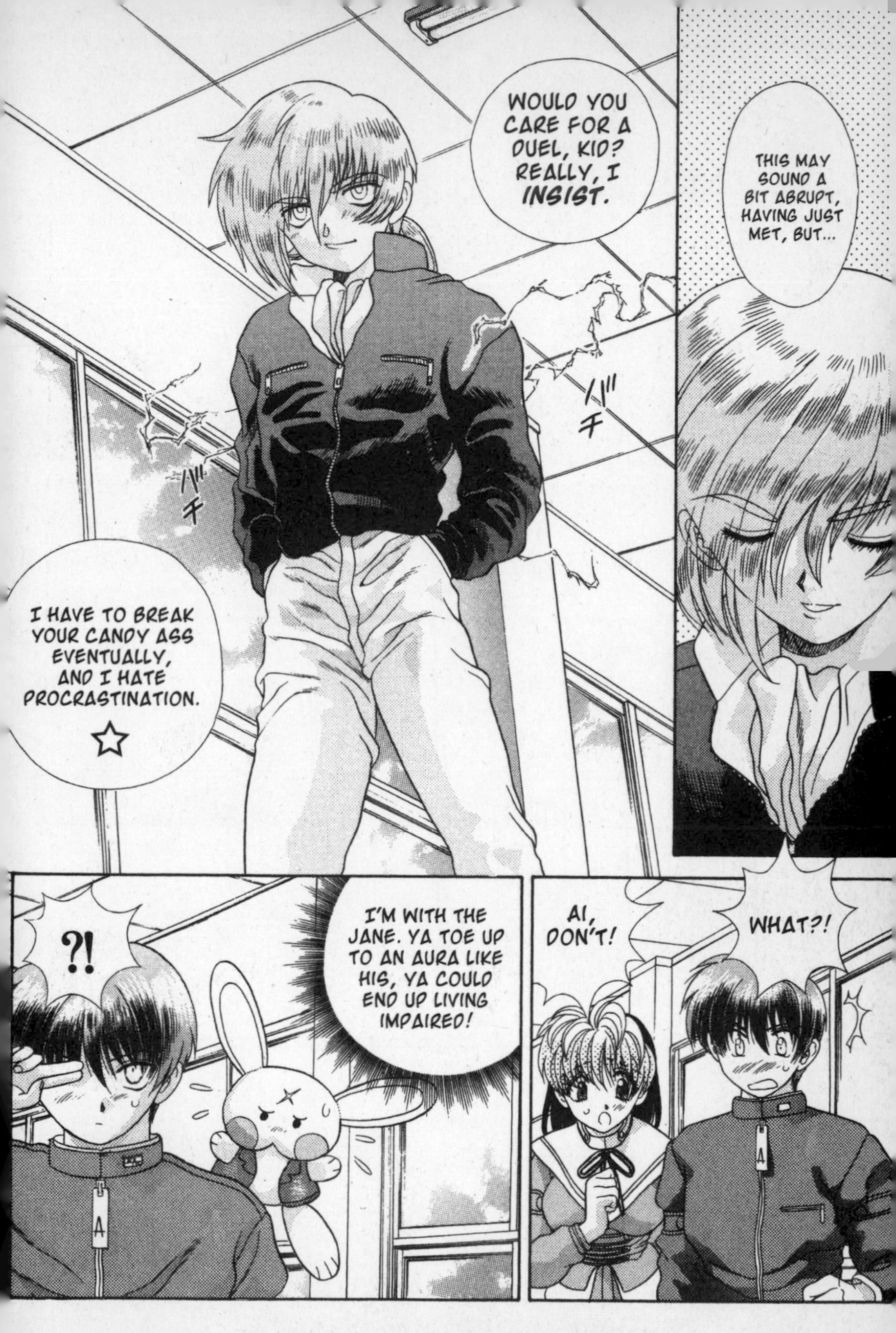
THIS MAY SOUND A BIT ABRUPT, HAVING JUST MET, BUT...
WOULD YOU CARE FOR A DUEL, KID? REALLY, I **INSIST**.
バチ
バチ
I HAVE TO BREAK YOUR CANDY ASS EVENTUALLY, AND I HATE PROCRASTINATION. ☆
WHAT?!
AI, DON'T!
I'M WITH THE JANE. YA TOE UP TO AN AURA LIKE HIS, YA COULD END UP LIVING IMPAIRED!
?!

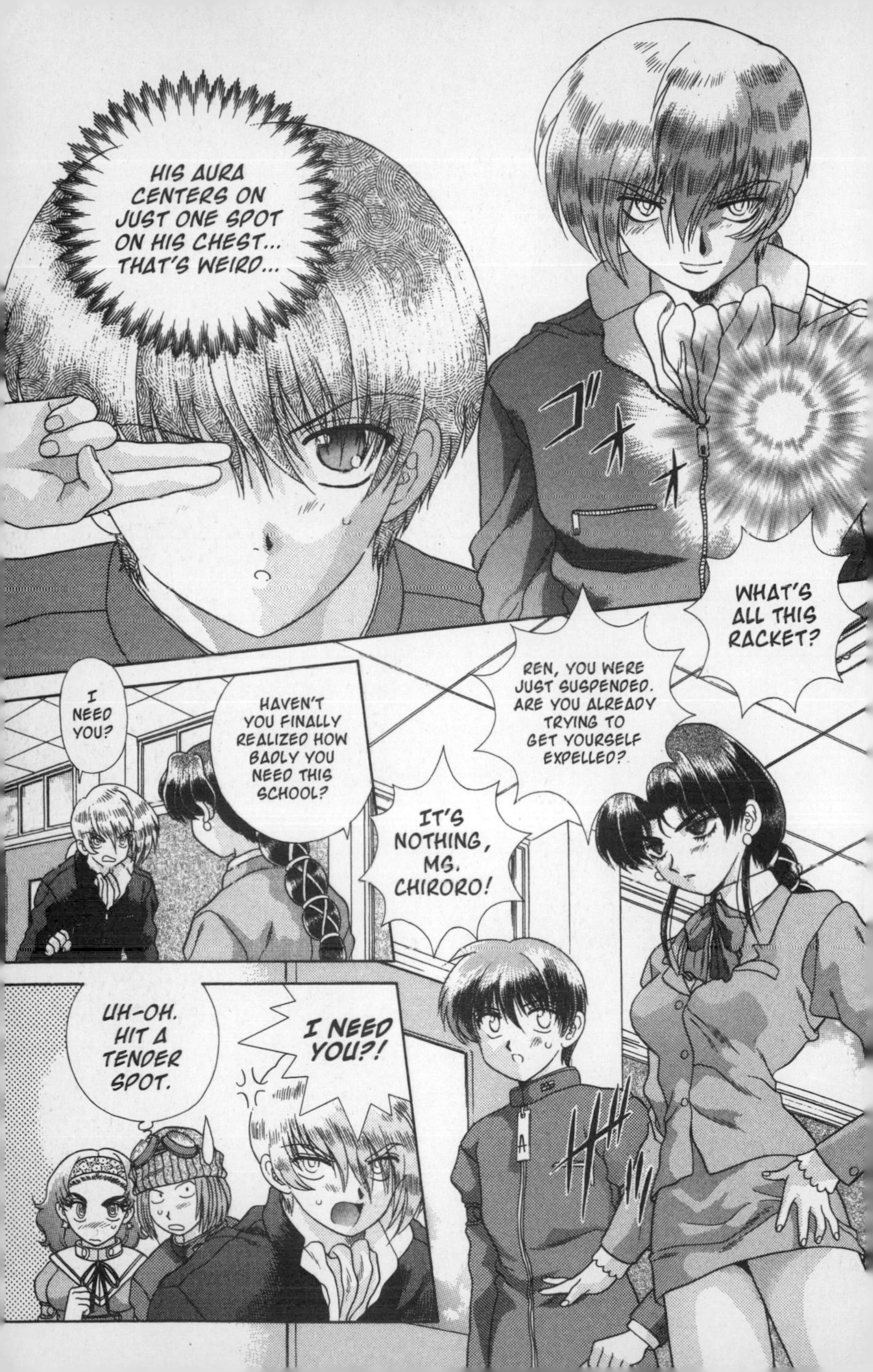
ゴオオ
WHAT'S ALL THIS RACKET?
HIS AURA CENTERS ON JUST ONE SPOT ON HIS CHEST... THAT'S WEIRD...
REN, YOU WERE JUST SUSPENDED. ARE YOU ALREADY TRYING TO GET YOURSELF EXPELLED?
IT'S NOTHING, MS. CHIRORO!
HAVEN'T YOU FINALLY REALIZED HOW BADLY YOU NEED THIS SCHOOL?
I NEED YOU?
I NEED YOU?!
UH-OH. HIT A TENDER SPOT.

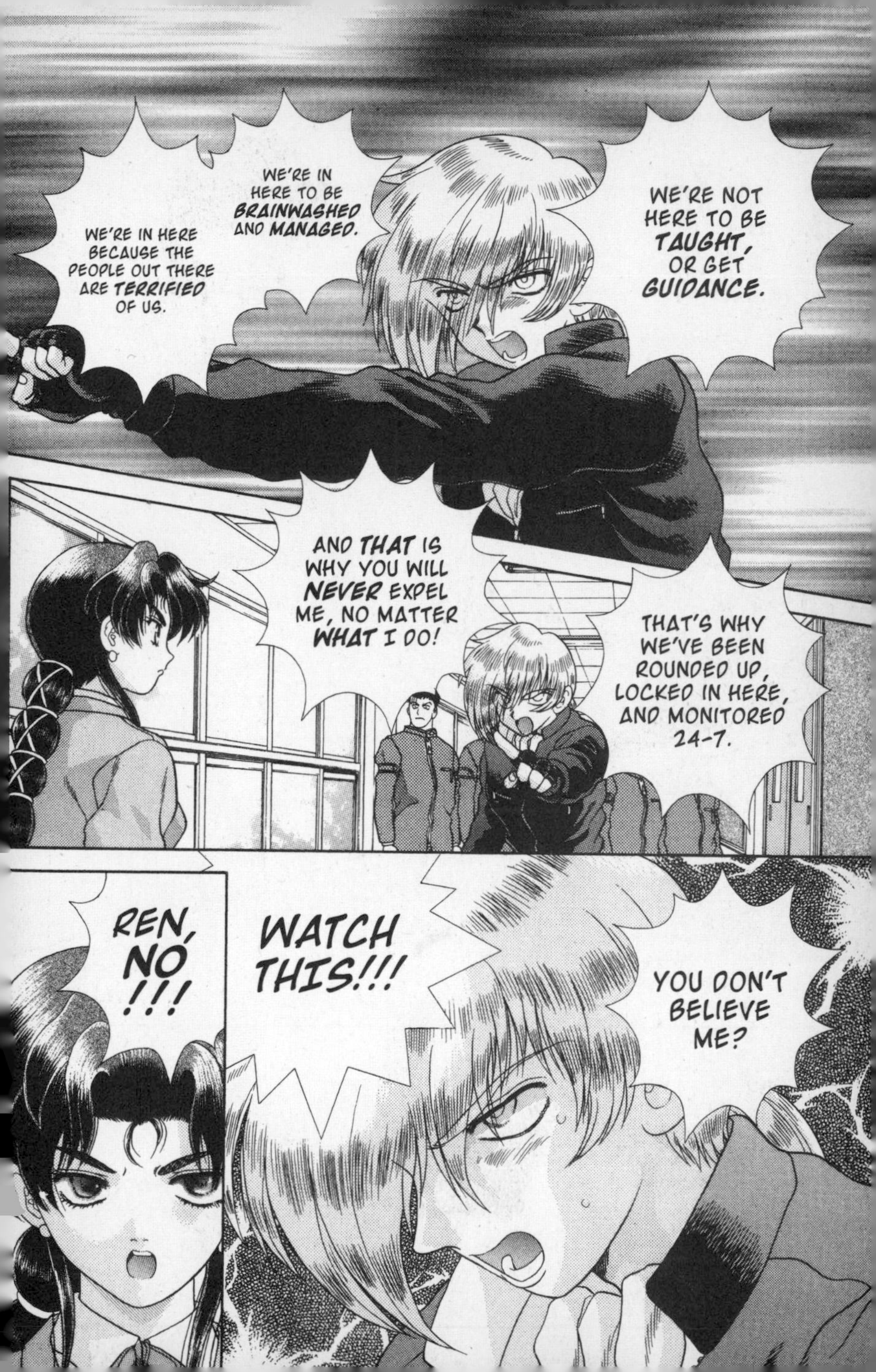
WE'RE NOT HERE TO BE TAUGHT, OR GET GUIDANCE.
WE'RE IN HERE TO BE BRAINWASHED AND MANAGED.
WE'RE IN HERE BECAUSE THE PEOPLE OUT THERE ARE TERRIFIED OF US.
THAT'S WHY WE'VE BEEN ROUNDED UP, LOCKED IN HERE, AND MONITORED 24-7.
AND THAT IS WHY YOU WILL NEVER EXPEL ME, NO MATTER WHAT I DO!
YOU DON'T BELIEVE ME?
WATCH THIS!!!
REN, NO!!!

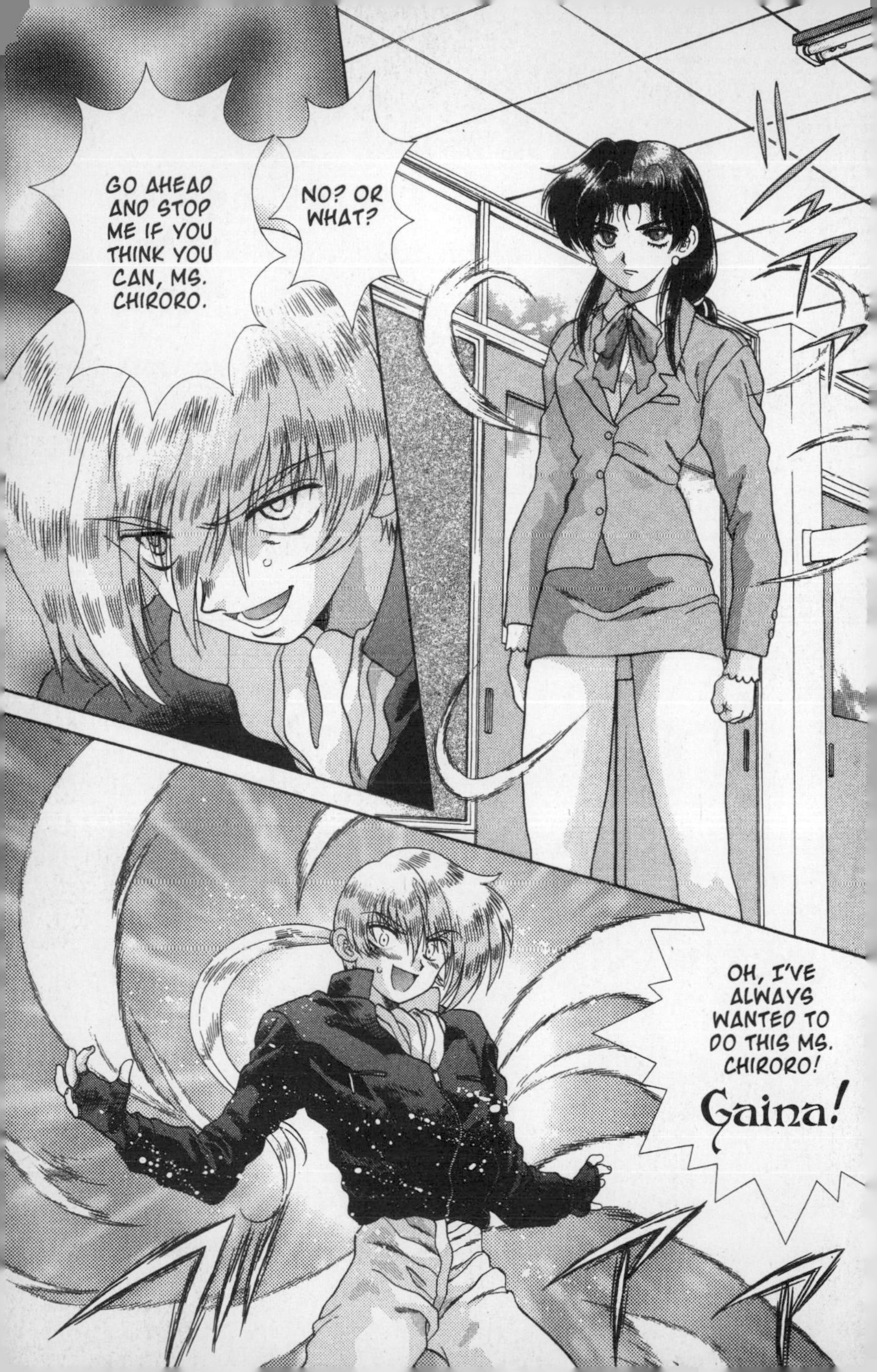
NO? OR WHAT?
GO AHEAD AND STOP ME IF YOU THINK YOU CAN, MS. CHIRORO.
OH, I'VE ALWAYS WANTED TO DO THIS MS. CHIRORO!
Gaina!

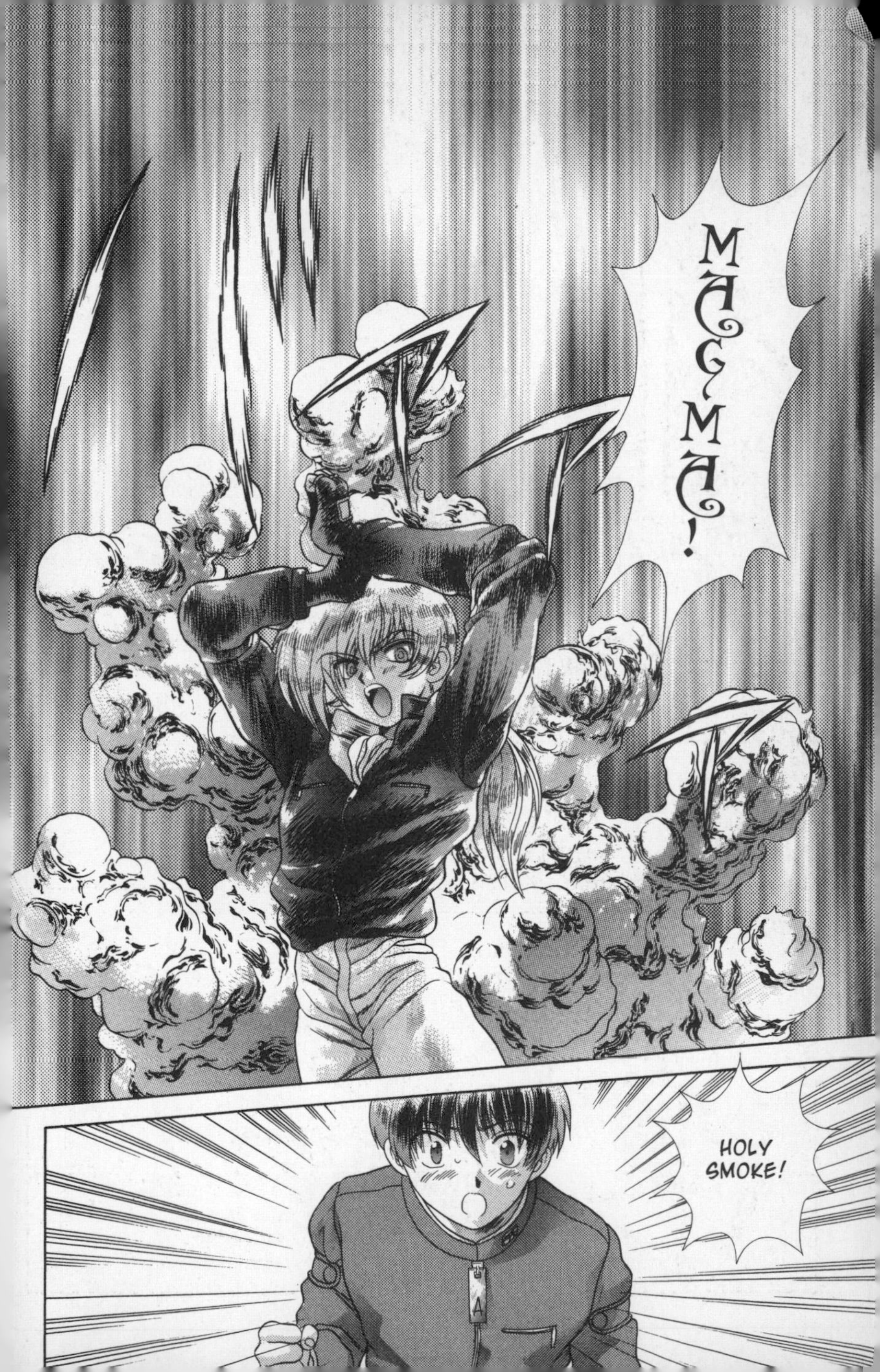
MAGMA!
HOLY SMOKE!

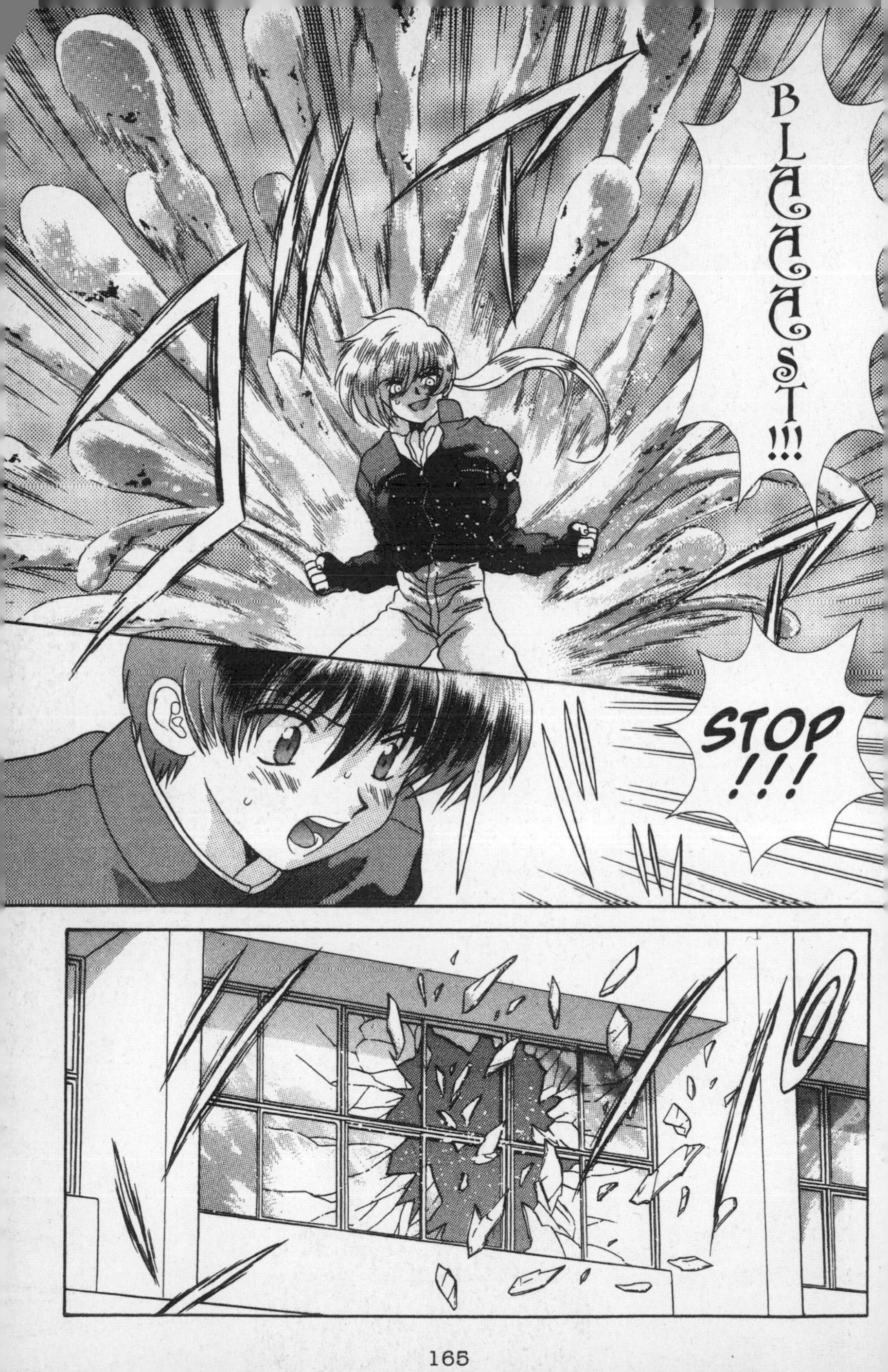
BLAAAST!!!
STOP!!!

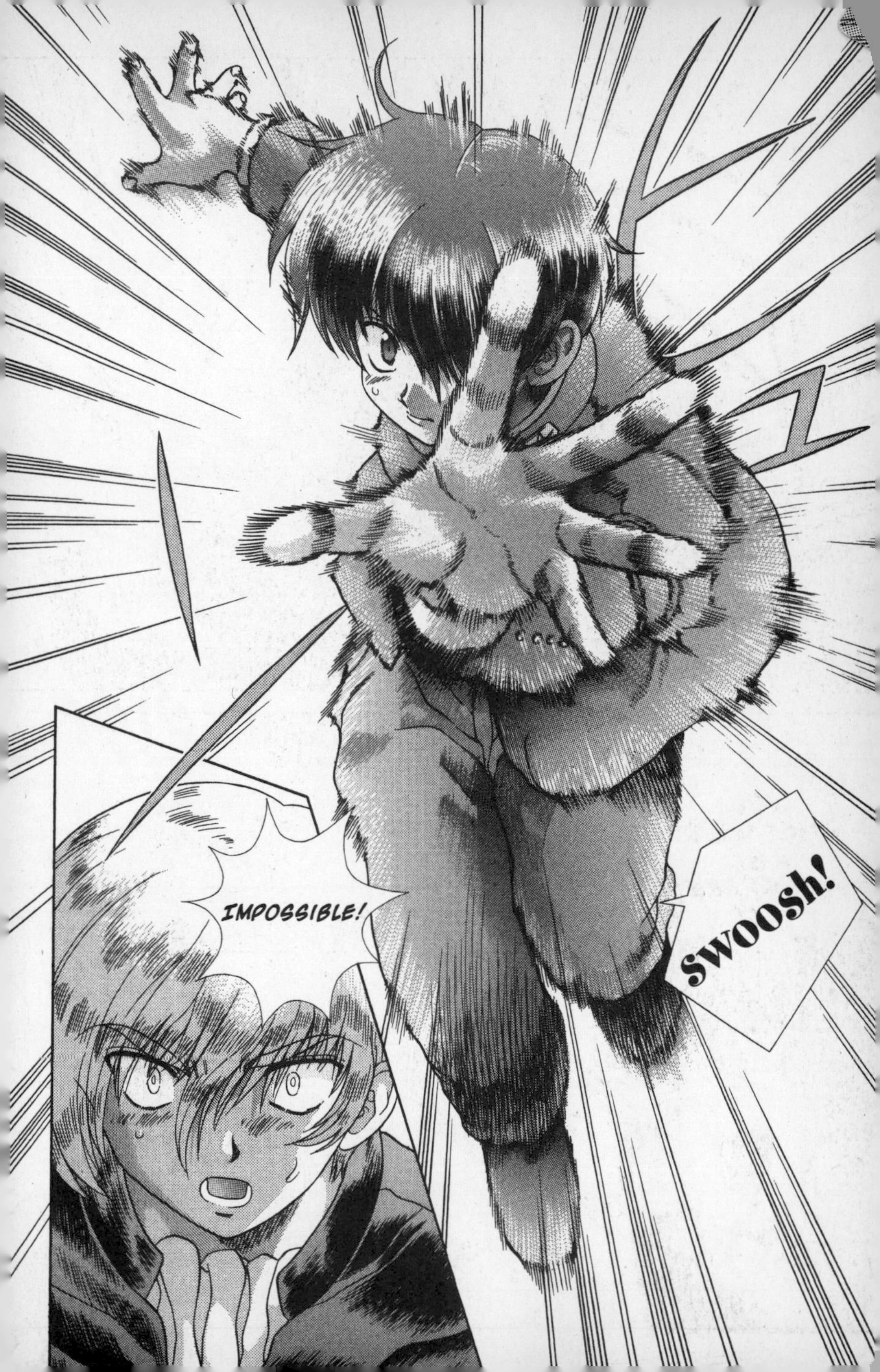
SWOOSH!
IMPOSSIBLE!

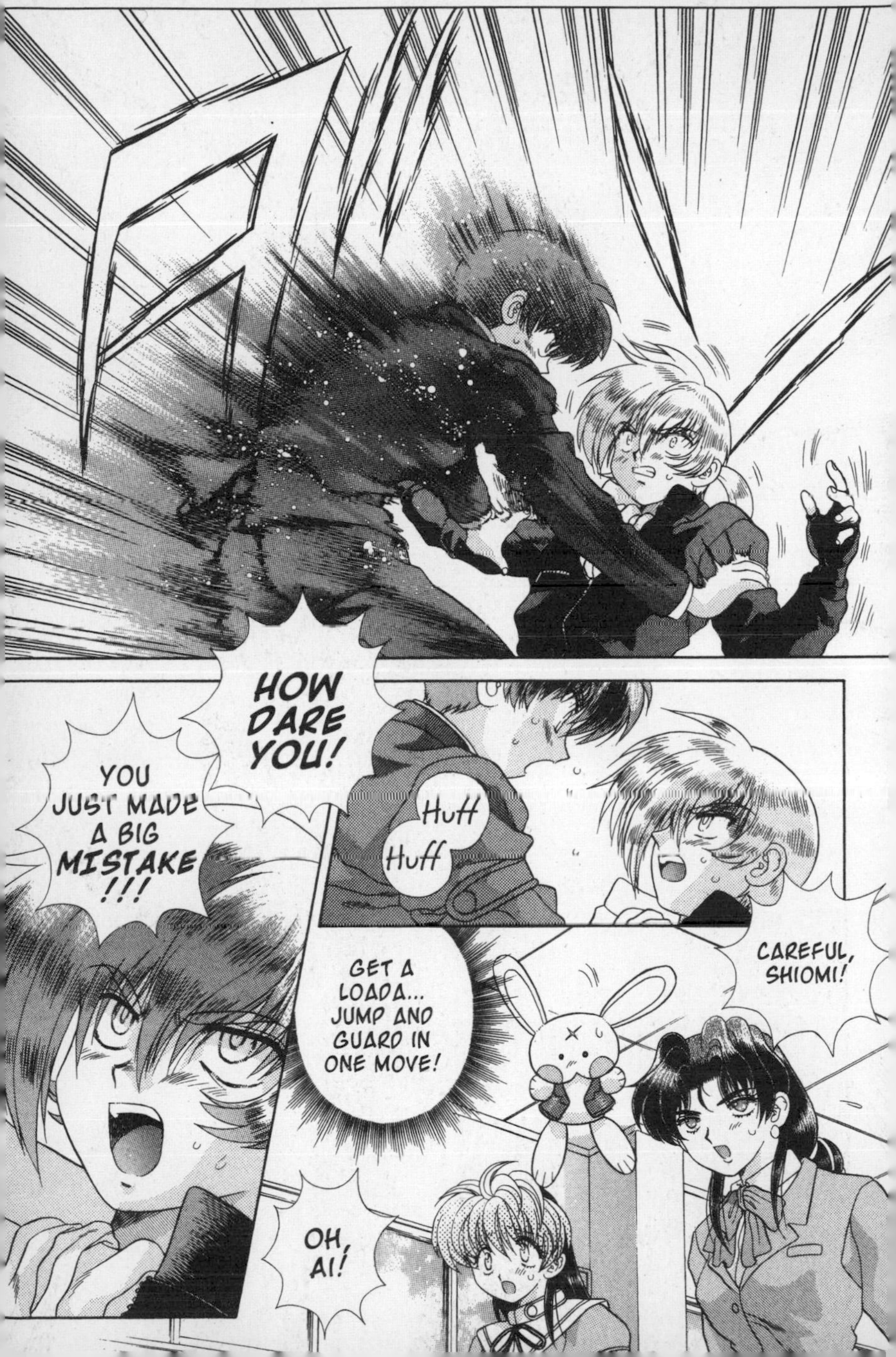
HOW DARE YOU!
Huff
Huff
YOU JUST MADE A BIG MISTAKE!!!
CAREFUL, SHIOMI!
GET A LOADA... JUMP AND GUARD IN ONE MOVE!
OH, AI!

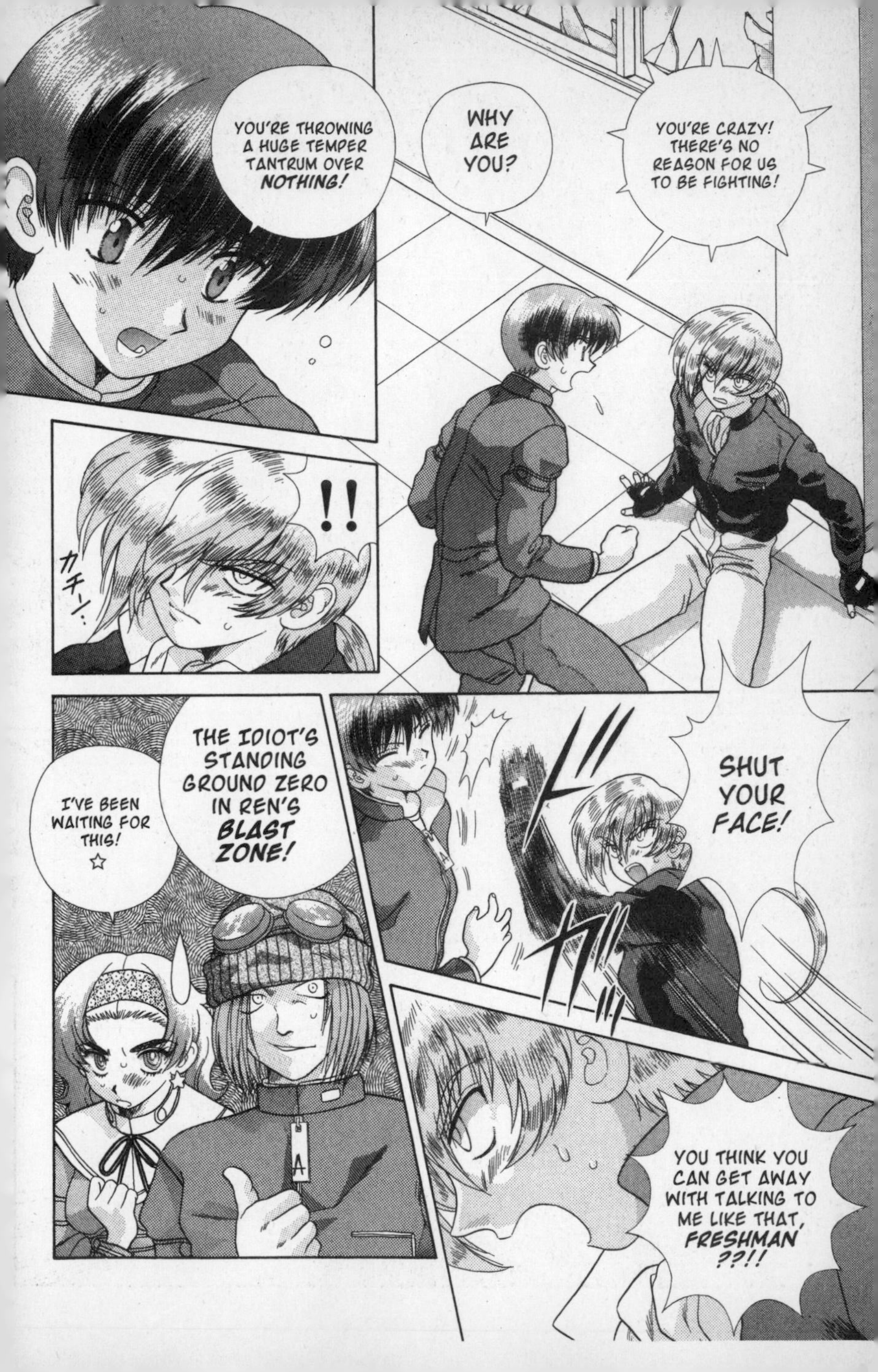
YOU'RE CRAZY! THERE'S NO REASON FOR US TO BE FIGHTING!
WHY ARE YOU?
YOU'RE THROWING A HUGE TEMPER TANTRUM OVER *NOTHING!*
!!
カチーン
SHUT YOUR *FACE!*
YOU THINK YOU CAN GET AWAY WITH TALKING TO ME LIKE THAT, *FRESHMAN* ??!!
THE IDIOT'S STANDING GROUND ZERO IN REN'S *BLAST ZONE!*
I'VE BEEN WAITING FOR THIS! ☆

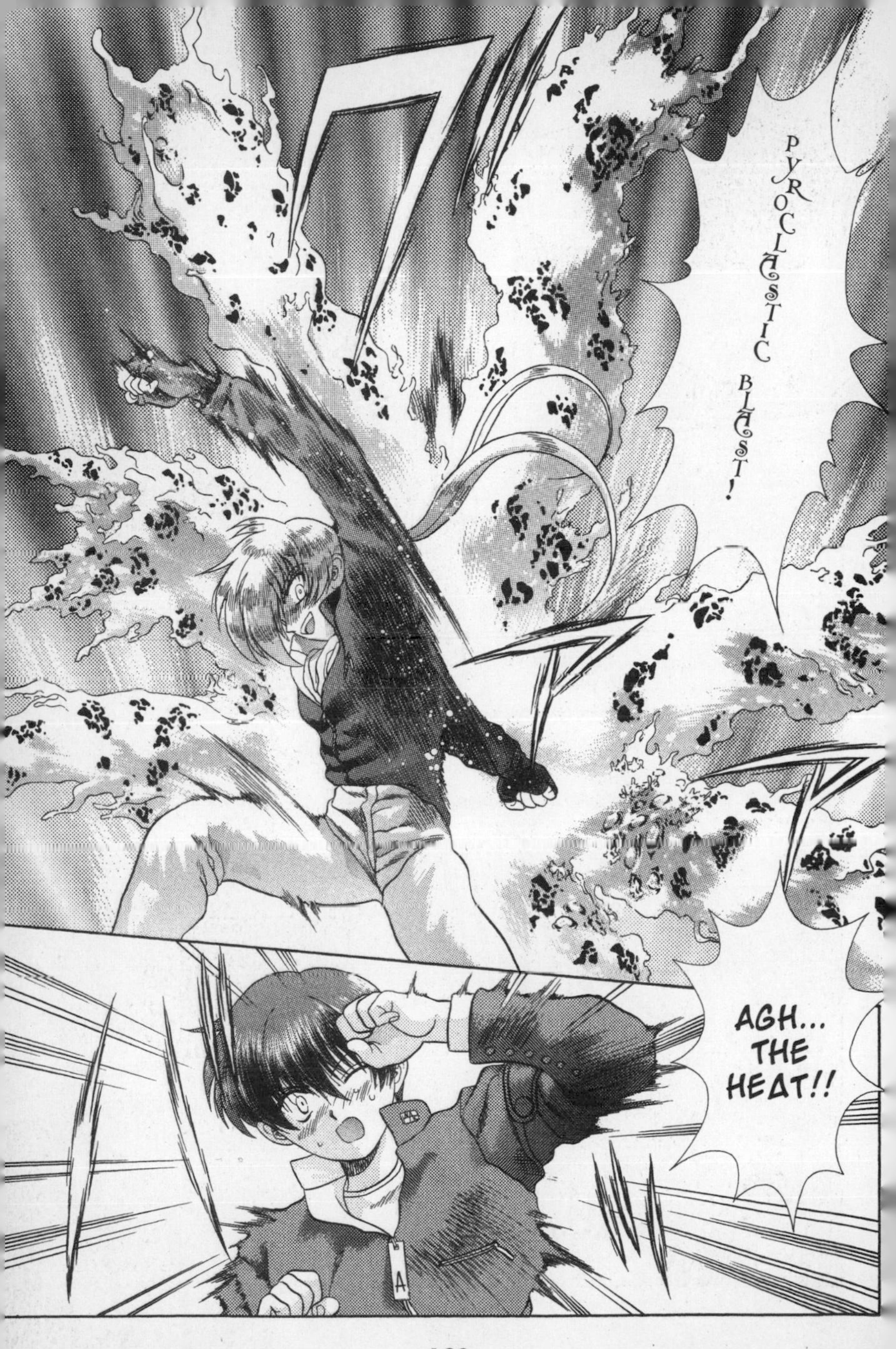
PYROCLASTIC BLAST!
AGH... THE HEAT!!

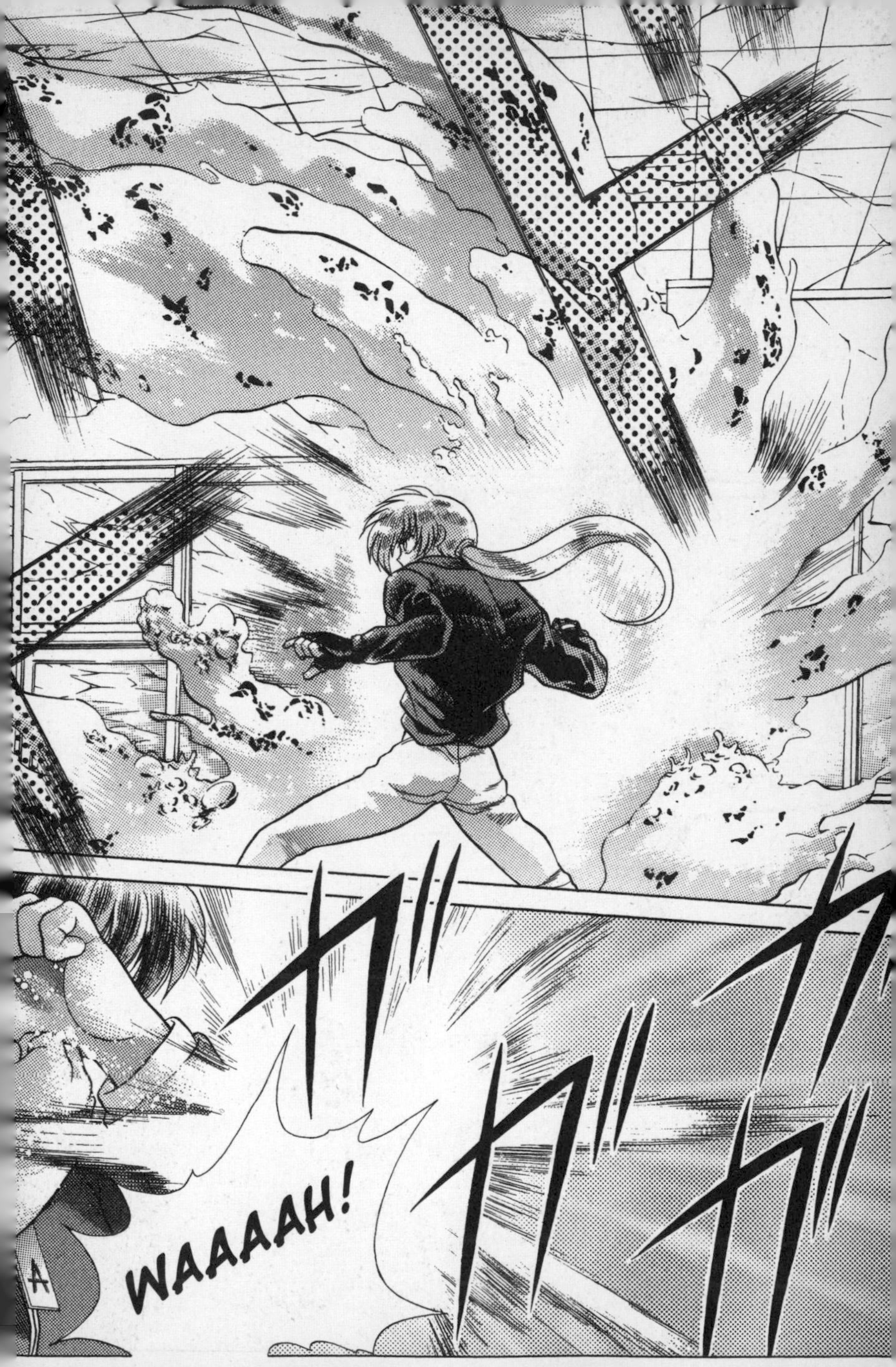
ガガガガ
WAAAAH!

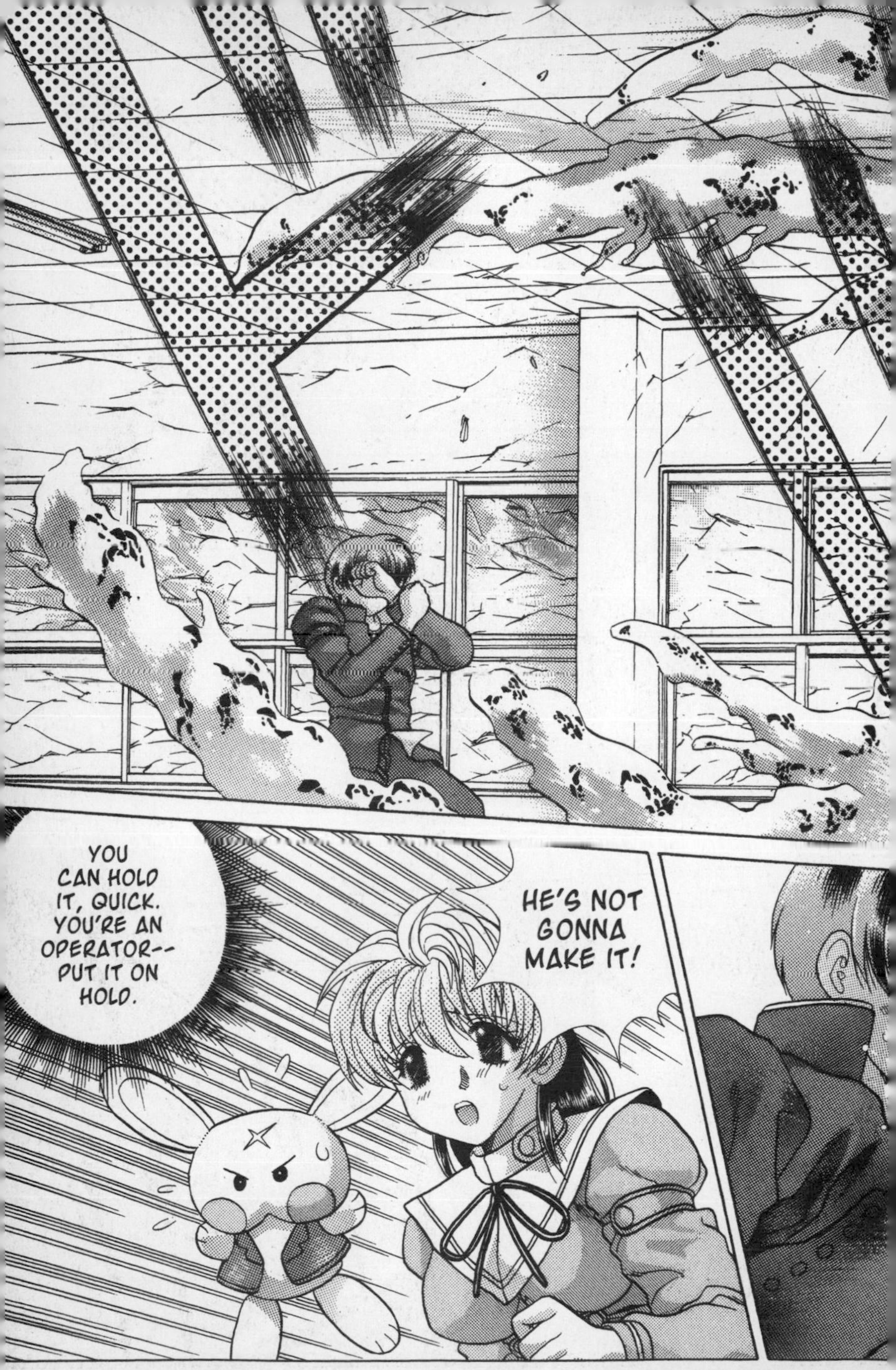
HE'S NOT GONNA MAKE IT!
YOU CAN HOLD IT, QUICK. YOU'RE AN OPERATOR--PUT IT ON HOLD.

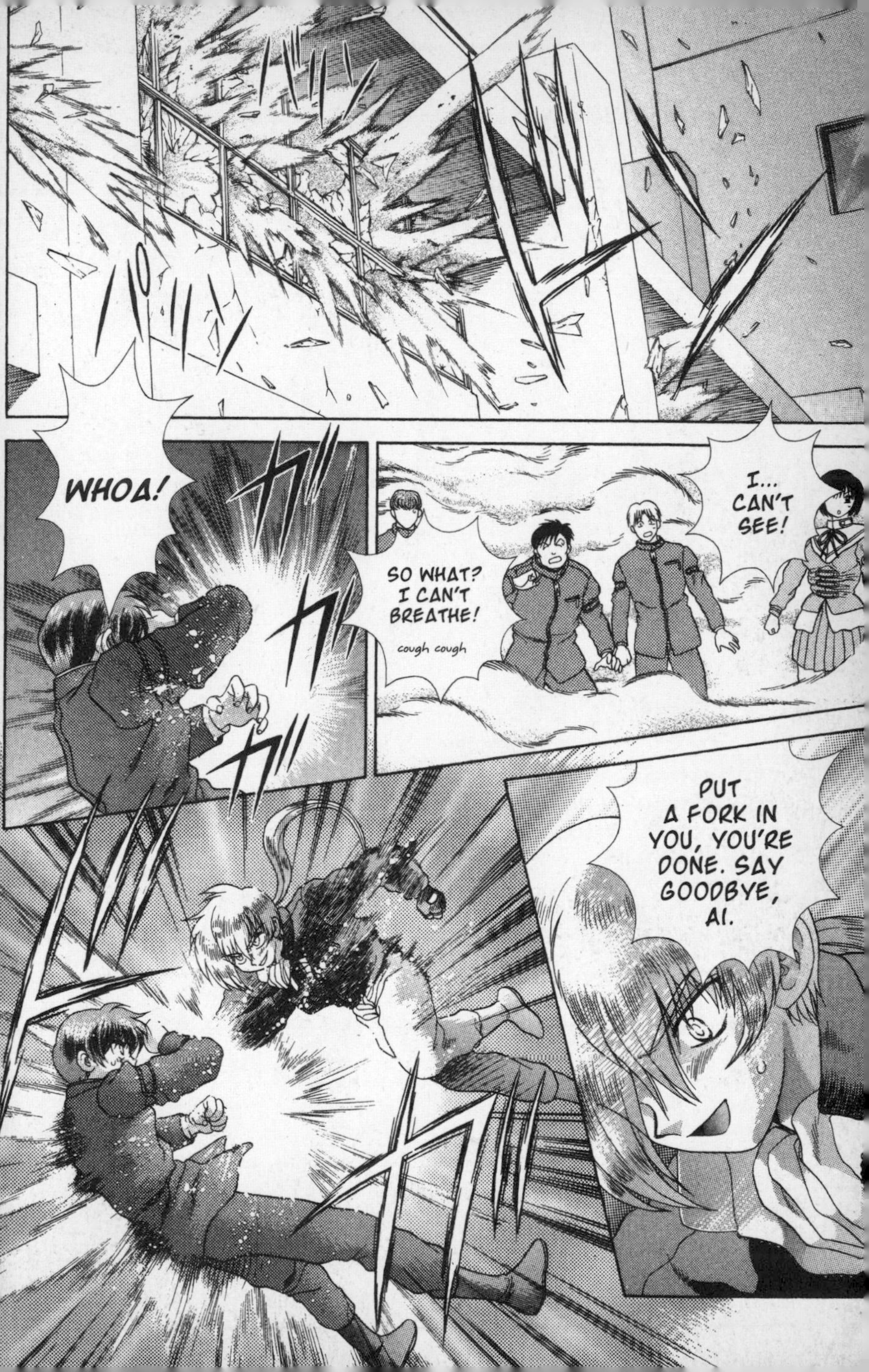
I... CAN'T SEE!
SO WHAT? I CAN'T BREATHE!
cough cough
WHOA!
PUT A FORK IN YOU, YOU'RE DONE. SAY GOODBYE, AI.

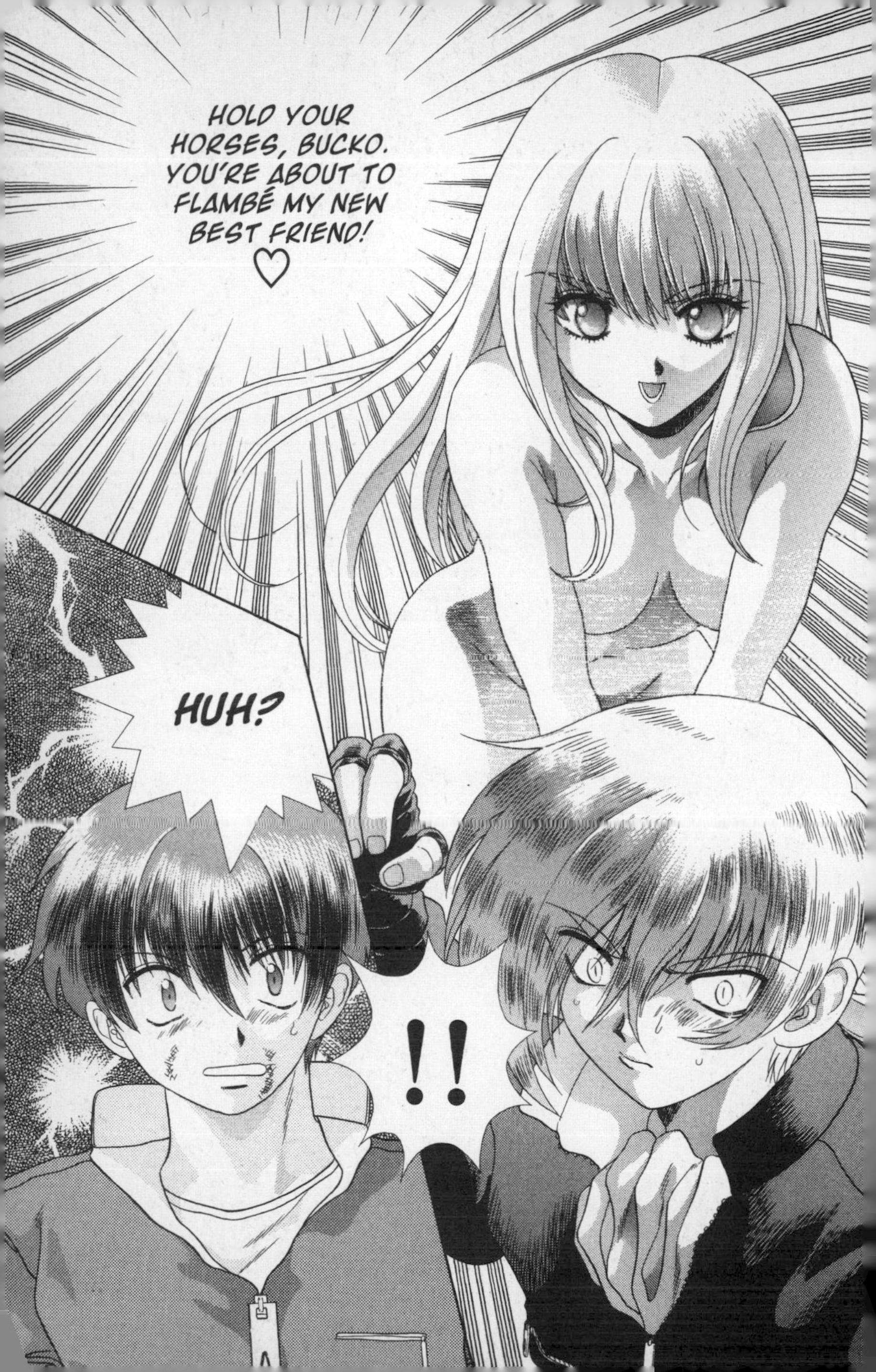
HOLD YOUR HORSES, BUCKO. YOU'RE ABOUT TO FLAMBÉ MY NEW BEST FRIEND! ♡
HUH?
!!

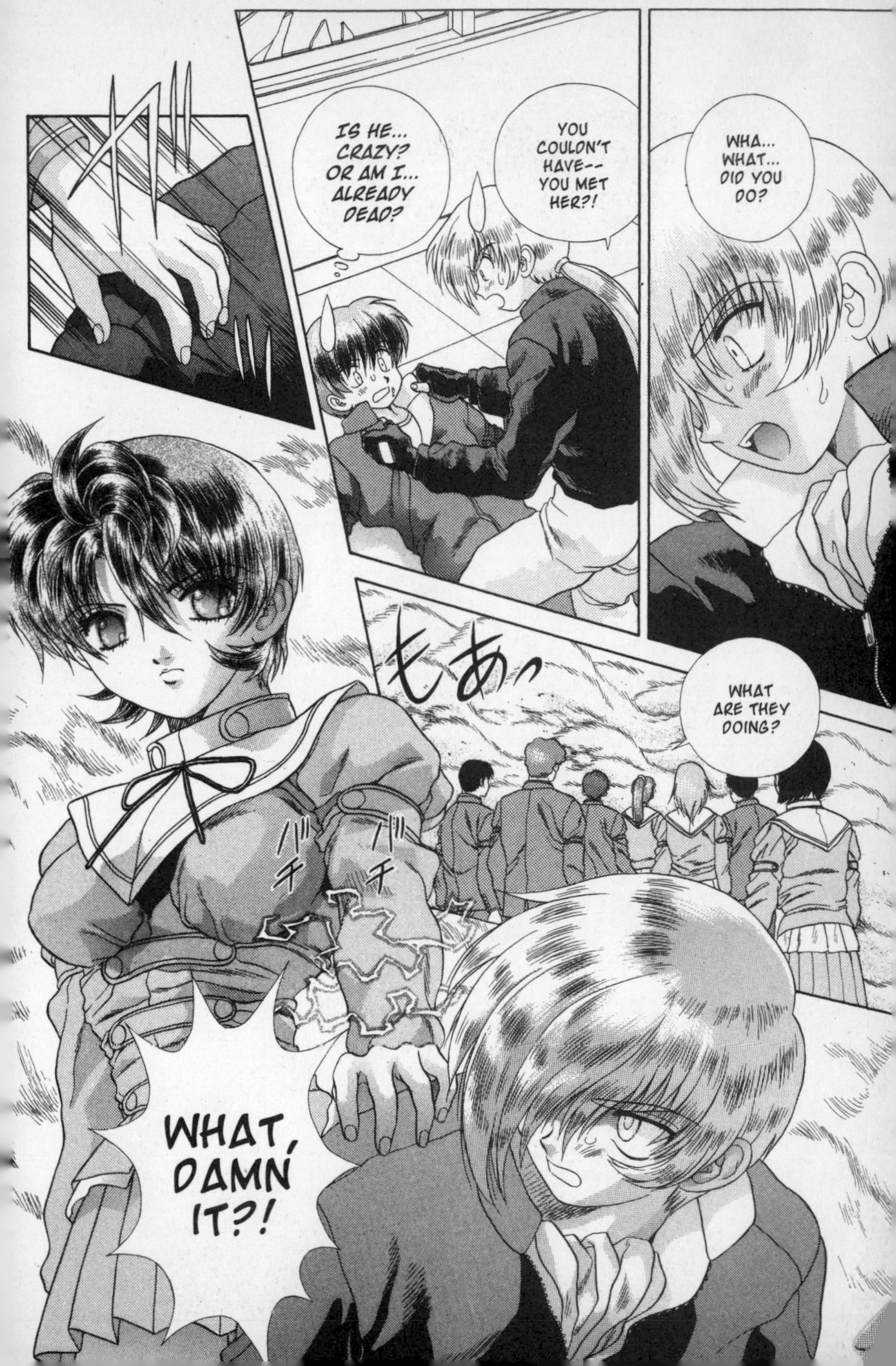
WHA... WHAT... DID YOU DO?
YOU COULDN'T HAVE-- YOU MET HER?!
IS HE... CRAZY? OR AM I... ALREADY DEAD?
もあ
WHAT ARE THEY DOING?
バチ
バチ
WHAT, DAMN IT?!

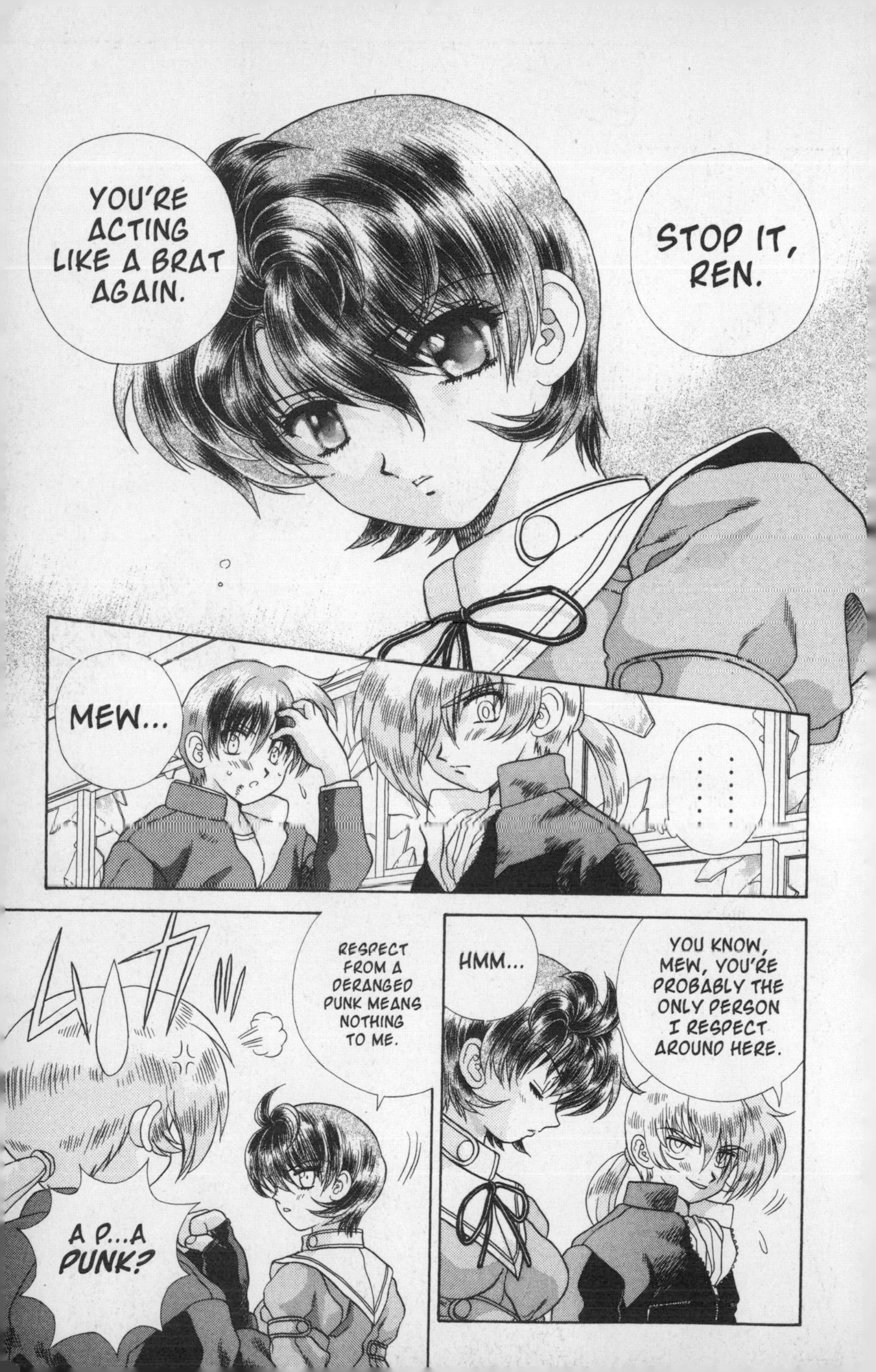
STOP IT, REN.
YOU'RE ACTING LIKE A BRAT AGAIN.
......
MEW...
YOU KNOW, MEW, YOU'RE PROBABLY THE ONLY PERSON I RESPECT AROUND HERE.
HMM...
RESPECT FROM A DERANGED PUNK MEANS NOTHING TO ME.
A P...A PUNK?

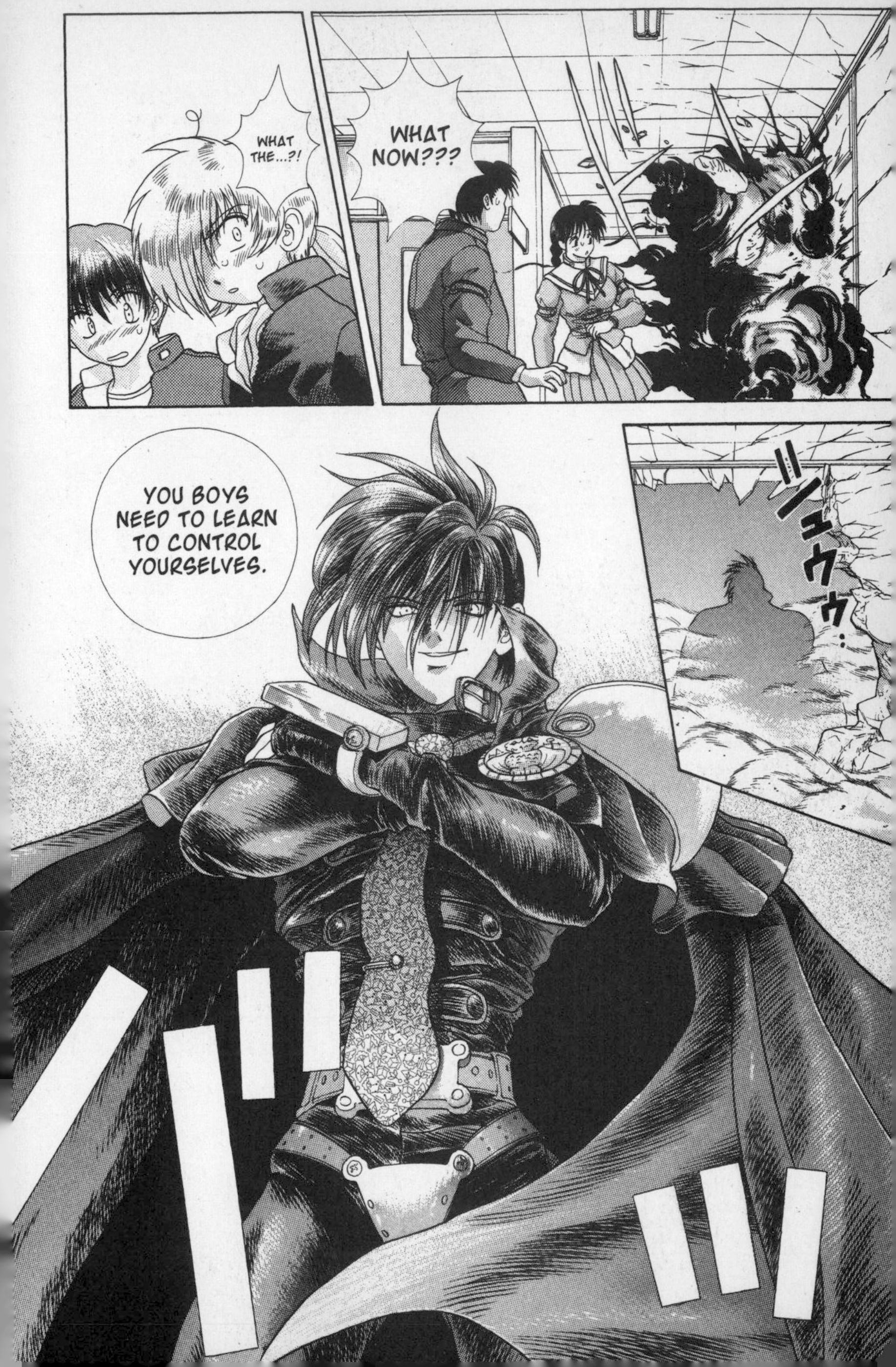
WHAT NOW???
WHAT THE...?!
シュウゥ…
YOU BOYS NEED TO LEARN TO CONTROL YOURSELVES.

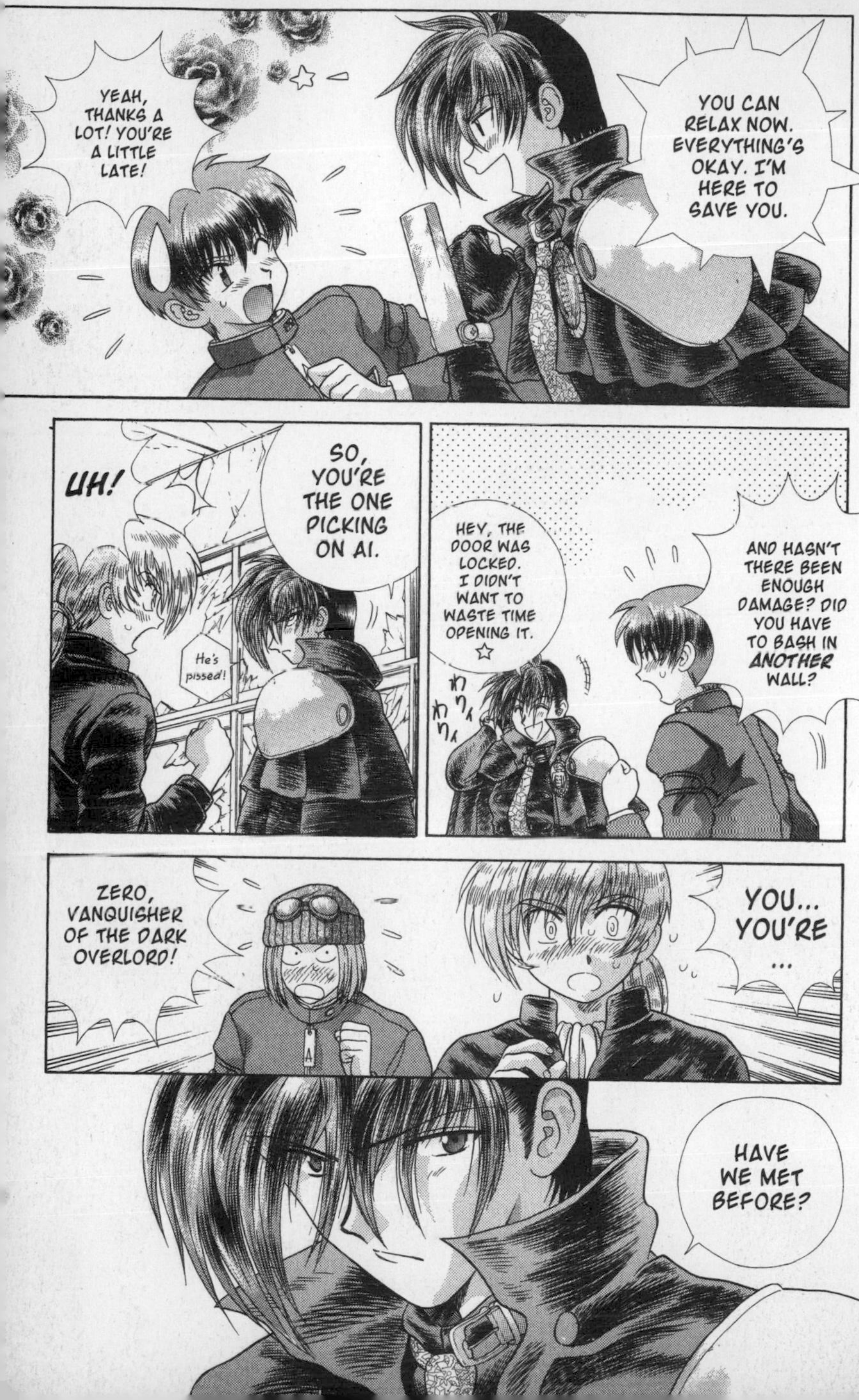
YOU CAN RELAX NOW. EVERYTHING'S OKAY. I'M HERE TO SAVE YOU.
YEAH, THANKS A LOT! YOU'RE A LITTLE LATE!
AND HASN'T THERE BEEN ENOUGH DAMAGE? DID YOU HAVE TO BASH IN ANOTHER WALL?
HEY, THE DOOR WAS LOCKED. I DIDN'T WANT TO WASTE TIME OPENING IT. ☆
SO, YOU'RE THE ONE PICKING ON AI.
UH!
He's pissed!
YOU... YOU'RE ...
ZERO, VANQUISHER OF THE DARK OVERLORD!
HAVE WE MET BEFORE?

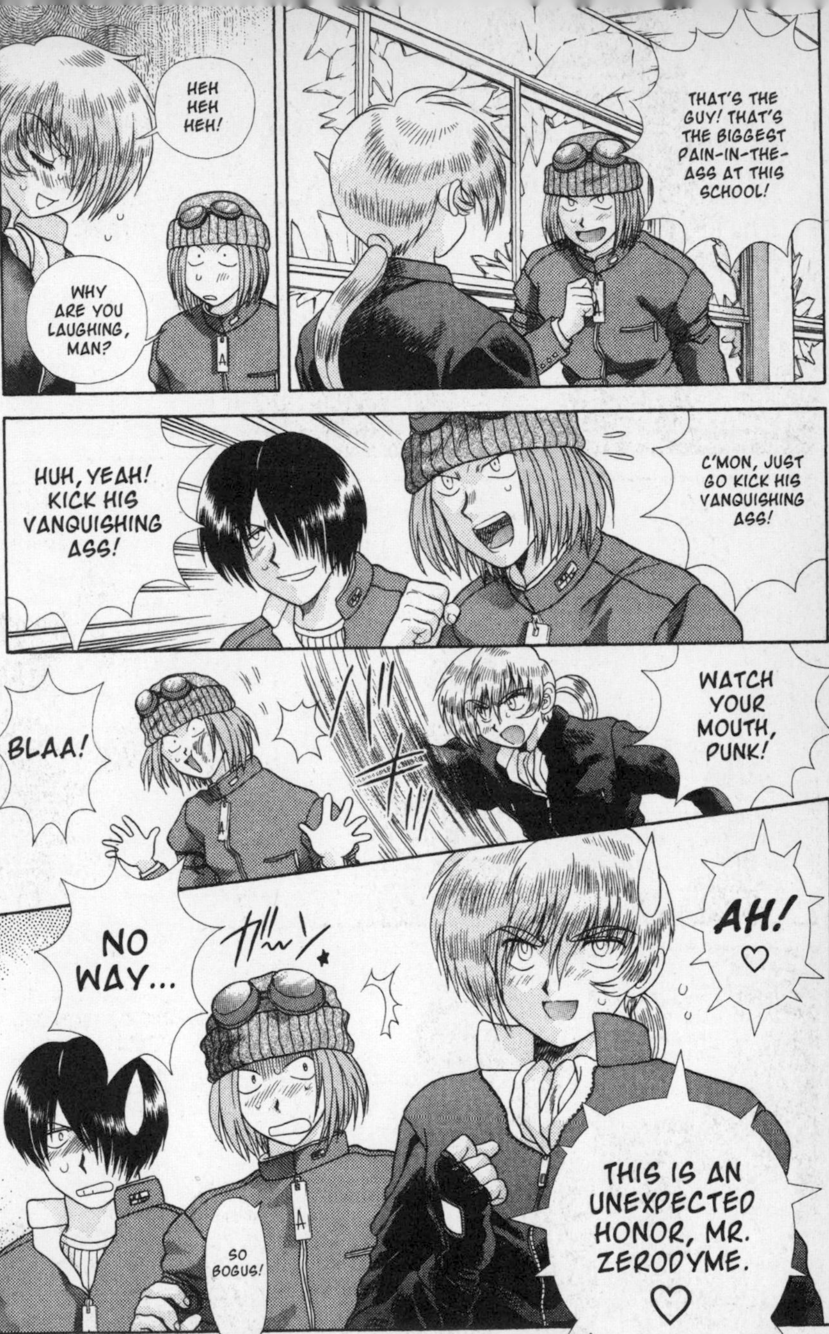
THAT'S THE GUY! THAT'S THE BIGGEST PAIN-IN-THE-ASS AT THIS SCHOOL!
HEH HEH HEH!
WHY ARE YOU LAUGHING, MAN?
C'MON, JUST GO KICK HIS VANQUISHING ASS!
HUH, YEAH! KICK HIS VANQUISHING ASS!
WATCH YOUR MOUTH, PUNK!
BLAA!
AH! ♡
THIS IS AN UNEXPECTED HONOR, MR. ZERODYME. ♡
NO WAY...
SO BOGUS!

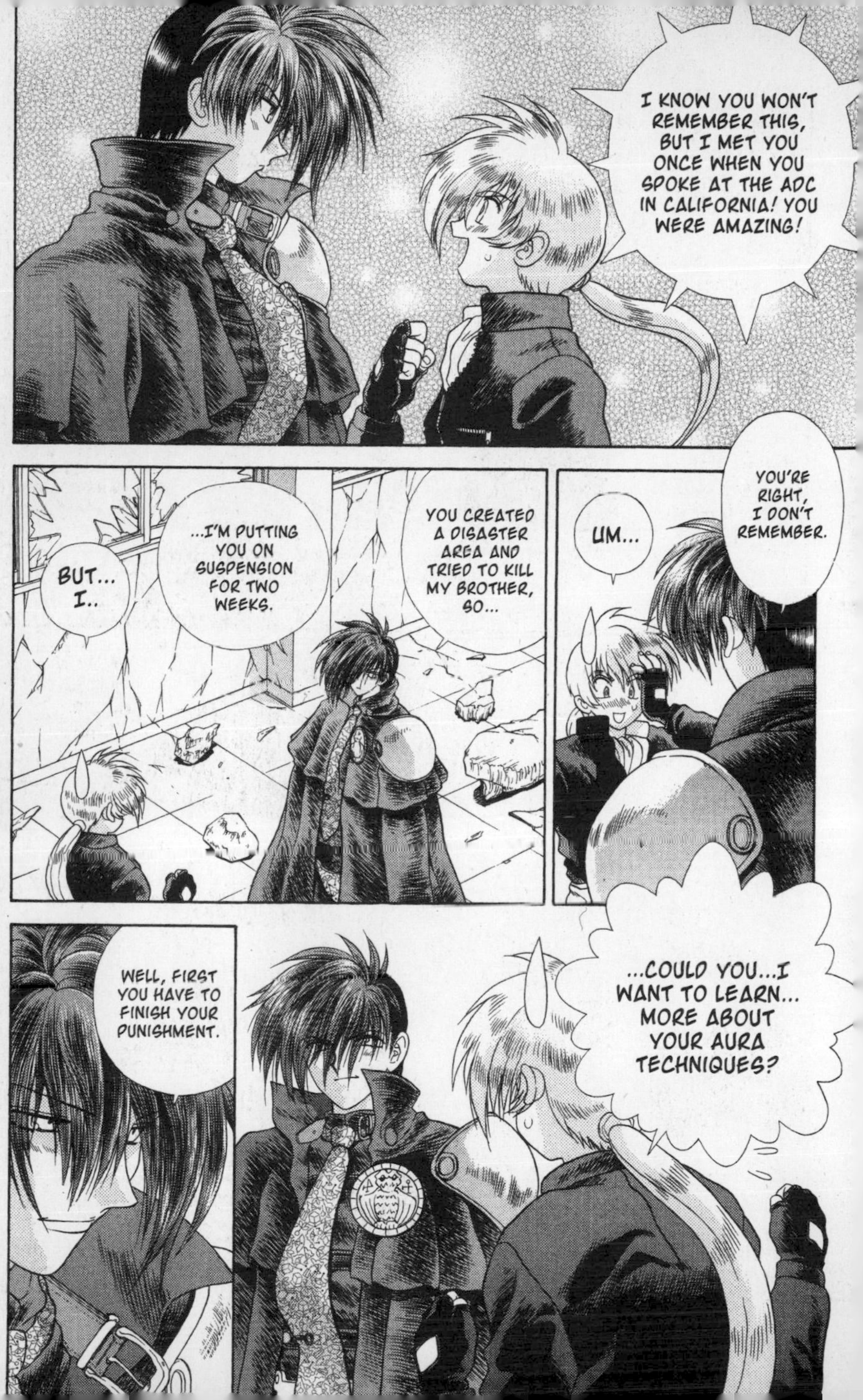
I KNOW YOU WON'T REMEMBER THIS, BUT I MET YOU ONCE WHEN YOU SPOKE AT THE ADC IN CALIFORNIA! YOU WERE AMAZING!
YOU'RE RIGHT, I DON'T REMEMBER.
UM...
YOU CREATED A DISASTER AREA AND TRIED TO KILL MY BROTHER, SO...
...I'M PUTTING YOU ON SUSPENSION FOR TWO WEEKS.
BUT... I...
...COULD YOU...I WANT TO LEARN... MORE ABOUT YOUR AURA TECHNIQUES?
WELL, FIRST YOU HAVE TO FINISH YOUR PUNISHMENT.

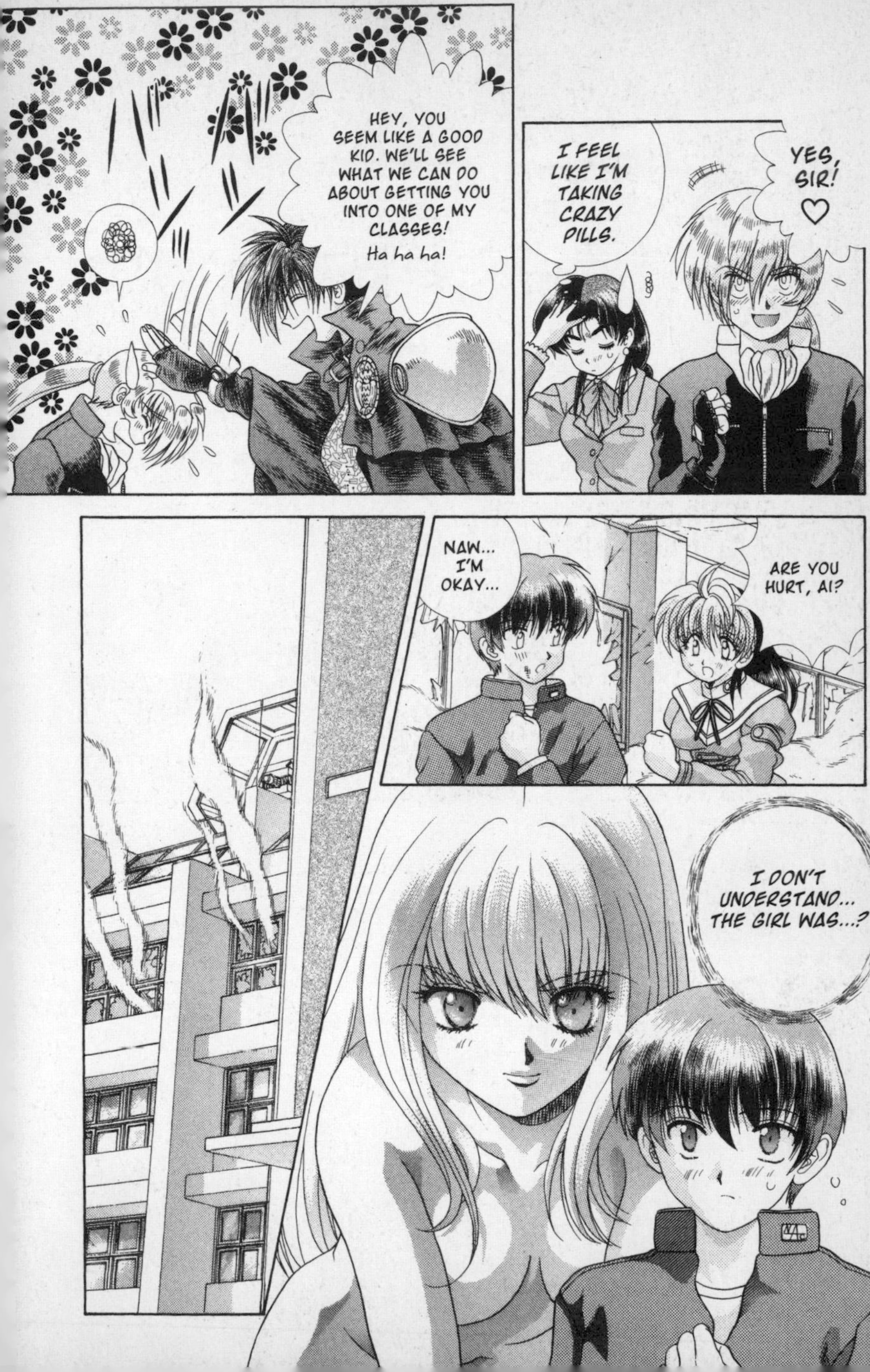
YES, SIR! ♡
I FEEL LIKE I'M TAKING CRAZY PILLS.
HEY, YOU SEEM LIKE A GOOD KID. WE'LL SEE WHAT WE CAN DO ABOUT GETTING YOU INTO ONE OF MY CLASSES!
Ha ha ha!
ARE YOU HURT, AI?
NAW... I'M OKAY...
I DON'T UNDERSTAND... THE GIRL WAS...?

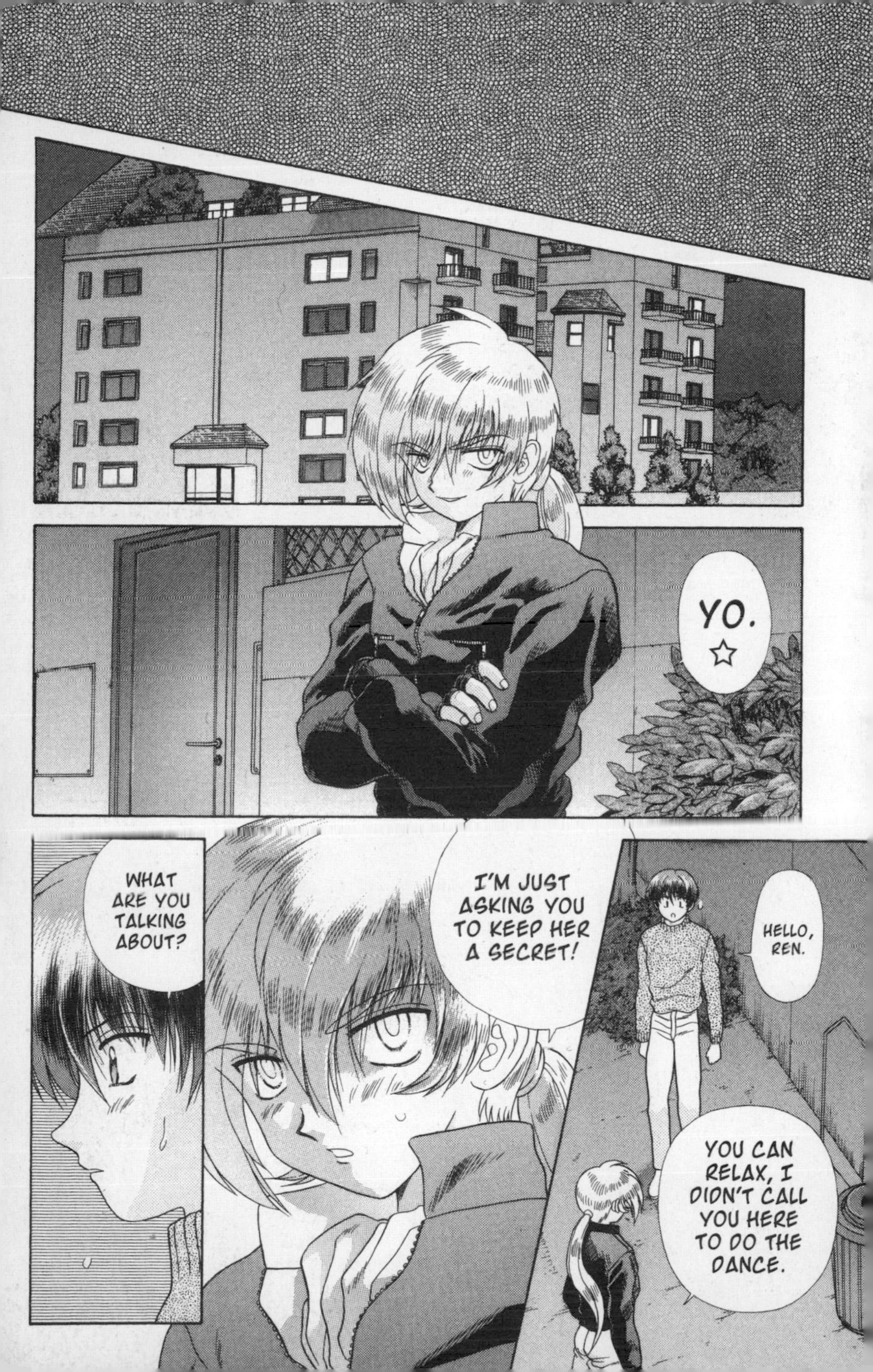
YO. ☆
HELLO, REN.
YOU CAN RELAX, I DIDN'T CALL YOU HERE TO DO THE DANCE.
I'M JUST ASKING YOU TO KEEP HER A SECRET!
WHAT ARE YOU TALKING ABOUT?

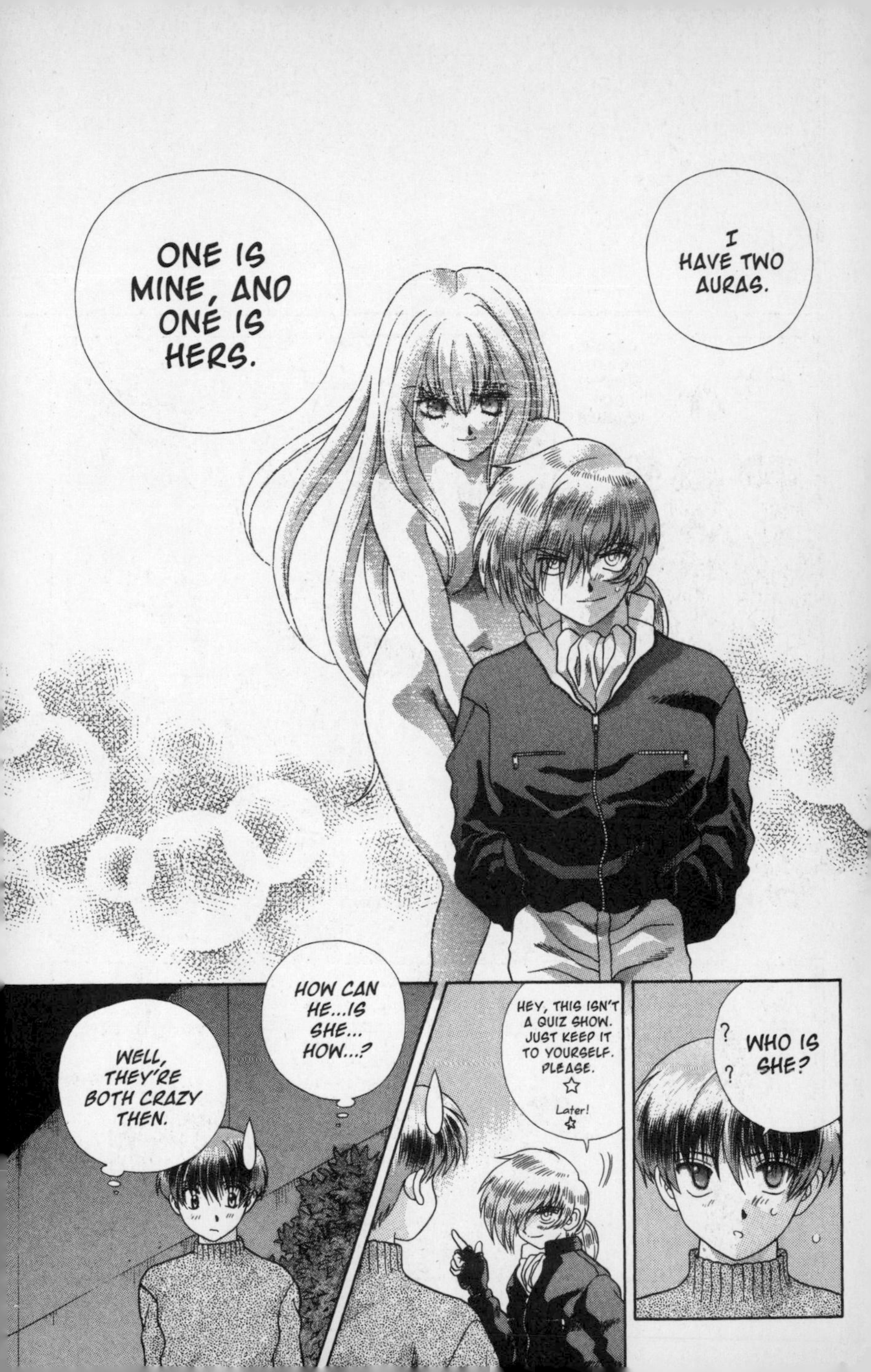
I HAVE TWO AURAS.
ONE IS MINE, AND ONE IS HERS.
? ?
WHO IS SHE?
HEY, THIS ISN'T A QUIZ SHOW. JUST KEEP IT TO YOURSELF. PLEASE. ☆
Later! ☆
HOW CAN HE...IS SHE... HOW...?
WELL, THEY'RE BOTH CRAZY THEN.

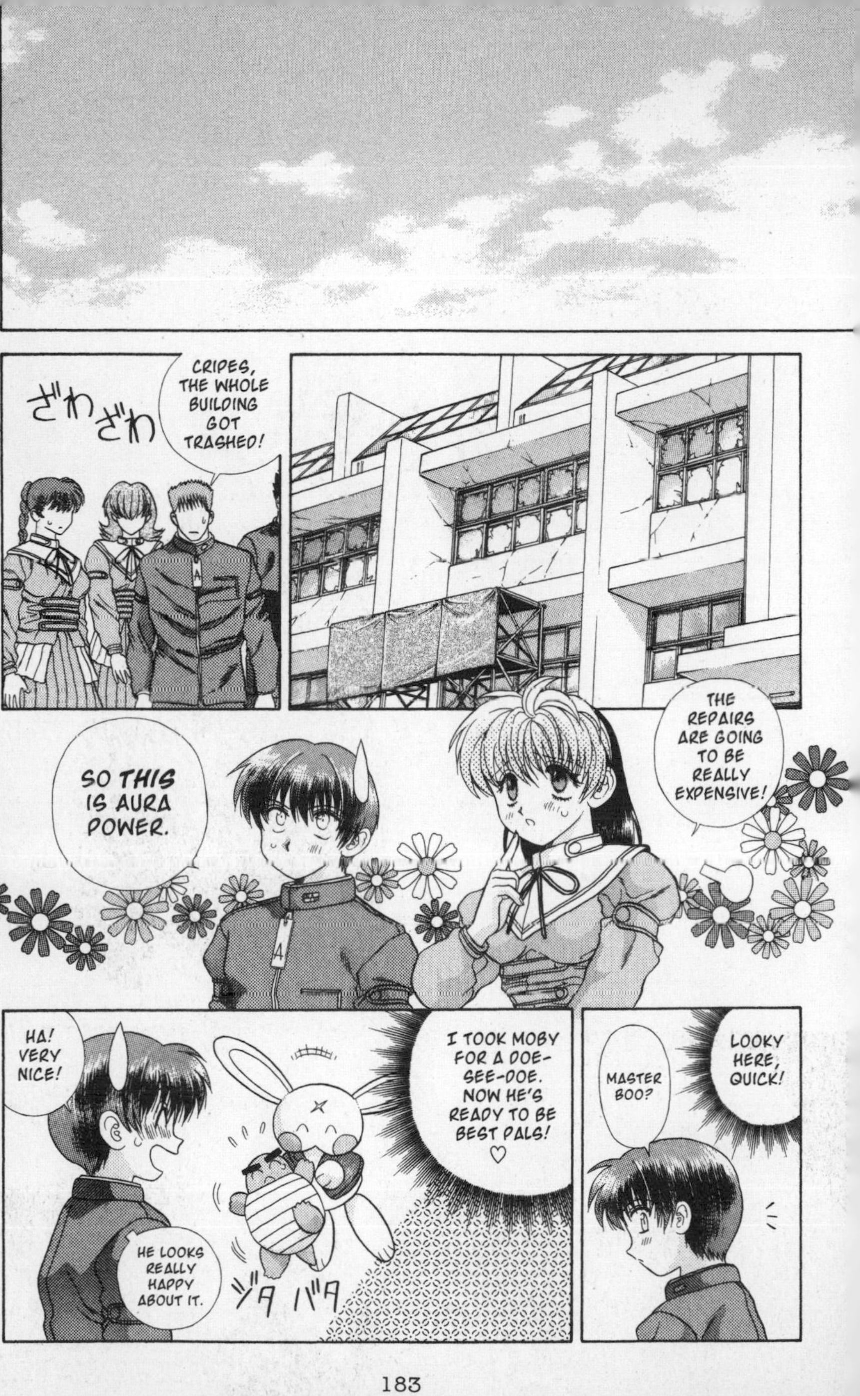
CRIPES, THE WHOLE BUILDING GOT TRASHED!
ざわざわ
THE REPAIRS ARE GOING TO BE REALLY EXPENSIVE!
SO THIS IS AURA POWER.
LOOKY HERE, QUICK!
MASTER BOO?
I TOOK MOBY FOR A DOE-SEE-DOE. NOW HE'S READY TO BE BEST PALS! ♡
HA! VERY NICE!
HE LOOKS REALLY HAPPY ABOUT IT.
ジタバタ

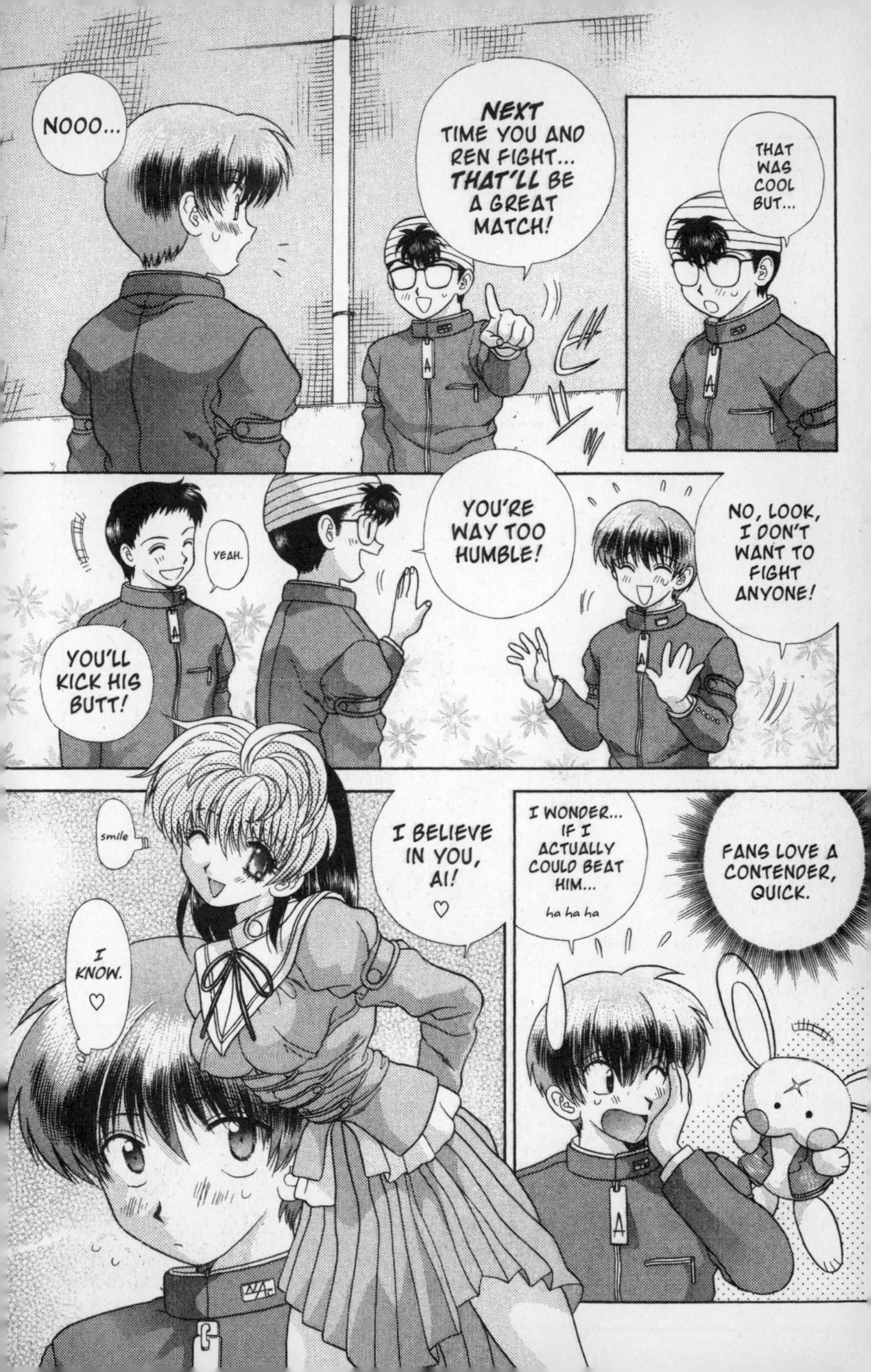
THAT WAS COOL BUT...
NEXT TIME YOU AND REN FIGHT... **THAT'LL** BE A GREAT MATCH!
NOOO...
NO, LOOK, I DON'T WANT TO FIGHT ANYONE!
YOU'RE WAY TOO HUMBLE!
YEAH.
YOU'LL KICK HIS BUTT!
FANS LOVE A CONTENDER, QUICK.
I WONDER... IF I ACTUALLY COULD BEAT HIM...
ha ha ha
I BELIEVE IN YOU, AI! ♡
smile
I KNOW. ♡

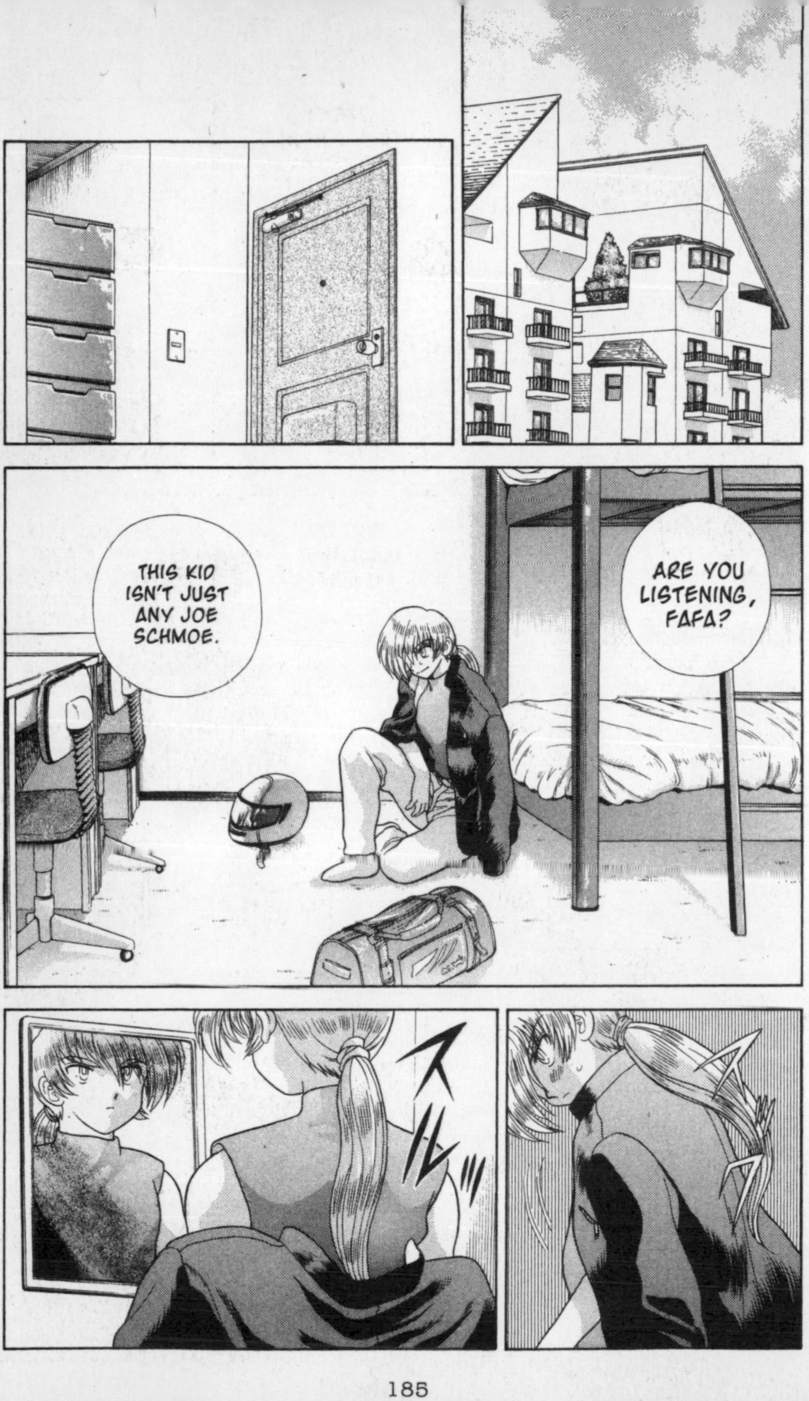
ARE YOU LISTENING, FAFA?
THIS KID ISN'T JUST ANY JOE SCHMOE.

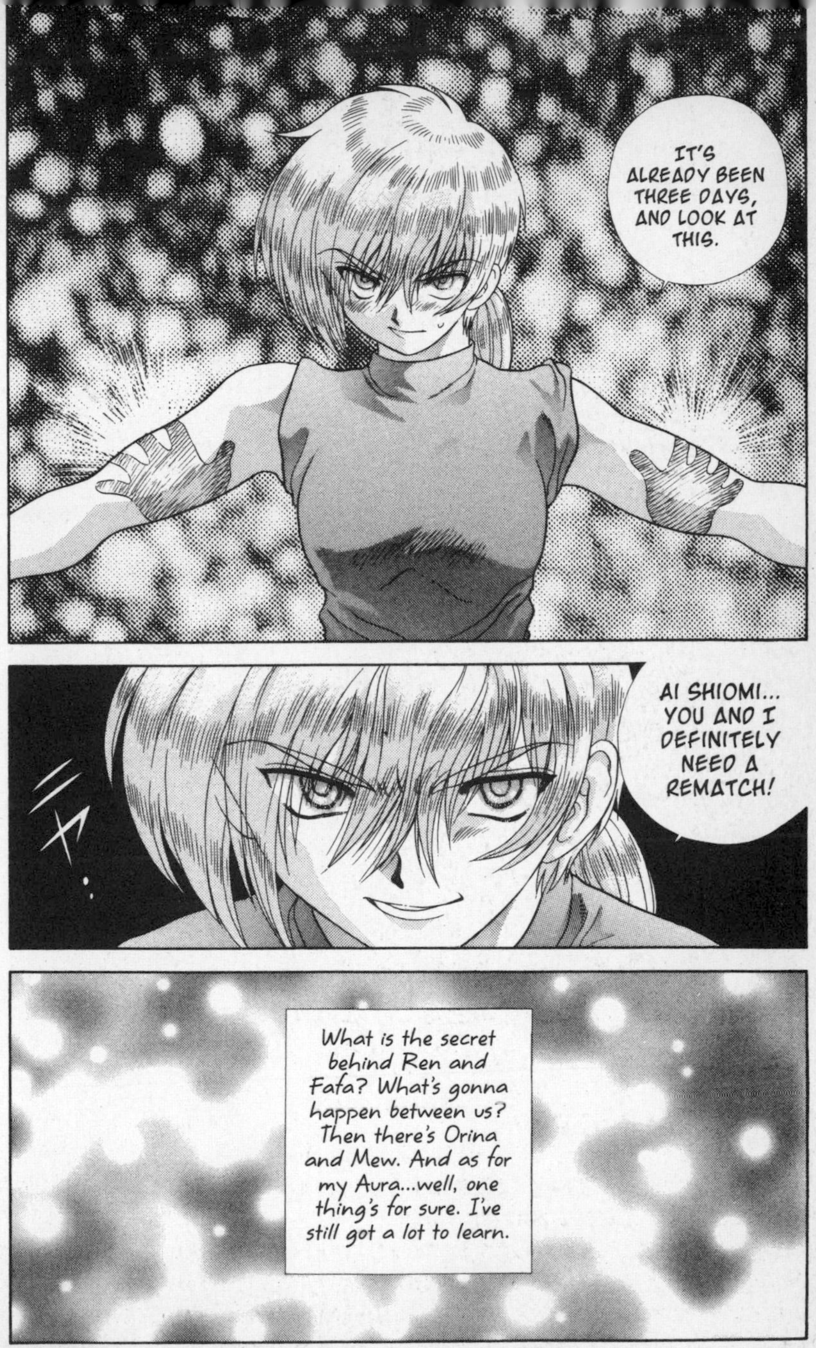
IT'S ALREADY BEEN THREE DAYS, AND LOOK AT THIS.
AI SHIOMI... YOU AND I DEFINITELY NEED A REMATCH!
What is the secret behind Ren and Fafa? What's gonna happen between us? Then there's Orina and Mew. And as for my Aura...well, one thing's for sure. I've still got a lot to learn.

Psychic Academy Volume 2 END

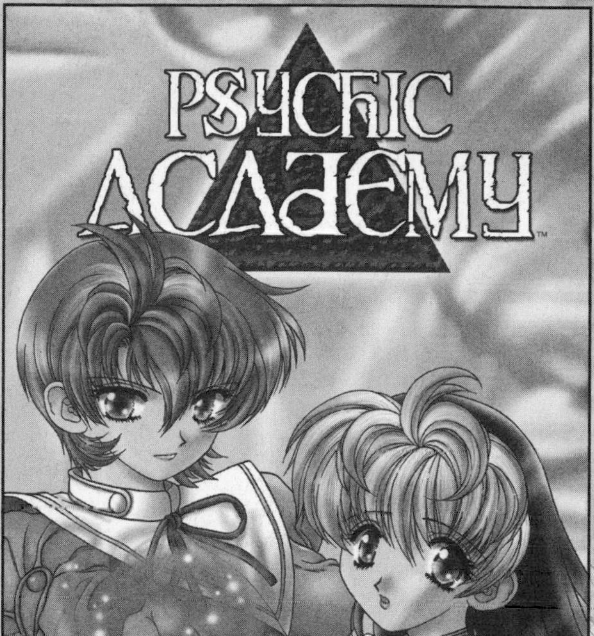
PSYCHIC ACADEMY™
3
PSYCHIC ACADEMY
KATSU AKI

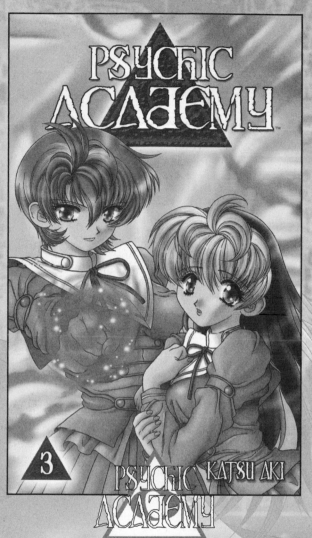

In the next volume...

The mysterious new girl Fafa sweeps into school and enchants Ai with the romantic notion of ditching class—a way to achieve, as she describes it, true "freedom." Ai, certainly not the rebellious type, but also not a big fan of school, attempts to embrace this new form of academic self-expression. When Mew shows up to drag him back to class she learns that Fafa won't surrender her new plaything without a fight!

When darkness is in your genes,
only love can steal it away.

D·N·ANGEL

CRESCENT MOON ™

From the dark side of the moon comes a shining new star...

TOKYOPOP

PLANET LADDER
PLANETES
PRIEST
PRINCESS AI
PSYCHIC ACADEMY
RAGNAROK
RAVE MASTER
REALITY CHECK
REBIRTH
REBOUND
REMOTE
RISING STARS OF MANGA
SABER MARIONETTE J
SAILOR MOON
SAINT TAIL
SAIYUKI
SAMURAI DEEPER KYO
SAMURAI GIRL REAL BOUT HIGH SCHOOL
SCRYED
SEIKAI TRILOGY, THE
SGT. FROG
SHAOLIN SISTERS
SHIRAHIME-SYO: SNOW GODDESS TALES
SHUTTERBOX
SKULL MAN, THE
SMUGGLER
SNOW DROP
SORCERER HUNTERS
STONE
SUIKODEN III
SUKI
THREADS OF TIME
TOKYO BABYLON
TOKYO MEW MEW
TOKYO TRIBES
TRAMPS LIKE US
UNDER THE GLASS MOON
VAMPIRE GAME
VISION OF ESCAFLOWNE, THE
WARRIORS OF TAO
WILD ACT
WISH
WORLD OF HARTZ
X-DAY
ZODIAC P.I.

MANGA NOVELS

CLAMP SCHOOL PARANORMAL INVESTIGATORS
KARMA CLUB
SAILOR MOON
SLAYERS

ART BOOKS

ART OF CARDCAPTOR SAKURA
ART OF MAGIC KNIGHT RAYEARTH, THE
PEACH: MIWA UEDA ILLUSTRATIONS

ANIME GUIDES

COWBOY BEBOP
GUNDAM TECHNICAL MANUALS
SAILOR MOON SCOUT GUIDES

TOKYOPOP KIDS

STRAY SHEEP

CINE-MANGA™

ALADDIN
ASTRO BOY
CARDCAPTORS
CONFESSIONS OF A TEENAGE DRAMA QUEEN
DUEL MASTERS
FAIRLY ODDPARENTS, THE
FAMILY GUY
FINDING NEMO
G.I. JOE SPY TROOPS
JACKIE CHAN ADVENTURES
JIMMY NEUTRON: BOY GENIUS, THE ADVENTURES OF
KIM POSSIBLE
LILO & STITCH
LIZZIE MCGUIRE
LIZZIE MCGUIRE MOVIE, THE
MALCOLM IN THE MIDDLE
POWER RANGERS: NINJA STORM
SHREK 2
SPONGEBOB SQUAREPANTS
SPY KIDS 2
SPY KIDS 3-D: GAME OVER
TEENAGE MUTANT NINJA TURTLES
THAT'S SO RAVEN
TRANSFORMERS: ARMADA
TRANSFORMERS: ENERGON

For more information visit www.TOKYOPOP.com

03.03.04T

MANGA

.HACK//LEGEND OF THE TWILIGHT
@LARGE
ABENOBASHI: MAGICAL SHOPPING ARCADE
A.I. LOVE YOU
AI YORI AOSHI
ANGELIC LAYER
ARM OF KANNON
BABY BIRTH
BATTLE ROYALE
BATTLE VIXENS
BRAIN POWERED
BRIGADOON
B'TX
CANDIDATE FOR GODDESS, THE
CARDCAPTOR SAKURA
CARDCAPTOR SAKURA - MASTER OF THE CLOW

CHOBITS
CHRONICLES OF THE CURSED SWORD
CLAMP SCHOOL DETECTIVES
CLOVER
COMIC PARTY
CONFIDENTIAL CONFESSIONS
CORRECTOR YUI
COWBOY BEBOP
COWBOY BEBOP: SHOOTING STAR
CRAZY LOVE STORY
CRESCENT MOON
CULDCEPT
CYBORG 009
D•N•ANGEL
DEMON DIARY
DEMON ORORON, THE
DEUS VITAE
DIGIMON
DIGIMON TAMERS
DIGIMON ZERO TWO
DOLL
DRAGON HUNTER
DRAGON KNIGHTS
DRAGON VOICE
DREAM SAGA
DUKLYON: CLAMP SCHOOL DEFENDERS
EERIE QUEERIE!
END, THE
ERICA SAKURAZAWA: COLLECTED WORKS
ET CETERA
ETERNITY
EVIL'S RETURN
FAERIES' LANDING
FAKE
FLCL
FORBIDDEN DANCE
FRUITS BASKET
G GUNDAM

GATEKEEPERS
GETBACKERS
GIRL GOT GAME
GRAVITATION
GTO
GUNDAM BLUE DESTINY
GUNDAM SEED ASTRAY
GUNDAM WING
GUNDAM WING: BATTLEFIELD OF PACIFISTS
GUNDAM WING: ENDLESS WALTZ
GUNDAM WING: THE LAST OUTPOST (G-UNIT)
GUYS' GUIDE TO GIRLS
HANDS OFF!
HAPPY MANIA
HARLEM BEAT
I.N.V.U.
IMMORTAL RAIN
INITIAL D
INSTANT TEEN: JUST ADD NUTS
ISLAND
JING: KING OF BANDITS
JING: KING OF BANDITS - TWILIGHT TALES
JULINE
KARE KANO
KILL ME, KISS ME
KINDAICHI CASE FILES, THE
KING OF HELL
KODOCHA: SANA'S STAGE
LAMENT OF THE LAMB
LEGAL DRUG
LEGEND OF CHUN HYANG, THE
LES BIJOUX
LOVE HINA
LUPIN III
LUPIN III: WORLD'S MOST WANTED
MAGIC KNIGHT RAYEARTH I
MAGIC KNIGHT RAYEARTH II
MAHOROMATIC: AUTOMATIC MAIDEN
MAN OF MANY FACES
MARMALADE BOY
MARS
MARS: HORSE WITH NO NAME
METROID
MINK
MIRACLE GIRLS
MIYUKI-CHAN IN WONDERLAND
MODEL
ONE
ONE I LOVE, THE
PARADISE KISS
PARASYTE
PASSION FRUIT
PEACH GIRL
PEACH GIRL: CHANGE OF HEART
PET SHOP OF HORRORS
PITA-TEN

03.03.04T

STOP!

This is the back of the book.
You wouldn't want to spoil a great ending!

This book is printed "manga-style," in the authentic Japanese right-to-left format. Since none of the artwork has been flipped or altered, readers get to experience the story just as the creator intended. You've been asking for it, so TOKYOPOP® delivered: authentic, hot-off-the-press, and far more fun!

DIRECTIONS

If this is your first time reading manga-style, here's a quick guide to help you understand how it works.

It's easy... just start in the top right panel and follow the numbers. Have fun, and look for more 100% authentic manga from TOKYOPOP®!